🐾 PETS R PERMITTED 🐾

HOTEL, MOTEL & KENNEL DIRECTORY

 PETS R PERMITTED

HOTEL, MOTEL & KENNEL DIRECTORY

Published by:

The Annenberg Communications Institute
Post Office Box 3099
Lakewood, CA 90711-3099 USA
(515) 224-4872

Library of Congress Cataloging in Publication Data
Annenberg Communications Institute, The
Pets-R-Permitted Hotel, Motel & Kennel Directory: The Pocket Directory of Places Pets Are Permitted
M. E. Nelson, Editor
1. Pets and Travel
2. Dogs--Transportation
3. Cats--Transportation
4. Travel--Handbooks, Manuals, etc.
I. Title

ISBN 1-56471-777-1: Softcover

WARNING!
THIS BOOK IS SELF DESTRUCTING AS YOU USE IT!

According to studies by the
American Hotel & Motel Association,
as many as 1 in 3 accomodations will be sold, change
names, or replace current management in the next year.
When management changes, so do phone numbers
and <u>pet policies</u>. To receive information on updates of
PETS-R-PERMITTED:

    1. Cut out this page
    2. Complete the registration form
    3. Fold in half and tape closed
    4. Affix first class (29 cents) postage
    5. MAIL TODAY!

**W
A
R
N
I
N
G
!**

NAME _____

ADDRESS _____

CITY _____ ST _____ ZIP _____

When purchased (approx) _____

Where purchased _____

Phone (optional) _____

WARNING!

fold here and tape shut

from

_____

_____

_____

PETS-R-PERMITTED
PURCHASE REGISTRATION PROCESSING
Post Office Box 3099
Lakewood, CA 90711-3099

TABLE OF CONTENTS

From the authors...

Like many pet owners, our pet is a pivotal part of our life. When we travel, we hate leaving him at home, even with the best pet sitter. When we do have to leave him we are constantly thinking about him...worrying that he may be lonely, wondering if he's getting enough exercise, wondering whether he's eating, and in general just missing him and talking about the cute things he does.

Traveling with our pet not only alleviates our worrying, it lets us bring our favorite creature comfort from home along with us on our trips.

Because we know we aren't the only ones who love our pets as much as we hate leaving them, we set out to help other pet owners by creating this directory. We hope it will be helpful to you. We encourage you to write us with suggestions for future updates to the directory. And, we want to hear about your travel experiences and any suggestions you might want to share with other pet travelers.

Here's hoping you have Happy Trails, full of Happy Tails!!!

How to use this directory...

To help you find accommodations easily, we have arranged all the listing alphabetically by geography. First, states are listed alphabetically. Then, within each state the towns are listed alphabetically. To further aid you, we've included page heading like you'd see in a dictionary, which list the beginning town and state that is listed on each page. We did this to provide you with a quick reference point as you flip through the directory.

If you cannot find an accommodation in a certain town, be sure to check nearby areas. To do this, refer to the zip code directory in the appendix. Look for zip codes that are sequentially similar to the area where you wish to stay. This method works because towns with similar zip codes are usually near each other geographically.

We have tried to include a postal address for each accommodation as well as a phone number. We've done this to help you in contacting the accommodations before you show up. Where possible we have also included toll free telephone numbers.

We have also endeavored to include an array of price ranges. This was easier to do in the cities than in the smaller towns. As a rule of thumb, you'll probably be able to find up-scale accommodations in the larger areas. In the smaller areas, most accommodations are in the mid to lower price ranges. For your convenience we have included guideline price ranges. These price ranges are by no means guaranteed.

When possible, we tried to gather information regarding the accommodations' SPECIFIC pet policies. Be reminded however, that hotel & motel managment and their policies change quite frequently. Notes regarding sizes allowed, deposits, fees and so forth are provided as guidelines. And just because an accommodation doesn't have any notes, it doesn't mean there aren't any restrictions. To get the current policy, be sure to call ahead!!

A few words about Hawaii & North Carolina...

State law in North Carolina forbids pets from sleeping in hotel or motel rooms. Therefore, if you intend to travel to North Carolina with your pet, please call a local kennel and reserve space well in advance of your trip. We have read in several articles that some hotels may have on-site kennels. Several late nights of telephone calls to North Carolina failed to locate any on-site kennels, however.

Hawaii currently has a four (4) month quarantine on incoming pets. Please contact your travel agent and veterinarian if you plan a trip to Hawaii with your pet.

PET TRAVEL SUPPLIES PACKING LIST

___pet first aid kit
___pet emergency care book
___health certificates (not just tags)
___grooming supplies
___regular food
___can opener & spoon (moist food)
___jug of water from home
___snack treats
___regular food & water bowls
___soap for cleaning pet bowls
___food mat to put under bowls

___bedding
___sturdy collar
___identification tags
___leash
___flashlight (for night walk)
___crate, carrier, cage
___pooper scooper or baggies
___litter box
___paper towels
___toys
___lint/hair remover if your pet sheds
___photos of your pet (in case it gets lost)

PET TRAVEL SAFETY

Make sure that your pet wars a sturdy collar with a firmly secured identification tag. The tag should include both your pet's name, and your name, address, and phone number. This information can help assure that your pet is returned to you if found roaming in an unfamiliar locale.

Because tags do fall off, a more permanant type of identification is available. The National Dog Registry and Tatoo-a-Pet offer nationwide recovery services. These services involve tatooing an i.d. number on your pet's ear or flank. This number is registered nationally to aid in your pet's recovery. Contact:

The National Dog Registry, Box 116, Woodstock, NY 12498, 914-679-2355
Tatoo-a-Pet, 1625 Emmons Ave., Brooklyn, NY 11235, 718-646-8200

Several simple measures can help to avoid the misfortune of losing your pet in unfamiliar surroundings.

Always maintain direct control of your pet...AT ALL TIMES!
By using a leash, cage or carrier you can assure that your pet will not break away from your care. Even when carrying your pet, it is wise to have a leash attached so you have something to grab onto in case your pet does manage to break lose.

Attach your dog's leash or cat's harness while your pet is in a secured, controlled environment. New environments can be frightening and distracting. Your pet may be prompted to run off before you have the chance to secure their leash or harness. For example, when making "pit stops" along your journey, unfamiliar surroundings can distract and disorient your pet. To avoid the danger of having your pet dash across a street, ALWAYS secure your pet's leash before opening the car door.

Same thing goes when leaving your room. To avoid knocking over other guests in the hallway, ALWAYS make sure your pet is securely leashed, crated, or caged before opening the door to your room.

PREPARING FOR TRAVEL - TEST TRIPS

Before taking your pet on a long trip, make an assessment of their "travelability". To do this, take your pet on a few trips in the car. Make each trip longer than the previous one. These trips will get them used to riding in the car and build their tolerance for longer rides.

If you have trouble "conditioning" your pet to trips in the car and your pet becomes anxious or unruly, you may want to discuss using a sedative with your vet or find a kennel or pet sitter. You might also try a travel crate. You can start "crating" your pet at home before your trip. Once your pet is used to the crate, go on a few short trips in the car with your pet in the crate. If this settles your pet, use the crate as their home away from home.

CAR DO'S & DONT'S

If you don't use a crate, train your pet to obey your commands while in the car. You must train your pet to sit in one place, not roam about the car, or stick its head out the window. As a general rule of thumb, it is wise to give your pet a pit stop about every two hours. Let your pet stretch and walk for about 10-15 minutes. Also offer your pet water at each pit stop. And always be sure to leash or harness your pet BEFORE opening the car door.

FIRST AID KIT SUPPLIES

__emergency pet care book	__cotton swabs	__cold pack
__small scissors	__antiseptic wipes	__rectal thermometer
__tweezers	__lubricating jelly	__flea shampoo
__gauze pads	__antibiotic cream	__oral dosage syringe
__gauze tape	__antiseptic burn cream	__ adhesive tape

VETERINARY EMERGENCY INFORMATION

From 9 AM - 5 PM (Mountain Time) Monday - Friday, the American Animal Hospital Association can help you locate a nearby veterinary hospital.

AAHA Veterinary Information Call 1-800-252-2242

PLANES, TRAINS, AND BUSES

Pets are not allowed on most trains and buses, however most airlines transport them. If you plan to transport your pet on an airline, do your homework and make your travel plans in advance. Air travel for pets is a serious undertaking and some pets should not fly. Air travel can be very unsafe for older, nervous, sickly, or pregnant animals.

Even if your pet is a good candidate for flying there are many details to attend to that are beyond the scope of this directory. The ASPCA prints a publication covering many of the details. It is entitled "Traveling With Your Pet". To order, send a check for $5.00 to ASPCA Public Relations, 441 E. 92nd Street, NY, NY 10028

The American Dog Owners Association also keeps up on the airlines' transportation of pets and keeps track of various airlines' performance. They also have a pamphlet on Canine Travel Tips and many other helpful pamphlets. Membership, which includes a newsletter, is a very reasonable $10/yr. for individuals and $15 for families. Their address is 1654 Columbia Turnpike, Castleton, NY 12033 Phone (518) 477-8469

What your host, the hotel or motel manager assumes...

DO NOT DISTURB
Your watchwords for keeping your pet in motels and hotels are: DO NOT DISTURB. Keep this in mind. To be a safe and courteous guest, your pet should NOT be seen and it should NOT be heard by the other guests.

BEST BEHAVIOR NOT <u>PEST</u> BEHAVIOR
Hotel and Motel owners will continue to Permit Pets ONLY if pet owners keep their pets from becoming pests. If you keep your pet from disturbing other guests and from doing damage, management will be more likely to continue to permit pets. If you allow your pet to be a pest, chances are you'll be asked to leave and you will ruin it for other pet owners who come looking for lodging. Strive to be a good example, or you'll be a dog-GONE example.

DON'T LEAVE 'EM ALONE
To help keep your pet from scratching, barking, crying and disturbing others, NEVER leave your pet alone in the room. Since the room will be a strange new place for your pet, it will bark or cry at every sound it hears outside the door. If left alone, your pet will try to get out of the room to investigate the strange sounds. This can result in costly nail marks on the door. To avoid costly damage and disturbing other guests, NEVER leave your pet alone in the room.

Check the local yellow pages if you need to kennel your pet for the day. Many tourist attractions have kennels of their own. Call the attraction directly to reserve kennel space for your pet. Remember to take your pet's health certificate when checking into the kennel.

PAYING THE PRICE
You must remember that you will have to take the time to help your pet to adjust to the strange new surroundings it will encounter as you travel. Giving words of reassurance, petting and comforting will help your pet to adjust. Keeping your pet calm and under control is the best way to insure that no thing or no person gets damaged...a small price to pay to avoid damage to persons and property.

Minimizing your pet's exposure to other people is the best way to keep your pet from becoming overexcited or aggressive. If you must encounter other people, always have your pet leased or caged. Even if your pet is normally friendly and outgoing, strange new surroundings may cause a change in temperament and tolerance. Lessening your pets interaction with other people will lessen the chance for unfriendly altercations.

If you keep your pet calm and under direct control, your travels should go off without a hitch. However, if your pet does get out of line, always report & volunteer to pay for any damages.

BRING BEDDING

Plan in advance where your pet will sleep. If your pet sleeps on a rug or a blanket or in a basket be sure to bring this along. If you are traveling with your pet in a cage, put the bedding in the cage and encourage your pet to sleep in the cage.

Never let your pet sleep in chairs or on the accommodation's bedding. If your pet MUST sleep on the bed with you, you MUST bring a bed covering to insure that the pet does not get on the accommodation's bedspreads or blankets. This will help minimize the pet hairs left on hotel beds and carpeting after you leave.

CLEAN INSIDE & OUTSIDE

Since the main purpose of hotels and motels is to provide lodging for human guests, always make the extra effort to remove all the traces of your pet from the room...and the grounds if your pet uses them for a rest room.

Before checking out, give your room a good once-over. Be sure to remove any empty food cans and clean up any spills, accidents and shed hair that remains.

CHOW TIME

Planning ahead for your pet's meals is a must. You need to bring your pet's food and water dishes and a mat on which to set them. Set the mat and dishes in the bathroom and don't feed your pet on the carpet.

A PLACE FOR EVERYTHING

When you register you will want to ask the management where they prefer you to walk your pet. As a general rule you should stay away from public areas, flower beds and pedestrian walkways. And, you should NEVER take your pet into public areas where other guests congregate such as the pool, lounge, children's playground or dining areas. As a general courtesy be sure to take a bag or pooper scooper to pick up what your pet leaves behind.

SPECIAL ACCOMMODATIONS

Some accommodations require you to keep your pet in their kennel rather than in your room. Others may require that only larger pets must be kept in their kennels. Furthermore, many accommodations will have special sections of rooms where pets are permitted and other sections where pets are not permitted. Many accommodations only have a limited number of pet rooms. That is why calling ahead for reservations is so important.

SEND US A NOTE

If you find more places where pets are permitted, please let us know. Also, if you have any comments about, or suggestions for improving our next directory, please drop us a note. Our aim is to serve you, the pet traveling public. Just let us know what we can do to help!

ACI
P.O. Box 3099
Lakewood, CA 90711-3099 USA

ALABAMA
ANNISTON
Hampton Inn
Hwy 21S. Jct. I-10 & SR 21
Anniston AL 36203
(205) 835-1492
(800) 426-7866
small pets only
Room rates $38-45

ATHENS
Days Inn
1322 Hwy 72 E.
Athens AL 35611
(205) 233-7500
(800) 325-2525
$20 pet deposit
Room rates $48-46

ATTALLA
Holiday Inn
801 Cleveland Ave.
Attalla AL 35954
(205) 538-7861
(800) 465-4329
Room rates $52-58

BESSEMER
EconomyInn
1011 9th Ave. SW
Bessemer AL 35020
(205) 424-9690
$4/pets
Room rates $30-44

Motel 6
1000 Shiloh Lane
Bessemer AL 35020
(205) 426-9646
1 small pet per room
Reservations (505) 891-6161
Room rates from $25

BIRMINGHAM
Hampton Inn
1466 Montgomery Hwy
Birmingham AL 35216
(205) 822-2224
(800) 426-7866
Room rates $46-49

Econo Lodge
130 Greenspring Hwy
Birmingham, AL 35209
(205) 942-1263
(800) 446-6900
$40-50

Days Inn
5101 Airport Hwy
Birmingham AL 35212
(205) 592-6110
(800) 325-2525
$4/pets
Room rates $45-65

Howard Johnson Hotel
1485 Montgomery Hwy.
Birmingham, AL 35216
(205) 823-4300
(800) 654-2000
$40-65

CULLMAN
Days Inn
1841 4th St. SW
Cullman AL 35055
(205) 739-3800
(800) 325-2525
$3/pets
Room rates $36-40

DECATUR
Quality Inn
3429 US 31 S.
Decatur AL 35602
(205) 355-0190
(800) 228-5151
Room rates $43-48

Days Inn
810 6th Ave
Decatur AL 35601
(205) 355-3520
(800) 325-2525
$5/pets
Room rates $44-48

Holiday Inn Downtown
1101 6th Ave. NE
Decatur AL 35601
(205) 355-3150
(800) 465-4329
Room rates $52-75

DOTHAN
Ramada Inn
3001 Ross Clark Circle
Dothan AL 36301
(205) 792-0031
(800) 228-2828
Room rates $52-56

Comfort Inn
3591 Ross Clark Circle NW
Dothan AL 36302
(205) 793-9090
(800) 228-5150
Room rates $47-51

Days Inn
2841 Ross Clark Circle SW
Dothan AL 36301
(205) 793-2550
(800) 325-2525
Room rates from $38

ENTERPRISE
Comfort Inn
615 US 84 Bypass
Enterprise AL 36330
(205) 393-2304
(800) 228-5150
Room rates $44-80

FLORENCE
Comfort Inn
400 S. Court St
Florence AL 35630
(205) 760-8888
(800) 228-5150
Room rates $40-47

Comfort Inn
400 S. Court St.
Florence AL 35630
(205) 760-8888
(800) 228-5150
Room rates $40-47

Florence Tourway Inn
1915 Florence Blvd.
Florence AL 35630
(205) 766-2620
small pets only
Room rates $38-42

FULTONDALE
Days Inn
616 Decatur Hwy
Fultondale AL 35068
(205) 849-0111
(800) 325-2525
$5/pets
Room rates $48-69

Always
Call
Ahead!

1

GADSDEN
Days Inn
1600 Rainbow Dr.
Gadsden AL 35901
(205) 543-1105
(800) 325-2525
$10 deposit required
Room rates $36-40

Econo Lodge
507 Cherry St.
Gadsden AL 35954
(205) 538-9925
(800) 553-2666
$20 deposit required
Room rates from $37

GREENVILLE
Econo Lodge
946 Fort Dale Rd.
Greenville AL 36037
(205) 382-3118
(800) 553-2666
Room rates from $33

GULF SHORES
Best Western on the Beach
SR 182
Gulf Shores AL 36542
(205) 948-7047
(800) 528-1234
$10 charge
Room rates $39-105

HOOVER
Days Inn
1535 Montgomery Hwy
Hoover AL 35216
(205) 822-6030
(800) 325-2525
small pets allowed
Room rates $38-56

HUNTSVILLE
Ramada Inn
3502 Memorial Parkway SW
Huntsville AL 35801
(205) 881-6120
(800) 228-2828
Room rates $47-52

Travelodge
2524 North Memorial Pkwy
Huntsville AL 35810
(205) 852-9200
(800) 255-3050
Room rates from $29

Motel 6
3200 W. University
Huntsville AL 35816
(205) 539-8448
1 small pet per room
Room rates $32-42

MADISON
Best Western
8716 Hwy 20
Madison AL 35758
(205) 772-0701
Room rates $50-57

Days Inn
102 Arlington Dr.
Madison AL 35758
(205) 772-9550
(800) 325-2525
Room rates $40-46

Days Inn - Huntsville Airport
102 Arlington Drive
Madison AL 35758
(205) 772-9550
(800) 325-2525
$4 extra charge
Room rates $40-43

MOBILE
Hampton Inn
4815 University Dr
Mobile AL 35816
(205) 830-9400
(800) 426-7866
Room rates $45-50

Hampton Inn
930 S. Beltine Hwy
Mobile AL 36609
(205) 344-4942
(800) 426-7866
Room rates $38-48

Days Inn
3650 Airport Blvd.
Mobile AL 36608
(205) 344-3410
(800) 325-2525
Room rates $35-55

Days Inn
1705 Dauphin Island Pkwy
Mobile AL 36605
(205) 471-6114
(800) 325-2525
Room rates $34-48

Motel 6
1520 Matzenger Dr.
Mobile AL 36605
(205) 473-1603
1 small pet per room
Reservations (505) 891-6161
Room rates from $25

Motel 6
5470 Tillman's Corner Pkwy
Mobile AL 36619
(205) 660-1483
1 small pet per room
Reservations (505) 891-6161
Room rates from $30

MONTGOMERY
Hampton Inn
1401 Eastern Blvd
Montgomery AL 36117
(205) 277-2400
(800) 426-7866
Room rates $40-46

Comfort Inn
5175 Carmichael Rd
Montgomery AL 36123-0175
(205) 277-1919
(800) 228-5150
Room rates $45-51

Days Inn
I-65 & 1150 W. South Blvd.
Montgomery AL 36105
(205) 281-8000
(800) 325-2525
$2/small dogs only
Room rates $33-42

Days Inn
I-65 & US 31
Montgomery AL 36043
(205) 281-7151
(800) 325-2525
$1 charge
Room rates from $35

Motel 6
1051 Eastern Bypass
Montgomery AL 36117
(205) 277-6748
1 small pet per room
Reservations (505) 891-6161
Room rates from $30

Howard Johnson Lodge
1110 East Blvd.
Montgomery, AL 36117
(205) 272-8800
(800) 654-2000
$32-50

MUSCLE SHOALS
Days Inn
2700 Woodward Ave.
Muscle Shoals AL 35661
(205) 383-3000
(800) 325-2525
Room rates $40-48

OPELIKA
Motel 6
1015 Columbus Pkwy
Opelika AL 36801
(205) 745-0988
1 small pet per room
Reservations (505) 891-6161
Room rates from $27

ORANGE BEACH
Days Inn
Hwy 182 East
Orange Beach AL 36561
(205) 981-9888
(800) 325-2525
Room rates $32-79

OXFORD
Days Inn
I-20 @ SR 21
Oxford AL 36203
(205) 835-0300
(800) 325-2525
Room rates $36-70

Motel 6
3202 Grace St.
Oxford AL 36203
(205) 831-5463
1 small pet per room
Reservations (505) 891-6161
Room rates from $24

PRATTVILLE
Ramada Inn
I-65 & US 31 North
Prattville AL 36067
(205) 365-3311
(800) 228-2828
Room rates from $44

SCOTTSBORO
Days Inn
1106 John T. Reid Pkwy
Scottsboro AL 35768
(205) 574-1212
(800) 325-2525
Room rates $34-50

SHEFFIELD
Ramada Inn
4205 Hatch Blvd
Sheffield AL 35660
(205) 381-3828
(800) 228-2828
Room rates $46-55

SHORTER
Days Inn
I-85 & Shorter Depot Rd.
Shorter AL 36075
(205) 727-6034
(800) 325-2525
Room rates $38-49

TILLMANS CORNER
Days Inn
5550 I-10 Service Rd.
Tillmans Corner AL 33619
(205) 661-8181
(800) 325-2525
Room rates $35-41

TUSCALOOSA
Motel 6
1700 McFarland Blvd
Tuscaloosa AL 35405
(205) 759-4942
1 small pet per room
Reservations (505) 891-6161
Room rates from $29

EconomyInn
3600 McFarland Blvd.
Tuscaloosa AL 35405
(205) 556-2010
Room rates $30-40

ALASKA
ANCHORAGE
Super 8 Motel
3501 Minnesota Dr.
Anchorage AK 99503
(907) 276-8884
(800) 848-8888
pets with deposit
Room rates $60-66

Clarion Inn
4800 Spenard Rd.
Anchorage AK 99517-3236
(907) 243-2300
(800) 458-6262
Room rates $135-200

FAIRBANKS
Super 8 Motel
1909 Airport Way
Fairbanks AK 99701
(907) 451-8888
(800) 848-8888
pets with deposit
Room rates $60-66

JUNEAU
Super 8 Motel
2295 Trout St.
Juneau AK 99801
(907) 789-4858
(800) 848-8888
pets with deposit
Room rates $61-68

Always
Call
Ahead!

KETCHIKAN
Super 8 Motel
2151 Sea Level Dr.
Ketchikan AK 99901
(907) 225-9088
(800) 848-8888
pets with deposit
Room rates $61-68

SITKA
Super 8 Motel
404 Sawmill Creek Rd.
Sitka AK 99835
(907) 747-8804
(800) 848-8888
pets with deposit
Room rates $66-73

ARIZONA
APACHE JUNCTION
Apache Junction Motel
1680 W. Apache Trail
Apache Junction AZ 85220
(602) 982-7702
Room rates $25-39

BENTONVILLE
Days Inn
1209 N. Walton
Bentonville AZ 72712
(501) 273-2451
(800) 325-2525
$5/pets
Room rates $50-56

BRINKLEY
Days Inn
I-40 & Hwy 49 North
Brinkley AZ 72021
(501) 734-1055
(800) 325-2525
$3/pets
Room rates $30-36

BULLHEAD CITY
Lake Mojave Resort
SR 68 & Davis Dam
Bullhead City AZ 86442
(602) 754-3245
Room rates $57-79

DOUGLAS
Motel 6
111 16th St
Douglas AZ 85607
(602) 364-2457
1 small pet per room
Reservations (505) 891-6161
Room rates $28-37

FLAGSTAFF
Super 8 Motel
3725 Kasper Ave.
Flagstaff AZ 86004
(602) 526-0818
(800) 848-8888
pets with permission
Room rates $28-45

Ramada Inn
2320 E Lucky Lane
Flagstaff AZ 86004
(602) 526-1150
(800) 228-2828
Room rates $55-78

Quality Inn
2000 S. Milton Rd.
Flagstaff AZ 86001
(602) 774-8771
(800) 228-5151
Room rates $53-78

Comfort Inn
914 S. Milton Rd
Flagstaff AZ 86001
(602) 774-7326
(800) 228-5150
Room rates $35-66

Days Inn
1000 West Business 40
Flagstaff AZ 86001
(602) 774-5221
(800) 325-2525
Room rates $44-70

Motel 6
2010 E. Butler Ave.
Flagstaff AZ 86001
(602) 774-1801
1 small pet per room
Reservations (505) 891-6161
Room rates $28-37

Motel 6
2745 South Woodlands Village
Flagstaff AZ 86001
(602) 779-3757
1 small pet per room
Reservations (505) 891-6161
Room rates $28-37

GRAND CANYON
El Tovar Hotel
South Rim Village
Grand Canyon National Park AZ
86023
(602) 638-2631
pets kept in kennels -$4-6.50
Room rates $90-130

Kachina Lodge
South Rim Village
Grand Canyon National Park AZ
86023
(602) 638-2631
Pets kept in kennels $4-6.50
Room rates $85-90

Maswik Lodge
South Rim Grand Canyon Village
Grand Canyon National Park AZ
86023
(602) 638-2631
pets kept in kennels $4-6.50
Room rates $57-85

Thunderbird Lodge
South Rim Grand Canyon Village
Grand Canyon National Park AZ
86023
(602) 638-2631
kennels $4-6.50 register @ Brite
Angel
Room rates $85-90

Yavapai Lodge
South Rim
Grand Canyon National Park AZ
86023
(602) 638-2631
kennels $4-6.50 open April -
October
Room rates $69-75

Always Call Ahead!

4

GREEN VALLEY
Quality Inn
111 S. La Canada
Green Valley AZ 85614
(602) 625-2250
(800) 228-5151
Room rates $55-88

HOLBROOK
Comfort Inn
2602 Navajo Blvd.
Holbrook AZ 86025
(602) 524-6131
(800) 228-5150
Room rates $44-64

Motel 6
2514 Navajo Blvd
Holbrook AZ 86025
(602) 524-6101
1 small pet per room
Reservations (505) 891-6161
Room rates $28-37

KINGMAN
Super 8 Motel
3401 E. Andy Devine Ave.
Kingman AZ 86401
(602) 757-4808
(800) 848-8888
pets with permission
Room rates $38-40

Quality Inn
1400 E. Andy Devine Ave.
Kingman AZ 86401
(602) 753-4747
(800) 228-5151
Room rates $45-59

Days Inn
3023 Andy Devine
Kingman AZ 86401
(602) 753-7500
(800) 325-2525
Room rates $39-45

Travelodge
3421 E. Andy Devine Ave.
Kingman AZ 86041
(602) 757-2158
(800) 255-3050
Room rates $35-37

Motel 6
424 E. Beale St.
Kingman AZ 86401
(602) 753-9222
1 small pet per room
Reservations (505) 891-6161
Room rates $28-37

LAKE HAVASU CITY
Super 8 Motel
305 London Bridge Rd.
Lake Havasu City AZ 86403
(602) 855-8844
(800) 848-8888
pets with permission
Room rates $39-46

Ramada Inn
1477 Queen's Bay Rd.
Lake Havasu City AZ 86403
(602) 855-0888
(800) 228-2828
Room rates $65-110

LAUGHLIN-BULLHEAD CITY
Motel 6
1616 Highway 95
Laughlin-Bullhead City AZ 86442
(602) 763-1002
1 small pet per room
Reservations (505) 891-6161
Room rates $28-37

MESA
Travelodge
22 South Country Club Dr.
Mesa AZ 85202
(602) 964-5694
(800) 255-3050
Room rates $35-52

Motel 6
336 W. Hampton Ave.
Mesa AZ 85202
(602) 844-8899
1 small pet per room
Reservations (505) 891-6161
Room rates $28-37

Always Call Ahead!

Motel 6
1511 S. Country Club Dr.
Mesa AZ 85202
(602) 834-0066
1 small pet per room
Reservations (505) 891-6161
Room rates $28-37

NOGALES
Super 8 Motel
700 W. Marisposa Rd.
Nogales AZ 85621
(602) 281-2242
(800) 848-8888
pets with permission
Room rates $41-47

Motel 6
1879 N. Grand Ave.
Nogales AZ 85621
(602) 281-2951
1 small pet per room
Reservations (505) 891-6161
Room rates $28-37

PHOENIX
Hampton Inn
8101 N. Black Canyon Hwy
Phoenix AZ 85021
(602) 864-6233
(800) 426-7866
Room rates $45-57

Howard Johnson Lodge
124 S. 24th St.
Phoenix, AZ 85034
(602) 244-8221
(800) 654-2000
$35-80

Super 8 Motel
4021 N. 27th Ave.
Phoenix AZ 85017
(602) 248-8880
(800) 848-8888
pets with permission
Room rates $41-48

Super 8 Motel
7171 W. Chandler Blvd.
Phoenix AZ 85226
(602) 961-3888
(800) 848-8888
pets with permission
Room rates $42-64

ARIZONA, Phoenix

Ramada Inn
12027 N 28th Dr.
Phoenix AZ 85029
(602) 866-7000
(800) 228-2828
small pets only
Room rates $46-75

Windom Hills
2641 W Union Hills Dr &I-17
Phoenix AZ 85027
(602) 978-2222
Room rates $69-89

Comfort Inn
1770 N. Dysart Rd.
Phoenix AZ 85338
(602) 923-9191
(800) 228-5150
Room rates $57-140

Quality Inn
951 W. Main St.
Phoenix AZ 85201
(602) 833-1231
(800) 228-5151
Room rates $42-99

Quality Inn
5121 E. La Puente Ave
Phoenix AZ 85044
(602) 893-3900
(800) 228-5151
Room rates $55-99

Quality Inn
3541 E. Van Buren Pkwy
Phoenix AZ 85008
(602) 273-7121
(800) 228-5151
Room rates $33-59

Howard Johnson Hotel
1500 N. 51st St.
Phoenix, AZ 85043
(602) 484-9009
(800) 654-2000
$55-125

Travelodge
8617 North Black Canyon Hwy
Phoenix AZ 85021
(602) 995-9500
(800) 255-3050
Room rates $37-42

Travelodge
8955 N.W. Grand Ave
Phoenix AZ 85345
(602) 979-7200
(800) 255-3050
Room rates $-42

Motel 6
2323 East Van Buren St.
Phoenix AZ 85006
(602) 267-7511
1 small pet per room
Reservations (505) 891-6161
Room rates $28-37

Motel 6
5315 East Van Buren
Phoenix AZ 85008
(602) 267-8555
1 small pet per room
Reservations (505) 891-6161
Room rates $28-37

Motel 6
1624 N. Black Canyon Hwy
Phoenix AZ 85009
(602) 269-6281
1 small pet per room
Reservations (505) 891-6161
Room rates $28-37

Motel 6
2330 W. Bell Rd.
Phoenix AZ 85023
(602) 993-2353
1 small pet per room
Reservations (505) 891-6161
Room rates $26-33

Motel 6
2735 W. Sweetwater Ave.
Phoenix AZ 85029
(602) 942-5030
1 small pet per room
Reservations (505) 891-6161
Room rates $28-37

Motel 6
1530 N. 52nd Dr.
Phoenix AZ 85043
(602) 272-0220
1 small pet per room
Reservations (505) 891-6161
Room rates $28-37

PRESCOTT
Super 8 Motel
1105 E. Sheldon St.
Prescott AZ 86301
(602) 776-1282
(800) 848-8888
pets with permission
Room rates $39-45

Motel 6
1111 E. Sheldon St.
Prescott AZ 86301
(602) 776-0160
1 small pet per room
Reservations (505) 891-6161
Room rates $28-37

SCOTTSDALE
Ramada Inn
6850 Main St.
Scottsdale AZ 85251
(602) 945-6321
(800) 228-2828
Room rates $55-132

Days Inn
4710 Scottsdale Rd.
Scottsdale AZ 85251
(602) 947-5411
(800) 325-2525
$5/pets
Room rates $71-125

Motel 6
6848 E. Camelback Rd.
Scottsdale AZ 85251
(602) 946-2280
1 small pet per room
Reservations (505) 891-6161
Room rates $28-37

SIERRA VISTA
Super 8 Motel
100 Fab Ave
Sierra Vista AZ 85635
(602) 459-5380
(800) 848-8888
pets with permission
Room rates from $45

Motel 6
1551 East Fry Blvd
Sierra Vista AZ 85635
(602) 459-5035
1 small pet per room
Reservations (505) 891-6161
Room rates $28-37

TEMPE
Super 8 Motel
1020 E. Apache Blvd.
Tempe AZ 85281
(602) 967-8891
(800) 848-8888
pets with permission
Room rates $46-66

Travelodge
1005 East Apache Blvd
Tempe AZ 85281
(602) 968-7871
(800) 255-3050
Room rates from $34

TUCSON
Ramada Inn
6944 E Tanque Verde
Tucson AZ 85715
(602) 886-9595
(800) 228-2828
Room rates $50-99

Quality Inn
1601 N. Oracle Rd.
Tucson AZ 85705
(602) 623-6666
(800) 228-5151
Room rates $46-62

Days Inn
88 E. Broadway Blvd.
Tucson AZ 85701
(602) 622-4000
(800) 325-2525
Room rates $52-77

Days Inn
3700 E. Irvington Rd.
Tucson AZ 85714
(602) 571-1400
(800) 325-2525
Room rates $47-60

Travelodge
222 South Freeway
Tucson AZ 85745
(602) 791-7511
(800) 255-3050
Room rates from $42

TUCSON
Motel 6
960 S. Freeway
Tucson AZ 85745
(602) 628-1339
1 small pet per room
Reservations (505) 891-6161
Room rates $28-37

Motel 6
1031 E. Benson Hwy
Tucson AZ 85713
(602) 628-1264
1 small pet per room
Reservations (505) 891-6161
Room rates $28-37

WILLCOX
Comfort Inn
724 N. Bisbee Ave
Willcox AZ 85643
(602) 384-4222
(800) 228-5150
Room rates $38-51

Motel 6
921 N. Bisbee
Willcox AZ 85643
(602) 384-2201
1 small pet per room
Reservations (505) 891-6161
Room rates $28-37

WILLIAMS
Travelodge
430 East Bill Williams Ave
Williams AZ 86046
(602) 635-2651
(800) 255-3050
Room rates $46-72

WINSLOW
Super 8 Motel
1916 W. 3rd St
Winslow AZ 86047
(602) 289-4606
(800) 848-8888
pets with permission
Room rates $35-37

Econo Lodge
1706 Park Dr.
Winslow, AZ 86047
(602) 289-4687
(800) 446-6900
$32-50

YOUNGTOWN
Motel 6
11133 Grand Ave.
Youngtown AZ 85363
(602) 977-1318
1 small pet per room
Reservations (505) 891-6161
Room rates $28-37

YUMA
Days Inn
Motel 6
1640 Arizona Ave.
Yuma AZ 85364
(602) 782-6561
1 small pet per room
Reservations (505) 891-6161
Room rates $28-37

Motel 6
1445 East 16th St.
Yuma AZ 85365
(602) 782-9521
1 small pet per room
Reservations (505) 891-6161
Room rates $28-37

ARKANSAS
ARKADELPHIA
Quality Inn
I-30 & SR 7
Arkadelphia AR 71923
(501) 246-5855
(800) 228-5151
Room rates $42-49

BENTONVILLE
Super 8 Motel
2301 SE Walton Blvd.
Bentonville AR 72712
(501) 273-1818
(800) 848-8888
pets with permission
Room rates $37-43

BLYTHEVILLE
Comfort Inn
I-55 & SR 18 E.
Blytheville AR 72316
(501) 763-7081
(800) 228-5150
Room rates $39-47

CLARKSVILLE
Super 8 Motel
1238 S. Rogers Ave.
Clarksville AR 72830
(501) 754-8800
(800) 848-8888
pets with permission
Room rates from $33

Days Inn
I-40
Clarksville AR 72830
(501) 754-8555
(800) 325-2525
Room rates $34-40

CONWAY
Ramada Inn
I-40 & US 64 Box 567
Conway AR 72032
(501) 329-8392
(800) 228-2828
Room rates $51-56

Comfort Inn
150 US 65 N.
Conway AR 72032
(501) 329-0300
(800) 228-5150
Room rates $44-72

Motel 6
H-65B & I-40/Box 567
Conway AR 72032
(501) 327-6623
1 small pet per room
Reservations (505) 891-6161
Room rates $26-33

CROSSETT
Ramada Inn
1400 Arkansas Hwy
Crossett AR 71635
(501) 364-4101
(800) 228-2828
Room rates $46-54

EL DORADO
Comfort Inn
2302 Junction City Rd.
El Dorado AR 71730
(501) 863-6677
(800) 228-5150
small pets only
Room rates $50-58

FAYETTEVILLE
Ramada Inn
3901 N College Ave
Fayetteville AR 72703
(501) 443-3431
(800) 228-2828
Room rates $44-50

Motel 6
2980 N. College
Fayetteville AR 72703
(501) 443-4351
1 small pet per room
Reservations (505) 891-6161
Room rates $26-33

FORT SMITH
Motel 6
6001 Rogers Ave.
Fort Smith AR 72903
(501) 484-0576
1 small pet per room
Reservations (505) 891-6161
Room rates $26-33

HARRISON
Ramada Inn
1222 North Main St.
Harrison AR 72601
(501) 741-7611
(800) 228-2828
Room rates $41-56

HOT SPRINGS
Days Inn
1125 E. Grand
Hot Springs AR 71901
(501) 624-3321
(800) 325-2525
Room rates $36-48

Best Western Sands Motel
1525 Central Ave.
Hot Springs Nat'l Park AR
71901
(501) 624-1258
(800) 528-1234
small pets only
Room rates $30-56

Holiday Inn Lake Hamilton
6100 Central Ave.
Hot Springs National Park AR
71902
(501) 525-1391
(800) 465-4329
small pets only
Room rates $55-69

JACKSONVILLE
Ramada Inn
200 Hwy 67 N
Jacksonville AR 72076
(501) 982-2183
(800) 228-2828
Room rates $39-54

JONESBORO
Super 8 Motel
2500 S. Caraway Rd.
Jonesboro AR 72401
(501) 972-0849
(800) 848-8888
pets with permission
Room rates $32-34

Motel 6
2300 South Caraway Rd.
Jonesboro AR 72401
(501) 932-1050
1 small pet per room
Reservations (505) 891-6161
Room rates $26-33

**Always
Call
Ahead!**

LITTLE ROCK
Super 8 Motel
7501 I-30
Little Rock AR 72209
(501) 568-8888
(800) 848-8888
pets with permission
Room rates $32-36

Comfort Inn
3200 Bankhead Dr.
Little Rock AR 72206
(501) 490-2010
(800) 228-5150
Room rates $45-54

Days Inn
2600 W. 65th St.
Little Rock AR 72209
(501) 562-1122
(800) 325-2525
Room rates $36-44

Motel 6
400 W. 29th St.
Little Rock AR 72114
(501) 758-5100
1 small pet per room
Reservations (505) 891-6161
Room rates $26-33

Motel 6
9525 30 Frontage Rd
Little Rock AR 72209
(501) 565-1388
1 small pet per room
Reservations (505) 891-6161
Room rates $26-33

MOUNTAIN HOME
Ramada Inn
1127 NE Hwy 62
Mountain Home AR 72653
(501) 425-9191
(800) 228-2828
Room rates $41-45

Holiday Inn
1350 Hwy 62 SW
Mountain Home AR 72653
(501) 425-5101
(800) 465-4329
Room rates $47-55

Always Call Ahead!

N. LITTLE ROCK
Economy Inn
3100 N. Main St.
N. Little Rock AR 72116
(501) 758-8110
$4 / day
Room rates $35-49

NEWPORT
Days Inn
101 Olivia Dr.
Newport AR 72112
(501) 523-6411
(800) 325-2525
Room rates $40-43

PRESCOTT
Comfort Inn
SR 24 W.
Prescott AR 71857
(501) 887-6641
(800) 228-5150
Room rates $36-44

RUSSELLVILLE
Motel 6
I-40 & County Rd.
Russellville AR 72801
(501) 968-3666
1 small pet per room
Reservations (505) 891-6161
Room rates $26-33

TEXARKANA
Super 8 Motel
325 E. 51st St.
Texarkana AR 75502
(501) 774-8888
(800) 848-8888
pets with permission
Room rates $31-33

Travelodge
4012 North State Line
Texarkana AR 75502
(501) 774-2771
(800) 255-3050
Room rates from $30

Motel 6
900 Realtor Ave.
Texarkana AR 75502
(501) 772-0678
1 small pet per room
Reservations (505) 891-6161
Room rates $26-33

Motel 6
900 Realtor Ave.
Texarkana AR 75502
(501) 772-0678
1 small pet per room
Reservations (505) 891-6161
Room rates $26-33

VAN BUREN
Super 8 Motel
106 N. Plaza Court
Van Buren AR 72956
(501) 471-8888
(800) 848-8888
pets with permission
Room rates $36-39

W. MEMPHIS
Motel 6
2501 So. Service Rd
W. Memphis AR 72301
(501) 735-0100
1 small pet per room
Reservations (505) 891-6161
Room rates $26-33

CALIFORNIA
ANAHEIM
Hampton Inn
300 E. Katella Way
Anaheim CA 92802
(714) 772-8713
(800) 426-7866
Room rates $61-70

Quality Hotel Conf. Center
616 Convention Way
Anaheim CA 92802
(714) 750-3131
(800) 228-5151
Room rates $67-85

Travelodge
505 West Katella Ave.
Anaheim CA 92802
(714) 774-8710
(800) 255-3050
Room rates from $39

Travelodge
2171 South Harbor Blvd
Anaheim CA 92802
(714) 750-3100
(800) 255-3050
Room rates $42-69

CALIFORNIA, Anaheim

Motel 6
921 South Beach Blvd
Anaheim CA 92804
(714) 220-2866
1 small pet per room
Reservations (505) 891-6161
Room rates $25-43

Motel 6
1440 N. State College
Anaheim CA 92806
(714) 956-9690
1 small pet per room
Reservations (505) 891-6161
Room rates $25-43

Motel 6
2920 W Chapman Ave
Anaheim CA 92668
(714) 634-2441
1 small pet per room
Reservations (505) 891-6161
Room rates $25-43

ARCADIA
Hampton Inn
311 E. Huntington Dr.
Arcadia CA 91006
(818) 574-5600
(800) 426-7866
Room rates $58-61

Motel 6
225 Colorado Pl
Arcadia CA 91006
(818) 446-2660
1 small pet per room
Reservations (505) 891-6161
Room rates $25-43

ARCATA
Super 8 Motel
4887 Valley W. Blvd.
Arcata CA 95521
(707) 822-8888
(800) 848-8888
pets with permission
Room rates $40-43

Quality Inn
3535 Janes Rd.
Arcata CA 95521
(707) 822-0409
(800) 228-5151
Room rates $76-81

Motel 6
4755 Valley West Blvd
Arcata CA 95521
(707) 822-7061
1 small pet per room
Reservations (505) 891-6161
Room rates $25-43

ATASCADERO
Motel 6
9400 El Camino Real
Atascadero CA 93422
(805) 466-6701
1 small pet per room
Reservations (505) 891-6161
Room rates $25-43

BAKERSFIELD
Quality Inn
1011 Oak St.
Bakersfield CA 93304
(805) 325-0772
(800) 228-5151
Room rates $42-55

Motel 6
350 Oak St.
Bakersfield CA 93304
(805) 326-1222
1 small pet per room
Reservations (505) 891-6161
Room rates $25-43

Motel 6
8223 E. Brundage Lane
Bakersfield CA 93307
(805) 366-7231
1 small pet per room
Reservations (505) 891-6161
Room rates $25-43

Motel 6
5241 Olive Tree Ct
Bakersfield CA 93308
(805) 392-9700
1 small pet per room
Reservations (505) 891-6161
Room rates $25-43

Motel 6
2727 White Lane
Bakersfield CA 93304
(805) 834-2828
1 small pet per room
Reservations (505) 891-6161
Room rates $25-43

BALDWIN PARK
Motel 6
14510 Garvey Ave
Baldwin Park CA 91706
(818) 960-5011
1 small pet per room
Reservations (505) 891-6161
Room rates $25-43

BANNING
Super 8 Motel
1690 W. Ramsey St.
Banning CA 92220
(714) 849-6887
(800) 848-8888
pets with permission
Room rates $36-40

BARSTOW
Quality Inn
1520 E. Main St.
Barstow CA 92311
(619) 256-6891
(800) 228-5151
Room rates $52-64

Motel 6
31951 East Main St
Barstow CA 92311
(619) 256-0653
1 small pet per room
Reservations (505) 891-6161
Room rates $25-43

BELLFLOWER
Motel 6
17220 Downey Ave
Bellflower CA 90706
(213) 531-3933
1 small pet per room
Reservations (505) 891-6161
Room rates $25-43

BERMUDA DUNES
Motel 6
78100 Varner Rd
Bermuda Dunes CA 92201
(619) 345-0550
1 small pet per room
Reservations (505) 891-6161
Room rates $25-43

BIG BEAR
Motel 6
1200 Big Bear Blvd
Big Bear CA 93215
(714) 585-6666
1 small pet per room
Reservations (505) 891-6161
Room rates $25-43

BIG BEAR LAKE
Cozy Hollow Lodge
40409 Big Bear Blvd.
Big Bear Lake CA 92315
(714) 866-8886
$50 refunded deposit
Room rates $45-130

Frontier Lodge & Motel
40472 Big Bear Blvd.
Big Bear Lake CA 92315
(714) 866-5888
$5 charge
Room rates $77-127

Grey Squirrel Resort
SR 18
Big Bear Lake CA 92315
(714) 866-4335
$5 night
Room rates $62-100

BLYTHE
Super 8 Motel
550 W. Donlon St.
Blythe CA 92225
(619) 922-8881
(800) 848-8888
pets with permission
Room rates $45-47

Comfort Inn
903 W. Hobson Way
Blythe CA 92225
(619) 922-4146
(800) 228-5150
Room rates $54-62

Motel 6
500 West Donlon St
Blythe CA 92225
(619) 922-6666
1 small pet per room
Reservations (505) 891-6161
Room rates $25-43

BUELLTON
Motel 6
333 McMurray Rd
Buellton CA 93427
(805) 688-7797
1 small pet per room
Reservations (505) 891-6161
Room rates $25-43

BUENA PARK
Motel 6
7051 Valley View
Buena Park CA 90622
(714) 522-1200
1 small pet per room
Reservations (505) 891-6161
Room rates $25-43

BURBANK
Burbank Airport Hilton
2500 Hollywood Way
Burbank CA 91505
(818) 843-6000
small pets only
Room rates $104-119

Holiday Inn - Burbank
150 East Angeleno
Burbank CA 91510
(818) 841-4770
(800) 465-4329
Room rates $106-115

BURLINGTON
Super 8 Motel
2100 Fay
Burlington CA 80807
(719) 346-5627
(800) 848-8888
limited rooms/$10 deposit
Room rates $31-35

BUTTONWILLOW
Motel 6
3810 Tracy Blvd
Buttonwillow CA 93206
(805) 764-5207
1 small pet per room
Reservations (505) 891-6161
Room rates $25-43

CAMARILLO
Motel 6
1641 East Daily Dr
Camarillo CA 93010
(805) 388-3467
1 small pet per room
Reservations (505) 891-6161
Room rates $25-43

CAMERON PARK
Super 8 Motel
3444 Coach Lane
Cameron Park CA 95682
(916) 677-7177
(800) 848-8888
pets with deposit
Room rates $47-50

Best Western Cameron Park
3361 Coach Lane
Cameron Park CA 95682
(916) 667-2203
(800) 528-1234
small, quiet pets
Room rates $56-65

CAMPBELL
Campbell Inn
675 E. Campbell Ave.
Campbell CA 95008
(408) 374-4300
$10 charge
Room rates $92-150

CANOGA PARK
Travelodge
20128 Roscoe Blvd
Canoga Park CA 91306
(818) 341-7200
(800) 255-3050
Room rates from $59

Warner Center Motor Inn
7132 DeSoto Ave.
Canoga Park CA 91303
(818) 346-5400
$10 charge
Room rates $50-70

CARLSBAD
Motel 6
1006 E. Elm Ave
Carlsbad CA 92008
(619) 434-7135
1 small pet per room
Reservations (505) 891-6161
Room rates $25-43

CALIFORNIA, Carlsbad

Motel 6
750 Raintree Dr
Carlsbad CA 92009
(619) 431-0745
1 small pet per room
Reservations (505) 891-6161
Room rates $25-43

CARMEL
Best Western - Carmel Mission
3665 Rio Rd.
Carmel CA 93922
(408) 624-1841
(800) 528-1234
ground floor old bldg only
Room rates $69-139

Wayside Inn
7th Ave. & Mission St.
Carmel CA 93921
(408) 624-5336
Room rates $70-175

Vagabond
4th & Delores St.
Carmel CA 93921
(408) 624-7738
(800) 522-1555
$10 charge
Room rates from $50

CARPINTERIA
Motel 6
4200 Via Real
Carpinteria CA 93013
(805) 684-6921
1 small pet per room
Reservations (505) 891-6161
Room rates $25-43

CARSON
Clarion Inn
2 Civic Plaza Dr.
Carson CA 90745
(213) 830-9200
(800) 458-6262
Room rates $90-100

CASTAIC
Comfort Inn
31558 Castaic Rd.
Castaic CA 91384
(805) 295-1100
(800) 228-5150
Room rates $48-60

CHICO
Motel 6
665 Manzabuta Court
Chico CA 95926
(916) 345-5500
1 small pet per room
Reservations (505) 891-6161
Room rates $25-43

Motel Orleans
655 Manzanita Ct.
Chico CA 95926
(916) 345-2533
$3 charge
Room rates $34-36

Safari Garden Motel
2352 Esplanade
Chico CA 95926
(916) 343-3201
$5 deposit
Room rates $40-44

Town House Motel
2231 Esplanade
Chico CA 95926
(916) 343-1621
small pets only
Room rates $34-45

CHINO
Motel 6
12266 Central Ave
Chino CA 91710
(714) 591-3877
1 small pet per room
Reservations (505) 891-6161
Room rates $25-43

CHULA VISTA
Motel 6
745 E St.
Chula Vista CA 92010
(619) 422-4200
1 small pet per room
Reservations (505) 891-6161
Room rates $25-43

Days Inn
225 Bay Blvd.
Chula Vista CA 92010
(619) 425-8200
(800) 325-2525
$4 charge
Room rates $50-80

CLAREMONT
Howard Johnson
721 Indian Hills Blvd.
Claremont CA 91711
(714) 626-2431
(800) 654-2000
domestic cats & dogs only
Room rates $47-69

COALINGA
Motel 6
25278 West Dorris
Coalinga CA 93210
(209) 935-2063
1 small pet per room
Reservations (505) 891-6161
Room rates $25-43

COLTON
Patriot Inn
2830 Iowa Ave.
Colton CA 92324
(714) 788-9900
small only
Room rates $40-49

COMMERCE
Ramada Inn
7272 Gage Ave
Commerce CA 90040
(213) 806-4777
(800) 228-2828
Room rates $67-75

CONCORD
Sheraton Hotel & Conf. Ctr
45 John Glenn Drive
Concord CA 94520
(415) 825-7700
(800) 325-3535
Room rates $42-140

CORNING
Days Inn
3475 Hwy 99 West
Corning CA 96021
(916) 824-2000
(800) 325-2525
$25 deposit/pets
Room rates $36-42

Always
Call
Ahead!

12

CORONA
Travelodge
1701 West Sixth St.
Corona CA 91720
(714) 735-5500
(800) 255-3050
Room rates $34-37

Motel 6
200 N. Lincoln
Corona CA 91719
(714) 735-6408
1 small pet per room
Reservations (505) 891-6161
Room rates $25-43

COSTA MESA
Residence Inn by Marriott
881 W. Baker St.
Costa Mesa CA 92626
(714) 241-8800
(800) 331-3131
$40-$60 fee + $7/day
Room rates $97-117

CULVER CITY
Ramada Hotel
6333 Bristol Pkwy
Culver City CA 90230
(213) 670-3200
(800) 228-2828
Room rates $90-100

CYPRESS
Ramada Inn
5865 Katella Ave.
Cypress CA 90630
(714) 827-1010
(800) 228-2828
Room rates from $84

Always Call Ahead!

DAVIS
Motel 6
4835 Chiles Rd
Davis CA 95616
(916) 753-3777
1 small pet per room
Reservations (505) 891-6161
Room rates $25-43

DESERT HOT SPRINGS
Stardust Motel
66634 5th St.
Desert Hot Springs CA 92240
(619) 329-5443
Room rates $40-42

DUNSMUIR
Travelodge
5400 Dunsmuir Ave.
Dunsmuir CA 96025
(916) 235-4395
(800) 255-3050
Room rates $40-45

EL CAJON
Penny Lodge
1556 E. Main
El Cajon CA 92021
(619) 442-9617
Room rates $40-48

Travelodge
471 North Magnolia Ave.
El Cajon CA 92020
(619) 447-3999
(800) 255-3050
Room rates $35-38

Motel 6
550 Montrose Ct.
El Cajon CA 92020
(619) 588-6100
1 small pet per room
Reservations (505) 891-6161
Room rates $25-43

EL CENTRO
Ramada Inn
1455 Ocotillo Dr
El Centro CA 92243
(619) 352-5152
(800) 228-2828
small pets only
Room rates $45-53

Motel 6
395 Smoketree Dr
El Centro CA 92243
(619) 353-6766
1 small pet per room
Reservations (505) 891-6161
Room rates $25-43

EL MONTE
Motel 6
3429 Peck Rd
El Monte CA 91731
(818) 448-6660
1 small pet per room
Reservations (505) 891-6161
Room rates $25-43

ESCONDIDO
Motel 6
900 N. Quince St
Escondido CA 92025
(619) 745-9252
1 small pet per room
Reservations (505) 891-6161
Room rates $25-43

Motel 6
509 W. Washington Ave
Escondido CA 92025
(619) 743-6669
1 small pet per room
Reservations (505) 891-6161
Room rates $25-43

EUREKA
Travelodge
4 Fourth St.
Eureka CA 95501
(707) 443-6345
(800) 255-3050
Room rates $59-69

Red Lion Inn
1929 4th St.
Eureka CA 95501
(707) 445-0844
Room rates $84-125

FAIRFIELD
Motel 6
1473 Holiday Lane
Fairfield CA 94533
(707) 425-4565
1 small pet per room
Reservations (505) 891-6161
Room rates $25-43

CALIFORNIA, Fairfield

Motel 6
2353 Magellan Rd
Fairfield CA 94533
(707) 427-0800
1 small pet per room
Reservations (505) 891-6161
Room rates $25-43

FALLBROOK
Travelodge
1608 S. Mission Rd.
Fallbrook CA 92028
(619) 723-1127
(800) 255-3050
Room rates from $

FONTANA
Motel 6
10195 Sierra Ave
Fontana CA 92335
(714) 823-8686
1 small pet per room
Reservations (505) 891-6161
Room rates $25-43

FREMONT
Econo Lodge
46019 Warm Springs Blvd.
Fremont, CA 94538
(415) 656-2800
(800) 446-6900
$35-60

Motel 6
34047 Fremont Blvd
Fremont CA 94536
(415) 793-4848
1 small pet per room
Reservations (505) 891-6161
Room rates $25-43

Motel 6
46101 Research Ave
Fremont CA 94539
(415) 490-4528
1 small pet per room
Reservations (505) 891-6161
Room rates $25-43

FRESNO
Motel 6
4245 N. Blackstone Ave
Fresno CA 93726
(209) 221-0800
1 small pet per room
Reservations (505) 891-6161
Room rates $25-43

Motel 6
933 North Pkwy Dr
Fresno CA 93728
(209) 233-3913
1 small pet per room
Reservations (505) 891-6161
Room rates $25-43

Motel 6
445 North Pkwy Dr
Fresno CA 93706
(209) 485-5011
1 small pet per room
Reservations (505) 891-6161
Room rates $25-43

Holiday Inn Centre Plaza
2233 Ventura St.
Fresno CA 93709
(209) 268-1000
(800) 465-4329
Room rates $73-79

GILROY
Super 8 Motel
8435 San Ysidro Ave.
Gilroy CA 95020
(408) 848-4108
(800) 848-8888
pets with permission
Room rates $38-40

Motel 6
6110 Monterey Hwy
Gilroy CA 95020
(408) 842-6061
1 small pet per room
Reservations (505) 891-6161
Room rates $25-43

HARBOR CITY
Motel 6
820 W. Sepulveda Blvd
Harbor City CA 90710
(213) 549-9560
1 small pet per room
Reservations (505) 891-6161
Room rates $25-43

HAYWARD
Travelodge
21598 Foothill Blvd
Hayward CA 94541
(415) 538-4380
(800) 255-3050
Room rates $45-47

HEMET
Super 8 Motel
3510 W. Florida
Hemet CA 92343
(714) 658-2281
(800) 848-8888
pets with permission
Room rates $43-47

Quality Inn
800 W. Florida Ave.
Hemet CA 92343
(714) 929-6366
(800) 228-5151
$25 deposit
Room rates $50-64

HOLLYWOOD
Best Western Hollywood
6141 Franklin Ave.
Hollywood CA 90028
(213) 464-5181
(800) 528-1234
$50 deposit, small only
Room rates $60-75

Holiday Inn Hollywood
1755 N. Highland Ave.
Hollywood CA 90028
(213) 462-7181
(800) 465-4329
Room rates $97-130

INDIO
Friendship Inn
84115 Indio Blvd.
Indio, CA 92201
(619) 342-4747
(800) 453-4511
#25-45

Super 8 Motel
81753 HWY 111
Indio, CA 92201
(619) 342-0264
(800) 848-8888
pets with permission
Rates from $44-48

Always Call Ahead!

Motel 6
82195 Indio Blvd
Indio CA 92201
(619) 342-6311
1 small pet per room
Reservations (505) 891-6161
Room rates $25-43

KING CITY
Motel 6
3 Broadway Circle
King City CA 93930
(408) 385-5000
1 small pet per room
Reservations (505) 891-6161
Room rates $25-43

LA JOLLA
La Jolla Palms Motel
6705 La Jolla Blvd.
La Jolla CA 92037
(619) 454-7101
small pets only
Room rates $46-99

LAKE TAHOE
(North Lake Tahoe)

TATAMI Cottage Resort
P.O. Box 138
7449 N. Lake Blvd.
Tahoe Vista, CA 96148
(916) 546-3523
Cottages $69-129

"Since 1925, we have taken pets.
We are next to a beaver pond
and a sandy beach. Pets are
free and stay in the room or
cottage. Cottages have kitchens,
fireplaces, lakeviews, and are
under giant pine trees"
Dave Bohm of TATAMI

LOMPOC
Motel 6
1415 East Ocean Ave
Lompoc CA 93436
(805) 736-6514
1 small pet per room
Reservations (505) 891-6161
Room rates $25-43

Porto Finale Inn
940 E. Ocean Ave.
Lompoc CA 93436
(805) 735-7731
$5 charge
Room rates $35-42

LONG BEACH
Travelodge
80 Atlantic Ave
Long Beach CA 90802
(213) 437-2471
(800) 255-3050
Room rates $52-55

Holiday Inn Long Beach Airport
2640 Lakewood Blvd.
Long Beach CA 90815
(213) 435-8511
(800) 465-4329
Room rates $80-85

Vagabond Inn
185 Atlantic Ave.
Long Beach CA 90802
(213) 435-3791
(800) 522-1555
$3 charge
Room rates $47-59

LOS ANGELES
Hampton Inn
10300 La Cienega Blvd
Los Angeles CA 90304
(213) 337-1000
(800) 426-7866
Room rates $67-75

Holiday Inn Convention Center
1020 S. Figueroa St.
Los Angeles CA 90015
(213) 748-1291
(800) 465-4329
small pets
Room rates $80-97

Holiday Inn - Downtown
750 Garland Ave. & 8th St.
Los Angeles CA 90017
(213) 628-5242
very small pets only
Room rates $72-78

Vagabond Inn
3101 S. Figueroa St.
Los Angeles CA 90007
(213) 746-1531
(800) 522-1555
$5 charge
Room rates $56-75

Neighborhood Suites Hotel
21902 Lassen St.
Los Angeles CA 91311
(818) 773-0707
Room rates $75-150

Holiday Inn @ LAX
9901 South La Cienega Blvd.
Los Angeles CA 90045
(213) 649-5151
(800) 465-4329
must remain crated
Room rates $96-109

Ma Maison Sofitel
8555 Beverly Blvd.
Los Angeles CA 90048
(213) 278-5444
$150 deposit required
Room rates $175-200

LOST HILLS
Motel 6
14685 Warren St
Lost Hills CA 93249
(805) 797-2346
1 small pet per room
Reservations (505) 891-6161
Room rates $25-43

MAMMOTH LAKES
Motel 6
3372 Main St
Mammoth Lakes CA 93546
(619) 934-6660
1 small pet per room
Reservations (505) 891-6161
Room rates $25-43

Royal Pines Resort
SR 203 & Viewpoint Rd.
Mammoth Lakes CA 93546
(619) 934-2306
$5 charge
Room rates $45-75

MARINA
Motel 6
100 Reservation Rd
Marina CA 93933
(408) 384-1000
1 small pet per room
Reservations (505) 891-6161
Room rates $25-43

MARINA DEL REY
Marina Del Rey Marriott
13480 Maxella Ave.
Marina Del Rey CA 90291
(213) 822-8555
Room rates $148-160

CALIFORNIA, Merced

MERCED
Motel 6
1410 V St
Merced CA 95340
(209) 384-2181
1 small pet per room
Reservations (505) 891-6161
Room rates $25-43

Motel 6
1983 E Childs Ave
Merced CA 95340
(209) 384-3702
1 small pet per room
Reservations (505) 891-6161
Room rates $25-43

MILPITAS
Best Western - Brookside Inn
400 Valley Way
Milpitas CA 95035
(408) 263-5566
(800) 528-1234
@ mgr's discretion
Room rates $55-60

Economy Inns of America
270 South Abbott Ave.
Milpitas CA 95035
(408) 946-8889
Room rates $3-47

MISSION VIEJO
Hampton Inn
26328 Oso Pkwy
Mission Viejo CA 92691
(714) 582-7100
(800) 426-7866
Room rates $73-80

MODESTO
Motel 6
722 Kansas Ave
Modesto CA 95351
(209) 524-3000
1 small pet per room
Reservations (505) 891-6161
Room rates $25-43

Best Western Town House
909 16th St.
Modesto CA 95354
(209) 524-7261
(800) 528-1234
small only
Room rates $50-55

Vagabond Inn
1525 McHenry Ave.
Modesto CA 95350
(209) 521-6340
(800) 522-1555
$3 charge
Room rates $55-60

MOJAVE
Travelodge
2201 Hwy 58
Mojave CA 93501
(805) 824-2441
(800) 255-3050
small only
Room rates from $40

Motel 6
16958 State Rte 58
Mojave CA 93501
(805) 824-4571
1 small pet per room
Reservations (505) 891-6161
Room rates $25-43

MONTEBELLO
Travelodge
525 West Washington Blvd
Montebello CA 90640
(213) 726-8222
(800) 255-3050
Room rates from $

MONTEREY
Bay Park Inn
1425 Munras Ave
Monterey CA 93940
(408) 649-1020
must be attended
Room rates $69-109

Motel 6
2124 N Fremont St
Monterey CA 93940
(408) 646-8585
1 small pet per room
Reservations (505) 891-6161
Room rates $25-43

Cypress Garden Motel
1150 Munras Ave.
Monterey CA 93940
(408) 373-2761
Room rates $50-100

Best Western - Monterey Bch
2600 Sand Dunes Drive
Monterey CA 93940
(408) 394-3321
(800) 528-1234
Room rates $90-170

Sand Dollar Inn
755 Abrego St.
Monterey CA 93940
(408) 372-7551
Room rates $60-100

MORENO VALLEY
Rodeway Inn
23330 Sunnymead Blvd.
Moreno Valley, CA 92388
(714) 242-0699
(800) 424-4777
$40-50

Motel 6
23581 Alessandro Blvd
Moreno Valley CA 92388
(714) 656-4451
1 small pet per room
Reservations (505) 891-6161
Room rates $25-43

Always
Call
Ahead!

16

MORRO BAY
Motel 6
298 Atascadero Rd
Morro Bay CA 93442
(805) 772-5641
1 small pet per room
Reservations (505) 891-6161
Room rates $25-43

MOUNT SHASTA
Best Western - The Tree House
I-5
Mount Shasta CA 96067
(916) 926-3101
(800) 528-1234
must be attended all times
Room rates $62-130

Mountain Air Lodge
1121 S. Mount Shasta Blvd.
Mount Shasta CA 96067
(916) 926-3411
$5 charge
Room rates $34-55

MOUNTAIN VIEW
Best Western Tropicana Lodge
1720 El Camino Real
Mountain View CA 94040
(415) 961-0220
(800) 528-1234
at manager's discretion
Room rates $56-70

MT. SHASTA
Motel 6
466 N. Weed Blvd.
Mt. Shasta CA 96094
(916) 938-4101
1 small pet per room
Reservations (505) 891-6161
Room rates $25-43

NAPA
Clarion Inn
3425 Solano Ave.
Napa CA 94558
(707) 253-7433
(800) 458-6262
$10 charge
Room rates $74-110

Motel 6
3380 Solano Ave
Napa CA 94558
(707) 257-6111
1 small pet per room
Reservations (505) 891-6161
Room rates $25-43

NEEDLES
Days Inn
1111 Pashard St.
Needles CA 92363
(619) 326-5660
(800) 325-2525
Room rates $43-510

Travelodge
1900 West Broadway
Needles CA 92363
(619) 326-3824
(800) 255-3050
Room rates from $40

Motel 6
1420 J St.
Needles CA 92363
(619) 326-3399
1 small pet per room
Reservations (505) 891-6161
Room rates $25-43

NEWARK
Motel 6
5600 Cedar Ct.
Newark CA 94560
(415) 791-5900
1 small pet per room
Reservations (505) 891-6161
Room rates $25-43

NEWBURY PARK
Motel 6
2850 Camino Dos Rios
Newbury Park CA 91320
(805) 499-0585
1 small pet per room
Reservations (505) 891-6161
Room rates $25-43

NEWPORT BEACH
Country Side Inn
325 Bristol St.
Newport Beach CA 92626
(714) 549-0300
small pets only
Room rates $80-100

NORTH HIGHLANDS
Motel 6
4600 Watt Ave.
North Highlands CA 95660
(916) 973-8637
1 small pet per room
Reservations (505) 891-6161
Room rates $25-43

OAKDALE
Ramada Inn
825 East F St.
Oakdale CA 95361
(209) 847-8181
(800) 228-2828
$50 deposit required
Room rates $70-90

OAKLAND
Days Inn
8350 Edes Ave.
Oakland CA 94621
(415) 568-1880
(800) 325-2525
$10 charge
Room rates $55-75

Motel 6
8480 Edes Ave.
Oakland CA 94621
(415) 638-1180
1 small pet per room
Reservations (505) 891-6161
Room rates $25-43

Motel 6
4919 Coliseum Way
Oakland CA 94601
(415) 261-7414
1 small pet per room
Reservations (505) 891-6161
Room rates $25-43

OCEANSIDE
Motel 6
3708 Plaza Dr
Oceanside CA 92056
(619) 941-1011
1 small pet per room
Reservations (505) 891-6161
Room rates $25-43

Motel 6
1403 Mission Ave.
Oceanside CA 92054
(619) 721-6662
1 small pet per room
Reservations (505) 891-6161
Room rates $25-43

CALIFORNIA, Ojai

OJAI
Best Western Casa Ojai
1302 E. Ojai Ave.
Ojai CA 93023
(805) 646-8175
(800) 528-1234
small pets only w/mgr approval
Room rates $55-80

Ojai Valley Inn & Country Club
SR 150
Ojai CA 93023
(805) 646-5511
small pets only
Room rates $170-220

ONTARIO
Travelodge
755 North Euclid Ave
Ontario CA 91762
(714) 984-1775
(800) 255-3050
Room rates from $

Motel 6
1560 E. Fourth St.
Ontario CA 91761
(714) 984-2424
1 small pet per room
Reservations (505) 891-6161
Room rates $25-43

Motel 6
1515 N. Mountain Ave.
Ontario CA 91762
(714) 986-6632
1 small pet per room
Reservations (505) 891-6161
Room rates $25-43

ORANGE
Hilton Suites - Anaheim
400 North State College Blvd.
Orange CA 92668
(714) 938-1111
(800) 445-8667
Room rates $125-160

OROVILLE
Motel 6
505 Montgomery St.
Oroville CA 95965
(916) 532-9400
1 small pet per room
Reservations (505) 891-6161
Room rates $25-43

OXNARD
Crown Sterling Suites
2101 Mandalay Beach Rd.
Oxnard CA 93035
(805) 984-2500
small pets only
Room rates $150-210

Vagabond Inn
1240 N. Oxnard Blvd.
Oxnard CA 93030
(805) 983-0251
(800) 522-1555
$3 charge
Room rates $45-50

PACIFIC GROVE
Best Western Butterfly Trees
1150 Lighthouse Ave.
Pacific Grove CA 93950
(408) 372-0503
(800) 528-1234
$10 nightly fee
Room rates $50-105

PALM SPRINGS
Super 8 Motel
1900 N. Palm Canyon Dr.
Palm Springs CA 92262
(619) 322-3757
(800) 848-8888
pets with permission
Room rates $56-60

Motel 6
660 S. Palm Canyon Dr.
Palm Springs CA 92262
(619) 327-4200
1 small pet per room
Reservations (505) 891-6161
Room rates $25-43

Motel 6
595 East Palm Canyon Dr.
Palm Springs CA 92262
(619) 325-6129
1 small pet per room
Reservations (505) 891-6161
Room rates $25-43

PALMDALE
Motel 6
407 West Palmdale Blvd
Palmdale CA 93551
(805) 272-0660
1 small pet per room
Reservations (505) 891-6161
Room rates $25-43

Vagabond Inn
130 E. Palmdale Blvd.
Palmdale CA 93550
(805) 273-1400
(800) 522-1555
$3 charge
Room rates $35-45

PALO ALTO
Travelodge
3255 El Camino Real
Palo Alto CA 94306
(415) 493-6340
(800) 255-3050
Room rates from $65

Motel 6
4301 El Camino Real
Palo Alto CA 94306
(415) 949-0833
1 small pet per room
Reservations (505) 891-6161
Room rates $25-43

PARADISE
Palos Verdes Motel
5423 Skyway
Paradise CA 95967
(916) 877-2127
small pets only
Room rates $35-40

Ponderosa Gardens Motel
7010 Skyway
Paradise CA 95969
(916) 872-9094
$2 charge
Room rates $42-57

PASADENA
Doubletree Hotel
191 N. Los Robles Ave.
Pasadena CA 91101
(818) 792-2727
Room rates from $89

Holiday Inn
303 E. Cordova St.
Pasadena CA 91101
(818) 449-4000
(800) 465-4329
small pets only + deposit
Room rates $100-105

Vagabond Inn
2863 E. Colorado Blvd.
Pasadena CA 91107
(818) 449-3020
(800) 522-1555
$3 charge
Room rates $55-60

PASO ROBLES
Travelodge
2701 Spring St.
Paso Robles CA 93446
(805) 238-0078
(800) 255-3050
Room rates from $50

PETALUMA
Quality Inn
5100 Montero Way
Petaluma CA 94954
(707) 664-1155
(800) 228-5151
Room rates $54-89

Motel 6
5135 Montero Way
Petaluma CA 94954
(707) 664-9090
1 small pet per room
Reservations (505) 891-6161
Room rates $25-43

PINOLE
Motel 6
1501 Fitzgerald Dr.
Pinole CA 94564
(415) 222-8174
1 small pet per room
Reservations (505) 891-6161
Room rates $25-43

PISMO BEACH
Motel 6
860 4th St.
Pismo Beach CA 93449
(805) 773-2665
1 small pet per room
Reservations (505) 891-6161
Room rates $25-43

Spyglass Inn
2705 Spyglass Dr.
Pismo Beach CA 93449
(805) 773-4855
$10/day pet fee
Room rates $65-95

Always Call Ahead!

PITTSBURG
Motel 6
2101 Loveridge Road
Pittsburg CA 94565
(415) 427-1600
1 small pet per room
Reservations (505) 891-6161
Room rates $25-43

PORTERVILLE
Motel 6
935 West Morton Ave.
Porterville CA 93257
(209) 781-7600
1 small pet per room
Reservations (505) 891-6161
Room rates $25-43

RANCHO CALIFORNIA
Motel 6
41900 Moreno Dr.
Rancho California CA 92390
(714) 676-7199
1 small pet per room
Reservations (505) 891-6161
Room rates $25-43

RANCHO CORDOVA
Comfort Inn
3240 Mather Field Rd.
Rancho Cordova CA 95670
(916) 363-3344
(800) 228-5150
$100 deposit
Room rates $60-99

Motel 6
10271 Folsom Blvd.
Rancho Cordova CA 95670
(916) 362-5800
1 small pet per room
Reservations (505) 891-6161
Room rates $25-43

Economy Inns of America
12249 Folsom Blvd.
Rancho Cordova CA 95670
(916) 351-1213
Room rates from $42

RED BLUFF
Super 8 Motel
203 Antelope Blvd.
Red Bluff CA 96080
(916) 527-8882
(800) 848-8888
pets with permission
Room rates $38-40

Motel 6
20 Williams Ave.
Red Bluff CA 96080
(916) 527-9200
1 small pet per room
Reservations (505) 891-6161
Room rates $25-43

REDDING
Motel 6
1250 Twin View Blvd.
Redding CA 96003
(916) 246-4470
1 small pet per room
Reservations (505) 891-6161
Room rates $25-43

Motel 6
1640 Hilltop Dr.
Redding CA 96001
(916) 221-1800
1 small pet per room
Reservations (505) 891-6161
Room rates $25-43

Best Western Hospitality House
532 N. Market St.
Redding CA 96003
(916) 241-6464
(800) 528-1234
small pets only
Room rates $42-46

Days Hotel
2180 Hilltop Dr.
Redding CA 96002
(916) 221-8200
(800) 325-2525
$35 deposit
Room rates $70-90

Vagabond Inn
536 E. Cypress Ave.
Redding CA 96002
(916) 223-1600
(800) 522-1555
$3 charge
Room rates $60-65

REDLANDS
Motel 6
1160 Arizona St.
Redlands CA 92374
(714) 792-3175
1 small pet per room
Reservations (505) 891-6161
Room rates $25-43

CALIFORNIA, Redwood City

REDWOOD CITY
Howard Johnson
485 Veterans Blvd.
Redwood City CA 94063
(415) 365-5500
(800) 654-2000
Room rates $69-85

RIDGECREST
Motel 6
535 S. China Lake Blvd.
Ridgecrest CA 93555
(619) 375-6866
1 small pet per room
Reservations (505) 891-6161
Room rates $25-43

RIVERSIDE
Motel 6
4045 University Ave.
Riverside CA 92501
(714) 686-6666
1 small pet per room
Reservations (505) 891-6161
Room rates $25-43

Motel 6
3663 La Sierra Ave.
Riverside CA 92505
(714) 351-0764
1 small pet per room
Reservations (505) 891-6161
Room rates $25-43

Motel 6
6830 Valley Way
Riverside CA 92509
(714) 681-6666
1 small pet per room
Reservations (505) 891-6161
Room rates $25-43

Holiday Inn
1200 University Ave.
Riverside CA 92507
(714) 682-8000
(800) 465-4329
small pets only
Room rates $72-80

ROHNERT PARK
Motel 6
6145 Commerce Blvd.
Rohnert Park CA 94928
(707) 585-8888
1 small pet per room
Reservations (505) 891-6161
Room rates $25-43

ROSEMEAD
Motel 6
1001 South San Gabriel Blvd
Rosemead CA 91770
(818) 572-6076
1 small pet per room
Reservations (505) 891-6161
Room rates $25-43

Vagabond Inn
3633 N. Rosemead Blvd.
Rosemead CA 91770
(818) 288-6661
(800) 522-1555
$3 charge
Room rates $42-65

ROWLAND HEIGHTS
Motel 6
78970 E Labin Ct
Rowland Heights CA 91748
(818) 964-5333
1 small pet per room
Reservations (505) 891-6161
Room rates $25-43

SACRAMENTO
Super 8 Motel
7216 55th St.
Sacramento CA 95823
(916) 427-7925
(800) 848-8888
pets with permission
Room rates $45-50

Motel 6
7780 Stockton Blvd.
Sacramento CA 95823
(916) 689-9141
1 small pet per room
Reservations (505) 891-6161
Room rates $25-43

Motel 6
7407 Elsie Ave.
Sacramento CA 95828
(916) 689-6555
1 small pet per room
Reservations (505) 891-6161
Room rates $25-43

Motel 6
7850 College Town Dr.
Sacramento CA 95826
(916) 383-8110
1 small pet per room
Reservations (505) 891-6161
Room rates $25-43

Motel 6
1415 30th St.
Sacramento CA 95816
(916) 457-0777
1 small pet per room
Reservations (505) 891-6161
Room rates $25-43

SALINAS
Motel 6
1010 Fairview Ave.
Salinas CA 93905
(408) 758-2122
1 small pet per room
Reservations (505) 891-6161
Room rates $25-43

Motel 6
1257 De La Torre Blvd.
Salinas CA 93905
(408) 757-3077
1 small pet per room
Reservations (505) 891-6161
Room rates $25-43

Vagabond Inn
131 Kern St.
Salinas CA 93905
(408) 758-4693
(800) 522-1555
$3 charge
Room rates $55-60

SAN BERNARDINO
Motel 6
1960 Ostrem's Way
San Bernardino CA 92407
(714) 887-8191
1 small pet per room
Reservations (505) 891-6161
Room rates $25-43

Motel 6
111 Redlands Blvd.
San Bernardino CA 92408
(714) 825-6666
1 small pet per room
Reservations (505) 891-6161
Room rates $25-43

SAN DIEGO
Travelodge
16929 West Bernardo Dr.
San Diego CA 92127
(619) 487-0445
(800) 255-3050
Room rates from $62

Travelodge
2380 Moore St.
San Diego CA 92110
(619) 291-9100
(800) 255-3050
Room rates $44-54

Motel 6
2424 Hotel Circle North
San Diego CA 92108
(619) 296-1612
1 small pet per room
Reservations (505) 891-6161
Room rates $25-43

Motel 6
5592 Clairemont Mesa Blvd.
San Diego CA 92117
(619) 268-9758
1 small pet per room
Reservations (505) 891-6161
Room rates $25-43

Howard Johnson
4545 Waring Rd.
San Diego CA 92120
(619) 286-7000
(800) 654-2000
Room rates $70-80

Hyatt Islandia
1441 Quivira Rd.
San Diego CA 92109
(619) 224-1234
(800) 233-1234
small dogs only
Room rates $130-170

SAN DIMAS
Motel 6
502 W Arrow Hwy
San Dimas CA 91773
(714) 592-5631
1 small pet per room
Reservations (505) 891-6161
Room rates $25-43

SAN FERNANDO
Days Inn
20128 Roscoe Blvd.
San Fernando CA 91306
(818) 341-7200
(800) 325-2525
$5/pets
Room rates $55-80

SAN FRANCISCO
Comfort Inn
401 E. Millbrae Ave.
San Francisco CA 94030
(415) 692-6363
(800) 228-5150
Room rates $100-135

San Francisco Hilton
330 O'Farrell St.
San Francisco CA 94102
(415) 771-1400
$5 charge
Room rates $150-230

Holiday Inn - Airport
245 S. Airport Blvd.
San Francisco CA 94080
(415) 589-7200
(800) 465-4329
Room rates $55-100

Rodeway Inn
1450 Lombard St.
San Francisco, CA 94123
(415) 673-0691
(800) 424-4777
$55-125

Days Inn
777 Airport Blvd.
San Francisco CA 94010
(415) 342-7772
(800) 325-2525
$4 charge
Room rates $65-80

Vagabond Inn - Airport
1640 Bayshore Hwy
San Francisco CA 94010
(415) 692-4040
(800) 522-1555
$3 charge
Room rates $60-75

SAN JOSE
Travelodge
1041 The Alameda
San Jose CA 95126
(408) 295-0159
(800) 255-3050
Room rates $55-58

Motel 6
2081 N. First St.
San Jose CA 95131
(408) 436-8180
1 small pet per room
Reservations (505) 891-6161
Room rates $25-43

Motel 6
2560 Fontaine Rd.
San Jose CA 95121
(408) 270-3131
1 small pet per room
Reservations (505) 891-6161
Room rates $25-43

Holiday Inn - Airport
1355 N. 4th St.
San Jose CA 95112
(408) 453-5340
(800) 465-4329
Room rates $65-75

Holiday Inn - Park Ctr Plaza
282 Almaden Blvd.
San Jose CA 95113
(408) 998-0400
(800) 465-4329
Room rates $65-75

SAN LUIS OBISPO
Motel 6
1433 Calle Joaquin
San Luis Obispo CA 93401
(805) 549-9595
1 small pet per room
Reservations (505) 891-6161
Room rates $25-43

Vagabond Inn
210 Madonna Rd.
San Luis Obispo CA 93401
(805) 544-4710
(800) 522-1555
$3 charge
Room rates $48-72

CALIFORNIA, San Mateo

SAN MATEO
Dunfey San Mateo Hotel
1770 S. Amphlett Blvd.
San Mateo CA 94402
(415) 573-7661
$15 per day charge
Room rates $95-130

Villa Hotel
4000 S. El Camino Real
San Mateo CA 94403
(415) 341-0966
Room rates $72-80

SAN SIMEON
Holiday Inn
9070 Castillo Dr.
San Simeon CA 93452
(805) 927-8691
(800) 465-4329
small pets only
Room rates $95-105

SAN YSIDRO
Motel 6
160 E. Calle Primaro
San Ysidro CA 92073
(619) 690-6663
1 small pet per room
Reservations (505) 891-6161
Room rates $25-43

SANTA ANA
Motel 6
1623 E. First St.
Santa Ana CA 92701
(714) 558-0500
1 small pet per room
Reservations (505) 891-6161
Room rates $25-43

Vagabond inn
1519 E. 1st St.
Santa Ana CA 92701
(714) 547-9426
(800) 522-1555
$3 charge
Room rates $43-59

SANTA BARBARA
Motel 6
443 Corona Del Mar
Santa Barbara CA 93103
(805) 564-1392
1 small pet per room
Reservations (505) 891-6161
Room rates $25-43

Motel 6
5897 Calle Real
Santa Barbara CA 93117
(805) 964-3596
1 small pet per room
Reservations (505) 891-6161
Room rates $25-43

Motel 6
3505 State St.
Santa Barbara CA 93105
(805) 687-5400
1 small pet per room
Reservations (505) 891-6161
Room rates $25-43

Vagabond Inn
2819 State St.
Santa Barbara CA 93105
(805) 687-6444
(800) 522-1555
$3 charge
Room rates $55-64

SANTA CLARA
Travelodge
3477 El Camino Real
Santa Clara CA 95051
(408) 984-3364
(800) 255-3050
Room rates from $54

Motel 6
3208 El Camino Real
Santa Clara CA 95051
(408) 241-0200
1 small pet per room
Reservations (505) 891-6161
Room rates $25-43

Vagabond Inn
3580 El Camino Real
Santa Clara CA 95051
(408) 241-0771
(800) 522-1555
$3 charge
Room rates $63-70

SANTA CRUZ
Vagabond Inn
1519 E. 1st St.
Santa Cruz CA 92701
(714) 547-9426
(800) 522-1555
$3 charge
Room rates $45-52

SANTA MARIA
Motel 6
2040 North Preisker Lane
Santa Maria CA 93454
(805) 928-8111
1 small pet per room
Reservations (505) 891-6161
Room rates $25-43

Motel 6
839 East Main St.
Santa Maria CA 93454
(805) 925-2551
1 small pet per room
Reservations (505) 891-6161
Room rates $25-43

SANTA MONICA
Travelodge
1525 Ocean Ave.
Santa Monica CA 90401
(213) 451-0761
(800) 255-3050
Room rates $75-80

Loews Santa Monica Beach
Hotel
1700 Ocean Ave.
Santa Monica CA 90401
(213) 458-6700
small pets only
Room rates $190-280

SANTA NELLA
Motel 6
12733 So. Hwy. 33
Santa Nella CA 95322
(209) 826-6644
1 small pet per room
Reservations (505) 891-6161
Room rates $25-43

Holiday Inn Mission de Oro
13070 Hwy 33 South
Santa Nella CA 95322
(209) 826-4444
(800) 465-4329
Room rates $42-55

SANTA ROSA
Travelodge
1815 Santa Rosa Ave.
Santa Rosa CA 95407
(707) 542-3472
(800) 255-3050
Room rates from $48

Travelodge
635 Healdsburg Ave.
Santa Rosa CA 95401
(707) 544-4141
(800) 255-3050
Room rates from $47

Motel 6
2760 Cleveland Ave.
Santa Rosa CA 95403
(707) 546-1500
1 small pet per room
Reservations (505) 891-6161
Room rates $25-43

SANTA YNEZ
Sanja Cota Motor Lodge
3099 Mission Dr.
Santa Ynez CA 93460
(805) 688-5525
$5 charge
Room rates $50-60

SEASIDE
Days Inn
1400 Del Monte Blvd.
Seaside CA 93955
(408) 394-5335
(800) 325-2525
Room rates $49-87

SELMA
Super 8 Motel
3142 S. Highland Ave.
Selma CA 93662
(209) 869-2800
(800) 848-8888
pets with permission
Room rates $40-44

SIMI VALLEY
Motel 6
2566 N. Erringer Rd.
Simi Valley CA 93065
(805) 526-3533
1 small pet per room
Reservations (505) 891-6161
Room rates $25-43

SOLVANG
Meadowlark Motel
2644 Mission Dr.
Solvang CA 93463
(805) 688-4631
Room rates $34-55

SOUTH LAKE TAHOE
Motel 6
P.O. Box 7756
2375 Lake Tahoe Blvd.
South Lake Tahoe CA 95731
(916) 542-1400
1 small pet per room
Reservations (505) 891-6161
Room rates $25-43

Alder Inn Motel
Off US 50 on Ski Run Blvd.
South Lake Tahoe CA 95729
(916) 544-4485
Room rates $35-86

Blue Lake Motel
Off US 50 on Ski Run Blvd.
South Lake Tahoe CA 95705
(916) 544-4853
$5 charge with $50 deposit
Room rates $35-86

Slalom Inn
1195 Ski Run Blvd.
South Lake Tahoe CA 95705
(916) 544-5765
small dogs only
Room rates $38-59

Tahoe Sands Inn
US 50 1 blk west of Ski Run Blvd.
South Lake Tahoe CA 95705
(916) 544-3476
$6 charge
Room rates $58-68

Tahoe Valley Motel
US 50 & SR 89 Tahoe Keys Blvd.
Box 7702
South Lake Tahoe CA 95731
(916) 541-0353
$5 extra charge
Room rates $39-85

STANTON
Motel 6
7450 Katella Ave.
Stanton CA 90680
(714) 891-0717
1 small pet per room
Reservations (505) 891-6161
Room rates $25-43

STOCKTON
Motel 6
4100 Waterloo Rd.
Stockton CA 95205
(209) 931-9511
1 small pet per room
Reservations (505) 891-6161
Room rates $25-43

Motel 6
1625 French Camp T-pike Rd.
Stockton CA 95206
(209) 467-3600
1 small pet per room
Reservations (505) 891-6161
Room rates $25-43

Eden Park Inn
1005 N. El Dorado St.
Stockton CA 95202
(209) 466-2711
short stays only
Room rates $32-41

La Quinta
2710 March Lane
Stockton CA 95207
(209) 952-7800
(800) 531-5900
small pets only
Room rates $54-75

Vagabond Inn
33 North Center St.
Stockton CA 95202
(209) 948-6151
(800) 522-1555
$3 charge
Room rates $36-50

Motel 6
775 N. Mathilda Ave.
Sunnyvale CA 94086
(408) 736-4595
1 small pet per room
Reservations (505) 891-6161
Room rates $25-43

SUNNYVALE
Motel 6
806 Ahwanee Ave.
Sunnyvale CA 94086
(408) 720-1222
1 small pet per room
Reservations (505) 891-6161
Room rates $25-43

Motel 6
775 N. Mathilda Ave.
Sunnyvale, CA 94086
(408) 736-4595
(505) 891-6161
1 small pet per room
$25-45

SYLMAR
Motel 6
12775 Encinitas Ave
Sylmar CA 91342
(818) 362-9491
1 small pet per room
Reservations (505) 891-6161
Room rates $25-43

TAHOE VISTA

TATAMI Cottage Resort
P.O. Box 138
7449 N. Lake Blvd.
Tahoe Vista, CA 96148
(916) 546-3523
Cottages $69-129

THOUSAND OAKS
Days Inn
1320 Newbury Rd.
Thousand Oaks CA 91320
(805) 499-5910
(800) 325-2525
$5 charge
Room rates $54-65

Howard Johnson
75 Thousand Oaks Blvd.
Thousand Oaks CA 91360
(805) 497-3701
(800) 654-2000
small cats & dogs only
Room rates $50-72

TRACY
Motel 6
3810 Tracy Blvd
Tracy CA 95376
(209) 836-4900
1 small pet per room
Reservations (505) 891-6161
Room rates $25-43

TRUCKEE
Super 8 Motel
11506 Deerfield Dr.
Truckee CA 95737
(916) 587-8888
(800) 848-8888
Room rates $69-79

TULARE
Motel 6
1111 North Blackstone
Tulare CA 93274
(209) 686-1611
1 small pet per room
Reservations (505) 891-6161
Room rates $25-43

TURLOCK
Motel 6
250 South Walnut Ave.
Turlock CA 95380
(209) 667-4100
1 small pet per room
Reservations (505) 891-6161
Room rates $25-43

UKIAH
Motel 6
1208 S. State St.
Ukiah CA 95482
(707) 468-5404
1 small pet per room
Reservations (505) 891-6161
Room rates $25-43

VACAVILLE
Super 8 Motel
101 Allison Court
Vacaville CA 95688
(707) 449-8884
(800) 848-8888
pets with permission
Room rates from $43

Motel 6
107 Lawrence Dr.
Vacaville CA 95688
(707) 447-5550
1 small pet per room
Reservations (505) 891-6161
Room rates $25-43

Best Western Heritage Inn
1420 E. Monte Vista Ave.
Vacaville CA 95688
(707) 448-8453
(800) 528-1234
small pets
Room rates $45-50

VALLEJO
Super 8 Motel
1596 Fairgrounds Dr.
Vallejo CA 94589
(707) 554-9655
(800) 848-8888
Room rates $55-60

Travelodge
160 E. Lincoln I-80
Vallejo CA 94591
(707) 552-7220
(800) 255-3050
Room rates $39-44

Motel 6
458 Fairgrounds Dr.
Vallejo CA 94589
(707) 642-7781
1 small pet per room
Reservations (505) 891-6161
Room rates $25-43

Motel 6
101 Maritime Academy Dr.
Vallejo CA 94590
(707) 557-0777
1 small pet per room
Reservations (505) 891-6161
Room rates $25-43

VENTURA
Motel 6
2145 E. Harbor Blvd.
Ventura CA 93001
(805) 643-5100
1 small pet per room
Reservations (505) 891-6161
Room rates $25-43

Motel 6
3075 Johnson Dr.
Ventura CA 93003
(805) 650-0080
1 small pet per room
Reservations (505) 891-6161
Room rates $25-43

VICTORVILLE
Travelodge
16868 Stoddard Wells Rd
Victorville CA 92392
(619) 243-7700
(800) 255-3050
Room rates from $27

Always
Call
Ahead!

Motel 6
16901 Stoddard Wells Rd.
Victorville CA 92392
(619) 243-0666
1 small pet per room
Reservations (505) 891-6161
Room rates $25-43

Holiday Inn
15494 Palmdale Rd.
Victorville CA 92392
(619) 245-6565
(800) 465-4329
$25 deposit required
Room rates $51-65

VISALIA
Holiday Inn Plaza Park
9000 West Airport Dr.
Visalia CA 93277
(209) 651-5000
(800) 465-4329
Room rates $76-82

WALNUT CREEK
Motel 6
2389 N. Main St.
Walnut Creek CA 94596
(415) 935-4010
1 small pet per room
Reservations (505) 891-6161
Room rates $25-43

WATSONVILLE
El Rancho Motel
976 Salinas Rd.
Watsonville CA 95076
(408) 722-2766
$5 charge
Room rates $33-55

WEST COVINA
Hampton Inn
3145 E Garvey Ave. N.
West Covina CA 91791
(818) 967-5800
(800) 426-7866
Room rates $55-65

Holiday Inn
3223 E Garvey Ave. N.
West Covina CA 91791
(818) 966-8311
(800) 465-4329
small pets only
Room rates $66-70

WESTMINISTER
Motel 6
6266 Westminister Ave.
Westminister CA 92683
(714) 891-5366
1 small pet per room
Reservations (505) 891-6161
Room rates $25-43

WHITTIER
Motel 6
8221 S Pioneer Blvd
Whittier CA 90606
(213) 692-9101
1 small pet per room
Reservations (505) 891-6161
Room rates $25-43

Vagabond Inn
14125 E Whittier Blvd.
Whittier CA 90605
(213) 698-9701
(800) 522-1555
$3 charge
Room rates $47-60

WILLIAMS
Comfort Inn
400 C St.
Williams CA 95987
(916) 473-2381
(800) 228-5150
Room rates $43-55

Motel 6
455 4th St.
Williams CA 95987
(916) 473-5337
1 small pet per room
Reservations (505) 891-6161
Room rates $25-43

WILLOWS
Super 8 Motel
457 Humboldt Ave.
Willows CA 95988
(916) 934-2871
(800) 848-8888
pets with permission
Room rates from $38

Best Western Golden Pheasant
249 N Humboldt Ave.
Willows CA 95988
(916) 934-4603
(800) 528-1234
small pets @ mgr's discretion
Room rates $45-60

WOODLAND
Motel 6
1564 East Main St.
Woodland CA 95695
(916) 666-6777
1 small pet per room
Reservations (505) 891-6161
Room rates $25-43

Motor Lodge
22621 Ventura Blvd.
Woodland Hills CA 91364
(818) 884-7777
$10 charge
Room rates $39-50

YREKA
Motel 6
1785 S. Main St.
Yreka CA 96097
(916) 842-4111
1 small pet per room
Reservations (505) 891-6161
Room rates $25-43

Best Western Miner's Inn
122 E Miner St.
Yreka CA 96097
(916) 842-4355
(800) 528-1234
Room rates $41-48

YUBA CITY
Motel 6
700 N. Polora Ave.
Yuba City CA 95991
(916) 674-1710
1 small pet per room
Reservations (505) 891-6161
Room rates $25-43

YUCCA VALLEY
Super 8 Motel
57096 29 Palms Hwy
Yucca Valley CA 92284
(619) 228-1773
(800) 848-8888
pets with permission
Room rates $39-43

COLORADO

AVON
Comfort Inn
0161 W. Beaver Creek Blvd.
Avon CO 81620
(303) 949-5511
(800) 228-5150
Room rates $49-195

BOULDER
Best Western Boulder Inn
770 28th St.
Boulder CO 80303
(303) 449-3800
(800) 528-1234
Room rates $56-67

Boulder Mountain Lodge
91 Four Mile Canyon Rd.
Boulder CO 80302
(303) 444-0882
$55 deposit required
Room rates $45-75

BRECKENRIDGE
Breckenridge Hilton
550 Village Rd
Breckenridge CO 80424
(303) 453-4500
$50 deposit required
Room rates $75-185

BRIGHTON
Super 8 Motel
1020 Old Brighton Rd.
Brighton CO 80601
(303) 659-6063
(800) 848-8888
pets with deposit
Room rates from $33

BURLINGTON
Econo Lodge
450 S. Lincoln
Burlington, CO 80807
(719) 346-5555
(800) 446-6900
$31-42

Super 8
2100 Fay
Burlington, CO 80807
(719) 346-5627
(800) 843-1991
pets with permission
$29-41

CANON CITY
Canon Inn
3075 E Hwy 50
Canon City CO 81212
(719) 275-8676
$10 deposit
Room rates $41-65

Old Town Inn
209 N. 19th St.
Canon City CO 81212
(719) 275-8687
Room rates $32-45

CASTLE ROCK
Super 8 Motel
1020 Park St.
Castle Rock CO 80104
(303) 688-0880
(800) 848-8888
pets with deposit
Room rates from $36

COLORADO SPRINGS
Hampton Inn
1410 Harrison Rd.
Colorado Springs CO 80906
(719) 579-6900
(800) 426-7866
Room rates $49-57

Ramada Inn
4440 N I-25
Colorado Springs CO 80907
(719) 594-0700
(800) 228-2828
Room rates $40-58

Comfort Inn
8280 State Hwy. 83
Colorado Springs CO 80920
(719) 598-6700
(800) 228-5150
Room rates $39-59

Motel 6
3228 N. Chestnut St.
Colorado Springs CO 80907
(719) 520-5400
1 small pet per room
Reservations (505) 891-6161
Room rates $26-28

Radisson Inn
1645 Newport Dr.
Colorado Springs CO 80916
(719) 597-7000
small pets only $25 deposit
Room rates $70-80

Quality Inn
555 W. Garden of Gods Rd.
Colorado Springs, CO 80907
(719) 593-9119
(800) 228-5151
$41-65

Holiday Inn Central
Cimmarron & 8th Streets
Colorado Springs CO 80905
(719) 473-5530
(800) 465-4329
Room rates $35-72

Rodeway Inn
2409 E. Pikes Peak Ave.
Colorado Springs CO 80909
(719) 471-0990
(800) 228-2000
small pets only
Room rates $37-45

Sheraton Co. Springs Hotel
2886 S. Circle Dr.
Colorado Springs CO 80906
(719) 579-5900
(800) 325-3535
Room rates $75-110

CORTEZ
Best Western Turqoise Inn
535 E. Main St.
Cortez CO 81321
(303) 565-3778
(800) 528-1234
small, supervised
Room rates $40-72

CRAIG
Super 8 Motel
200 Hwy 13
Craig CO 81625
(303) 824-3471
(800) 848-8888
pets with permission
Room rates $31-47

Holiday Inn
300 S. Hwy 13
Craig CO 81625
(303) 824-9455
(800) 465-4329
Room rates $29-60

DENVER
Ramada Inn
3737 Quebec St.
Denver CO 80207
(303) 388-6161
(800) 228-2828
Room rates $57-73

Quality Inn
6300 E. Hampden Ave.
Denver CO 80222
(303) 758-2211
(800) 228-5151
Room rates $39-61

Comfort Inn
7201 E. 36th Ave
Denver CO 80207
(303) 393-7666
(800) 228-5150
Room rates $43-58

Comfort Inn
3440 S. Vance St.
Denver CO 80227
(303) 989-5500
(800) 228-5150
Room rates $50-65

Quality Inn
110 W. 104th Ave
Denver CO 80234
(303) 451-1234
(800) 228-5151
Room rates $47-52

Days Inn
4590 Quebec
Denver CO 80216
(303) 320-0260
(800) 325-2525
Room rates $44-68

Days Inn
1150 E. Colfax
Denver CO 80218
(303) 831-7700
(800) 325-2525
Room rates $40-54

Days Inn
1680 S. Colorado Blvd.
Denver CO 80222
(303) 691-2223
(800) 325-2525
Room rates $36-45

Motel 6
12020 E. 39th Ave.
Denver CO 80239
(303) 371-1980
1 small pet per room
Reservations (505) 891-6161
Room rates $26-28

Motel 6
480 Wadsworth Blvd.
Denver CO 80226
(303) 232-4924
1 small pet per room
Reservations (505) 891-6161
Room rates $26-28

Hotel Denver Downtown
1450 Glenarm Place
Denver CO 80202
(303) 573-1450
$25 deposit required
Room rates $65-88

DURANGO
Days Inn
1700 County Road 203
Durango CO 81301
(303) 259-1430
(800) 325-2525
Room rates $39-72

Holiday Inn
800 Camino Del Rio
Durango CO 81301
(303) 247-5393
(800) 465-4329
Room rates $49-89

National 9
2855 N. Main Ave.
Durango CO 81301
(303) 247-2653
Room rates $30-56

Always Call Ahead!

ENGLEWOOD
Days Inn
9201 E. Arapahoe Rd.
Englewood CO 80111
(303) 790-8220
(800) 325-2525
$6/pets
Room rates $35-65

Arapahoe Inn
9009 E. Arapahoe Rd.
Englewood CO 80112
(303) 790-1421
$25 deposit
Room rates $40-52

ESTES PARK
Holiday Inn
101 S. St. Vrain Ave.
Estes Park CO 80517
(303) 586-2332
(800) 465-4329
Room rates $52-82

EVANS
Motel 6
3015 8th Ave.
Evans CO 80620
(303) 351-6481
1 small pet per room
Reservations (505) 891-6161
Room rates $26-28

FT. COLLINS
Comfort Inn
1638 E. Mulberry St.
Ft. Collins, CO 80524
(303) 484-2444
(800) 228-5150
$45-75

Days Inn
3625 E. Mulberry
Ft. Collins CO 80524
(303) 221-5490
(800) 325-2525
small pets allowed
Room rates $19-35

Motel 6
3900 E. Mulberry
Ft. Collins CO 80524
(303) 482-6466
1 small pet per room
Reservations (505) 891-6161
Room rates $26-28

COLORADO, Fort Collins

Holiday Inn
3836 E. Mulberry St.
Ft. Collins CO 80524
(303) 484-4660
(800) 465-4329
small pets, outside rooms
Room rates $44-64

GLENWOOD SPRINGS
Ramada Inn
124 W. 6th St.
Glenwood Springs CO 81601
(303) 945-2500
(800) 228-2828
Room rates $49-80

GOLDEN
Days Inn
15059 W. Colfax Ave.
Golden CO 80401
(303) 277-0200
(800) 325-2525
$6/pets
Room rates $37-65

Holiday Inn West
14707 W. Colfax Ave.
Golden CO 80401
(303) 279-7611
(800) 465-4329
Room rates $55-66

GRAND JUNCTION
Super 8 Motel
728 Horizon Dr.
Grand Junction CO 81506
(303) 248-8080
(800) 848-8888
pets with permission
Room rates $31-40

Ramada Inn
2790 Crossroads Blvd @
Horizon Dr.
Grand Junction CO 81506
(303) 241-8411
(800) 228-2828
Room rates $40-60

Motel 6
776 Horizon Dr.
Grand Junction CO 81501
(303) 243-2628
1 small pet per room
Reservations (505) 891-6161
Room rates $26-28

GREELEY
Holiday Inn
609 8th Ave.
Greeley CO 80631
(303) 356-3000
(800) 465-4329
Room rates $44-51

GUNNISON
Days Inn
701 West Hwy 50
Gunnison CO 81230
(303) 641-0608
(800) 325-2525
$3/pets
Room rates $33-45

LAKEWOOD
Hampton Inn
3605 S. Wadsworth Blvd.
Lakewood CO 80235
(303) 989-6900
(800) 426-7866
Room rates $46-48

LAMAR
Best Western Cow Place Inn
1301 N. Main St.
Lamar CO 81052
(719) 336-7753
(800) 528-1234
Room rates $50-65

LONGMONT
Super 8 Motel
10805 Turner Ave.
Longmont CO 80504
(303) 772-0888
(800) 848-8888
pets with permission
Room rates from $31

LOVELAND
Super 8 Motel
1655 E. Eisenhower Blvd.
Loveland CO 80537
(303) 663-7000
(800) 848-8888
pets with permission
Room rates from $30

MONTROSE
Super 8 Motel
1705 E. Main
Montrose CO 81401
(303) 249-9294
(800) 848-8888
pets with deposit
Room rates $31-39

NORTHGLENN
Days Inn
36 E. 120th Ave.
Northglenn CO 80233
(303) 457-0688
(800) 325-2525
$6/pets
Room rates from $59

PAGOSA SPRINGS
Super 8 Motel
34 Piedra Rd.
Pagosa Springs CO 81147
(303) 731-4005
(800) 848-8888
pets with permission
Room rates $24-44

PARACHUTE
Super 8 Motel
252 Green St.
Parachute CO 81635
(303) 285-7936
(800) 848-8888
Room rates from $39

PUEBLO
Super 8 Motel
1100 Hwy 50 W.
Pueblo CO 81008
(719) 545-4104
(800) 848-8888
pets with permission
Room rates from $31

Motel 6
4103 N. Elizabeth
Pueblo CO 81008
(719) 543-6221
1 small pet per room
Reservations (505) 891-6161
Room rates $26-28

Plaza Quality Inn
800 Hwy 50 West
Pueblo CO 81008
(719) 543-6820
Room rates $45-65

STEAMBOAT SPRINGS
Super 8 Motel
US Hwy. 40 E.
Steamboat Springs CO 80477
(303) 879-5230
(800) 848-8888
pets with permission
Room rates $32-49

28

Holiday Inn
3190 Lincoln
Steamboat Springs CO 80477
(303) 879-2250
(800) 465-4329
one pet per room
Room rates $75-150

STERLING
Days Inn
12881 Hwy 61
Sterling CO 80751
(303) 522-6660
(800) 325-2525
Room rates $34-55

THORNTON
Motel 6
6 W. 83rd Place
Thornton CO 80221
(303) 429-1550
1 small pet per room
Reservations (505) 891-6161
Room rates $26-28

WHEAT RIDGE
Motel 6
9920 W. 49th Ave.
Wheat Ridge CO 80033
(303) 424-0658
1 small pet per room
Reservations (505) 891-6161
Room rates $26-28

Motel 6
10300 So. I-70 Frontage Rd.
Wheat Ridge CO 80033
(303) 467-3172
1 small pet per room
Reservations (505) 891-6161
Room rates $26-28

YUMA
Harvest Motel
421 W. 8th Ave.
Yuma CO 80759
(303) 848-5853
$5 night fee
Room rates $32-35

CONNECTICUT
BRIDGEPORT
Days Inn
815 Lafayette Blvd.
Bridgeport CT 06604
(203) 366-5421
(800) 325-2525
pet deposit required
Room rates $68-95

DANBURY
Hilton
18 Old Ridgebury Rd.
Danbury CT 06810
(203) 794-0600
(800) 445-8667
Room rates $75-160

Holiday Inn
80 Newtown Rd.
Danbury CT 06810
(203) 792-4000
(800) 465-4329
Room rates $55-90

Ramada Inn
I-84
Danbury CT 06810
(203) 792-3800
(800) 228-2828
Room rates $70-115

DARIEN
Comfort Inn
50 Ledge Rd.
Darien CT 06820
(203) 655-8211
(800) 228-5150
Room rates $66-85

EAST HARTFORD
Ramada Inn
100 E. River Dr.
East Hartford CT 06108
(203) 528-9703
(800) 228-2828
Room rates $86-106

Comfort Inn
191 Spencer St.
East Hartford, CT 06040
(203) 643-5811
(800) 228-5150
$70-150

EAST WINDSOR
Comfort Inn
260 Main St.
East Windsor CT 06088
(203) 627-6585
(800) 228-5150
small pets only
Room rates $60-70

ENFIELD
Motel 6
11 Hazard Ave.
Enfield CT 06082
(203) 741-3685
1 small pet per room
Reservations (505) 891-6161
Room rates $31-36

Red Roof Inn
5 Hazard Ave.
Enfield CT 06082
(203) 741-2571
(800) 843-7663
Room rates $40-50

GREENWICH
Howard Johnson
1141 Post Rd.
Greenwich CT 06878
(203) 637-3691
(800) 654-2000
Room rates $75-100

HARTFORD
Super 8 Motel
57 W. Service Rd.
Hartford CT 06120
(203) 246-8888
(800) 848-8888
pets with permission
Room rates $46-48

Always
Call
Ahead!

Ramada Inn
440 Asylum St.
Hartford CT 06103
(203) 246-6591
(800) 228-2828
Room rates $72-112

Comfort Inn
111 Berlin Rd.
Hartford, CT 06416
(203) 635-4100
(800) 228-5150
$46-58

Sheraton
305 Trumbull St.
Hartford CT 06103
(203) 728-5151
(800) 325-3535
small pets w/reservations
Room rates $125-175

Holiday Inn
363 Roberts St.
Hartford CT 06108
(203) 528-9611
(800) 465-4329
Room rates $75-100

MERIDEN
Hampton Inn
10 Bee St.
Meriden CT 06450
(203) 235-5154
(800) 426-7866
small pets only
Room rates $47-59

Ramada Inn
275 Research Pkwy
Meriden CT 06450
(203) 238-2380
(800) 228-2828
Room rates $99-119

Days Inn
900 E. Main St.
Meriden CT 06450
(203) 238-1211
(800) 325-2525
Room rates $45-55

MILFORD
Hampton Inn
129 Plains Rd.
Milford CT 06460
(203) 874-4400
(800) 426-7866
Room rates $56-66

Holiday Inn
1212 Boston Post Rd.
Milford CT 06460
(203) 878-6561
(800) 465-4329
small pets only
Room rates $75-110

Red Roof Inn
10 Rowe Ave.
Milford CT 06460
(203) 877-6060
(800) 843-7663
small pets only
Room rates $50-60

NEW HAVEN
Howard Johnson hotel
400 Sargent Dr.
New Haven, CT 06511
(203) 562-1111
(800) 654-2000
$53-65

Quality Inn
100 Pond Lily Ave.
New Haven CT 06525
(203) 387-6651
(800) 228-5151
Room rates $75-120

Holiday Inn
30 Whalley Ave.
New Haven CT 06511
(203) 777-6221
(800) 465-4329
Room rates $75-115

NEW LONDON
Red Roof Inn
707 Colman St.
New London CT 06320
(203) 444-0001
(800) 843-7663
Room rates $45-60

NORTH HAVEN
HolidayInn
201 Washington Ave.
North Haven CT 06473
(203) 239-4225
small pets only, $10 nightly
Room rates $80-100

NORWALK
Comfort Inn
50 Ledge Rd.
Norwalk CT 06820
(203) 655-8211
(800) 228-5150
Room rates from $70

Holiday Inn
789 Conneticut Ave.
Norwalk CT 06854
(203) 853-3477
(800) 465-4329
$100 deposit
Room rates $60-100

NORWICH
Sheraton
1 Sheraton Plaza
Norwich CT 06360
(203) 889-5201
(800) 325-3535
Room rates $75-90

SHELTON
Residence Inn by Marriott
1001 Bridgeport Ave.
Shelton CT 06484
(203) 926-9000
(800) 331-3131
$10 charge
Room rates $100-150

SOUTHINGTON
Motel 6
625 Queen St.
Southington CT 06489
(203) 621-7351
1 small pet per room
Reservations (505) 891-6161
Room rates $31-36

Howard Johnson
30 Laning St.
Southington CT 06489
(203) 628-0921
(800) 654-2000
Room rates $50-70

STAMFORD
Ramada Inn
19 Clark Hills Ave.
Stamford CT 06902
(203) 327-4300
(800) 228-2828
Room rates $44-64

TRUMBULL
Marriott
180 Hawley Lane
Trumbull CT 06611
(203) 378-1400
(800) 228-9290
small pets only
Room rates $90-165

VERNON
Howard Johnson
451 Hartford Turnpike
Vernon CT 06066
(203) 875-0781
(800) 654-2000
Room rates $50-65

WATERBURY
Quality Inn
88 Union St.
Waterbury CT 06702
(203) 575-1500
Room rates $65-90

WEST HAVEN
Days Hotel
490 Sawmill Rd.
West Haven CT 06516
(203) 933-0344
(800) 325-2525
Room rates $75-95

WETHERSFIELD
Motel 6
1341 Silas Deane Hwy.
Wethersfield CT 06109
(203) 563-5900
1 small pet per room
Reservations (505) 891-6161
Room rates $31-36

WINDSOR LOCKS
Motel 6
3 National Dr.
Windsor Locks CT 06096
(203) 292-6200
1 small pet per room
Reservations (505) 891-6161
Room rates $31-36

Ramada Inn
5 Ella T Grasso Turnpike
Windsor Locks CT 06096
(203) 623-9494
(800) 228-2828
Room rates $65-100

DELAWARE
DOVER
Sheraton
1570 N. Du Pont Hwy
Dover DE 19901
(302) 678-8500
(800) 325-3535
small pets only
Room rates $70-75

NEW CASTLE
Travelodge
1213 West Ave
New Castle DE 19720
(302) 654-5544
(800) 255-3050
Room rates $42-45

NEWARK
Hampton Inn
Three Concord Lane
Newark DE 19713
(302) 737-3900
(800) 426-7866
Room rates $55-65

Quality Inn
1120 S. College Ave.
Newark DE 19713
(302) 368-8715
(800) 228-5150
small pets only
Room rates $42-54

Red Roof Inn
415 Stanton Christiana Rd.
Newark DE 19713
(302) 292-2870
(800) 843-7663
Room rates $45-51

WILMINGTON
Motel 6
1200 West Ave.
Wilmington DE 19720
(302) 571-1200
1 small pet per room
Reservations (505) 891-6161
Room rates from $28

DISTRICT OF COLUMBIA
WASHINGTON
Econo Lodge
1600 New York Ave. NE
Washington, DC 20002
(202) 832-3200
(800) 446-6900
$48-55

Quality Inn
7200 Baltimore Blvd
Washington DC 20740
(301) 864-5820
(800) 228-5151
Room rates $44-64

Comfort Inn
16216 Frederick Rd.
Washington DC 20877
(301) 330-0023
(800) 228-5150
Room rates $69-78

Comfort Inn
20260 Goldenrod Ln.
Washington DC 20874
(301) 428-1300
(800) 228-5150
Room rates $39-85

Comfort Suites
14402 Laurel Pl.
Washington DC 20707
(301) 206-2600
(800) 228-5150
Room rates $59-100

Quality Inn
6461 Edsall Rd.
Washington DC 22312
(703) 354-4400
(800) 228-5151
Room rates $50-65

Comfort Inn
5716 S. Van Dorn St.
Washington DC 22310
(703) 922-9200
(800) 228-5150
Room rates $52-85

DISTRICT OF COLUMBIA, Washington

Quality Inn
6111 Arlington Blvd.
Washington DC 22044
(703) 534-9100
(800) 228-5151
Room rates $57-80

Travelodge
4202 Inn St.
Washington DC 22172
(703) 221-1115
(800) 255-3050
Room rates $46-52

FLORIDA
ALACHUA
Days Inn
I-75 & US.. 441
Alachua FL 32615
(904) 462-3251
(800) 325-2525
small pets allowed
Room rates $42-85

ALTAMONTE SPRINGS
La Quinta
150 Westmonte Drive
Altamonte Springs FL 32714
(407) 788-1411
(800) 531-5900
small pets only
Room rates $70-75

BOCA RATON
Crown Sterling Suites
701 NW 53rd St.
Boca Raton FL 33487
(407) 994-8200
$25 fee
Room rates $85-130

BONIFAY
Budget Inn
114 W. Hwy 90
Bonifay FL 32425
(904) 547-4167
$5/pets
Room rates $28-35

Econo Lodge
2210 S. Waukesha St.
Bonifay, FL 32425
(904) 547-9345
(800) 446-6900
$35-50

BRADENTON
Days Inn
644 67th St. Circle East
Bradenton FL 34208
(813) 746-2505
(800) 325-2525
$5/pets
Room rates $35-50

Motel 6
660 67th St. Circle East
Bradenton FL 34208
(813) 747-6005
1 small pet per room
Reservations (505) 891-6161
Room rates $25-42

Park Inn
4450 47th St. West
Bradenton FL 34210
(813) 795-4633
Room rates $65-75

CAPE CORAL
Quality Inn
1538 Cape Coral Pkwy
Cape Coral FL 33904
(813) 542-2121
(800) 228-5151
$10 charge
Room rates $45-80

CLEARWATER
Super 8 Motel
13260 34th St.
Clearwater FL 34622
(813) 572-8881
(800) 848-8888
small pets with permission
Room rates $41-59

Rodeway Inn
20967 US 19N
Clearwater, FL 34625
(813) 799-1181
(800) 424-4777
$38-80

La Quinta
3301 Ulmerton Rd.
Clearwater FL 34622
(813) 572-7222
(800) 531-5900
small pets only
Room rates $50-70

Park Inn
13625 Icot Blvd.
Clearwater FL 34620
(813) 536-7275
small pets only
Room rates $60-70

COCOA
Ramada Inn
900 Friday Rd. I-90 @ Exit 76
Cocoa FL 32926
(407) 631-1210
(800) 228-2828
small pets only
Room rates $40-60

Econo Lodge
3220 N. Cocoa Blvd.
Cocoa FL 32926
(407) 632-4561
(800) 553-2666
small pets only
Room rates $35-50

Days Inn
5600 N. Atlantic Ave.
Cocoa Beach FL 32931
(407) 783-7621
(800) 325-2525
$5/pets - pets under 15lbs.
Room rates $47-69

Motel 6
3701 North Atlantic Ave.
Cocoa Beach FL 32931
(407) 783-3103
1 small pet per room
Reservations (505) 891-6161
Room rates $25-42

CRESTVIEW
Days Inn
I-10 & FL 85
Crestview FL 32536
(904) 682-8842
(800) 325-2525
Room rates $29-45

Always Call Ahead!

CRYSTAL RIVER
Comfort Inn
4486 N. Suncoast Blvd.
Crystal River FL 32629
(904) 563-1500
(800) 228-5150
Room rates $35-55

Days Inn
2380 NW Hwy 19 N.
Crystal River FL 32639
(904) 795-2111
(800) 325-2525
$3/small pets
Room rates $35-55

DANIA BEACH
Motel 6
825 E. Dania Beach Blvd.
Dania Beach FL 33004
(305) 921-5505
1 small pet per room
Reservations (505) 891-6161
Room rates $25-42

DAYTONA
Days Inn
839 S. Atlantic Ave
Daytona FL 32176
(904) 677-6600
(800) 325-2525
$6/pet charge
Room rates $37-130

Days Inn
2900 Volusia Ave.
Daytona FL 32124
(904) 255-0541
(800) 325-2525
$4/pets
Room rates $43-85

Days Inn
1909 S. Atlantic Ave.
Daytona FL 32118
(904) 255-4492
(800) 325-2525
small pets
Room rates $29-130

DAYTONA BEACH
Comfort Inn
507 S. Atlantic Ave.
Daytona Beach FL 32074
(904) 677-8550
(800) 228-5150
Room rates $43-99

Quality Inn
1567 N. US 1
Daytona Beach FL 32174
(904) 672-8621
(800) 228-5151
Room rates $43-99

Howard Johnson Lodge
2725 Volusia Ave.
Daytona Beach, FL 32114
(904) 255-7412
(800) 654-2000
$45-60

DE LAND
Hilton
350 International Speedway Blvd.
De Land FL 32724
(904) 734-3146
(800) 445-8667
Room rates $65-100

Quality Inn
2801 New York Ave. East
De Land FL 32724
(904) 736-3440
(800) 228-5151
$5 charge
Room rates $40-120

DEERFIELD BEACH
Quality Suites
1050 E. Newport Ctr Dr.
Deerfield Beach FL 33442
(305) 570-8888
(800) 228-5151
Room rates $105-134

Days Inn
50 SE 20th Ave.
Deerfield Beach FL 33441
(305) 428-0650
(800) 325-2525
$10 charge
Room rates $44-109

**Always
Call
Ahead!**

DESTIN
Days Inn
1029 Hwy 98 E.
Destin FL 32541
(904) 837-2599
(800) 325-2525
$10/pets
Room rates $35-80

ENGLEWOOD
Days Inn
2540 South McCall Road
Englewood FL 34224
(813) 474-5544
(800) 325-2525
$4/pets
Room rates $48-80

FLORIDA CITY
Hampton Inn
124 Palm Dr.
Florida City FL 33034
(305) 247-8833
(800) 426-7866
Room rates $50-65

Knights Inn
401 US 1
Florida City FL 33034
(305) 245-2800
(800) 722-7220
small pets only
Room rates $35-55

FORT WALTON
Days Inn
135 Miracle Strip Pkwy
Fort Walton FL 32548
(904) 244-6184
(800) 325-2525
$3/pets
Room rates $38-55

FT. LAUDERDALE
Comfort Suites Conv. Center
1800 S. Federal Hwy
Ft. Lauderdale FL 33316
(305) 767-8700
(800) 228-5150
Room rates $75-105

Days Inn
1595 W. Oakland Park Blvd.
Ft. Lauderdale FL 33311
(305) 484-9290
(800) 325-2525
Room rates $40-85

FLORIDA, Fort Lauderdale

Days Inn
3355 N. Federal Hwy
Ft. Lauderdale FL 33306
(305) 566-4301
(800) 325-2525
$10 charge
Room rates $53-95

Days Inn
2711 South Ocean Drive
Ft. Lauderdale FL 33019
(305) 922-8200
(800) 325-2525
$10 charge
Room rates $39-120

Motel 6
1801 State Road 84
Ft. Lauderdale FL 33315
(305) 760-7999
1 small pet per room
Reservations (505) 891-6161
Room rates $25-42

Days Inn Downtown
1700 Broward Blvd.
Ft. Lauderdale FL 33312
(305) 463-2500
(800) 325-2525
$10 charge
Room rates $35-70

Guest Quarters Suites
2670 Sunrise Blvd.
Ft. Lauderdale FL 33304
(305) 565-3800
$10 charge
Room rates $110-210

Howard Johnson Lodge
2075 SR 84
Ft. Lauderdale, FL 33315
(305) 525-4232
(800) 654-2000
$44-80

FT. MYERS
Days Inn
11435 Cleveland Ave.
Ft. Myers FL 33907
(813) 936-1311
(800) 325-2525
$5/pets
Room rates $39-65

Days Inn
11435 Cleveland Ave.
Ft. Myers FL 33907
(813) 936-1211
(800) 325-2525
$4 charge
Room rates $40-65

Knights Inn
3350 Marina Town Blvd.
Ft. Myers FL 33903
(813) 656-5544
(800) 722-7220
Room rates $40-65

La Quinta
4850 Cleveland Ave.
Ft. Myers FL. 33907
(813) 275-3300
(800) 531-5900
Room rates $50-80

Sheraton
2500 Edwards Dr.
Ft. Myers FL 33901
(813) 337-0300
(800) 325-3535
Room rates $90-150

Wellesly Inn
4400 Ford St. Extension
Ft. Myers FL 33916
(813) 278-3949
$10 charge
Room rates $40-100

FT. WALTON
Econo Lodge
100 Miracle Strip Way
Ft. Walton FL 32548
(904) 244-0121
(800) 553-2666
Room rates $35-52

GAINESVILLE
Super 8 Motel
4202 SW 40th Blvd.
Gainesville FL 32608
(904) 378-3888
(800) 848-8888
pets with permission
Room rates $36-38

Motel 6
4000 S.W. 40th Blvd.
Gainesville FL 32608
(904) 373-1604
1 small pet per room
Reservations (505) 891-6161
Room rates $25-42

Daystop
2820 13th St. NW
Gainesville FL 32609
(904) 376-1211
small pets only
Room rates $29-35

Econo Lodge
2649 13th St. SW
Gainesville FL 32608
(904) 373-7816
(800) 553-2666
small pets only
Room rates $35-40

Econo Lodge
700 75th St. NW
Gainesville FL 32607
(904) 332-2346
(800) 553-2666
$5 charge
Room rates $64-40

HOLIDAY
Best Western - Tahitian Resort
2337 US 19
Holiday FL 34691
(813) 937-4121
(800) 528-1234
$3 charge, small only
Room rates $45-80

HOMESTEAD
Days Inn
51 South Homestead Blvd.
Homestead FL 33030
(305) 245-1260
(800) 325-2525
Room rates $44-48

JACKSONVILLE
Hampton Inn
1170 Airpport Entrance Rd.
Jacksonville FL 32218
(904) 741-4980
(800) 426-7866
Room rates $44-50

Quality Inn
4660 Salisbury Rd.
Jacksonville FL 32256
(904) 281-0900
(800) 228-5151
Room rates $39-48

Econo Lodge
2300 Phillips Hwy.
Jacksonville, FL 32207
(904) 396-2301
(800) 446-6900
$25-80

Econo Lodge
5018 University Blvd.
Jacksonville, FL 32216
(904) 731-0800
(800) 446-6900
$25-80

Super 8 Motel
4280 Eldridge Ave.
Jacksonville, FL 32073
(904) 269-8887
(800) 843-1991
Pets with permission
$31-49

Motel 6
10885 Harts Rd.
Jacksonville FL 32218
(904) 757-8600
1 small pet per room
Reservations (505) 891-6161
Room rates $25-42

Motel 6
6107 Youngerman Circle
Jacksonville FL 32244
(904) 777-6100
1 small pet per room
Reservations (505) 891-6161
Room rates $25-42

**Always
Call
Ahead!**

Best Western - Executive Inn
10888 Harts Rd.
Jacksonville FL 32218
(904) 751-5600
(800) 528-1234
$25 deposit required
Room rates $40-45

Best Western Inn
5221 University Blvd.
Jacksonville FL 32216
(904) 737-1690
(800) 528-1234
small only @ mgr's option
Room rates $35-40

Budgetel Inn
3199 Hartley Rd.
Jacksonville FL 32257
(904) 468-9999
(800) 428-3438
Room rates $39-45

Comfort Suites
8333 Dix Ellis Rd.
Jacksonville FL 32256
(904) 739-1155
(800) 228-5150
$25 charge
Room rates $45-75

Ramada Inn
5624 Cagle Rd.
Jacksonville FL 32216
(904) 737-8000
(800) 228-2828
$25 deposit and $5 per day
Room rates $30-35

Rodeway Inn
3233 Emerson St.
Jacksonville FL 322207
(904) 398-3331
(800) 228-2000
Room rates $35-40

KEY WEST
Ramada Inn
3420 N. Roosevelt Blvd
Key West FL 33040
(305) 294-5541
(800) 228-2828
$5/pets - $25 deposit
Room rates $49-209

KISSIMMEE
Best Western
2661 E. Irlo Bronson Hwy
Kissimmee FL 34745-0128
(407) 846-2221
$5 / day
Room rates $33-75

Comfort Inn
7571 W. Irlo Bronson Hwy
Kissimmee FL 34746
(407) 396-7500
(800) 228-5150
Room rates $36-94

Motel 6
7455 W. Irlo Bronson Hwy.
Kissimmee FL 34746
(407) 396-6422
1 small pet per room
Reservations (505) 891-6161
Room rates $25-42

Motel 6
5731 W. Irlo Bronson Hwy.
Kissimmee FL 32741
(407) 396-6333
1 small pet per room
Reservations (505) 891-6161
Room rates $25-42

Howard Johnson
2323 Irlo Bronson Hwy
Kissimmee FL 34744
(407) 846-4900
(800) 654-2000
$5 charge
Room rates $40-100

Holiday Inn
5678 Irlo Bronson Hwy
Kissimmee FL 34746
(407) 396-4488
(800) 465-4329
small pets only
Room rates $70-105

LAKE BUENA VISTA
Comfort Inn
8442 Palm Plaza
Lake Buena Vista FL 32830
(407) 239-7300
(800) 228-5150
small pets only
Room rates $31-65

Days Inn
I-4 & US 27
Lake Buena Vista FL 32830
(813) 424-2596
(800) 325-2525
$5/pets
Room rates $40-70

LAKE CITY
Quality Inn
5600 US 90 W. Rte 13
Lake City FL 32055
(904) 752-7550
(800) 228-5151
$3/pet
Room rates $34-40

Days Inn
I-75 & US-90 Rt#13 Box 1140
Lake City FL 32055
(904) 752-9350
(800) 325-2525
$4/pets
Room rates $34-48

Motel 6
U.S. 90 West & Hall of Fame Dr.
Lake City FL 32055
(904) 755-4664
1 small pet per room
Reservations (505) 891-6161
Room rates $25-42

LAKELAND
Crossroads Motor Lodge
I-4 & 3223 US 98
Lakeland FL 33805
(813) 688-6031
$4/pets
Room rates $22-25

Motel 6
3120 U.S. 98 N.
Lakeland FL 33805
(813) 682-0643
1 small pet per room
Reservations (505) 891-6161
Room rates $25-42

LANTANA
Motel 6
1300 Lantana Rd.
Lantana FL 33462
(407) 585-5833
1 small pet per room
Reservations (505) 891-6161
Room rates $25-42

LEESBURG
Super 8 Motel
1392 N. Blvd. W.
Leesburg FL 34748
(904) 787-6363
(800) 848-8888
pets with permission
Room rates $44-46

Days Inn
1308 N. 14th St.
Leesburg FL 34748
(904) 787-1210
(800) 325-2525
Room rates $35-65

MARATHON
Days Inn
13201 Overseas Hwy
Marathon FL 33050
(305) 289-0222
(800) 325-2525
$6/pets
Room rates $71-102

MARIANNA
Comfort Inn
I-10 @ SR 71
Marianna FL 32446
(904) 526-5600
(800) 228-5150
Room rates $48-58

MELBOURNE
Days Inn
4555 W. New Haven Ave.
Melbourne FL 32904
(407) 724-5840
(800) 325-2525
Room rates $32-50

Howard Johnson - Airport
440 Harbor City Blvd.
Melbourne FL 32901
(407) 723-3661
(800) 654-2000
Room rates $35-65

MIAMI
Ramada Inn
7600 N. Kendall Dr.
Miami FL 33156
(305) 595-6000
(800) 228-2828
Room rates $59-89

Quality Inn
14501 S. Dixie Hwy. (US 1)
Miami FL 33176
(305) 251-2000
(800) 228-5151
small pets only
Room rates $60-93

Days Inn - Airport
3401 Le Jeune Rd. NW
Miami FL 33142
(305) 871-4221
(800) 325-2525
$10 charge, 30 lb max
Room rates $75-85

Residence Inn by Marriott
1212 82nd Ave. NW
Miami FL 33126
(305) 591-2211
(800) 331-3131
$60 fee + $6/day
Room rates $125-155

Hampton Inn
5125 NW 36th St.
Miami Springs FL 33166
(305) 887-2153
(800) 426-7866
Room rates $49-65

Ramada Inn
16805 NW 12th Ave.
Miami, FL 33169
(305) 624-8401
(800) 228-2828
$40-100

Hampton Inn
2500 Brickell Ave.
Miami, FL 33129
(305) 854-2070
(800) HAMPTON
$60-80

N. SEFFNER
Days Inn
6010 SR 579
N. Seffner FL 33584
(813) 621-4681
(800) 325-2525
$3/pets
Room rates $32-49

NAPLES
Wellesley Inn
1555 5th Ave.
Naples FL 33942
(813) 793-4646
(800) 654-2000
$10 charge
Room rates $40-100

NICEVILLE
Comfort Inn
101 SR 85 N.
Niceville FL 32578
(904) 678-8077
(800) 228-5150
Room rates $51-75

OCALA
Quality Inn
3767 NW Blitchton Rd.
Ocala FL 32675
(904) 732-2300
(800) 228-5151
$6/pets
Room rates $32-50

Days Inn
4040 W. Silver Springs Blvd.
Ocala FL 32675
(904) 629-8850
(800) 325-2525
$4/pets
Room rates $35-55

Travelodge
4020 Northwest Blitchton Rd
Ocala North FL 32675
(904) 732-2510
(800) 255-3050
Room rates $30-34

ORANGE CITY
Comfort Inn
445 S. Volusia Ave.
Orange City FL 32763
(904) 775-7444
(800) 228-5150
Room rates $39-135

ORANGE PARK
Super 8 Motel
4280 Eldridge Ave.
Orange Park FL 32073
(904) 269-8887
(800) 848-8888
small only
Room rates $36-38

ORLANDO
Quality Inn
7600 International Dr.
Orlando FL 32189
(407) 351-1600
(800) 228-5151
Room rates $29-53

Quality Inn
9000 International Dr.
Orlando FL 32819
(407) 345-8585
(800) 228-5151
pets under 15 lbs. only
Room rates $29-53

Days Inn
901 N. Orlando Ave.
Orlando FL 32789
(407) 644-8000
(800) 325-2525
$35 per stay fee
Room rates $66-80

Days Inn
2500 W. 33rd
Orlando FL 32809
(407) 841-3731
(800) 325-2525
$5/pets
Room rates $36-95

Days Inn
2323 McCoy Rd.
Orlando FL 32809
(407) 859-6100
(800) 325-2525
$4/pets
Room rates $42-65

Days Inn
7200 International Dr.
Orlando FL 32819
(407) 351-1200
(800) 325-2525
$4/pets
Room rates $42-76

Days Inn
1221 W. Landstreet Rd.
Orlando FL 32824
(407) 859-7700
(800) 325-2525
$8/pets
Room rates $32-79

Days Inn
7980 Irlo Bronson Mem. Hwy
Orlando FL 34746
(407) 396-1000
(800) 325-2525
Room rates $35-90

Motel 6
5350 Adanson Rd.
Orlando FL 32810
(407) 647-1444
1 small pet per room
Reservations (505) 891-6161
Room rates $25-42

Inns of America
8222 Jamaican Court
Orlando FL 32819
(407) 345-1172
small pets only
Room rates $34-60

Howard Johnson Lodge
8820 S. Orange Blossom Trail
Orlando, FL 32809
(407) 851-8200
(800) 654-2000
$40-80

PALM BEACH GARDEN
Holiday Inn
4431 PGA Blvd.
Palm Beach Garden FL 33410
(407) 622-2260
(800) 465-4329
Room rates $45-125

37

FLORIDA, Panama City

PANAMA CITY
Best Western - Bayside Inn
711 Beach Dr.
Panama City FL 32401
(904) 763-4622
(800) 528-1234
small pets only
Room rates $45-65

Super 8
207 Hwy 231 North
Panama City FL 32405
(904) 784-1988
(800) 848-8888
$25 deposit
Room rates $34-40

PENSACOLA
Ramada Inn
6550 Pensacola Blvd
Pensacola FL 32505
(904) 477-0711
(800) 228-2828
Room rates $50-57

Howard Johnson
6911 Pensacola Blvd
Pensacola FL 32516
(904) 479-3800
small only
Room rates $43-56

Comfort Inn
6911 Pensacola Blvd
Pensacola FL 32505
(904) 478-4499
(800) 228-5150
Room rates $34-50

Days Inn
7051 Pensacola Blvd.
Pensacola FL 32505
(904) 476-9090
(800) 325-2525
$5/pet
Room rates $45-65

Motel 6
7226 Plantation Rd.
Pensacola FL 32504
(904) 474-1060
1 small pet per room
Reservations (505) 891-6161
Room rates $25-42

Motel 6
5829 Pensacola Blvd.
Pensacola FL 32505
(904) 477-7522
1 small pet per room
Reservations (505) 891-6161
Room rates $25-42

Hilton
200 Gregory St.
Pensacola FL 32501
(904) 433-3336
(800) 445-8667
$50 charge
Room rates $83-98

POMPANO BEACH
Motel 6
1201 N.W. 31st Ave.
Pompano Beach FL 33069
(305) 977-8011
1 small pet per room
Reservations (505) 891-6161
Room rates $25-42

Days Inn
2700 Ocean Blvd.
Riviera Beach FL 33404
(407) 848-8661
(800) 325-2525
$5/pets
Room rates $49-114

RIVIERA BEACH
Motel 6
3651 Blue Heron Blvd.
Riviera Beach FL 33404
(407) 863-1011
1 small pet per room
Reservations (505) 891-6161
Room rates $25-42

RUSHKIN
Days Inn
611 Destiny Dr.
Rushkin FL 33570
(813) 645-3291
(800) 325-2525
$5/pets
Room rates $49-80

SANFORD
Days Inn
4650 SR 46
Sanford FL 32771
(407) 323-6500
(800) 325-2525
$4/pets
Room rates $30-47

SARASOTA
Comfort Inn
4800 N. Tamiami Trail
Sarasota FL 34234
(813) 355-7091
(800) 228-5150
Room rates $45-80

Days Inn
4900 N. Tamiami Tr.
Sarasota FL 34234
(813) 355-9721
(800) 325-2525
$4/pets
Room rates $35-60

ST. AUGUSTINE
Quality Inn
2445 SR 16
St. Augustine FL 32092
(904) 829-1999
(800) 228-5151
Room rates $34-48

Comfort Inn
1111 Ponce De Leon Blvd.
St. Augustine FL 32084
(904) 824-5554
(800) 228-5150
$5/pets
Room rates $42-100

Days Inn
2560 SR 16
St. Augustine FL 32092
(904) 824-4341
(800) 325-2525
$4/pets
Room rates $32-49

Days Inn
2800 Ponce de Leon Blvd.
St. Augustine FL 32084
(904) 829-6581
(800) 325-2525
$10/small pets
Room rates $37-60

ST. PETERSBURG
Days Inn
9359 US Hwy 19 North
St. Petersburg FL 34666
(813) 577-3838
(800) 325-2525
Room rates $41-85

38

STARKE
Days Inn
I-75 to I-10 to Rt. 301
Starke FL 32091
(904) 964-7600
(800) 325-2525
Room rates $47-62

STUART
Days Suites
8605 SE Federal Hwy
Stuart FL 33455
(407) 546-3600
(800) 325-2525
limited pet rooms -fee charged
Room rates $40-69

TALLAHASSE
Motel 6
1481 Timberlane Drive
Tallahasse FL 32308
(904) 668-2600
1 small pet per room
Reservations (505) 891-6161
Room rates $25-42

Days Inn
2800 N. Monroe St.
Tallahassee FL 32303
(904) 385-0136
(800) 325-2525
$3/pets
Room rates $42-44

Days Inn
722 Apalachee Pkwy
Tallahassee FL 32303
(904) 224-2181
(800) 325-2525
$10 charge
Room rates $41-47

TAMPA
Ramada Inn
5303 W. Kennedy Blvd
Tampa FL 33609
(813) 877-0534
(800) 228-2828
Room rates $59-79

Ramada Inn
400 E Bears Ave.
Tampa FL 33613
(813) 961-1000
(800) 228-2828
small pets only
Room rates $40-45

Days Inn
11736 US 19 & FL 52
Tampa FL 34668
(813) 863-1502
(800) 325-2525
Room rates $25-115

Days Inn
701 E. Fletcher Ave.
Tampa FL 33612
(813) 977-1550
(800) 325-2525
$4/pets
Room rates $30-51

Days Inn
2901 E. Busch Blvd.
Tampa FL 33612
(813) 933-6471
(800) 325-2525
$4/pets
Room rates $37-64

Days Inn
2520 N. 50th St.
Tampa FL 33619
(813) 247-3300
(800) 325-2525
$10 charge
Room rates $30-75

Motel 6
333 East Fowler Ave.
Tampa FL 33612
(813) 932-4948
1 small pet per room
Reservations (505) 891-6161
Room rates $25-42

Sheraton
7401 Hillsborough Ave.
Tampa FL 33610
(813) 626-0999
(800) 325-3535
small pets only
Room rates $75-90

TITUSVILLE
Days Inn
3480 Garden St.
Titusville FL 32796
(407) 269-9310
(800) 325-2525
Room rates $55-65

Travelodge
3810 South Washington Ave.
Titusville FL 32780
(407) 267-9111
(800) 255-3050
Room rates $35-45

VENICE
Motel 6
281 Venice Bypass
Venice FL 34292
(813) 485-8255
1 small pet per room
Reservations (505) 891-6161
Room rates $25-42

W. PALM BEACH
Days Inn
2300 45th St.
W. Palm Beach FL 33407
(407) 689-0450
(800) 325-2525
$10 charge
Room rates $39-89

Days Inn
6255 Okeechobee Blvd.
W. Palm Beach FL 33417
(407) 686-6000
(800) 325-2525
$10 daily charge only 1 pet
Room rates $40-82

WHITE SPRINGS
Days Inn
SR 126 & I-75
White Springs FL 32096
(904) 397-2155
(800) 325-2525
Room rates $32-40

ZEPHYRHILLS
Economy Inn
I-75 & SR 54 W.
Zephyrhills FL 33543
(813) 973-0155
small only - $5/night
Room rates $35-57

GEORGIA
ACKWORTH
Best Western Frontier Inn
SR 92 & I-75
Ackworth GA 30101
(404) 974-0116
(800) 528-1234
Room rates $40-50

ADEL
Quality Inn
1103 W. 4th St.
Adel GA 31620
(912) 896-2244
(800) 228-5151
Room rates $26-29

Days Inn
1200 W. 4th St.
Adel GA 31620
(912) 896-4574
(800) 325-2525
Room rates $26-29

ALBANY
Super 8 Motel
2444 N. Slappey Blvd.
Albany GA 31701
(912) 888-8388
(800) 848-8888
pets with permission
Room rates $37-39

Ramada Inn
2505 N. Slappey Blvd.
Albany GA 31701
(912) 883-3211
(800) 228-2828
Room rates $56-60

Days Inn
422 Oglethorpe Ave.
Albany GA 31701
(912) 888-2632
(800) 325-2525
kennels for larger dogs
Room rates $43-53

Motel 6
301 S. Thornton Dr.
Albany GA 31705
(912) 439-0078
1 small pet per room
Reservations (505) 891-6161
Room rates $25-32

ASHBURN
Quality Inn
I-75 & SR 159
Ashburn GA 31714
(912) 567-3334
(800) 228-5151
Room rates from $39

ATHENS
Ramada Inn
513 W. Broad St.
Athens GA 30601
(404) 546-8122
(800) 228-2828
Room rates $55-62

Quality Inn
295 E. Dougherty St.
Athens GA 30601
(404) 546-0410
(800) 228-5151
Room rates $45-90

Days Inn
166 Finley St.
Athens GA 30306
(404) 369-7000
(800) 325-2525
Pets allowed 2-days
Room rates $43-65

Days Inn
2741 Atlanta Hwy
Athens GA 30606
(404) 546-9750
(800) 325-2525
$5/pet fee
Room rates $30-45

ATLANTA
Hampton Inn
1975 N. Druid Hills Rd
Atlanta GA 30319
(404) 320-6600
(800) 426-7866
Room rates $44-53

Super 8 Motel
1451 Hudson Bridge Rd.
Atlanta GA 30281
(404) 474-5758
(800) 848-8888
pets with permission
Room rates $33-35

Ramada Inn
4225 Fulton Industrial Blvd.
Atlanta GA 30336
(404) 691-4100
(800) 228-2828
small pets only
Room rates $57-73

Quality Inn
2960 NE Expwy.
Atlanta GA 30341
(404) 451-5231
(800) 228-5151
Room rates from $48

Quality Inn
330 Peachtree St.
Atlanta GA 30308
(404) 577-1980
(800) 228-5151
Room rates $59-93

Quality Inn
1470 Spring St. NW
Atlanta GA 30309
(404) 872-5821
(800) 228-5151
$20 fee, small pets only
Room rates $56-66

Howard Johnson Lodge
2700 Curtis Drive
Atlanta, GA 30080
(404) 435-4990
(800) 654-2000
$45-65

Hampton Inn
3398 Piedmont Rd. NE
Atlanta, GA 30305
(404) 223-5656
(800) 426-7866
$49-65

Hampton Inn
3400 Northlake Pkwy
Atlanta, GA 30345
(404) 493-1966
(800) 426-7866
$40-55

Always Call Ahead!

Comfort Inn
1363 Klondike Rd.
Atlanta GA 30207
(404) 760-0300
(800) 228-5150
Room rates $50-65

Comfort Inn
775 George Busbee Pkwy
Atlanta GA 30144
(404) 424-7666
(800) 228-5150
Room rates $55-60

Comfort Inn
2945 SR 317
Atlanta GA 30174
(404) 945-1608
(800) 228-5150
Room rates $43-56

Motel 6
3585 Chamblee
Atlanta GA 30341
(404) 455-8000
1 small pet per room
Reservations (505) 891-6161
Room rates $25-32

Motel 6
4100 Wendell Dr.
Atlanta GA 30336
(404) 696-0757
1 small pet per room
Reservations (505) 891-6161
Room rates $25-32

Marriott Suites
6210 Peachtree
Atlanta GA 30328
(404) 668-0808
(800) 228-9290
small $45-125 fee
Room rates $70-140

Holiday Inn Perimeter-Dunwoody
4386 Chamblee-Dunwoody Rd.
Atlanta GA 30341
(404) 457-6363
(800) 465-4329
Room rates $50-85

AUGUSTA
Hampton Inn
3030 Washington Rd.
Augusta GA 30907
(404) 737-1122
(800) 426-7866
Room rates $39-45

Howard Johnson
601 Bobby Jones Expressway
Atlanta, GA 30907
(404) 863-2882
(800) I GO HOJO
Rooms $30-42

Ramada Inn
1365 Gordon Hwy
Augusta GA 30901
(404) 722-4344
(800) 228-2828
Room rates $42-45

Days Inn
I-20 & 3026 Washington Rd.
Augusta GA 30907
(404) 738-0131
(800) 325-2525
$4/pets
Room rates $33-43

Motel 6
2650 Center West Pkwy.
Augusta GA 30909
(404) 736-1934
1 small pet per room
Reservations (505) 891-6161
Room rates $25-32

BRUNSWICK
Ramada Inn
3241 Glynn Ave
Brunswick GA 31523
(912) 264-8611
(800) 228-2828
Room rates $51-55

Ramada Inn
I-95 & US 341
Brunswick GA 31520
(912) 264-3621
(800) 228-2828
Room rates $51-55

Always
Call
Ahead!

Comfort Inn
490 New Jesup Hwy
Brunswick GA 31520
(912) 264-6540
(800) 228-5150
$5/pets
Room rates $49-67

Days Inn
409 New Jesup Hwy
Brunswick GA 31520
(912) 264-4330
(800) 325-2525
$4/pets
Room rates $37-54

Motel 6
403 Butler Dr.
Brunswick GA 31520
(912) 264-8582
1 small pet per room
Reservations (505) 891-6161
Room rates $25-32

Holiday Inn
3302 Glynn Ave.
Brunswick GA 31520
(912) 264-9111
(800) 465-4329
Room rates $55-65

BRYON
Economy Inn
I-75
Bryon GA 31008
(912) 956-5300
$5/pets
Room rates $32-40

CAIRO
Comfort Inn
2800 E. US 84
Cairo GA 31728
(912) 377-8000
(800) 228-5150
Room rates $43-57

CALHOUN
Days Inn
742 Hwy 53 SE
Calhoun GA 30701
(404) 629-8271
(800) 325-2525
$4/pets
Room rates $30-42

CARROLLTON
Ramada Inn
1202 S. Park St.
Carrollton GA 30117
(404) 834-7700
(800) 228-2828
Room rates $52-57

Days Inn
180 Centennial Rd.
Carrollton GA 30117
(404) 830-1000
(800) 325-2525
Room rates $45-53

CARTERSVILLE
Days Inn
851 Cass-White Rd.
Cartersville GA 30120
(404) 386-0350
(800) 325-2525
$5/pets
Room rates $29-39

Comfort Inn
28 Hwy 294 SE
Cartersville GA 30120
(404) 387-1800
(800) 228-5150
Room rates $32-40

Econo Lodge
I-75 N. Box 746
Cartersville, GA 30120
(404) 386-3303
(800) 446-6900
$30-35

Friendship Inn
5667 SR 20 NE
Cartersville, GA 30120
(404) 386-1449
(800) 453-4511
$30-35

COLLEGE PARK
Knights Inn
3860 Flat Shoals Rd.
College Park GA 30349
(404) 969-0110
(800) 722-7220
Room rates $35-45

COLUMBUS
Comfort Inn
3443 Macon Rd.
Columbus GA 31907-2528
(404) 568-3300
(800) 228-5150
Room rates $45-51

Days Inn
3452 Macon Rd.
Columbus GA 31907
(404) 561-4400
(800) 325-2525
$4/pets
Room rates $42-55

Motel 6
3050 Victory Dr.
Columbus GA 31903
(404) 687-7214
1 small pet per room
Reservations (505) 891-6161
Room rates $25-32

Sheraton - Airport
5351 Simmons Blvd.
Columbus GA 31904
(404) 327-6868
(800) 325-3535
$100 deposit
Room rates $55-80

CORDELE
Ramada Inn
I-75 & US 280
Cordele GA 31015
(912) 273-5000
(800) 228-2828
Room rates $39-45

Holiday Inn
Jct I-75 & US 280
Cordele GA 31015
(912) 273-4117
(800) 465-4329
Room rates $50-55

CUMMINGS
Days Inn
875 Lanier 400 Pkwy
Cummings GA 30130
(404) 889-3045
(800) 325-2525
Room rates $44-48

DALTON
Quality Inn
2107 Chattanooga Rd.
Dalton GA 30720
(404) 278-1448
(800) 228-5151
Room rates $38-43

Days Inn
1518 W. Walnut Ave.
Dalton GA 30720
(404) 278-0850
(800) 325-2525
$4/pets
Room rates $38-47

Motel 6
2200 Chattanooga Rd.
Dalton GA 30720
(404) 278-5522
1 small pet per room
Reservations (505) 891-6161
Room rates $25-32

DECATUR
Days Inn
4200 Wesley Club Dr.
Decatur GA 30034
(404) 288-7110
(800) 325-2525
Room rates $35-42

Motel 6
2565 Wesley Chapel Rd.
Decatur GA 30035
(404) 288-6911
1 small pet per room
Reservations (505) 891-6161
Room rates $25-32

DOUGLAS
Super 8 Motel
1610 S. Peterson Ave.
Douglas GA 31533
(912) 384-0886
(800) 848-8888
pets with permission
Room rates $34-36

Days Inn
907 N. Peterson
Douglas GA 31533
(912) 384-5190
(800) 325-2525
Room rates $34-40

EAST POINT
Motel 6
4427 Commerce Dr.
East Point GA 30344
(404) 762-5201
1 small pet per room
Reservations (505) 891-6161
Room rates $25-32

Sheraton - Airport
1325 Virginia Ave.
East Point GA 30344
(404) 768-6660
(800) 325-3535
Room rates $90-110

Holiday Inn
1380 Virginia Ave.
East Point GA 30344
(404) 762-8411
(800) 465-4329
Room rates $40-50

FOLKSTON
Days Inn
1201 S. 2nd St.
Folkston GA 31537
(912) 495-2514
(800) 325-2525
Room rates $32-39

FORSYTH
Hampton Inn
I-75 @ Tift College Dr.
Forsyth GA 31029
(912) 994-9697
(800) 426-7866
Room rates $38-46

Days Inn
I-75 & GA 42
Forsyth GA 31029
(912) 994-5168
(800) 325-2525
$4/pets
Room rates $28-39

GAINESVILLE
Days Inn
US 129 & I-985
Gainesville GA 30503
(404) 532-7531
(800) 325-2525
$4/pets
Room rates from $38

Holiday Inn
726 Jesse Jewel Pkwy
Gainesville GA 30501
(404) 536-4451
(800) 465-4329
Room rates $55-60

JEKYLL ISLAND
Clarion Resort
85 S. Beachview Dr.
Jekyll Island GA 31520
(912) 635-2261
(800) 458-6262
$5/pets
Room rates $55-160

Comfort Inn
711 Beachview Dr.
Jekyll Island GA 31520
(912) 635-2211
(800) 228-5150
$5/pets
Room rates $55-159

Days Inn
60 S. Beachview Dr.
Jekyll Island GA 31520
(912) 653-3319
(800) 325-2525
$5/pets
Room rates $39-99

KINGSLAND
Super 8 Motel
I-95 & Hwy 40
Kingsland GA 31548
(912) 729-6888
(800) 848-8888
pets with permission
Room rates $37-39

Comfort Inn
I-95 & SR 40
Kingsland GA 31548
(912) 729-6979
(800) 228-5150
Room rates $43-58

Days Inn
1050 E. King Ave.
Kingsland GA 31548
(912) 729-5454
(800) 325-2525
$5/pets
Room rates $29-65

LA GRANGE
Comfort Inn
1601 LaFayette Pkwy
La Grange GA 30240
(404) 882-9540
(800) 228-5150
Room rates $44-45

LAKE PARK
Red CarpetInn
I-75 & Rt.5
Lake Park GA 31636
(912) 559-7902
Room rates $25-33

MACON
Hampton Inn
3680 Riverside Dr.
Macon GA 31210
(912) 471-0660
(800) 426-7866
Room rates $43-48

Quality Inn
2720 Riverside Dr.
Macon GA 31204
(912) 743-1482
(800) 228-5151
under 20 lbs.
Room rates $39-48

Comfort Inn
2690 Riverside Dr.
Macon GA 31204
(912) 746-8855
(800) 228-5150
Room rates $46-60

Days Inn
2737 Sheraton Dr.
Macon GA 31204-1197
(912) 745-8521
(800) 325-2525
$5/pets
Room rates $32-28

Economy Inn
4295 Pio Nono Ave.
Macon GA 31206
(912) 788-8910
$5/pets
Room rates $34-49

GEORGIA, Macon

Motel 6
4991 Harrison Rd.
Macon GA 31206
(912) 474-2870
1 small pet per room
Reservations (505) 891-6161
Room rates $25-32

Macon Downtown Hotel
108 1st St.
Macon GA 31202
(912) 746-1461
under 25 lbsRoom rates $60-70

MADISON
Days Inn
2001 Eatonton Hwy
Madison GA 30650
(404) 342-1839
(800) 325-2525
$10 charge
Room rates $38-44

MARIETTA
Motel 6
2360 Delk Rd.
Marietta GA 30067
(404) 952-8161
1 small pet per room
Reservations (505) 891-6161
Room rates $25-32

Hampton Inn
455 Franklin Rd.
Marietta GA 30067
(404) 425-9977
(800) 426-7866
Room rates $45-50

MCDONOUGH
Economy Inn
1311 McDonough Rd.
McDonough GA 30253
(404) 957-5818
$5/pets
Room rates $32-45

MILLEDGEVILLE
Days Inn
3001 Hwy 441 N. (Heritage Rd)
Milledgeville GA 31061
(912) 453-3551
(800) 325-2525
$2/pets
Room rates $32-42

NEWNAN
Econo Lodge
1310 Hwy 29 S.
Newnan GA 30263
(404) 253-1499
(800) 553-2666
Room rates $35-40

NORCROSS
Motel 6
6015 Oakbrook Pkwy.
Norcross GA 30093
(404) 446-2311
1 small pet per room
Reservations (505) 891-6161
Room rates $25-32

PERRY
Quality Inn
I-75 @ US 341
Perry GA 31069
(912) 987-1345
(800) 228-5151
Room rates $40-55

Days Inn
800 Valley Dr.
Perry GA 31069
(912) 987-2142
(800) 325-2525
Room rates $24-49

RICHMOND HILL
Days Inn
I-95 & US 17
Richmond Hill GA 31324
(912) 756-3371
(800) 325-2525
$4/pets
Room rates $30-52

Travelodge
I-95 & US-17 South
Richmond Hill GA 31324
(912) 756-3325
(800) 255-3050
Room rates from $36

Motel 6
I-95 & U.S. Hwy 17
Richmond Hill GA 31324
(912) 756-3543
1 small pet per room
Reservations (505) 891-6161
Room rates $25-32

RINGGOLD
Super 8 Motel
401 South
Ringgold GA 30736
(404) 965-7080
(800) 848-8888
pets with permission
Room rates $37-40

Travelodge
I-75 & Exit 142
Ringgold GA 30736
(404) 891-9894
(800) 255-3050
Room rates from $28

ROME
Ramada Inn
707 Turner McCall Blvd.
Rome GA 30161
(404) 291-0101
(800) 228-2828
Room rates $48-54

Days Inn
840 Turner McCall Blvd.
Rome GA 30161
(404) 295-0400
(800) 325-2525
Room rates $46-53

SAVANNAH
Super 8 Motel
I-95 @ Hwy 204
Savannah GA 31419
(912) 927-8550
(800) 848-8888
pets with permission
Room rates $39-43

Quality Inn
231 W. Boundary St.
Savannah GA 31401
(912) 232-3200
(800) 228-5151
Room rates $40-75

Always
Call
Ahead!

Quality Inn
Rt. 5
Savannah GA 31408
(912) 964-1421
(800) 228-5151
Room rates $41-130

Quality Inn
300 W. Bay St.
Savannah GA 31401
(912) 236-6321
(800) 228-5151
Room rates $45-58

Travelodge
11516 Abercorn St.
Savannah GA 31419
(912) 927-6274
(800) 255-3050
Room rates $30-75

Sheraton
612 Wilmington Island Rd.
Savannah GA 31410
(912) 897-1612
(800) 325-3535
small pets only
Room rates $85-120

STOCKBRIDGE
Motel 6
7233 Davidson Pkwy.
Stockbridge GA 30281
(404) 389-1142
1 small pet per room
Reservations (505) 891-6161
Room rates $25-32

SUWANEE
Days Inn
3103 Hwy 317
Suwanee GA 30174
(404) 945-8372
(800) 325-2525
$5/per pet
Room rates from $36

Comfort Inn
2945 Hwy 317
Suwanee GA 30174
(404) 945-1608
(800) 228-5150
Room rates $34-36

THOMASVILLE
Days Inn
US 19 Bypass & US 319
Thomasville GA 31792
(912) 226-6025
(800) 325-2525
$4/pets
Room rates $32-36

TIFTON
Ramada Inn
I-75 & US 82
Tifton GA 31794
(912) 382-8500
(800) 228-2828
Room rates $43-44

Quality Inn
1103 King Rd.
Tifton GA 31794
(912) 386-2100
(800) 228-5151
Room rates $43-66

Economy Inn
I-75 & US 82
Tifton GA 31793
(912) 382-8100
$5 nightly fee
Room rates $33-40

Holiday Inn
US 82 & 319
Tifton GA 31793
(912) 382-6687
(800) 465-4329
Room rates $45-50

UNADILLA
Days Inn
I-75 & US 41
Unadilla GA 31091
(912) 627-3211
(800) 325-2525
$2/pets
Room rates $29-37

VALDOSTA
Hampton Inn
1705 Gornto Rd
Valdosta GA 31601
(912) 244-8800
(800) 426-7866
Room rates $42-46

Ramada Inn
I-75 & GA 84
Valdosta GA 31603
(912) 242-1225
(800) 228-2828
Room rates from $45

Quality Inn
1902 W. Hill Ave.
Valdosta GA 31601
(912) 244-4520
(800) 228-5151
Room rates $46-65

Travelodge
1330 St. Augustine Rd.
Valdosta GA 31601
(912) 242-3464
(800) 255-3050
Room rates from $34

Motel 6
2003 West Hill Ave.
Valdosta GA 31601
(912) 333-0047
1 small pet per room
Reservations (505) 891-6161
Room rates $25-32

VANDALIA
Days Inn
I-70 & US 40
Vandalia GA 62471
(618) 283-1400
(800) 325-2525
Room rates $38-48

VILLA RICA
Super 8 Motel
195 Hwy 61 Connector
Villa Rica GA 30180
(404) 459-8888
(800) 848-8888
Room rates $35-37

Comfort Inn
128 SR 61 connector
Villa Rica GA 30180
(404) 459-8000
(800) 228-5150
Room rates $37-55

WARNER ROBBINS
Radisson Inn
2725 Watson Blvd.
Warner Robbins GA 31093
(912) 953-3000
(800) 333-3333
Room rates $50-80

GEORGIA, Waycross

WAYCROSS
Super 8 Motel
132 Havanna Ave.
Waycross GA 31501
(912) 285-8885
(800) 848-8888
pets with permission
Room rates $34-36

IDAHO
BOISE
Super 8 Motel
2773 Elder St.
Boise ID 83705
(208) 344-8871
(800) 848-8888
pets with deposit
Room rates $36-40

Quality Inn
2717 Vista Ave.
Boise ID 83705
(208) 343-7505
(800) 228-5151
Room rates $56-64

Travelodge
1314 Grove St.
Boise ID 83706
(208) 342-9351
(800) 255-3050
Room rates $34-35

Motel 6
2323 Airport Way
Boise ID 83705
(208) 344-3506
1 small pet per room
Reservations (505) 891-6161
Room rates $25-33

CALDWELL
Comfort Inn
901 Sprecht Ave.
Caldwell ID 83605
(208) 454-2222
(800) 228-5150
Room rates $52-66

Comfort Inn
280 W. Appleway
Coeur D'Alene ID 83814
(208) 765-5500
(800) 228-5150
Room rates $48-85

COEUR D'ALENE
Days Inn
2200 Northwest Blvd.
Coeur D'Alene ID 83814
(208) 667-8668
(800) 325-2525
small pets
Room rates $40-49

Motel 6
416 Appleway
Coeur D'Alene ID 83814
(208) 664-6600
1 small pet per room
Reservations (505) 891-6161
Room rates $25-33

Holiday Inn
414 Appleway
Coeur D'Alene ID 83814
(208) 765-3200
(800) 465-4329
Room rates $65-85

IDAHO FALLS
Super 8 Motel
705 Lindsay Blvd.
Idaho Falls ID 83402
(208) 522-8880
(800) 848-8888
pets with permission
Room rates $36-39

Motel 6
1448 W. Broadway
Idaho Falls ID 83402
(208) 522-0112
1 small pet per room
Reservations (505) 891-6161
Room rates $25-33

LEWISTON
Ramada Inn
621 21st St.
Lewiston ID 83501
(208) 799-1000
(800) 228-2828
Room rates $64-76

Super 8 Motel
3120 North South Hwy
Lewiston, ID 83501
(208) 743-8808
(800) 843-1991
pets with permission
$31-55

MOSCOW
Super 8 Motel
175 Peterson Dr.
Moscow ID 83843
(208) 883-1503
(800) 848-8888
Room rates $32-35

Motel 6
101 Baker St.
Moscow ID 83843
(208) 882-5511
1 small pet per room
Reservations (505) 891-6161
Room rates $25-33

NAMPA
Super 8 Motel
I-84 @ Nampa Blvd.
Nampa ID 83651
(208) 467-2888
(800) 848-8888
pets with permission
Room rates $38-39

POCATELLO
Super 8 Motel
1330 Bench Rd.
Pocatello ID 83204
(208) 234-0888
(800) 848-8888
pets with permission
Room rates $35-37

Quality Inn
1555 Pocatello Creek Rd.
Pocatello ID 83201
(208) 233-2200
(800) 228-5151
Room rates $50-62

Motel 6
291 W. Burnside Ave.
Pocatello ID 83201
(208) 237-7880
1 small pet per room
Reservations (505) 891-6161
Room rates $25-33

REXBURG
Best Western Cotton Tree Inn
450 4th St. S.
Rexburg ID 83440
(208) 356-4646
(800) 528-1234
$20 deposit, mgr approval
Room rates $45-50

SANDPOINT
Super 8 Motel
3245 Hwy 95 N.
Sandpoint ID 83864
(208) 263-2210
(800) 848-8888
pets with permission
Room rates $37-38

Quality Inn
807 N. 5th Ave.
Sandpoint ID 83864
(208) 263-2111
(800) 228-5151
open credit card deposit
Room rates $44-64

TWIN FALLS
Econo Lodge
320 Main Ave.
Twin Falls, ID 83301
(208) 733-8770
(800) 446-6900
$28-45

Motel 6
1472 Blue Lakes Blvd. N.
Twin Falls ID 83301
(208) 734-3993
1 small pet per room
Reservations (505) 891-6161
Room rates $25-33

ILLINOIS
ALTON
Super 8 Motel
1800 Homer Adams Pkwy
Alton IL 62002
(618) 465-8885
(800) 848-8888
pets with permission
Room rates $36-38

Holiday Inn
3800 Homer Adams Pwy
Alton IL 62002
(618) 462-1220
(800) 465-4329
Room rates $65-75

ARLINGTON HEIGHTS
Motel 6
441 W. Algonquin Rd.
Arlington Heights IL 60005
(708) 806-1230
1 small pet per room
Reservations (505) 891-6161
Room rates $29-35

Howard Johnson Lodge
8201 W. Higgins Rd.
Arlington Heights, IL 60631
(312) 693-2323
(800) 654-2000
$60-125

BENTON
Days Inn
711 W. Main
Benton IL 62812
(618) 439-3183
(800) 325-2525
Room rates $32-39

BLOOMINGTON
Ramada Inn
401 Brock Dr.
Bloomington IL 61701
(309) 829-7602
(800) 228-2828
Room rates $40-50

Days Inn
1707 W. Market St.
Bloomington IL 61701
(309) 829-6292
(800) 325-2525
Room rates $40-50

Days Inn
1803 E. Empire
Bloomington IL 61704
(309) 663-1361
(800) 325-2525
Room rates $38-54

Holiday Inn
1219 Holiday Lane
Bloomington IL 61704
(309) 662-5311
(800) 465-4329
Room rates $60-75

BRAIDWOOD
Days Inn
140 S. Hickory St.
Braidwood IL 60408
(815) 458-2812
(800) 325-2525
$50 deposit
Room rates $36-43

CARBONDALE
Super 8 Motel
1180 E. Main
Carbondale IL 62901
(618) 457-8822
(800) 848-8888
pets with permission
Room rates $37-39

Holiday Inn
800 Main St.
Carbondale IL 62901
(618) 529-1100
(800) 465-4329
Room rates $60-75

CHAMPAIGN
Comfort Inn
305 Market View Dr.
Champaign IL 61821
(217) 352-4055
(800) 228-5150
Room rates $40-55

Motel 6
1906 N. Cunningham Ave.
Champaign IL 61801
(217) 344-1082
1 small pet per room
Reservations (505) 891-6161
Room rates $20-26

Holiday Inn
1505 Neil St.
Champaign IL 61820
(217) 359-1601
(800) 465-4329
Room rates $50-60

CHICAGO
Hampton Inn
5200 W. Lincoln Hwy
Chicago IL 60443
(708) 481-3900
(800) 426-7866
Room rates $58-65

Howard Johnson Hotel
5615 N. Cumberland Ave.
Chicago, IL 60631
(312) 693-5800
(800) 654-2000
$55-165

**Always
Call
Ahead!**

Comfort Inn
2175 E. Touhy Ave.
Chicago IL 60018
(708) 635-1300
(800) 228-5150
Room rates $52-82

Quality Inn
3830 179th St
Chicago IL 46323
(219) 844-2140
(800) 228-5151
Room rates $43-46

Comfort Inn
135 S. Larkin Ave.
Chicago IL 60435
(815) 744-1770
(800) 228-5150
Room rates $49-60

Comfort Suites
17 W. 445 Roosevelt Rd.
Chicago IL 30181
(708) 916-1000
(800) 228-5150
Room rates $75-82

Quality Inn
10 W. Roosevelt Rd.
Chicago IL 60181
(708) 941-9100
(800) 228-5151
Room rates $48-62

Howard Johnson Hotel
5615 N. Cumberland Ave.
Chicago, IL 60631
(312) 693-5800
(800) 654-2000
$55-165

Ramada Inn
933 Rt 83 S.
Chicago, IL 60126
(708) 279-0700
(800) 228-2828
$54-70

Comfort Inn
3235 Norman Ave.
Chicago, IL 60435
(815) 436-5141
(800) 228-5150
$46-70

Comfort Inn
383 Lynch Dr.
Chicago IL 61832
(217) 443-8004
(800) 228-5150
Room rates $40-50

Essex Inn
800 Michigan Ave. @ 8th St.
Chicago IL 60605
(312) 939-2800
crated only
Room rates $95-115

Holiday Inn
350 Orleans
Chicago IL 60654
(312) 836-5000
(800) 465-4329
Room rates $120-150

COLLINSVILLE
Super 8 Motel
2 Gateway Dr.
Collinsville IL 62234-6106
(618) 345-8008
(800) 848-8888
pets with permission
Room rates $37-39

Quality Inn
475 N. Bluff Rd.
Collinsville IL 62234
(618) 344-7171
(800) 228-5151
Room rates $45-65

DANVILLE
Super 8 Motel
377 Lynch Dr.
Danville IL 61832
(217) 443-4499
(800) 848-8888
pets with permission
Room rates $38-41

Friendship Inn
400 N. Vermillion
Danville, IL 61832
(217) 443-1550
(800) 453-4511
$32-40

Ramada Inn
I-74 & Lynch Rd
Danville IL 61832
(217) 446-2400
(800) 228-2828
Room rates $47-60

Lincoln Inn
77 Gilbert St.
Danville IL 61832
(217) 443-6600
Room rates $55-65

DE KALB
Motel 6
1116 W. Lincoln Hwy.
De Kalb IL 60115
(815) 756-3398
1 small pet per room
Reservations (505) 891-6161
Room rates $21-27

Days Inn
1212 W. Lincoln Hwy
Dekalb IL 60115
(815) 758-8661
(800) 325-2525
Room rates $48-60

DECATUR
Holiday Inn Conference Resort
US 36 & Wyckles Rd.
Decatur IL 62522
(217) 422-8800
(800) 465-4329
Room rates $35-60

DIXON
Super 8 Motel
1800 S. Galena Ave.
Dixon IL 61021
(815) 284-1800
(800) 848-8888
pets with permission
Room rates $35-37

DOWNERS GROVE
Best Inns of America
3010 Finley Rd.
Downers Grove IL 60515
(708) 515-1500
(800) 237-8466
small pets only
Room rates $48-55

Always
Call
Ahead!

Red Roof Inn
1113 Butterfield Rd.
Downers Grove IL 60515
(708) 963-4205
(800) 843-7663
small pets only
Room rates $45-50

EAST HAZELCREST
Motel 6
17214 Halsted St.
East Hazelcrest IL 60429
(708) 957-9233
1 small pet per room
Reservations (505) 891-6161
Room rates $27-32

EFFINGHAM
Super 8 Motel
1400 Thelma Keller Ave.
Effingham IL 62401
(217) 342-6888
(800) 848-8888
Room rates $37-39

Ramada Inn
I-70/57 & Rte 32-33
Effingham IL 62401
(217) 342-2131
(800) 228-2828
Room rates $56-75

US Inn
1606 Fayette Ave.
Effingham IL 62401
(217) 342-4667
Room rates $35-40

Days Inn
W. Fayette Rd. & I-57
Effingham IL 62401
(217) 342-9271
(800) 325-2525
Room rates $30-40

ELGIN
Ramada Inn
500 W. River Rd
Elgin IL 60123
(708) 695-3000
$25 deposit
Room rates $50-55

Holiday Inn
345 River Rd.
Elgin IL 60123
(708) 695-5000
(800) 465-4329
Room rates $65-70

ELK GROVE VILLAGE
Motel 6
1601 Oakton St.
Elk Grove Village IL 60007
(708) 981-9766
1 small pet per room
Reservations (505) 891-6161
Room rates $27-33

ELMHURST
Ramada Inn
933 S. Rte 83
Elmhurst IL 60126
(708) 279-0700
(800) 228-2828
small pets only
Room rates $52-80

FAIRVIEW HEIGHTS
Super 8 Motel
45 Ludwig Dr.
Fairview Heights IL 62208
(618) 398-8338
(800) 848-8888
pets with permission
Room rates $39-41

FORSYTH
Comfort Inn
134 Barnett Ave.
Forsyth IL 62535
(217) 875-1166
(800) 228-5150
Room rates $40-50

FREEPORT
Holiday Inn
1300 South St.
Freeport IL 61032
(815) 235-3121
(800) 465-4329
Room rates $60-70

GALENA
Best Western Quiet House Suite
9915 Hwy 20 East
Galena IL 61036
(815) 777-2577
(800) 528-1234
pet restrictions - call ahead
Room rates $75-125

GALESBURG
Comfort Inn
907 W. Carl Sandburg Dr.
Galesburg IL 61401
(309) 344-5445
(800) 228-5150
Room rates $38-45

Days Inn
29 Public Square
Galesburg IL 61401
(309) 343-9161
(800) 325-2525
Room rates $45-50

GLENVIEW
Motel 6
1535 Milwaukee Ave.
Glenview IL 60025
(708) 390-7200
1 small pet per room
Reservations (505) 891-6161
Room rates $29-35

HARVEY
Motel 6
17003 Halsted St.
Harvey IL 60426
(708) 596-7470
1 small pet per room
Reservations (505) 891-6161
Room rates $27-33

HOFFMAN ESTATES
Budgetel Inn
2075 Barrington Rd.
Hoffman Estates IL 60195
(708) 882-8848
(800) 428-3438
Room rates $45-50

JACKSONVILLE
Super 8 Motel
1003 W. Morton Rd.
Jacksonville IL 62650
(217) 479-0303
(800) 848-8888
pets with permission
Room rates $37-40

Motel 6
1716 W. Morton Dr.
Jacksonville IL 62650
(217) 243-7157
1 small pet per room
Reservations (505) 891-6161
Room rates $21-27

ILLINOIS, Jacksonville

Holiday Inn
1717 Morton Ave.
Jacksonville IL 62650
(217) 245-9571
(800) 465-4329
Room rates $52-60

JOLIET
Motel 6
1850 McDonough Rd.
Joliet IL 60436
(815) 729-2800
1 small pet per room
Reservations (505) 891-6161
Room rates $25-31

Red Roof Inn
1750 McDonough St.
Joliet IL 60436
(815) 741-2304
(800) 843-7663
$3 charge
Room rates $40-45

KANKAKEE
Days Inn
1975 E. Court
Kankakee IL 60901
(815) 939-7171
(800) 325-2525
$4/pets
Room rates $49-59

LANSING
Best Western
2505 Bernice Rd.
Lansing IL 60438
(708) 895-7810
(800) 528-1234
small pets only
Room rates $50-70

LITCHFIELD
Super 8 Motel
I-55 & IL 16 W.
Litchfield IL 62056
(217) 324-7788
(800) 848-8888
pets with permission
Room rates from $37

MACOMB
Super 8 Motel
313 University Ave.
Macomb IL 61455
(309) 836-8888
(800) 848-8888
pets with permission
Room rates from $35

Holiday Inn
1400 Lafayette St.
Macomb IL 61455
(309) 833-5511
(800) 465-4329
Room rates $55-60

MARION
Super 8 Motel
I-57 & Rt.13
Marion IL 62959
(618) 993-5577
(800) 848-8888
pets with permission
Room rates from $35

Holiday Inn
I-57
Marion IL 62959
(618) 997-2326
(800) 465-4329
Room rates $55-60

MATTOON
Super 8 Motel
Rt. 16 E. & I-57
Mattoon IL 61938
(217) 235-8888
(800) 848-8888
pets with permission
Room rates from $37

MENDOTA
Super 8 Motel
508 Hwy 34 E.
Mendota IL 61342
(815) 539-7429
(800) 848-8888
pets with permission
Room rates from $37

MOLINE
Hampton Inn
6920 27th St.
Moline IL 61265
(309) 762-1711
(800) 426-7866
Room rates $42-48

Comfort Inn
2600 52nd Ave.
Moline IL 61265
(309) 762-7000
(800) 228-5150
Room rates $40-50

Holiday Inn
6902 27th St.
Moline IL 61265
(309) 762-8811
(800) 465-4329
Room rates $60-75

MORRIS
Comfort Inn
70 W. Gore Rd.
Morris IL 60450
(815) 942-1433
(800) 228-5150
Room rates $45-55

MT. VERNON
Super 8 Motel
401 S
Mt. Vernon IL 62864
(618) 242-8800
(800) 848-8888
pets with permission
Room rates from $37

Ramada Inn
222 Potomac Blvd.
Mt. Vernon IL 62864
(618) 244-7100
(800) 228-2828
$10 charge
Room rates $52-95

Daystop
750 S. 10th
Mt. Vernon IL 62864
(618) 244-3224
(800) 325-2525
$3/pets
Room rates $33-37

Motel 6
I-57 & IL 15
Mt. Vernon, IL 62864
(618) 244-2383
(505) 891-6161
$22-36

Red Roof Inn
1698 Diehl Rd.
Naperville IL 60540
(708) 369-2500
(800) 843-7663
Room rates $40-50

NILES
Travelodge
7247 North Waukegan Rd.
Niles IL 60648
(708) 647-9444
(800) 255-3050
Room rates from $50

NORMAL
Super 8 Motel
Traders Circle
Normal IL 61761
(309) 454-5858
(800) 848-8888
Room rates from $41

Motel 6
1600 North Main St.
Normal IL 61761
(309) 452-0422
1 small pet per room
Reservations (505) 891-6161
Room rates from $

O'FALLON
Comfort Inn
1100 S. East Gate Dr.
O'Fallon IL 62269
(618) 624-6060
(800) 228-5150
Room rates $43-76

OAKBROOK
Days Inn
407 Ogden Ave.
Oakbrook IL 60514
(708) 325-2500
(800) 325-2525
pets with permission
Room rates $43-53

Days Inn
115 E. Ogden Ave.
Oakbrook IL 60559
(708) 969-5200
(800) 325-2525
pets with permission
Room rates $37-47

PALATINE
Motel 6
1450 E. Dundee Rd.
Palatine IL 60067
(708) 359-0046
1 small pet per room
Reservations (505) 891-6161
Room rates $26-32

PEORIA
Super 8 Motel
4025 W. War Memorial Dr.
Peoria IL 61614
(309) 688-8074
(800) 848-8888
pets with permission
Room rates from $39

Comfort Suites
4025 War Memorial
Peoria IL 61614
(800) 221-2222
(800) 228-5150
Room rates $47-50

Motel 6
104 West Camp St.
Peoria IL 61611
(309) 699-7281
1 small pet per room
Reservations (505) 891-6161
Room rates $25-31

PERU
Motel 6
1900 May Rd.
Peru IL 61354
(815) 224-2785
1 small pet per room
Reservations (505) 891-6161
Room rates from $20

PONTIAC
Super 8 Motel
I-55 & Rt. 116 E.
Pontiac IL 61764
(815) 844-6888
(800) 848-8888
pets with permission
Room rates from $37

QUINCY
Travelodge
200 South 3rd St.
Quincy IL 62301
(217) 222-5620
(800) 255-3050
Room rates from $39

Holiday Inn
201 3rd St.
Quincy IL 62301
(217) 222-2666
(800) 465-4329
small pets only
Room rates $60-70

ROCKFORD
Motel 6
4205 11th St.
Rockford IL 61109
(815) 398-0066
1 small pet per room
Reservations (505) 891-6161
Room rates from $21

Exel Inn
220 Lyford Rd.
Rockford IL 61108
(815) 332-4915
Room rates $34-38

ROLLING MEADOWS
Motel 6
1800 Winnetka Circle
Rolling Meadows IL 60008
(708) 818-8088
1 small pet per room
Reservations (505) 891-6161
Room rates from $28

SALEM
Super 8 Motel
1704 W. Main St.
Salem IL 62881
(618) 548-5882
(800) 848-8888
requires deposit
Room rates from $35

Days Inn
1812 W. Main St.
Salem IL 62881
(618) 548-4212
(800) 325-2525
small pets
Room rates $37-40

SCHILLER PARK
Motel 6
9408 W. Lawrence ave.
Schiller Park IL 60176
(708) 671-4282
1 small pet per room
Reservations (505) 891-6161
Room rates from $30

SPRINGFIELD
Super 8 Motel
1330 S. Dirksen Pkwy
Springfield IL 62703
(217) 528-8889
(800) 848-8888
pets with deposit
Room rates from $34

Super 8 Motel
3675 S. 6th St.
Springfield IL 62703
(217) 529-8898
(800) 848-8888
pets with deposit
Room rates from $34

Quality Inn
400 N. 9th St.
Springfield IL 62702
(217) 522-7711
(800) 228-5151
Room rates $41-45

Days Inn
3000 Stevenson Dr.
Springfield IL 62703
(217) 529-0171
(800) 325-2525
Room rates $42-47

Capitol Plaza Hotel
418 E. Jefferson St.
Springfield IL 62701
(217) 525-1700
under 20 lbs
Room rates from $43

Motel 6
3125 Wide Track Dr.
Springfield IL 62703
(217) 789-1063
1 small pet per room
Reservations (505) 891-6161
Room rates from $22

Motel 6
3125 Wide Track Drive
Springfield IL 62703
(217) 789-1063
1 small pet per room
Reservations (505) 891-6161
Room rates from $

Holiday Inn Conference Center
3100 Dirksen Pkwy
Springfield IL 62703
(217) 529-7171
(800) 465-4329
Room rates $60-75

Howard Johnson
3190 Dirksen Pkwy
Springfield IL 62703
(217) 529-9100
(800) 654-2000
small pets only
Room rates $35-45

TUSCOLA
Super 8 Motel
Rt. 36
Tuscola IL 61953
(217) 253-5488
(800) 848-8888
pets with permission
Room rates from $37

URBANA
Howard Johnson Lodge
1990 N. Cunningham
Urbana, IL 61801
(217) 367-8331
(800) 654-2000
$46-90

Motel 6
1906 N. Cunningham Ave.
Urbana IL 61801
(217) 344-1082
1 small pet per room
Reservations (505) 891-6161
Room rates from $20

Best Western - Lincoln Lodge
403 University Ave.
Urbana IL 61801
(217) 367-1111
(800) 528-1234
$10 charge
Room rates $40-50

VANDALIA
Comfort Inn
I-70@ US 51
Vandalia IL 62471
(618) 283-4400
(800) 228-5150
Room rates $35-46

Travelodge
1500 North 6th St.
Vandalia IL 62471
(618) 283-2363
(800) 255-3050
Room rates from $33

WAUKEGAN
Airport Inn
3651 Lewis Ave.
Waukegan IL 60087
(708) 249-7777
$5 charge
Room rates $36-41

INDIANA
ANDERSON
Comfort Inn
2205 E. 59th St.
Anderson IN 46013IN
(317) 644-4422
(800) 228-5150
Room rates $44-55

Friendship Inn
583 Broadway
Anderson, IN 46012
(317) 643-6685
(800) 453-4511
$27-50

**Always
Call
Ahead!**

Motel 6
5810 Scatterfield Rd.
Anderson IN 46013
(317) 642-9023
1 small pet per room
Reservations (505) 891-6161
Room rates $25-33

Best Western
5901 Scatterfield Rd.
Anderson IN 46013
(317) 649-0451
$20 charge
Room rates $60-70

BLOOMINGTON
Super 8 Motel
1000 W. State Rd.
Bloomington IN 47401
(812) 323-8000
(800) 848-8888
pets with permission
Room rates $40-45

Motel 6
126 S. Franklin Rd.
Bloomington IN 47401
(812) 332-0337
1 small pet per room
Reservations (505) 891-6161
Room rates $25-33

Holiday Inn
2601 Walnut
Bloomington IN 47402
(812) 332-9453
(800) 465-4329
Room rates $50-65

CLARKSVILLE
Lakeview Hotel
505 Marriot Dr.
Clarksville IN 47130
(812) 283-4411
$10 deposit
Room rates $54-150

COLUMBUS
Days Inn
3445 Jonathon Moore Pike
Columbus IN 47201
(812) 376-9951
(800) 325-2525
Room rates $50-75

Holiday Inn
2480 Jonathon Moore Pike
Columbus IN 47201
(812) 372-1541
(800) 465-4329
Room rates $60-90

CRAWFORDSVILLE
Days Inn
1040 Corey Blvd.
Crawfordsville IN 47933
(317) 362-0300
(800) 325-2525
Room rates $39-59

DALEVILLE
Super 8 Motel
I-69 & SR 67
Daleville IN 46017
(317) 378-0888
(800) 848-8888
pets with permission
Room rates from $37

ELKHART
Days Inn
2820 Cassapolis St.
Elkhart IN 46514
(219) 262-3541
(800) 325-2525
Room rates $31-46

Red Roof Inn
2902 Cassopolis St.
Elkhart IN 46514
(219) 262-3691
(800) 843-7663
Room rates $35-40

EVANSVILLE
Super 8 Motel
4600 Morgan Ave.
Evansville IN 47715
(812) 476-4008
(800) 848-8888
pets with permission
Room rates $38-42

Travelodge
701 1st Ave.
Evansville IN 47710
(812) 422-3886
(800) 255-3050
$25 deposit
Room rates $30-40

Motel 6
4201 US 41 North
Evansville IN 47711
(812) 424-6431
1 small pet per room
Room rates $30-40

FRANKLIN
Days Inn
2180 E. King
Franklin IN 46131
(317) 736-8000
(800) 325-2525
small pets
Room rates $47-57

FT. WAYNE
Super 8 Motel
522 Coliseum Blvd.
Ft. Wayne IN 46805
(219) 484-8326
(800) 848-8888
pets with permission
Room rates from $38

Days Inn
5250 Distribution Dr
Ft. Wayne IN 46825
(219) 484-9681
(800) 325-2525
Room rates $32-42

Days Inn
3730 E. Washington Blvd.
Ft. Wayne IN 46803
(219) 424-1980
(800) 325-2525
Room rates $32-36

Motel 6
3003 Coliseum Blvd. W.
Ft. Wayne IN 46808
(219) 482-3972
1 small pet per room
Reservations (505) 891-6161
Room rates $25-33

INDIANA, Fort Wayne

Motel 6
1020 Coliseum Blvd. N.
Ft. Wayne IN 46805
(219) 422-8551
1 small pet per room
Reservations (505) 891-6161
Room rates $25-33

Marriott
305 Washington Center Rd.
Ft. Wayne IN 46825
(219) 484-0411
(800) 228-9290
small pets only
Room rates $70-110

Ramada Inn
1212 Magnavox Way
Ft. Wayne, IN 46804
(219) 432-0511
(800) 228-2828
$47-67

HAMMOND
Motel 6
3840 179th St.
Hammond IN 46324
(219) 845-0330
1 small pet per room
Reservations (505) 891-6161
Room rates $25-33

INDIANAPOLIS
Super 8 Motel
4530 E. Emerson Ave.
Indianapolis IN 46203
(317) 788-0955
(800) 848-8888
$10 charge
Room rates from $39

Super 8 Motel
4502 S. Harding St.
Indianapolis IN 46217
(317) 788-4774
(800) 848-8888
pets allowed with $10 charge
Room rates from $38

Econo Lodge
4326 Sellers St.
Indianapolis, IN 46226
(317) 542-1031
(800) 446-6900
$29-85

Comfort Inn
3880 W. 92nd St.
Indianapolis IN 46268
(822) 221-2222
(800) 228-5150
Room rates $44-55

Days Inn
7314 E. 21st St.
Indianapolis IN 46219
(317) 359-5500
(800) 325-2525
small pets only
Room rates $35-40

Days Inn
450 Bixler Rd.
Indianapolis IN 46227
(317) 788-0811
(800) 325-2525
$5/pets
Room rates $37-42

Motel 6
2851 Shadeland Ave.
Indianapolis IN 46219
(317) 546-5864
1 small pet per room
Reservations (505) 891-6161
Room rates $25-33

Hilton
31 Ohio St.
Indianapolis IN 46204
(317) 635-2000
(800) 445-8667
$50 charge, under 10 lbs
Room rates $90-120

JASPER
Days Inn
Jct Hwys 162 & 164
Jasper IN 47546
(812) 482-6000
(800) 325-2525
$2/pets
Room rates $44-48

JEFFERSONVILLE
Ramada Inn
700 Riverside Dr.
Jeffersonville IN 47130
(812) 284-6711
(800) 228-2828
Room rates $58-88

Motel 6
2016 Old Hwy 31 East
Jeffersonville IN 47130
(812) 283-7703
1 small pet per room
Reservations (505) 891-6161
Room rates $25-33

KOKOMO
Comfort Inn
522 Essex Dr.
Kokomo IN 46901
(317) 452-5050
(800) 228-5150
Room rates $44-55

LAFAYETTE
Days Inn
400 Sagamore Pkwy S.
Lafayette IN 47905
(317) 447-4131
(800) 325-2525
Room rates $45-55

Howard Johnson
4343 SR 26 East
Lafayette IN 47905
(317) 447-0575
(800) 654-2000
Room rates $70-90

Super 8 Motel
8300 Louisianna St.
Merrillville IN 46410
(219) 736-8383
(800) 848-8888
pets with permission
Room rates from $35

MERRILLVILLE
La Quinta
8210 Louisiana St.
Merrillville IN 46410
(219) 738-2870
(800) 531-5900
Room rates $45-55

MICHIGAN CITY
Red Roof Inn
110 Kieffer Rd.
Michigan City IN 46360
(219) 874-5251
(800) 843-7663
Room rates $35-40

MUNCIE
Comfort Inn
4011 W. Bethel
Muncie IN 47305
(317) 282-6666
(800) 228-5150
Room rates $44-55

Holiday Inn
3400 Madison
Muncie IN 47302
(317) 288-1911
(800) 465-4329
$50 deposit
Room rates $45-50

The Hotel Roberts
420 High St.
Muncie IN 47305
(317) 741-7777
$100 deposit + $50 fee
Room rates $45-75

PLYMOUTH
Motel 6
2535 N. Michigan
Plymouth IN 46563
(219) 935-5911
1 small pet per room
Reservations (505) 891-6161
Room rates $25-33

PORTAGE
Motel 6
6101 Melton Rd.
Portage IN 46368
(219) 763-3121
1 small pet per room
Reservations (505) 891-6161
Room rates $25-33

Days Inn
6161 Melton Rd.
Portage IN 46368
(219) 762-2136
(800) 654-2000
crated only
Room rates $45-70

REMINGTON
Days Inn
I-65 & US 24
Remington IN 47977
(219) 261-2178
(800) 325-2525
$2/pets
Room rates $29-32

RICHMOND
Quality Inn
5501 National Rd. E
Richmond IN 47374
(317) 966-7511
(800) 228-5151
Room rates $55-125

Days Inn
540 W. Eaton Pike
Richmond IN 47374
(317) 966-7591
(800) 325-2525
small pets $5 charge
Room rates $36-42

Best Western Imperial Lodge
3020 Main St.
Richmond IN 47374
(317) 966-1505
(800) 528-1234
small pets only
Room rates $32-40

Howard Johnson
US 27 & I-70
Richmond IN 47374
(317) 962-7576
(800) 654-2000
Room rates $55-90

SEYMOUR
Days Inn
302 S. Commerce Dr.
Seymour IN 47274
(812) 522-3678
(800) 325-2525
$3/pets
Room rates $33-48

SHELBYVILLE
Super 8 Motel
20 Rampart Dr.
Shelbyville IN 46176
(317) 392-6239
(800) 848-8888
pets allowed with $10 charge
Room rates from $38

SOUTH BEND
Days Inn
52757 Bus. US 31 North
South Bend IN 46637
(219) 277-0510
(800) 325-2525
$3/pets
Room rates $31-50

Motel 6
52624 US 31/33
South Bend IN 46637
(219) 272-7072
1 small pet per room
Reservations (505) 891-6161
Room rates $25-33

Holiday Inn
515 Dixie Way
South Bend IN 46637
(219) 272-6600
(800) 465-4329
Room rates $55-80

Howard Johnson
52939 US 33 North
South Bend IN 46637
(219) 272-1500
(800) 654-2000
Room rates $45-85

SPEEDWAY
Motel 6
6330 Debonair Lane
Speedway IN 46224
(317) 293-3220
1 small pet per room
Reservations (505) 891-6161
Room rates $25-33

SULLIVAN
Days Inn
Jct 41 & 154
Sullivan IN 47882
(812) 268-6391
(800) 325-2525
Room rates $40-50

INDIANA, Tell City

TELL CITY
Days Inn
Hwy 66 & 14th St.
Tell City IN 47586
(812) 547-3474
(800) 325-2525
Room rates $36-40

TERRE HAUTE
Super 8 Motel
3089 S. 1st St.
Terre Haute IN 47802
(812) 232-4890
(800) 848-8888
pets with deposit
Room rates from $34

Days Inn
2800 S. Dixie Bee Rd.
Terre Haute IN 47802
(812) 234-4268
(800) 325-2525
Room rates $41-57

Travelodge
530 South 3rd St.
Terre Haute IN 47807
(812) 232-7075
(800) 255-3050
Room rates from $38

VALPRAISO
Bridgeview Inn
559 West St.
Valpraiso IN 46383
(219) 464-8555
$50 deposit plus
permission
Room rates $45-47

VINCENNES
Holiday Inn
600 Wheatland Rd.
Vincennes IN 47591
(812) 886-9900
(800) 465-4329
Room rates $48-55

WARSAW
Comfort Inn
2605 E. Center St.
Warsaw IN 46580
(219) 267-7337
(800) 228-5150
$25 deposit
Room rates $53-65

IOWA

AMES
Comfort Inn
1605 S. Dayton Ave.
Ames IA 50010
(515) 232-0689
(800) 228-5150
Room rates $39-51

BURLINGTON
Comfort Inn
3051 Kirkwood
Burlington IA 52601
(319) 753-0000
(800) 228-5150
Room rates $38-55

CARROLL
Super 8 Motel
Hwy 17 N.
Carroll IA 51401
(712) 792-4753
(800) 848-8888
pets with permission
Room rates from $31

CEDAR RAPIDS
Comfort Inn
5055 Rockwell Dr.
Cedar Rapids IA 52402
(319) 393-8247
(800) 228-5150
Room rates $42-50

Comfort Inn
390 33rd Ave SW
Cedar Rapids IA 52404
(319) 363-7934
(800) 228-5150
Room rates $37-50

Days Inn
3245 Southgate Place S.W.
Cedar Rapids IA 52404
(319) 365-4339
(800) 325-2525
pets allowed with permission
Room rates $40-50

CLINTON
Days Inn
1522 Lincolnway
Clinton IA 52732
(319) 243-8841
(800) 325-2525
$10 pet deposit with permission
Room rates $39-54

Travelodge
302 6th Ave.
Clinton IA 52732
(319) 243-4730
(800) 255-3050
Room rates from $34

CORALVILLE
Comfort Inn
209 W. 9th ST
Coralville IA 52241
(319) 351-8144
(800) 228-5150
Room rates $46-50

Motel 6
810 1st Ave.
Coralville IA 52241
(319) 354-0030
1 small pet per room
Reservations (505) 891-6161
Room rates $28-33

COUNCIL BLUFFS
Super 8 Motel
2712 S. 24th St.
Council Bluffs IA 51501
(712) 322-2888
(800) 848-8888
pets with permission
Room rates from $30

Motel 6
1846 N. 16th St.
Council Bluffs IA 51501
(712) 328-8300
1 small pet per room
Reservations (505) 891-6161
Room rates $28-33

Comfort Inn
3208 S. 7th St.
Council Bluffs IA 51501
(712) 366-9699
(800) 228-5150
Room rates $33-40

**Always
Call
Ahead!**

DAVENPORT
Hampton Inn
3330 E. Kimberly Rd.
Davenport IA 52807
(319) 359-3921
(800) 426-7866
Room rates $42-48

Ramada Inn
6263 N. Brady
Davenport IA 52806
(319) 386-1940
(800) 228-2828
Room rates $55-60

Comfort Inn
7222 Northwest Blvd.
Davenport IA 52806
(319) 391-8222
(800) 228-5150
Room rates $36-80

Days Inn
101 W. 65th St.
Davenport IA 52807
(319) 388-9999
(800) 325-2525
pets allowed with permission
Room rates $35-55

Days Inn
3202 E. Kimberly Rd.
Davenport IA 52807
(319) 355-1190
(800) 325-2525
pets allowed with permission
Room rates $40-50

Motel 6
6111 N. Brady St.
Davenport IA 52806
(319) 391-8997
1 small pet per room
Reservations (505) 891-6161
Room rates $28-33

DECORAH
Super 8 Motel
Hwy 9
Decorah IA 52101
(319) 382-8771
(800) 848-8888
pets with deposit
Room rates from $38

DES MOINES
Econo Lodge
5626 Douglas Ave.
Des Moines, IA 50310
(515) 278-1601
(800) 446-6900
$31-37

Econo Lodge
11000 Douglas Ave.
Des Moines, IA 50322
(515) 278-4601
(800) 446-6900
$35-55

Super 8 Motel
4755 Merle Hay Rd.
Des Moines IA 50323
(505) 278-8858
(800) 848-8888
pets with permission
Room rates from $37

Ramada Inn
4685 NE 14th St.
Des Moines IA 50313
(515) 265-5671
(800) 228-2828
Room rates $40-49

Comfort Inn
5231 Fleur Dr.
Des Moines IA 50321
(515) 287-3434
(800) 228-5150
Room rates $44-75

Days Inn
3501 E. 14th St.
Des Moines IA 50316
(515) 265-2541
(800) 325-2525
small pets only
Room rates $34-63

Travelodge
4845 Merle Hay Rd.
Des Moines IA 50322
(515) 278-5511
(800) 255-3050
Room rates from $36

Motel 6
4817 Fleur Dr.
Des Moines IA 50321
(515) 287-6364
1 small pet per room
Reservations (505) 891-6161
Room rates $28-33

Motel 6
4940 NE 14th St.
Des Moines IA 50313
(515) 266-5456
1 small pet per room
Reservations (505) 891-6161
Room rates $28-33

DUBUQUE
Comfort Inn
4055 Dodge St.
Dubuque IA 52001
(319) 556-3006
(800) 228-5150
Room rates $42-50

FT. MADISON
Super 8 Motel
Hwy 61 W.
Ft. Madison IA 52627
(319) 372-8500
(800) 848-8888
pets with permission
Room rates from $34

IOWA CITY
Howard Johnson
2216 Dodge St.
Iowa City IA 52240
(319) 351-1010
(800) 654-2000
Room rates $40-55

KEOKUK
Days Inn
4th & Main St.
Keokuk IA 52632
(319) 524-8000
(800) 325-2525
$5/pets
Room rates $45-50

MASON CITY
Travelodge
24 5th St.
Mason City IA 50401
(515) 424-2910
(800) 255-3050
Room rates from $36

IOWA, Muscatine

MUSCATINE
Super 8 Motel
Hwys 61 & 38
Muscatine IA 52761
(319) 263-9100
(800) 848-8888
pets with depsoit
Room rates from $37

NEWTON
Super 8 Motel
1635 S. 12th Ave.
Newton IA 50208
(515) 792-8868
(800) 848-8888
pets with permission
Room rates from $38

OTTUMWA
Days Inn
206 Church St.
Ottumwa IA 52501
(515) 682-8131
(800) 325-2525
Room rates $42-59

SERGEANT BLUFF
Motel 6
6166 Harbor Dr.
Sergeant Bluff IA 51054
(712) 277-3131
1 small pet per room
Reservations (505) 891-6161
Room rates $28-33

SIOUX CITY
Holiday Inn
1401 Zenith Dr.
Sioux City IA 51103
(712) 277-3211
(800) 465-4329
Room rates $50-60

SPENCER
Super 8 Motel
209 11th St. SW
Spencer IA 51301
(712) 262-8500
(800) 848-8888
Room rates from $31

SPIRIT LAKE
Super 8 Motel
2501 Hwy 71
Spirit Lake IA 51360
(712) 336-4901
(800) 848-8888
small pets in smoking rooms
Room rates from $32

URBANDALE
Comfort Inn
5900 Sutton Pl.
Urbandale IA 50322
(515) 270-1037
(800) 228-5150
Room rates $40-50

WALCOTT
Super 8 Motel
Walcott I-80 Industrial Park
Walcott IA 52773
(319) 284-5083
(800) 848-8888
pets with deposit
Room rates from $34

WATERLOO
Super 8 Motel
1825 LaPorte Rd.
Waterloo IA 50702
(319) 233-1800
(800) 848-8888
pets with permission
Room rates from $38

Comfort Inn
1945 LaPorte Rd.
Waterloo IA 50702
(319) 234-7411
(800) 228-5150
Room rates $40-50

WEBSTER CITY
Super 8 Motel
305 Closz Dr.
Webster City IA 50595
(515) 832-2000
(800) 848-8888
pets with permission
Room rates from $35

WILLIAMSBURG
Super 8 Motel
RR 2
Williamsburg IA 52361
(319) 668-2800
(800) 848-8888
pets with permission
Room rates from $36

KANSAS
ABILENE
Super 8 Motel
I-70 @ N. Buckeye Ave.
Abilene KS 67410
(913) 263-4545
(800) 848-8888
pets with permission
Room rates from $35

ATCHINSON
Best Western Atchinson Inn
401 S. 10th
Atchinson KS 66002
(913) 367-7000
(800) 528-1234
small pets only
Room rates $35-45

COFFEYVILLE
Best Western - Fountain Plaza
104 11th St.
Coffeyville KS 67337
(316) 251-2250
(800) 528-1234
small pets only
Room rates $35-45

COLBY
Super 8 Motel
1040 Zelfer Ave.
Colby KS 67701
(913) 462-8248
(800) 848-8888
pets with permission
Room rates from $33

Ramada Inn
1950 S Range
Colby KS 67701
(913) 462-3933
(800) 228-2828
Room rates $39-49

DODGE CITY
Super 8 Motel
1708 W. Wyatt Earp Blvd.
Dodge City KS 67801
(316) 225-3924
(800) 848-8888
Room rates $37-42

Always
Call
Ahead!

EMPORIA
Super 8 Motel
2913 W. Hwy 50
Emporia KS 66801
(316) 342-7567
(800) 848-8888
pets with permission
Room rates from $35

Quality Inn
3021 W. US 50
Emporia KS 66801
(316) 342-3770
(800) 228-5151
Room rates $40-46

Days Inn
3032 W. Hwy 50
Emporia KS 66801
(316) 342-1787
(800) 325-2525
Room rates $38-47

Econo Lodge
2630 W. 18th Ave.
Emporia, KS 66801
(316) 343-1240
(800) 446-6900
$29-40

GARDEN CITY
Hilton Inn
1911 Kansas
Garden City KS 67846
(316) 275-7471
(800) 445-8667
under 20 lbs
Room rates $45-60

GOODLAND
Motel 6
I-70 & Hwy 27
Goodland KS 67735
(913) 899-5672
1 small pet per room
Reservations (505) 891-6161
Room rates $27-32

GREAT BEND
Super 8 Motel
3500 10th St.
Great Bend KS 67530
(316) 793-8486
(800) 848-8888
pets with permission
Room rates from $36

HAYS
Hampton Inn
3801 Vine St.
Hays KS 67601
(913) 625-8103
(800) 426-7866
Room rates from $44

Motel 6
3404 Vine St.
Hays KS 67601
(913) 625-4282
1 small pet per room
Reservations (505) 891-6161
Room rates $27-32

HUTCHINSON
Super 8 Motel
1305 E. 11th Ave.
Hutchinson KS 67501
(316) 662-6394
(800) 848-8888
pets with permission
Room rates from $34

Quality Inn
15 W. 4th St.
Hutchinson KS 67501
(316) 663-1211
(800) 228-5151
Room rates $45-69

Comfort Inn
1621 Super Plaza
Hutchinson KS 67501
(316) 663-7822
(800) 228-5150
Room rates $45-69

JUNCTION CITY
Days Inn
1024 S. Washington
Junction City KS 66441
(913) 762-2727
(800) 325-2525
Room rates $32-48

KANSAS CITY
Riverview Inn
42 Minnesota Ave.
Kansas City KS 66101
(913) 342-6919
Room rates $50-70

LAWRENCE
Super 8 Motel
515 McDonald Dr.
Lawrence KS 66044
(913) 842-5721
(800) 848-8888
pets with permission
Room rates from $38

Days Inn
2309 Iowa St.
Lawrence KS 66046
(913) 843-9100
(800) 325-2525
Room rates $29-42

Travelodge
801 Iowa St.
Lawrence KS 66049
(913) 842-5100
(800) 255-3050
Room rates $39-41

LEAVENWORTH
Ramada Inn
3rd & Delaware Streets
Leavenworth KS 66048
(913) 651-5500
(800) 228-2828
Room rates $40-55

LENEXA
Motel 6
9725 Lenexa Dr.
Lenexa KS 66215
(913) 541-8558
1 small pet per room
Reservations (505) 891-6161
Room rates $27-32

Motel 6
9725 Lenexa Dr.
Lenexa KS 66215
(913) 541-8558
1 small pet per room
Reservations (505) 891-6161
Room rates $27-32

KANSAS, Lenexa

Holiday Inn
12601 95th St.
Lenexa KS 66215
(913) 888-6670
(800) 465-4329
Room rates $50-85

LIBERAL
Super 8 Motel
747 E. Pancake Blvd.
Liberal KS 67901
(316) 624-8880
(800) 848-8888
pets with permission
Room rates from $34

MANHATTAN
Days Inn
1501 Tuttle Creek Blvd.
Manhattan KS 66502
(913) 539-5391
(800) 325-2525
Room rates $36-56

Motel 6
510 Tuttle Creek Blvd.
Manhattan KS 66502
(913) 537-1022
1 small pet per room
Reservations (505) 891-6161
Room rates $27-32

MCPHERSON
Super 8 Motel
2110 E. Kansas
McPherson KS 67460
(316) 241-8881
(800) 848-8888
pets with permission
Room rates from $34

NEWTON
Super 8 Motel
1620 E. 2nd St.
Newton KS 67114
(316) 283-7611
(800) 848-8888
pets with permission
Room rates from $32

OLATHE
Holiday Inn
101 151st St.
Olathe KS 66061
(913) 829-4000
(800) 465-4329
Room rates $60-75

OVERLAND PARK
Econo Lodge
7508 Shawnee Mission Pkwy.
Overland Park, KS 66202
(913) 262-9600
(800) 446-6900
$30-47

Marriott
108 Metcalf Ave.
Overland Park KS 66212
(913) 451-8000
(800) 228-9290
Room rates $100-140

SALINA
Park Inn International
453 Broadway
Salina KS 67402
(913) 827-5533
Room rates $23-35

TOPEKA
Comfort Inn
1518 SW Wanamaker Rd.
Topeka KS 66604913
(913) 273-5365
(800) 228-5150
Room rates $41-65

Days Inn
1510 S. Wanamaker Rd.
Topeka KS 66604
(913) 272-8538
(800) 325-2525
Room rates $40-50

Motel 6
3846 S. Topeka Ave.
Topeka KS 66609
(913) 267-1222
1 small pet per room
Reservations (505) 891-6161
Room rates $27-32

Motel 6
709 Fairlawn Rd.
Topeka KS 66606
(912) 272-8283
1 small pet per room
Reservations (505) 891-6161
Room rates $27-32

Holiday Inn
605 Fairlawn Rd.
Topeka KS 66606
(913) 272-8040
(800) 465-4329
small pets only
Room rates $60-70

WICHITA
Comfort Inn
4849 S. Laura
Wichita KS 67216
(316) 522-1800
(800) 228-5150
Room rates $52-56

Motel 6
5736 W. Kellogg
Wichita KS 67209
(316) 945-8440
1 small pet per room
Reservations (505) 891-6161
Room rates $27-32

Tudor Inn
9100 Kellogg
Wichita KS 67207
(316) 685-0371
$10 deposit
Room rates $45-60

Park Inn International
1000 Broadway
Wichita KS 67214
(316) 267-6211
small pets only
Room rates $40-65

Holiday Inn
7335 Kellogg
Wichita KS 67207
(316) 685-1281
(800) 465-4329
Room rates $60-80

KENTUCKY
ASHLAND
Knights Inn
7216 SR 60
Ashland KY 41101
(606) 928-9501
(800) 722-7220
Room rates $29-39

Always
Call
Ahead!

BARDSTOWN
Holiday Inn
US 31 & Blue Grass Pkwy
Bardstown KY 40004
(502) 348-9253
(800) 465-4329
small pets only
Room rates $55-70

BEREA
Days Inn
Rt. 595 & I-75
Berea KY 40403
(606) 986-7373
(800) 325-2525
$5/pets
Room rates $36-49

BOWLING GREEN
Hampton Inn
233 Three Springs Rd
Bowling Green KY 42104
(502) 842-4100
(800) 426-7866
Room rates $45-55

Ramada Inn
4767 Scottsville Rd.
Bowling Green KY 42101
(502) 781-3000
(800) 228-2828
Room rates $53-66

Econo Lodge
760 Interstate Dr.
Bowling Green, KY 42101
(502) 781-6181
(800) 446-6900
$32-40

Motel 6
3139 Scottsville Rd.
Bowling Green KY 42101
(502) 843-0140
1 small pet per room
Reservations (505) 891-6161
Room rates $28-31

CARROLLTON
Days Inn
Jct I-71 & US 227
Carrollton KY 41008
(502) 732-9301
(800) 325-2525
Room rates from $40

CAVE CITY
Quality Inn
Mammoth Cave Rd.
Cave City KY 42127
(502) 773-2181
(800) 228-5151
Room rates $30-62

Days Inn
I-65 & Hwys 90 & 70
Cave City KY 42127
(502) 773-2151
(800) 325-2525
Room rates from $29

CORBIN
Super 8 Motel
I-75 & US 25-E
Corbin KY 40701
(606) 528-8888
(800) 848-8888
Room rates from $26

Quality Inn
I-75 & US 25 E.
Corbin KY 40701
(606) 528-4802
(800) 228-5151
Room rates $32-40

Days Inn
I-75 & US 25 W.
Corbin KY 40701
(606) 528-8150
(800) 325-2525
Room rates $31-36

COVINGTON
Holiday Inn
600 3rd St.
Covington KY 41011
(606) 291-4300
(800) 465-4329
Room rates $39-65

ELIZABETHTOWN
Days Inn
I-65 & US 62
Elizabethtown KY 42701
(502) 769-5522
(800) 325-2525
No show dogs
Room rates $32-37

Motel 6
Hwy 62 & I 65
Elizabethtown KY 42701
(502) 769-3102
1 small pet per room
Reservations (505) 891-6161
Room rates $28-31

Howard Johnson
708 Dixie Hwy.
Elizabethtown KY 42701
(502) 765-2185
(800) 654-2000
Room rates $35-45

ERLANGER
Days Inn
599 Donaldson Rd.
Erlanger KY 41018
(606) 342-7111
(800) 325-2525
Room rates $30-36

FLORENCE
Motel 6
7937 Dream St.
Florence KY 41042
(606) 283-0909
1 small pet per room
Reservations (505) 891-6161
Room rates $28-31

FRANKFORT
Super 8 Motel
1225 US Hwy 127 S.
Frankfort KY 40602
(502) 875-3220
(800) 848-8888
pets with permission
Room rates from $37

Ramada Inn
855 Louisville Rd
Frankfort KY 40601
(502) 227-2282
(800) 228-2828
Room rates $60-70

FRANKLIN
Super 8 Motel
1805 Scottsville Rd.
Franklin KY 42134
(502) 586-8885
(800) 848-8888
pets with permission
Room rates from $33

FT. WRIGHT
Days Inn
1945 Dixie Hwy
Ft. Wright KY 41011
(606) 341-8801
(800) 325-2525
Room rates $35-37

FULTON
Quality Inn
US 51 & Purchase Pkwy
Fulton KY 42401
(502) 472-2342
(800) 228-5151
Room rates $39-48

GEORGETOWN
Travelodge
401 Delaplain Rd.
Georgetown KY 40324-0926
(502) 863-1166
Room rates $43-50

Days Inn
I-75 & Delaplain Rd.
Georgetown KY 40324
(502) 863-5000
(800) 325-2525
$4/pets
Room rates $32-42

HENDERSON
Days Inn
2044 US 41 North
Henderson KY 42420
(502) 826-6600
(800) 325-2525
Room rates $45-57

HOPKINSVILLE
Best Western
4101 Ft. Campbell Blvd.
Hopkinsville KY 42240
(502) 886-9000
(800) 528-1234
$4 charge
Room rates $40-45

LEXINGTON
Econo Lodge
5527 Athens-Boonesboro Rd.
Lexington, KY 40509
(606) 263-5101
(800) 446-6900
$28-35

Motel 6
2260 Elkhorn Rd.
Lexington KY 40505
(606) 293-1431
1 small petRoom rates $30-45

Quality Inn
1050 Newtown Pike
Lexington KY 40511
(606) 233-0561
(800) 228-5151
Room rates $36-46

Days Inn
5575 Athens-Boonesboro Rd.
Lexington KY 40509
(606) 263-3100
(800) 325-2525
$3/pets
Room rates $32-38

Travelodge
1987 North Broadway
Lexington KY 40505
(606) 299-1202
(800) 255-3050
Room rates $29-33

Holiday Inn
1950 Newtown Pike
Lexington KY 40511
(606) 233-0512
(800) 465-4329
Room rates $70-85

LONDON
Ramada Inn
1025 W. 92 Bypass
London KY 40741
(606) 864-7331
(800) 228-2828
Room rates $50-60

LOUISVILLE
Ramada Inn
1921 Bishop Lane
Louisville KY 40218
(502) 456-4411
(800) 228-2828
Room rates $52-64

Quality Hotel
100 E. Jefferson St.
Louisville KY 40202
(502) 582-2481
(800) 228-5151
Room rates $54-300

Days Inn
1620 Arthur St.
Louisville KY 40217
(502) 636-3781
(800) 325-2525
Room rates $40-58

Airport Inn
3315 Bardstown Rd.
Louisville KY 40218
(502) 452-1501
Room rates $40-50

Travelodge
401 S 2nd St
Louisville KY 40202
(502) 583-2841
(800) 255-3050
Room rates from $36

Motel 6
3304 Bardstown Rd.
Louisville KY 40218
(502) 456-2861
1 small pet per room
Reservations (505) 891-6161
Room rates $28-31

MADISONVILLE
Days Inn
Hwy 41-41A North
Madisonville KY 42431
(502) 821-8620
(800) 325-2525
Room rates $45-57

MT. STERLING
Days Inn
705 Maysville Rd.
Mt. Sterling KY 40353
(606) 498-4680
(800) 325-2525
$4/pets
Room rates $34-39

OWENSBORO
Days Inn
3720 New Hartford Rd.
Owensboro KY 42301
(502) 684-9621
(800) 325-2525
$1 charge
Room rates $48-40

Motel 6
4886 Fredrica St.
Owensboro KY 42301
(502) 686-8606
1 small pet per room
Reservations (505) 891-6161
Room rates $28-31

PADUCAH
Quality Inn
1380 S. Irvin Cobb Dr.
Paducah KY 42001
(502) 443-8751
(800) 228-5151
Room rates from $40

Friendship Inn
4050 Clarks River Rd.
Paducah, KY 42003
(502) 442-3595
(800) 453-4511
$20-26

RADCLIFF
Super 8 Motel
395 Redmar Blvd. off 31 W.
Radcliff KY 40160
(502) 352-1888
(800) 848-8888
pets with deposit
Room rates from $37

RICHMOND
Motel 6
1698 Northgate Dr.
Richmond KY 40475
(606) 623-0880
1 small pet per room
Reservations (505) 891-6161
Room rates $28-31

Holiday Inn
100 Eastern Bypass
Richmond KY 40475
(606) 623-9220
(800) 465-4329
Room rates $45-55

SHEPHERDSVILLE
Travelodge
Paroquet Springs Dr.
Shepherdsville KY 40165
(502) 543-4400
$6.50 / night pet fee
Room rates $43-95

Days Inn
Exit 117
Shepherdsville KY 40165
(502) 543-3011
(800) 325-2525
Room rates $34-37

WALTON
Days Inn
11177 Frontage Rd.
Walton KY 41094
(606) 485-4151
(800) 325-2525
Room rates $35-39

WILLIAMSTOWN
Days Inn
211 KY 36 W.
Williamstown KY 41097
(606) 824-5025
(800) 325-2525
Room rates $31-36

LOUISIANA
ABERDEEN
Days Inn
783 West Bel Air Ave.
Aberdeen LA 21001
(301) 272-8500
(800) 325-2525
Room rates $42-46

ALEXANDRIA
Days Inn
2300 N. MacArthur Dr.
Alexandria LA 71301
(318) 443-7331
(800) 325-2525
Room rates $40-49

Travelodge
1146 MacArthur Dr.
Alexandria LA 71303
(318) 443-1841
(800) 255-3050
Room rates $36-38

Motel 6
546 MacArthur Dr.
Alexandria LA 71301
(318) 445-2336
1 small pet per room
Reservations (505) 891-6161
Room rates $27-30

BATON ROUGE
Motel 6
10445 Rieger Rd.
Baton Rouge LA 70809
(504) 291-4912
1 small pet per room
Reservations (505) 891-6161
Room rates $27-30

Howard Johnson Lodge
2365 College Dr.
Baton Rouge, LA 70808
(504) 925-2451
(800) 654-2000
$43-60

Comfort Inn
2455 S. Acadian Thruway
Baton Rouge, LA 70726
(504) 927-5790
(800) 228-5150
$30-55

BOSSIER CITY
Days Inn
200 John Wesley Blvd.
Bossier City LA 71112
(318) 742-9200
(800) 325-2525
$5/pets - small pets only
Room rates $31-41

Motel 6
210 John Wesley Blvd.
Bossier City LA 71112
(318) 742-3472
1 small pet per room
Reservations (505) 891-6161
Room rates $27-30

Sheraton
2015 Old Minden Rd.
Bossier City LA 71111
(318) 742-9700
(800) 325-3535
Room rates $55-75

Always Call Ahead!

HARVEY
Best Western - Westbank Hotel
1700 Lapalco Blvd.
Harvey LA 70058
(504) 366-5369
(800) 528-1234
small pets only
Room rates from $50

LAFAYETTE
Super 8 Motel
2224 NE Evageline Thwy
Lafayette LA 70501
(318) 232-8826
(800) 848-8888
pets with permission
Room rates from $32

Super 8 Motel
2224 NE Evangeline Thwy.
Lafayette, LA 70501
(318) 232-8826
(800) 843-1991
$27-40

Comfort Inn
1421 SE Evangeline Thruway
Lafayette LA 70501
(318) 232-9000
(800) 228-5150
Room rates $48-54

Days Inn
1620 N. University @ I-10
Lafayette LA 70506
(318) 237-8880
(800) 325-2525
$5/small pets
Room rates $40-45

Motel 6
2724 NE Evageline Thruway
Lafayette LA 70507
(318) 233-2055
1 small pet per room
Reservations (505) 891-6161
Room rates $27-30

LAKE CHARLES
Days Inn
1010 N. Hwy 171
Lake Charles LA 70601
(318) 433-1711
(800) 325-2525
$4/pets
Room rates $36-40

Motel 6
335 Hwy 171
Lake Charles LA 70601
(318) 433-1773
1 small pet per room
Reservations (505) 891-6161
Room rates $27-30

MONROE
Comfort Inn
196 Frontage Rd.
Monroe LA 71202
(318) 345-2220
(800) 228-5150
Room rates $38-42

Motel 6
1501 US 165 Bypass
Monroe LA 71202
(318) 322-5430
1 small pet per room
Reservations (505) 891-6161
Room rates $27-30

NATCHITOCHES
Super 8 Motel
801 Hwy 3110 Bypass
Natchitoches LA 71457
(318) 352-1700
(800) 848-8888
pets with permission
Room rates from $31

NEW ORLEANS
Quality Inn
5353 Paris Rd.
New Orleans LA 70043
(504) 277-5353
(800) 228-5151
Room rates $44-89

Quality Inn
3900 Tulane Ave
New Orleans LA 70119
(504) 486-5541
(800) 228-5151
Room rates $49-60

Best Western - Patio Downtown
2820 Tulane Ave.
New Orleans LA 70119
(504) 822-0200
(800) 528-1234
$6 charge, small only
Room rates $50-75

Hilton - Airport
901 Airline Hwy.
New Orleans LA 70063
(504) 469-5000
(800) 445-8667
Room rates $100-130

HoJo Inn
4200 Old Gentilly Rd.
New Orleans, LA 70126
(504) 944-0151
(800) 654-2000
$36-60

PORT ALLEN
Days Inn
215 Lobdell Hwy
Port Allen LA 70767
(504) 387-0671
(800) 325-2525
$5/pets
Room rates from $29

Motel 6
2800 I-10 Frontage Rd.
Port Allen LA 70767
(504) 343-5945
1 small pet per room
Reservations (505) 891-6161
Room rates $27-30

SHREVEPORT
Days Inn
4935 W. Monkhouse Rd.
Shreveport LA 71109
(318) 636-0080
(800) 325-2525
$5/pets
Room rates $31-41

Always Call Ahead!

Motel 6
4915 Monkhouse Dr.
Shreveport LA 71109
(318) 631-9691
1 small pet per room
Reservations (505) 891-6161
Room rates $27-30

SLIDELL
Ramada Inn
I-10 @ Gause Blvd.
Slidell LA 70461
(504) 643-9960
(800) 228-2828
Room rates $45-58

Days Inn
1645 Gause Blvd.
Slidell LA 70458
(504) 641-3450
(800) 325-2525
$4/pets
Room rates $35-45

Motel 6
136 Taos St.
Slidell LA 70458
(504) 649-7925
1 small pet per room
Reservations (505) 891-6161
Room rates $27-30

THIBODAUX
Howard Johnson
201 North Canal Blvd.
Thibodaux, LA 70301
(504) 447-9071
(800) 654-2000
$40-75

MAINE
AUGUSTA
Best Western - Senator Inn
284 Western Ave.
Augusta ME 04330
(207) 622-5804
(800) 528-1234
small pets only
Room rates $55-85

BANGOR
Comfort Inn
750 Hogan Rd.
Bangor ME 04401
(207) 942-7899
(800) 228-5150
$6/pets
Room rates $51-71

Econo Lodge
482 Odlin Rd.
Bangor ME 04401
(207) 942-6301
(800) 553-2666
$5 charge
Room rates $45-80

Ramada Inn
357 Odlin Rd.
Bangor ME 04401
(207) 947-6961
(800) 228-2828
Room rates $70-110

Red Carpet Inn
480 Main St.
Bangor ME 04401
(207) 942-5281
Room rates $40-65

ELLSWORTH
Holiday Inn
High St.
Ellsworth ME 04605
(207) 667-9341
(800) 465-4329
Room rates $45-100

FARMINGTON
Mount Blue Motel
US 2 & SR 4
Farmington ME 04938
(207) 778-6004
$7 charge
Room rates $36-50

FREEPORT
Eagle Motel
US 1
Freeport ME 04032
(207) 865-3106
Room rates $50-80

GLEN COVE
Sea View Motel
US 1
Glen Cove ME 04846
(207) 594-8479
Room rates $55-65

GREENVILLE
Greenwood Motel
SR 6 & 15
Greenville ME 04442
(207) 695-3321
$7 charge
Room rates $35-50

KENNEBUNK
Friendship Inn
SR 35
Kennebunk ME 04094
(207) 985-6525
(800) 553-2666
Room rates $40-70

The Colony
Ocean Ave. & Kings Rd.
Kennebunkport ME 04046
(207) 967-3331
$15 charge
Room rates $110-275

KITTERY
Charter House Hotel
I-95
Kittery ME 03904
(207) 439-2000
Room rates $55-75

PORTLAND
Howard Johnson
155 Riverside St.
Portland ME 04103
(207) 774-5861
(800) 654-2000
$50 deposit
Room rates $55-125

**Always
Call
Ahead!**

MAINE, Rumford

RUMFORD
Linnell Inn
US 2
Rumford ME 04276
(207) 364-4511
Room rates $40-55

SANFORD
Bar-H Motel
SR 109
Sanford ME 04073
(207) 324-4662
Room rates $35-55

SEARSPORT
Yardarm Motel
US 1
Searsport ME 04974
(207) 548-2404
$3 charge
closed winters
Room rates $30-55

SOUTH PORTLAND
Comfort Inn
90 Maine Mall Rd.
South Portland ME 04106
(207) 775-0409
(800) 228-5150
Room rates $50-87

Howard Johnson
675 Main St.
South Portland ME 04106
(207) 775-5343
(800) 654-2000
$50 charge
Room rates $60-110

WATERVILLE
Econo Lodge
455 Kennedy Memorial Dr.
Waterville, ME 04901
(207) 872-5577
(800) 446-6900
$39-75

MARYLAND
ABERDEEN
Howard Johnson
7923 Bel Air Ave.
Aberdeen MD 21001
(301) 272-6000
Room rates $55-80

Econo Lodge
820 Bel Air Ave.
Aberdeen MD 21001
(301) 272-5500
(800) 553-2666
Room rates $40-50

ANNAPOLIS
Holiday Inn
210 Holiday Ct.
Annapolis MD 21401
(301) 224-3150
(800) 465-4329
small pets only
Room rates $70-85

Howard Johnson
170 Revell Hwy.
Annapolis MD 21401
(301) 757-1600
(800) 654-2000
small pets only
Room rates $45-85

BALTIMORE
Hampton Inn
829 Elkridge Landing Rd
Baltimore MD 21090
(301) 850-0600
(800) 426-7866
Room rates $64-67

Quality Inn
5625 O'Donnell St
Baltimore MD 21224
(301) 633-9500
(800) 228-5151
Room rates $74-225

Quality Inn
5801 Baltimore National Pike
Baltimore MD 21228
(301) 774-5000
(800) 228-5151
Room rates $49-59

Comfort Inn
6921 Baltimore-Annap. Blvd
Baltimore MD 21225
(301) 789-9100
(800) 228-5150
Room rates $76-80

Quality Inn
1015 York Rd.
Baltimore MD 21204
(301) 825-9190
(800) 228-5151
Room rates $54-79

Marriott
1743 Nursery Rd.
Baltimore MD 21240
(301) 859-8300
(800) 228-9290
small pets only
Room rates $60-140

Holiday Inn
890 Elkridge Landing Rd.
Baltimore MD 21090
(301) 859-8400
(800) 465-4329
Room rates $115-145

Howard Johnson Hotel
5701 Baltimore National Pike
Baltimore, MD 21228
(301) 747-8900
(800) 654-2000
$38-53

Holiday Inn
1100 Cromwell Bridge Rd.
Baltimore MD 21204
(301) 823-4410
(800) 465-4329
Room rates $50-110

BELTSVILLE
Ramada Inn
4050 Powder Mill Rd.
Beltsville MD 20705
(301) 572-7100
(800) 228-2828
Room rates $39-73

BETHESDA
Marriott
5151 Parks Hill Rd.
Bethesda MD 20814
(301) 897-9400
(800) 228-9290
Room rates $110-300

 Always Call Ahead!

CAMBRIDGE
Quality Inn
US 50 & Crusader Rd.
Cambridge MD 21613
(301) 228-6900
(800) 228-5151
Room rates $44-50

CAMP SPRINGS
Motel 6
5701 Allentown Rd.
Camp Springs MD 20746
(301) 702-1061
1 small pet per room
Reservations (505) 891-6161
Room rates $31-40

CAPITOL HEIGHTS
Motel 6
75 Hampton Park Blvd.
Capitol Heights MD 20743
(301) 499-0800
1 small pet per room
Reservations (505) 891-6161
Room rates $31-40

COLUMBIA
Columbia Inn
10207 Wincopin Circle
Columbia MD 21044
(301) 730-3900
$75 deposit
Room rates $105-125

EASTON
Days Inn
Route 50
Easton MD 21601
(301) 822-4600
(800) 325-2525
Room rates $52-60

Econo Lodge
8175 Ocean Gateway
Easton, MD 21601
(301) 820-5555
(800) 446-6900
$37-50

ELKTON
Motel 6
223 Belle Hill Rd.
Elkton MD 21921
(301) 392-5020
1 small pet per room
Reservations (505) 891-6161
Room rates $31-40

FREDERICK
Super 8 Motel
5579 Spectrum Dr.
Frederick MD 21701
(301) 695-2881
(800) 848-8888
Room rates from $47

Quality Inn
7400 Quality Ct.
Frederick MD 21701
(301) 694-7704
(800) 228-5151
Room rates $50-80

Holiday Inn
999 Patrick St.
Frederick MD 21701
(301) 662-5141
(800) 465-4329
Room rates $70-95

Sheraton
5400 Sheraton Dr.
Frederick MD 21701
(301) 694-7500
(800) 325-3535
Room rates $70-90

FROSTBURG
Comfort Inn
SR 36 Frostburg Industrial Park
Frostburg MD 21532
(301) 689-2050
(800) 228-5150
Room rates from $49

GRANTSVILLE
Holiday Inn
US Rt. 48 & Rt. 219 N.
Grantsville MD 21536
(301) 895-5993
Room rates $48-54

HAGERSTOWN
Econo Lodge
Rt. #6
Hagerstown MD 21740
(301) 791-3560
(800) 553-2666
$2.50 charge
Room rates $35-40

Holiday Inn
900 Dual Hwy
Hagerstown MD 21740
(301) 739-9050
(800) 465-4329
Room rates $55-65

Ramada Inn
901 Dual Hwy.
Hagerstown MD 21740
(301) 733-5100
(800) 228-2828
Room rates $65-70

HAVRE DE GRACE
Super 8 Motel
929 Pulaski Hwy
Havre De Grace MD 21078
(301) 939-1880
(800) 848-8888
pets with permission
Room rates from $42

HUNT VALLEY
Hampton Inn
11200 York Rd.
Hunt Valley MD 21031
(301) 527-1500
(800) 426-7866
small pets only
Room rates $45-70

LANKAM
Holiday Inn
5910 Princess Garden Pkwy
Lankam MD 20706
(301) 459-1000
small pets only
Room rates $39-180

LAUREL
Knights Inn
3380 Fort Meade Rd.
Laurel MD 20707
(301) 498-5553
(800) 722-7220
Room rates $40-50

**Always
Call
Ahead!**

OCEAN CITY
Days Inn
4201 Coastal Hwy
Ocean City MD 21842
(301) 289-6488
(800) 325-2525
Room rates $59-109

HoJo Inn
102 60th St.
Ocean City, MD 21842
(301) 524-5634
(800) 654-2000
$30-60

POCOMOKE
Days Inn
UA 13
Pocomoke MD 21851
(301) 957-3000
(800) 325-2525
Room rates $40-46

Quality Inn
825 Ocean Hwy
Pocomoke City MD 21851
(301) 957-1300
(800) 228-5151
Room rates $39-88

ROCKVILLE
Ramada Inn
1251 W. Montgomery Ave.
Rockville MD 20850
(301) 424-4940
(800) 228-2828
under 50 lbs.
Room rates $63-96

Days Inn
16001 Shady Grove Rd.
Rockville MD 20850
(301) 948-4300
(800) 325-2525
small pets only
Room rates $45-64

SALISBURY
Super 8 Motel
2615 N. Salisbury Blvd.
Salisbury MD 21801
(301) 749-5131
(800) 848-8888
pets with permission
Room rates from $39

Comfort Inn
US 13 N.
Salisbury MD 21801
(301) 543-4666
(800) 228-5150
Room rates $43-57

Days Inn
Rt. 13 N.- RR #6 Box 978
Salisbury MD 21801
(301) 749-6200
(800) 325-2525
$5/pets
Room rates $46-52

TOWSON
Days Inn
8801 Loch Raven Blvd.
Towson MD 21204
(301) 882-0900
(800) 325-2525
$25 pet deposit
Room rates $52-56

WALDORF
Super 8 Motel
5050 Hwy 301 St.
Waldorf MD 20603
(301) 932-8957
(800) 848-8888
pets with permission
Room rates from $41

WESTMINSTER
Quality Inn
451 WMC Dr.
Westminster MD 21157
(301) 857-1900
(800) 228-5151
Room rates $51-55

Days Inn
25 S. Cranberry Rd.
Westminster MD 21157
(301) 857-0500
(800) 325-2525
Room rates $50-62

WILLIAMSPORT
Days Inn
310 W. Potomac St.
Williamsport MD 21795
(301) 582-3500
(800) 325-2525
$4/pets
Room rates $49-55

MASSACHUSETTS
AMHERST
University Lodge
345 Pleasant St.
Amherst MA 01002
(413) 256-8111
Room rates $50-75

ANDOVER
Ramada Inn
131 River Rd.
Andover MA 01810
(508) 685-6200
Room rates $75-100

BOSTON
Comfort Inn
1668 Worcester Rd.
Boston MA 01701
(508) 620-0500
(800) 228-5150
Room rates $48-65

Quality Inn
60 Forbes Blvd.
Boston MA 02048
(508) 339-2323
(800) 228-5151
Room rates $59-77

Morgan Inn
SR 9
Boston MA 01581
(508) 366-0202
Room rates $49-70

Days Hotel
131 River Rd.
Boston MA 01810
(508) 685-6200
(800) 325-2525
Room rates $49-97

Hilton
40 Dalton St.
Boston MA 02115
(617) 236-1100
(800) 445-8667
small pets only
Room rates $150-215

BRAINTREE
Days Inn
190 Wood Rd.
Braintree MA 02184
(617) 848-1260
(800) 325-2525
Room rates $60-80

Motel 6
125 Union St.
Braintree, MA 02184
(617) 848-7890
(505) 891-6161
$28-36

CAPE COD
Quality Inn
291 Jones Rd.
Cape Cod MA 02540
(508) 540-2000
(800) 228-5151
Room rates $58-119

CONCORD
Howard Johnson
740 Elm St.
Concord MA 01742
(508) 369-6100
(800) 654-2000
Room rates $75-90

DANVERS
Howard Johnson
65 Newbury St.
Danvers MA 01923
(508) 774-8045
(800) 654-2000
$25 deposit
Room rates $80-85

EDGARTOWN
Clarion Inn
227 Upper Main St.
Edgartown MA 02539
(508) 627-5161
(800) 458-6262
Room rates $85-115

FALL RIVER
Hampton Inn
53 Old Bedford Rd.
Fall River MA 02790
(508) 675-8500
(800) 426-7866
Room rates $69-71

Days Inn
332 Milliken Blvd.
Fall River MA 02721
(508) 676-1991
(800) 325-2525
Room rates $39-65

FALMOUTH
Mariner Motel
555 Main St.
Falmouth MA 02540
(508) 548-1331
dogs only
Room rates $40-80

FRAMINGHAM
Days Inn
30 Worcester Rd.
Framingham MA 01701
(508) 875-6151
(800) 325-2525
Room rates $49-86

GREENFIELD
Candlelight Motor Inn
208 Mohawk Trail
Greenfield MA 01301
(413) 772-0101
$5 charge
Room rates $40-85

HADLEY
Howard Johnson
401 Russel St.
Hadley MA 01035
(413) 586-0114
(800) 654-2000
Room rates $55-85

HAVERHILL
Best Western
401 Lowell Ave.
Haverhill MA 01832
(508) 373-1511
$10 deposit
Room rates $60-100

HYANNIS
Hampton Inn
1470 Rt. 132
Hyannis MA 02601
(508) 771-4804
(800) 426-7866
Room rates $54-71

LAWRENCE
Hampton Inn
224 Winthrop Ave.
Lawrence MA 01843
(508) 975-4050
(800) 426-7866
Room rates from $59

LOWELL
Town House
850 Chelmsford St.
Lowell MA 01851
(508) 454-5606
Room rates $55-75

Howard Johnson Hotel
187 Chelmsford St.
Lowell, MA 01824
(508) 256-7511
(800) 654-2000
$42-75

MANSFIELD
Quality Inn
60 Forbes Blvd.
Mansfield MA 02048
(508) 339-2323
(800) 228-5151
Room rates $65-85

MIDDLEBORO
Days Inn
I-495 & 105E to Clark St.
Middleboro MA 02346
(508) 946-4400
(800) 325-2525
small pets only
Room rates $52-59

**Always
Call
Ahead!**

MASSACHUSETTS, New Bedford

NEW BEDFORD
Days Inn
500 Hathaway Rd.
New Bedford MA 02740
(508) 997-1231
(800) 325-2525
$5/night
Room rates $65-75

NORTH EASTHAM
The Dolphin Inn
US 6
North Eastham MA 02651
(508) 255-1159
$7 charge
Room rates $45-75

PROVINCETOWN
Holiday Inn
SR 6A/Shore Drive
Provincetown MA 02657
(508) 487-1711
(800) 465-4329
Room rates $50-125

SOUTH DEERFIELD
Motel 6
Rt. 5-10
South Deerfield MA 01373
(413) 665-7161
1 small pet per room
Reservations (505) 891-6161
Room rates from $32

SPRINGFIELD
Best Western Black Horse
500 Riverdale St.
Springfield MA 01089
(413) 733-2161
(800) 528-1234
small pets only
Room rates $70-100

Monarch Place
1080 Riverdale St.
Springfield MA 01089
(413) 781-1010
small pets only
Room rates $90-125

STURBRIDGE
Days Inn
Hwy I-90/I-84 & US 20
Sturbridge MA 01566
(508) 347-9311
(800) 325-2525
Room rates $40-79

Service Host Hotel
366 Main St.
Sturbridge MA 01566
(508) 347-7393
small pets only
Room rates $90-135

WESTBOROUGH
Westborough Marriott
5400 Computer Dr.
Westborough MA 01581
(508) 366-5511
Room rates $115-125

WESTPORT
Hampton Inn
53 Old Bedford Rd.
Westport MA 02790
(508) 675-8500
(800) 426-7866
Room rates $65-75

WORCESTER
Hampton Inn
110 Summer St.
Worcester MA 01608
(508) 757-0400
(800) 426-7866
Room rates $69-74

Super 8 Motel
880 Donald J. Lynch Blvd.
Worcester MA 01752
(508) 460-1000
(800) 848-8888
Room rates from $50

MICHIGAN
ALPENA
Holiday Inn
1000 Hwy 23 North
Alpena MI 49707
(517) 356-2151
(800) 465-4329
Room rates $65-75

ANN ARBOR
Howard Johnson Lodge
2380 Carpenter Rd.
Ann Arbor, MI 48108
(313) 971-0700
(800) 654-2000
$52-70

Comfort Inn
2455 Carpenter Rd.
Ann Arbor MI 48108
(313) 973-6100
(800) 228-5150
Room rates $54-120

Knights Inn
3764 State St.
Ann Arbor MI 48108
(313) 665-9900
(800) 722-7220
Room rates $40-45

Red Roof Inn
3621 Plymouth Rd.
Ann Arbor MI 48105
(313) 996-5800
(800) 843-7663
$3 charge
Room rates $40-45

AUBURN HILLS
Knights Inn
14711 Opdyke Rd.
Auburn Hills MI 48057
(313) 373-8440
(800) 722-7220
$3 charge
Room rates $41-45

BARAGA
Super 8 Motel
790 Michigan Ave.
Baraga MI 49908
(906) 353-6680
(800) 848-8888
pets with permission
Room rates from $38

BATTLE CREEK
Motel 6
4775 Beckley Rd.
Battle Creek, MI 49017
(616) 979-1141
(505) 891-6161
$28-36

Howard Johnson
2590 Capital Ave. SW
Battle Creek MI 49015
(616) 965-3201
(800) 654-2000
Room rates $50-65

Knights Inn
2595 Capital Ave. SW
Battle Creek MI 49015
(616) 694-2600
(800) 722-7220
Room rates from $40

BAY CITY
Holiday Inn
501 Saginaw St.
Bay City MI 48708
(517) 892-3501
(800) 465-4329
Room rates $60-75

BELLEVILLE
Super 8 Motel
45707 S. I-94
Belleville MI 48111
(313) 699-1888
(800) 848-8888
pets with permission
Room rates from $38

BENTON HARBOR
Super 8 Motel
1950 E. Napier Ave.
Benton Harbor MI 49022
(616) 926-1371
(800) 848-8888
pets with permission
Room rates from $38

Motel 6
2063 Pipestone Rd.
Benton Harbor, MI 49022
(616) 925-5100
(505) 891-6161
$28-36

Ramada Inn
798 Ferguson Dr.
Benton Harbor MI 49022
(616) 927-1172
(800) 228-2828
Room rates $57-73

Comfort Inn
1598 Mall Dr.
Benton Harbor MI 49022
(616) 925-1880
(800) 228-5150
Room rates $40-55

Days Inn
2699 Michigan Rt. 139
Benton Harbor MI 49022
(616) 925-7021
(800) 325-2525
Room rates $46-53

Knights Inn
2063 Pipestone Rd.
Benton Harbor MI 49022
(616) 925-5100
(800) 722-7220
Room rates $35-40

BLOOMFIELD HILLS
Holiday Inn
1801 Telegraph Rd.
Bloomfield Hills MI 48013
(313) 334-2444
(800) 465-4329
Room rates $65-80

CANTON
Super 8 Motel
3933 Lotz Rd.
Canton MI 48188
(313) 722-8880
(800) 848-8888
pets with permission
Room rates from $39

Knights Inn
41216 Ford Rd.
Canton MI 48188
(313) 981-5000
(800) 722-7220
Room rates $40-42

CHEBOYGAN
Continental Moter Inn
613 Main St.
Cheboygan MI 49721
(616) 627-7164
Room rates $35-55

CLAWSON
Super 8 Motel
1145 W. Maple
Clawson MI 48017
(313) 435-8881
(800) 848-8888
pets with permission
Room rates from $42

CLIO
Travelodge
4254 W. Vienna Rd.
Clio MI 48420
(313) 687-2240
(800) 255-3050
Room rates from $43

COLDWATER
Quality Inn
1000 Orleans Blvd.
Coldwater MI 49036
(517) 278-2017
(800) 228-5151
Room rates $62-110

DEARBORN
Holiday Inn
22900 Michigan Ave.
Dearborn MI 48124
(313) 278-4800
(800) 465-4329
Room rates $70-90

DETROIT
Comfort Inn
29235 Buckingham
Detroit MI 48154
(313) 458-7111
(800) 228-5150
Room rates $50-90

Comfort Inn
9501 Middlebelt Rd.
Detroit MI 48174
(313) 946-4300
(800) 228-5150
Room rates $54-83

Comfort Inn
11401 Hall Rd.
Detroit MI 48317
(313) 739-7111
(800) 228-5150
Room rates $47-74

Knights Inn
37527 Grand River Rd.
Detroit MI 48335
(313) 477-3200
small pets
Room rates $32-37

**Always
Call
Ahead!**

MICHIGAN, Detroit

Days Hotel
17017 West Nine Mile Rd.
Detroit MI 48075
(313) 557-4800
(800) 325-2525
Room rates $69-85

FARMINGTON
Knights Inn
37527 Grand River Ave.
Farmington MI 48024
(313) 477-3200
(800) 722-7220
Room rates $40-42

FARMINGTON HILLS
Motel 6
38300 Grand River Hills Ave.
Farmington Hills MI 48331
(313) 471-0590
1 small pet per room
Reservations (505) 891-6161
Room rates $27-31

FLINT
Super 8 Motel
3033 Claude Ave.
Flint MI 48507
(313) 230-7888
(800) 848-8888
pets with permission
Room rates from $37

Mr. Gibby's Inn
G-3129 Miller Rd.
Flint MI 48507
(313) 235-8561
$25 deposit
Room rates $50-75

Days Inn
2207 W. Bristol Rd.
Flint MI 48507
(313) 239-4681
(800) 325-2525
$5/pets
Room rates $33-48

Sheraton
4300 Pierson Rd.
Flint MI 48504
(313) 732-0400
(800) 325-3535
Room rates $55-65

GAYLORD
Holiday Inn
833 Main St
Gaylord MI 49735
(517) 732-2431
(800) 465-4329
Room rates $60-90

GRAND BLANC
Travelodge
G-2435 W. Grand Blanc Rd
Grand Blanc MI 48439
(313) 655-4681
(800) 255-3050
Room rates from $42

GRAND RAPIDS
Hampton Inn
4981 28th St. SE
Grand Rapids MI 49512
(616) 956-9304
(800) 426-7866
Room rates $47-53

Quality Inn
4495 28th St. SE
Grand Rapids MI 49512
(616) 956-8080
(800) 228-5151
Room rates $59-92

Motel 6
3524 28th St. SE
Grand Rapids MI 49508
(616) 957-3511
1 small pet per room
Reservations (505) 891-6161
Room rates $27-31

Holiday Inn
3333 28th St. SE
Grand Rapids MI 49508
(616) 949-9222
(800) 465-4329
Room rates $60-90

HAZEL PARK
Holiday Inn
1 Nine Mile Rd.
Hazel Park MI 48030
(313) 399-5800
(800) 465-4329
Room rates $55-65

HOUGHTON LAKE
Holiday Inn
9285 M-55 @ US 27
Houghton Lake MI 48629
(517) 422-5175
(800) 465-4329
Room rates $55-90

IMLAY CITY
Super 8 Motel
6951 Newark Rd.
Imlay City MI 48444
(313) 724-5501
(800) 848-8888
pets with deposit
Room rates from $38

IRONWOOD
Super 8 Motel
160 E. Cloverland Dr.
Ironwood MI 49938
(906) 932-3395
(800) 848-8888
pets with permission
Room rates $37-41

JACKSON
Super 8 Motel
2001 Shirley Dr.
Jackson MI 49202
(517) 788-8780
(800) 848-8888
pets with permission
Room rates from $38

Days Inn
901 Rosehill Dr.
Jackson MI 49202
(517) 787-1111
(800) 325-2525
well behaved only
Room rates $35-48

Holiday Inn
2000 Holiday Inn Dr.
Jackson MI 49202
(517) 783-2681
(800) 465-4329
Room rates $55-70

KALAMAZOO
Days Inn
1912 E. Kilgore Fr.
Kalamazoo MI 49002
(616) 382-2303
(800) 325-2525
$2-3/pets
Room rates $40-49

Sheraton
3600 Cork St.
Kalamazoo MI 49001
(616) 385-3922
(800) 325-3535
Room rates $80-95

LANSING
Super 8 Motel
910 American Rd.
Lansing MI 48911
(517) 393-8008
(800) 848-8888
pets with permission
Room rates from $37

Best Western Inn
1000 Ramada Dr.
Lansing MI 48911
(517) 393-5500
(800) 228-2828
Room rates $44-53

Motel 6
112 E. Main St.
Lansing MI 48933
(517) 484-8722
1 small pet per room
Reservations (505) 891-6161
Room rates $27-31

Howard Johnson Lodge
6741 S. Cedar St.
Lansing, MI 48911
(517) 694-0454
(800) 654-2000
$32-40

LIVONIA
Super 8 Motel
28512 Schoolcraft Rd.
Livonia MI 48150
(313) 425-5150
(800) 848-8888
pets with permission
Room rates from $41

LUDINGTON
Ramada Inn
4079 W US 10 @ Brye Rd
Ludington MI 49431
(616) 845-7311
(800) 228-2828
Room rates $55-90

MACKINAW CITY
Ramada Inn
450 S. Nicolet
Mackinaw City MI 49701
(616) 436-5535
(800) 228-2828
Room rates $38-84

American Motel
SR 108 & Nicolet St.
Mackinaw City MI 49701
(616) 436-5231
Room rates $20-40

Econo Lodge
412 Nicolet St.
Mackinaw City MI 49701
(616) 436-5026
(800) 553-2666
small pets only
Room rates $35-75

Scottish Inns
701 Huron St.
Mackinaw City MI 49701
(616) 436-5493
small only, closed winter
Room rates $30-85

MADISON HEIGHTS
Hampton Inn
32420 Stephenson Hwy
Madison Heights MI 48071
(313) 585-8881
(800) 426-7866
Room rates $55-65

Motel 6
32700 Barrington Rd.
Madison Heights MI 48071
(313) 583-0500
1 small pet per room
Reservations (505) 891-6161
Room rates $27-31

Knights Inn
32703 Stephenson Hwy.
Madison Heights MI 48071
(313) 583-7700
(800) 722-7200
Room rates $35-42

MANISTIQUE
Ramada Inn
US 2 E. Lakeshore Dr.
Manistique MI 49854
(906) 341-6911
(800) 228-2828
Room rates $55-75

Howard Johnson
726 Lakeshore Dr.
Manistique MI 49854
(906) 341-6981
(800) 654-2000
$7 charge
Room rates $40-75

MARQUETTE
Ramada Inn
412 W. Washington St.
Marquette MI 49855
(906) 228-6000
(800) 228-2828
Room rates $58-65

MIDLAND
Holiday Inn
1500 Wackerly
Midland MI 48640
(517) 631-4220
(800) 465-4329
Room rates $65-90

MONROE
Knights Inn
1250 Dixie Hwy.
Monroe MI 48161
(313) 243-0597
(800) 722-7200
Room rates $35-40

MT.PLEASANT
Comfort Inn
2424 S. Mission St.
Mt.Pleasant MI 48858
(517) 772-4000
(800) 228-5150
Room rates $50-110

MUNISING
Comfort Inn
SR 28 E. Box 276
Munising, MI 49862
(906) 387-5292
(800) 228-5150
$39-75

MUSKEGON
Comfort Inn
1675 E. Sherman Blvd.
Muskegon MI 69666
(616) 739-9092
(800) 228-5150
Room rates $49-89

NEW BALTIMORE
Travelodge
29101 Twenty-three Mile Rd
New Baltimore MI 48047
(313) 949-4520
(800) 255-3050
Room rates from $45

NEW BUFFALO
Comfort Inn
11539 O'Brien Ct.
New Buffalo MI 49117
(616) 469-4440
(800) 228-5150
Room rates $50-90

NOTHVILLE
Hampton Inn
20600 Haggerty Rd.
Nothville MI 48167
(313) 462-1119
(800) 426-7866
Room rates $49-60

NOVI
Hilton
21111 Haggerty Rd.
Novi MI 48050
(313) 349-4000
(800) 445-8667
under 20 lbs
Room rates $75-175

OKEMOS
Comfort Inn
2209 University Park Dr.
Okemos MI 48864
(517) 349-8700
(800) 228-5150
Room rates $52-80

PETOSKEY
Days Inn
630 W. Mitchell
Petoskey MI 49770
(616) 347-8717
(800) 325-2525
Room rates $41-84

PLAINWELL
Comfort Inn
622 Allegan ST.
Plainwell MI 49080
(616) 685-9891
(800) 228-5150
Room rates $50-85

PORT HURON
Econo Lodge
1720 Hancock St.
Port Huron MI 48060
(313) 984-2661
(800) 553-2666
$2.50 charge
Room rates $50-55

ROMULUS
Super 8 Motel
9863 Middlebelt Rd.
Romulus MI 48174
(313) 946-8808
(800) 848-8888
pets with permission
Room rates from $41

Knights Inn
8500 Wickham Rd.
Romulus MI 48174
(313) 722-8500
(800) 722-7220
Room rates $35-40

Radisson Hotel
8000 Merriman Rd.
Romulus MI 48174
(313) 729-2600
(800) 333-3333
small only
Room rates $110-125

ROSEVILLE
Super 8 Motel
20445 Erin St.
Roseville MI 48066
(313) 296-1730
(800) 848-8888
pets with permission
Room rates from $36

SAGINAW
Comfort Inn
3425 Holland Ave
Saginaw MI 48601
(517) 753-2461
(800) 228-5150
Room rates $43-55

Best Western
3325 Davenport Ave.
Saginaw MI 48602
(517) 793-2080
(800) 528-1234
Room rates $40-50

SOUTHFIELD
Hampton Inn
27500 Northwestern Hwy.
Southfield MI 48034
(313) 356-5500
(800) 426-7866
Room rates $45-75

ST. IGNACE
Bay View Motel
1133 State St.
St. Ignace MI 49781
(906) 643-9444
$5 charge open 5/15 - 10/15
Room rates $25-55

STERLING HEIGHTS
Super 8 Motel
34550 Van Dyke
Sterling Heights MI 48312
(313) 795-8800
(800) 848-8888
pets with permission
Room rates from $39

Comfort Inn
11401 Hall Rd.
Sterling Heights, MI 48317
(313) 739-7111
(800) 228-5150
$45-80

Days Inn
34858 Van Dyke
Sterling Heights MI 48077
(313) 939-5300
(800) 325-2525
Room rates $39-49

TAYLOR
Super 8 Motel
15101 Huron St.
Taylor MI 48180
(313) 283-8830
(800) 848-8888
pets with permission
Room rates from $42

TRAVERSE CITY
Knights Inn
618 Front St.
Traverse City MI 49684
(616) 929-0410
(800) 722-7220
Room rates $35-60

TROY
Holiday Inn
2537 Rochester Ct.
Troy MI 48083
(313) 689-7500
(800) 465-4329
Room rates $80-100

WALKER
Motel 6
777 Three Mile Rd.
Walker MI 49504
(616) 784-9375
1 small pet per room
Reservations (505) 891-6161
Room rates $27-31

WARREN
Motel 6
8300 Chicago Rd.
Warren MI 48093
(313) 826-9300
1 small pet per room
Reservations (505) 891-6161
Room rates $27-31

Knights Inn
7500 Miller Dr.
Warren MI 48092
(313) 978-7500
(800) 722-7220
Room rates $35-40

WESTHAVEN
Knights Inn
21880 West Rd.
Westhaven MI 48183
(313) 676-8550
(800) 722-7220
Room rates $35-40

MINNESOTA
ALBERT LEA
Super 8 Motel
2019 E. Main St.
Albert Lea MN 56007
(507) 377-0591
(800) 848-8888
pets with deposit
Room rates from $38

Days Inn
2306 E. Main St.
Albert Lea MN 56007
(507) 373-6471
(800) 325-2525
Room rates $49-60

ALEXANDRIA
Super 8 Motel
4620 Hwy 29 S.
Alexandria MN 56308
(612) 763-6552
(800) 848-8888
pets with permission
Room rates from $37

ANOKA
Super 8 Motel
1129 W. Main St
Anoka MN 55303
(612) 422-8000
(800) 848-8888
pets with permission
Room rates from $39

AUSTIN
Super 8 Motel
1401 14th St. NW
Austin MN 55912
(507) 433-1801
(800) 848-8888
pets with deposit
Room rates from $38

Holiday Inn
I-90 & 4th St.
Austin MN 55912
(507) 433-1000
(800) 465-4329
Room rates $50-75

BAXTER
Super 8 Motel
Hwy 371 N.
Baxter MN 56425
(218) 828-4288
(800) 848-8888
pets with deposit
Room rates from $35

BEMIDJI
Days Inn
2420 Paul Bunyon Dr.
Bemidji MN 56601
(218) 751-0390
(800) 325-2525
snall pets allowed
Room rates $34-50

BLOOMINGTON
Super 8 Motel
7800 2nd Ave. S.
Bloomington MN 55420
(612) 888-8800
(800) 848-8888
pets with permission
Room rates from $42

Comfort Inn
1321 E. 78th St.
Bloomington MN 55425
(612) 854-3400
(800) 228-5150
Room rates $46-70

Days Inn
8000 Bridge Rd.
Bloomington MN 55437
(612) 831-9595
(800) 325-2525
small pets allowed
Room rates $39-49

BRAINERD
Days Inn
Hwy 371 & 210 W.
Brainerd MN 56401
(218) 829-0391
(800) 325-2525
Room rates $35-60

Econo Lodge
2655 US 371 S.
Brainerd, MN 56401
(218) 828-0027
(800) 446-6900
$30-50

Holiday Inn
SR 371
Brainerd MN 56401
(218) 829-1441
(800) 465-4329
Room rates $55-70

BUFFALO
Super 8 Motel
303 10th Ave. S.
Buffalo MN 55313
(612) 682-5930
(800) 848-8888
pets with permission
Room rates from $37

BURNSVILLE
Super 8 Motel
1101 Burnsville Pkwy
Burnsville MN 55337
(612) 894-3400
(800) 848-8888
pets with permission
Room rates from $36

CHANHASSEN
Chanhassen Inn
531 79th St.
Chanhassen MN 55317
(612) 934-7373
$15 deposit
Room rates $35-40

CHASKA
Heritage Inn
830 Yellow Brick Rd.
Chaska MN 55318
(612) 448-7030
$10 deposit
Room rates $32-40

CHISAGO CITY
Super 8 Motel
11650 Lake Blvd.
Chisago City MN 55013
(612) 257-8088
(800) 848-8888
pets with deposit
Room rates from $35

DETROIT LAKES
Super 8 Motel
400 Morrow Ave.
Detroit Lakes MN 56501
(218) 847-1651
pets with permission
Room rates from $37

DULUTH
Best Western Edgewater West
2211 London Rd.
Duluth MN 55812
(218) 728-5141
(800) 528-1234
attended all times
Room rates $50-80

Best Western Downtown Motel
131 2nd St.
Duluth MN 55801
(218) 727-6851
(800) 528-1234
Room rates $25-55

EVELETH
Super 8 Motel
Hwy 53
Eveleth MN 55734
(218) 744-1661
(800) 848-8888
pets with permission
Room rates from $35

FARIBAULT
Comfort Inn
I-35 & SR 60
Faribault MN 55021
(507) 334-2051
(800) 228-5150
Room rates $36-49

GLENCOE
Super 8 Motel
717 Morningside Dr.
Glencoe MN 55336
(612) 864-6191
(800) 848-8888
pets with permission
Room rates from $36

GRAND MARAIS
Super 8 Motel
Hwy 61 W.
Grand Marais MN 55604
(218) 387-2448
(800) 848-8888
pets with permission
Room rates $40-50

Econo Lodge
US 61 E. Box 667
Grand Marais, MN 55604
(218) 389-2547
(800) 446-6900
$35-60

GRAND RAPIDS
Days Inn
311 E. Hwy 2
Grand Rapids MN 55744-3155
(218) 326-3457
(800) 325-2525
Only reported small pets
Room rates $45-50

HIBBING
Days Inn
1520 Hwy 37 E.
Hibbing MN 55746
(218) 263-8306
(800) 325-2525
small pets allowed
Room rates $26-44

INTERNATIONAL FALLS
Days Inn
Hwy 53
International Falls MN 56679
(218) 283-9441
(800) 325-2525
small pets
Room rates $40-65

LAKEVILLE
Super 8 Motel
20800 Kenrick Ave.
Lakeville MN 55044
(612) 469-1134
(800) 848-8888
pets with deposit
Room rates from $45

Days Inn
11274 210th St.
Lakeville MN 55044
(612) 469-1900
(800) 325-2525
Room rates $31-35

MANKATO
Days Inn
1285 Range St.
Mankato MN 56001
(507) 387-3332
(800) 325-2525
pets allowed with permission
Room rates $40-50

Holiday Inn
101 Main St.
Mankato MN 56001
(507) 345-1234
(800) 465-4329
Room rates $45-60

MAPLEWOOD
Days Inn
1780 E. County Rd.
Maplewood MN 55109
(612) 770-2811
(800) 325-2525
small pets only
Room rates $52-60

**Always
Call
Ahead!**

Super 8
285 N. Century Ave.
Maplewood MN 55119
(612) 738-1600
Room rates $39-49

MARSHALL
Super 8 Motel
Hwys 59 & 23
Marshall MN 56258
(507) 537-1461
(800) 848-8888
pets with deposit
Room rates from $36

Comfort Inn
1511 E. College Dr.
Marshall MN 56258
(507) 532-3070
(800) 228-5150
Room rates $36-40

MINNEAPOLIS
Super 8 Motel
7125 80th St.
Minneapolis, MN 55016
(612) 458-0313
(800) 843-1991
pets with permission
$35-50

Days Inn
1501 Freeway Blvd.
Minneapolis MN 55430
(612) 566-4140
(800) 325-2525
Room rates $60-68

Days Inn
2955 Empire Lane
Minneapolis MN 55447
(612) 559-2400
(800) 325-2525
Room rates $38-54

Holiday Inn
1313 Nicollet Mall
Minneapolis MN 55403
(612) 332-0371
(800) 465-4329
Room rates $90-100

Holiday Inn
1500 Washington Ave.
Minneapolis MN 55454
(612) 333-4646
(800) 465-4329
Room rates $80-90

MONTICELLO
Comfort Inn
200 E. Oakwood Dr.
Monticello MN 55362
(612) 295-1111
(800) 228-5150
Room rates $38-42

MOORHEAD
The Madison
600 30th Ave. S.
Moorhead MN 56560
(218) 233-6171
quiet pets only
Room rates $39-64

NEW ULM
Super 8 Motel
1901 S. Broadway
New Ulm MN 56073
(507) 359-2400
(800) 848-8888
Room rates from $36

OWATONNA
Super 8 Motel
I-35 & Hwy 14 W.
Owatonna MN 55060
(507) 451-0380
(800) 848-8888
pets with permission
Room rates from $35

RICHFIELD
Motel 6
7640 Cedar Ave. S.
Richfield MN 55423
(612) 861-4491
1 small pet per room
Reservations (505) 891-6161
Room rates $28-33

ROCHESTER
Super 8 Motel
1230 S. Broadway
Rochester MN 55901
(507) 288-8288
(800) 848-8888
pets with deposit
Room rates from $38

Super 8 Motel
1608 2nd St. SW
Rochester MN 55902
(507) 281-5100
(800) 848-8888
pets with permission
Room rates from $40

Comfort Inn
111 SE 28th St.
Rochester MN 55904
(507) 286-1001
(800) 228-5150
Room rates $43-53

Days Inn
Hwy 52 take 2nd St. SW
Rochester MN 55901
(507) 282-2733
(800) 325-2525
Room rates $32-44

Days Inn
106 SE 21st St.
Rochester MN 55904
(507) 282-1756
(800) 325-2525
$25 deposit
Room rates $39-49

Travelodge
426 2nd St. S.W.
Rochester MN 55901
(507) 289-4095
(800) 255-3050
Room rates from $43

Motel 6
2107 W. Frontage Rd.
Rochester MN 55901
(507) 282-6625
1 small pet per room
Reservations (505) 891-6161
Room rates $28-33

Holiday Inn
220 Broadway
Rochester MN 55904
(507) 288-3231
(800) 465-4329
Room rates $60-100

Radisson Hotel
150 Broadway
Rochester MN 55904
(507) 281-8000
(800) 333-3333
$25 deposit
Room rates $65-100

MINNESOTA, Rogers

ROGERS
Super 8 Motel
21130 134th Ave. N.
Rogers MN 55374
(612) 428-4000
(800) 848-8888
pets with permission
Room rates from $36

ROSEVILLE
Motel 6
2300 Cleveland Ave. N.
Roseville MN 55113
(612) 639-3988
1 small pet per room
Reservations (505) 891-6161
Room rates $28-33

S. BURNSVILLE
Days Inn
13080 Aldrich Ave. S.
S. Burnsville MN 55337
(612) 894-8280
(800) 325-2525
Room rates $36-48

ST. CLOUD
Super 8 Motel
50 Park Ave. S.
St. Cloud MN 56301
(612) 253-5530
(800) 848-8888
pets with permission
Room rates from $37

Holiday Inn
SR 15 Box 1104
St. Cloud MN 56302
(612) 253-9000
(800) 465-4329
Room rates $55-80

ST. JOSEPH
Super 8 Motel
Minnesota St. & County Rd. 75
St. Joseph MN 56374
(612) 363-7711
(800) 848-8888
pets with permission
Room rates from $37

ST. PAUL
Comfort Inn
1321 E. 78th St.
St. Paul, MN 55425
(612) 854-3400
(800) 228-5150
$46-70

Ramada Hotel
1870 Old Hudson Rd.
St. Paul, MN 55119
(612) 735-2330
(800) 228-2828
$60-80

WILLMAR
Super 8 Motel
2655 S. 1st
Willmar MN 56201
(612) 235-7260
(800) 848-8888
pets with deposit
Room rates from $36

WINONA
Super 8 Motel
1025 Sugar Loaf Rd.
Winona MN 55987
(507) 454-6066
(800) 848-8888
pets with deposit
Room rates from $37

Days Inn
420 Cottonwood Dr.
Winona MN 55897
(507) 454-6930
(800) 325-2525
small pets allowed
Room rates $39-47

WORTHINGTON
Super 8 Motel
I-90 & 266
Worthington MN 56187
(507) 372-7755
(800) 848-8888
pets with deposit
Room rates from $36

ZUMBROTA
Super 8 Motel
1432 N. Star Dr.
Zumbrota MN 55992
(507) 732-7852
(800) 848-8888
pets with permission
Room rates from $36

MISSISSIPPI

BATESVILLE
Days Inn
Rt. 2
Batesville MS 38606
(601) 563-4999
(800) 325-2525
small pets only
Room rates $30-40

BILOXI
Quality Inn
1865 Beach Blvd.
Biloxi MS 39531
(601) 388-3212
(800) 228-5151
Room rates $48-70

Motel 6
2476 Beach Blvd.
Biloxi MS 39531
(601) 388-5130
1 small pet per room
Reservations (505) 891-6161
Room rates $27-30

CORINTH
Econo Lodge
US 72 & 45, Box 540
Corinth, MS 38834
(601) 287-4421
(800) 446-6900
$32-55

COLUMBUS
Holiday Inn
506 Hwy. 45 North
Columbus MS 39701
(601) 328-5202
(800) 465-4329
small pets only
Room rates $45-55

GREENVILLE
Ramada Inn
2700 US 82 E.
Greenville MS 38701
(601) 332-4411
(800) 228-2828
Room rates $40-55

Days Inn
2500 Hwy 82 E.
Greenville MS 38701
(601) 335-1999
(800) 325-2525
$3/pets
Room rates $35-40

GREENWOOD
Ramada Inn
900 W. Park Ave.
Greenwood MS 38930
(601) 455-2321
(800) 228-2828
Room rates $40-49

Days Inn
621 Hwy 82 W.
Greenwood MS 38930
(601) 453-0030
(800) 325-2525
Room rates $47-49

GULFPORT
Motel 6
9355 US 49
Gulfport MS 39503
(601) 863-1890
1 small pet per room
Reservations (505) 891-6161
Room rates $27-30

HATTIESBURG
Howard Johnson Lodge
6553 Hwy 49 N.
Hattiesburg, MS 39401
(601) 268-2251
(800) 654-2000
$32-50

Days Inn
3113 Hwy 49N.
Hattiesburg MS 39401
(601) 544-6300
(800) 325-2525
$5 pet fee
Room rates $32-34

Motel 6
3109 Hwy 49 N.
Hattiesburg MS 39401
(601) 544-6096
1 small pet per room
Reservations (505) 891-6161
Room rates $27-30

JACKSON
Ramada Inn
400 Greymont Ave.
Jackson MS 39202
(601) 969-2141
(800) 228-2828
Room rates $45-58

Friendship Inn
3880 I-55
Jackson, MS 39212
(601) 373-1244
(800) 453-4511
$30-45

Super 8 Motel
2655 I-55 S.
Jackson, MS 39204
(601) 372-1006
(800) 843-1991
$29-37

Motel 6
970 I-20 West
Jackson MS 39201
(601) 969-3423
1 small pet per room
Reservations (505) 891-6161
Room rates $27-30

LAUREL
Ramada Inn
1105 Sawmill Rd.
Laurel MS 39440
(601) 649-9100
(800) 228-2828
Room rates $45-55

MCCOMBS
Ramada Inn
I-55 @ Delaware Exit
McCombs MS 39648
(601) 684-5566
(800) 228-2828
Room rates $44-52

MERIDIAN
Comfort Inn
2901 St. Paul St.
Meridian MS 39301
(601) 485-2722
(800) 228-5150
Room rates $40-45

Days Inn
1521 Tom Bailey Dr.
Meridian MS 39301
(601) 483-3812
(800) 325-2525
small pets
Room rates $34-49

Motel 6
2309 S. Frontage Rd.
Meridian MS 39301
(601) 482-1182
1 small pet per room
Reservations (505) 891-6161
Room rates $27-30

Holiday Inn
Hwy. 45 South @ I-20
Meridian MS 39302
(601) 693-4521
(800) 465-4329
Room rates $35-45

NATCHEZ
Days Inn
109 Hwy 61 S.
Natchez MS 39120
(601) 445-8291
(800) 325-2525
small pets only
Room rates $35-45

NEWTON
Days Inn
I-20 & Hwy 15
Newton MS 39345
(601) 683-3361
(800) 325-2525
Room rates $35-40

SOUTHHAVEN
Best Western Inn
8945 Hamilton Rd.
Southhaven MS 38671
(601) 393-4174
(800) 528-1234
Room rates $40-70

TUPELO
Holiday Inn
923 Gloster St.
Tupelo MS 38801
(601) 842-8811
(800) 465-4329
Room rates $50-65

MISSOURI

BLUE SPRINGS
Motel 6
901 W. Jefferson St.
Blue Springs MO 64015
(816) 228-9133
1 small pet per room
Reservations (505) 891-6161
Room rates $27-33

BOONVILLE
Comfort Inn
I-70 & SR 5
Boonville MO 65233
(816) 882-5317
(800) 228-5150
Room rates $43-53

BRANSON
Days Inn
Hwy 76
Branson MO 65616
(417) 334-5544
(800) 325-2525
small pets, $7.50/day
Room rates $32-52

Lakeshore Resort
Lake Shore Dr.
Branson MO 65616
(417) 334-6262
$4 charge
Room rates $40-85

BRIDGETON
Motel 6
3657 Pennridge Dr.
Bridgeton MO 63044
(314) 298-7550
1 small pet per room
Reservations (505) 891-6161
Room rates $27-33

CAPE GIRARDEAU
Thrifty Inn
Jct I-55 & Rt. K
Cape Girardeau MO 63701
(314) 334-3000
Room rates $36-45

COLUMBIA
Ramada Inn
1100 Vandiver Dr.
Columbia MO 65202
(314) 449-0051
(800) 228-2828
Room rates $51-70

Days Inn
1900 I-70 Dr.
Columbia MO 65203
(314) 445-8511
(800) 325-2525
$10 deposit
Room rates $43-59

Motel 6
1718 N. Providence Rd.
Columbia MO 65203
(314) 442-9300
1 small pet per room
Reservations (505) 891-6161
Room rates $27-33

Holiday Inn
1612 Providence Rd.
Columbia MO 65202
(314) 449-2491
(800) 465-4329
Room rates $60-70

EDWARSVILLE
Days Inn
Jct. I-270 & IL 157
Edwarsville MO 62025
(618) 656-3000
(800) 325-2525
Room rates $42-46

EUREKA
Ramada Inn
I-44 & Allentown Rd.
Eureka MO 63025
(314) 938-6661
(800) 228-2828
Room rates $54-109

Super 8 Motel
1733 5th St.
Eureka MO 63025
(314) 938-4368
(800) 848-8888
$10 deposit
Room rates $30-50

HANNIBAL
Days Inn
4070 Market St.
Hannibal MO 63401
(314) 248-1700
(800) 325-2525
Room rates $35-55

Holiday Inn
4141 Market St.
Hannibal MO 63401
(314) 221-6610
(800) 465-4329
small pets only
Room rates $50-75

HAYTI
Comfort Inn
I-55 & SR 84
Hayti MO 63851
(314) 359-0023
(800) 228-5150
Room rates from $45

HIGGINSVILLE
Super 8 Motel
Hwy 13 @ I-70
Higginsville MO 64037
(816) 584-7781
(800) 848-8888
pets with deposit
Room rates from $35

INDEPENDENCE
Red Roof Inn
13712 42nd Terrace
Independence MO 64055
(816) 373-2800
(800) 843-7663
Room rates $30-40

JEFFERSON
Ramada Inn
1510 Jefferson
Jefferson MO 65109
(314) 635-7171
(800) 228-2828
Room rates $45-59

Days Inn
US 50 E
Jefferson MO 65101
(314) 636-5101
(800) 325-2525
Room rates $45-54

Motel 6
1624 Jefferson St.
Jefferson City MO 65109
(314) 634-4220
1 small pet per room
Reservations (505) 891-6161
Room rates $27-33

**Always
Call
Ahead!**

JOPLIN
Ramada Inn
3320 Rangeline Rd.
Joplin MO 64804
(417) 781-0500
(800) 228-2828
Room rates $56-64

Days Inn
3500 Rangeline Rd.
Joplin MO 64804
(417) 623-0100
(800) 325-2525
Room rates $39-48

Motel 6
3031 S. Range Line Rd.
Joplin MO 64804
(417) 781-6400
1 small pet per room
Reservations (505) 891-6161
Room rates $27-33

Holiday Inn
3615 Range Line Rd.
Joplin MO 64804
(417) 782-1000
(800) 465-4329
Room rates $65-80

KANSAS CITY
Ramada Inn
6101 E. 87th St.
Kansas City MO 64138
(816) 765-4331
(800) 228-2828
$25/pets
Room rates $50-68

Econolodge
8500 E. SR 350
Kansas City MO 64133
(816) 353-3000
$5/pets
Room rates $32-61

Econo Lodge
11300 NW Prairieview Rd.
Kansas City, MO 64153
(816) 464-5082
(800) 446-6900
$33-60

Days Inn
5100 E. Linwood Blvd.
Kansas City MO 64128
(816) 923-7777
(800) 325-2525
$5/pets
Room rates from $34

American Inn
11801 Blue Ridge Blvd.
Kansas City MO 64134
(816) 763-0600
deposit
Room rates $37-47

Motel 6
8230 NW Prairie View Rd.
Kansas City MO 64152
(816) 741-6400
1 small pet per room
Reservations (505) 891-6161
Room rates $27-33

Holiday Inn
7333 Parvin Rd.
Kansas City MO 64117
(816) 455-1060
(800) 465-4329
Room rates $50-85

Holiday Inn
4011 Blue Ridge Cutoff
Kansas City MO 64133
(816) 353-5300
(800) 465-4329
Room rates $65-90

KIRKSVILLE
Days Inn
Hwy 63 S.
Kirksville MO 63501
(816) 665-8244
(800) 325-2525
Room rates $53-58

LEBANON
Super 8 Motel
1831 W. Elm
Lebanon MO 65536
(417) 588-2574
(800) 848-8888
pets with permission
Room rates from $37

MARYVILLE
Super 8 Motel
Hwy 71 S.
Maryville MO 64468
(816) 582-8088
(800) 848-8888
pets with deposit
Room rates from $36

N. KANSAS CITY
Days Inn
2232 Taney St.
N. Kansas City MO 64116
(816) 421-6000
(800) 325-2525
small pets allowed
Room rates $37-47

NEVADA
Super 8 Motel
2301 E. Austin
Nevada MO 64772
(417) 667-8880
(800) 848-8888
pets with permission
Room rates from $34

OSAGE BEACH
Scottish Inns
US 54
Osage Beach MO 65065
(314) 348-3123
Room rates $25-50

Holiday Inn
4234 Butter Hill Rd.
Osage Beach MO 63129
(314) 894-0700
(800) 465-4329
Room rates $60-85

OZARK
Super 8 Motel
299 N. 20th
Ozark MO 65721
(417) 458-8800
(800) 848-8888
pets with permission
Room rates from $37

MISSOURI, Platte City

PLATTE CITY
Comfort Inn
1200 SR 92.
Platte City MO 64079
(816) 431-5430
(800) 228-5150
Room rates $47-53

ROLLA
Days Inn
1207 Kings Hwy
Rolla MO 65401
(314) 341-3700
(800) 325-2525
$3/pets
Room rates $25-35

SEDALIA
Days Inn
3501 W. Broadway
Sedalia MO 65301
(816) 826-8400
(800) 325-2525
$6/pets
Room rates $45-57

SIKESTON
Hampton Inn
1330 S. Main
Sikeston MO 63801
(314) 471-3930
(800) 426-7866
Room rates from $52

SPRINGFIELD
Quality Inn
3050 N. Kentwood
Springfield MO 65803
(417) 833-3108
(800) 228-5151
Room rates $52-64

Comfort Inn
Battlefield Rd. @ US 65
Springfield MO 65804
(417) 833-6200
(800) 228-5150
Room rates $63-71

Motel 6
2455 N. Glenstone Ave.
Springfield MO 65803
(417) 869-4343
1 small pet per room
Reservations (505) 891-6161
Room rates $27-33

Days Inn
2700 Glenstone Ave.
Springfield MO 65803
(417) 865-5511
(800) 325-2525
Room rates $35-50

Howard Johnson
2610 Glenstone
Springfield MO 65803
(417) 866-6671
(800) 654-2000
Room rates $45-75

ST. CHARLES
Knights Inn
3800 Harry S Truman Dr.
St. Charles MO 63301
(314) 925-2020
(800) 722-7220
Room rates $35-40

ST. JOSEPH
Ramada Inn
4016 Frederick
St. Joseph MO 64506
(816) 233-6192
(800) 228-2828
Room rates $54-61

Days Inn
4312 Frederick Ave.
St. Joseph MO 64506
(816) 279-1671
(800) 325-2525
Room rates $39-41

ST. LOUIS
Hampton Inn
2211 Market St.
St. Louis MO 63103
(314) 241-3200
(800) 426-7866
Room rates $69-79

Motel 6
4576 Woodson Rd.
St. Louis, MO 63134
(314) 427-1313
(505) 891-6161
$28-36

Ramada Inn
12031 Lackland St.
St. Louis MO 63146
(314) 878-1400
(800) 228-2828
Room rates $55-68

Clarion Inn
200 S. 4th St.
St. Louis MO 63102
(314) 241-9500
(800) 458-6262
Room rates $70-100

Comfort Inn
3730 S. Lindbergh Blvd.
St. Louis MO 63127-1397
(314) 842-1200
(800) 228-5150
Room rates $40-53

Days Inn
2560 S. Outer Rd.
St. Louis MO 63367
(314) 625-1711
(800) 325-2525
$2/pets
Room rates $44-53

Days Inn
333 Washington Ave.
St. Louis MO 63102
(314) 621-7900
(800) 325-2525
Room rates $49-99

Motel 6
4576 Woodson Rd.
St. Louis MO 63134
(314) 427-1313
1 small pet per room
Reservations (505) 891-6161
Room rates $27-33

Motel 6
1405 Dunn Rd.
St. Louis MO 63138
(314) 869-9400
1 small pet per room
Reservations (505) 891-6161
Room rates $27-33

SULLIVAN
Super 8 Motel
601 N. Service Rd.
Sullivan MO 63080
(314) 468-8076
(800) 848-8888
Room rates from $32

82

WARRENSBURG
Super 8 Motel
440 Russell Ave.
Warrensburg MO 64093
(816) 429-2183
(800) 848-8888
pets with permission
Room rates from $32

WAYNESVILLE
Super 8 Motel
I-44 & Hwy 28
Waynesville MO 65583
(314) 336-3036
(800) 848-8888
pets with permission
Room rates from $32

Ramada Inn
US 66 West, Box L
Waynesville MO 65583
(314) 336-3121
(800) 228-2828
Room rates $49-62

Daystop
Rt. 1
Waynesville MO 65583
(314) 774-2255
(800) 325-2525
Room rates $28-36

WENTZVILLE
Ramada Inn
900 Corporate Pkwy
Wentzville MO 63385
(314) 327-7001
(800) 228-2828
Room rates $49-61

Comfort Inn
1400 Continential Dr.
Wentzville MO 63385
(314) 327-5515
(800) 228-5150
Room rates $37-51

WEST PLAINS
Ramada Inn
Bypass 63 & 160
West Plains MO 65775
(417) 256-8191
(800) 228-2828
Room rates $38-54

**Always
Call
Ahead!**

MONTANA
BELGRADE
Super 8 Motel
6450 Jackrabbit Lane
Belgrade MT 59714
(406) 388-1493
(800) 848-8888
pets with permission
Room rates from $35

BILLINGS
Super 8 Motel
5400 Southgate Dr.
Billings MT 59102
(406) 248-8842
(800) 848-8888
small only
Room rates from $34

Daystop
843 Parkway Lane
Billings MT 59101
(406) 252-4007
(800) 325-2525
Room rates $30-40

Motel 6
5400 Midland Rd.
Billings MT 59101
(406) 252-0093
1 small pet per room
Reservations (505) 891-6161
Room rates $28-30

Quality Inn
2036 Overland Ave.
Billings. MT 59102
(406) 652-1320
(800) 228-5151
Room rates $50-59

BOZEMAN
Holiday Inn
5 Baxter Lane
Bozeman MT 59715
(406) 587-4561
(800) 465-4329
Room rates $50-60

BUTTE
Townhouse Inn
2777 Harrison Ave.
Butte MT 59701
(406) 494-8850
$3 charge
Room rates $42-50

COLUMBUS
Super 8 Motel
602 8th Ave. N.
Columbus MT 59019
(406) 322-4101
(800) 848-8888
pets w/permission & $3
Room rates from $34

CONRAD
Super 8 Motel
215 N. Main St.
Conrad MT 59425
(406) 278-7676
(800) 848-8888
pets with permission
Room rates from $33

DEER LODGE
Super 8 Motel
1150 N. Main
Deer Lodge MT 59722
(406) 846-2370
(800) 848-8888
pets with permission
Room rates from $34

DILLON
Sundowner Motel
500 Montana St.
Dillon MT 59725
(406) 683-2375
Room rates $20-30

EAST GLACIER PARK
Many Glacier Hotel
On Swiftcurrent Lake
East Glacier Park MT 59434
(406) 226-5551
leashed
Room rates $60-75

Rising Sun Motor Inn
Off Going-to-the-Sun Hwy.
East Glacier Park MT 59434
(406) 226-5551
leashed
Room rates $40-55

MONTANA, Gardiner

GARDINER
Super 8 Motel
Hwy 89
Gardiner MT 59030
(406) 848-7401
(800) 848-8888
Room rates from $40

Yellowstone Village North
US 89
Gardiner MT 59030
(406) 848-7417
$5 charge
Room rates $25-60

GLENDIVE
Super 8 Motel
1904 N. Merrill Ave.
Glendive MT 59330
(406) 365-5671
(800) 848-8888
pets with permission
Room rates from $31

Days Inn
2000 N. Merrill Ave.
Glendive MT 59330
(406) 365-6011
(800) 325-2525
small pets allowed
Room rates $32-40

GREAT FALLS
Super 8 Motel
1214 13th St.
Great Falls MT 59405
(406) 727-7600
(800) 848-8888
pets with deposit
Room rates from $34

Quality Inn
1411 10th Ave. S.
Great Falls MT 59405
(406) 761-4600
(800) 228-5151
Room rates $56-65

HAVRE
Super 8 Motel
1901 Hwy 2 W.
Havre MT 59501
(406) 265-1411
(800) 848-8888
pets with permission
Room rates from $35

HELENA
Days Inn
2001 Prospect Ave.
Helena MT 59601
(406) 442-3280
(800) 325-2525
small pets allowed
Room rates $35-55

Motel 6
800 N. Oregon
Helena MT 59601
(406) 442-9990
1 small pet per room
Reservations (505) 891-6161
Room rates $28-30

KALISPELL
Motel 6
1540 Hwy 93 S.
Kalispell MT 59901
(406) 752-6355
1 small pet per room
Reservations (505) 891-6161
Room rates $28-30

LIBBY
Super 8 Motel
Hwy 2 W.
Libby MT 59923
(406) 293-2771
(800) 848-8888
Room rates from $35

LIVINGSTON
Yellowstone Inn
1515 West Park
Livingston MT 59047
(406) 222-6110
Room rates $35-60

MILES CITY
Super 8 Motel
I-94 exit 138
Miles City MT 59301
(406) 323-5261
(800) 848-8888
pets with permission
Room rates from $30

Motel 6
1314 Haynes Ave.
Miles City MT 59301
(406) 232-7040
1 small pet per room
Reservations (505) 891-6161
Room rates $28-30

MISSOULA
Super 8 Motel
3901 S. Brooks
Missoula MT 59801
(406) 251-2255
(800) 848-8888
pets extra
Room rates from $33

Village Red Lion Inn
100 Madison
Missoula MT 59802
(406) 728-3100
Room rates $60-80

POLSON
Super 8 Motel
Jct of 93 & 35
Polson MT 59860
(406) 883-6266
(800) 848-8888
pets with permission
Room rates from $41

RED LODGE
Super 8 Motel
1223 S. Broadway
Red Lodge MT 59068
(406) 446-2288
(800) 848-8888
pets with permission
Room rates $30-35

ST. REGIS
Super 8 Motel
I-90 exit 33
St. Regis MT 59866
(406) 649-2422
(800) 848-8888
pets with deposit
Room rates from $33

W. YELLOWSTONE
Quality Inn
315 Yellowstone Ave.
W. Yellowstone MT 59758
(406) 646-7365
(800) 228-5151
Room rates $36-60

Best Western Cross Winds Inn
201 Firehole
W. Yellowstone MT 59758
(406) 646-9557
(800) 528-1234
Room rates $40-70

WHITEFISH
Super 8 Motel
8th St. & Spokane Ave.
Whitefish MT 59937
(406) 862-8255
(800) 848-8888
pets with permission
Room rates from $35

NEBRASKA
ALLIANCE
Super 8 Motel
1419 W. 3rd St.
Alliance NE 69301
(308) 762-8300
(800) 848-8888
pets with permission
Room rates from $35

BELLEVUE
American Family Inn
1110 Fort Crook Rd.
Bellevue NE 68005
(402) 291-0804
Room rates $35-45

CHADRON
Super 8 Motel
Hwys 20 W. & 385
Chadron NE 69337
(308) 432-4471
(800) 848-8888
pets with permission
Room rates from $31

COLUMBUS
New World Inn
265 33rd Ave.
Columbus NE 68601
(402) 564-1492
Room rates $45-60

GRAND ISLAND
Super 8 Motel
2603 S. Locust St.
Grand Island NE 68801
(308) 384-4380
(800) 848-8888
pets with permission
Room rates from $33

Econo Lodge
3205 Locust
Grand Island NE 68801
(308) 384-1333
(800) 553-2666
Room rates $25-35

Holiday Inn
2503 Locust St.
Grand Island NE 68801
(308) 384-1330
(800) 465-4329
Room rates $50-60

HASTINGS
Holiday Inn
US 34 & 281
Hastings NE 68901
(402) 463-6721
(800) 465-4329
Room rates $40-50

KEARNEY
Holiday Inn
301 2nd Ave.
Kearney NE 68848
(308) 237-3141
(800) 465-4329
Room rates $55-65

Ramada Inn
SR 44
Kearney NE 68848
(308) 237-5971
(800) 228-2828
Room rates $50-60

KIMBALL
Super 8 Motel
I-80 & 71 Interchange
Kimball NE 69145
(308) 235-4888
(800) 848-8888
pets with permission
Room rates from $31

LINCOLN
Ramada Inn
2301 NW 12th St.
Lincoln NE 68521
(402) 475-4400
(800) 228-2828
Room rates $44-54

Comfort Inn
2940 NW 12th St.
Lincoln NE 68521
(402) 475-2200
(800) 228-5150
Room rates $39-50

Days Inn
2920 NW 12th St.
Lincoln NE 68521
(402) 475-3616
(800) 325-2525
Room rates $33-50

Travelodge
3245 Cornhusker Hwy
Lincoln NE 68504
(402) 466-2341
(800) 255-3050
Room rates from $30

Motel 6
3001 NW 12th St.
Lincoln NE 68521
(402) 475-3211
1 small pet per room
Reservations (505) 891-6161
Room rates $29-30

Hilton
141 9th St.
Lincoln NE 68508
(402) 475-4011
(800) 445-8667
Room rates $65-85

MCCOOK
Super 8 Motel
1103 E. B St.
McCook NE 69001
(308) 345-1141
(800) 848-8888
pets with permission
Room rates from $30

Best Western Chief Motel
612 West "B" St.
McCook NE 69001
(308) 345-3700
(800) 528-1234
Room rates $40-50

Always
Call
Ahead!

NORFOLK
Super 8 Motel
1223 Omaha Ave.
Norfolk NE 68701
(402) 379-2220
(800) 848-8888
pets with permission
Room rates from $34

NORTH PLATTE
Super 8 Motel
220 Eugene Ave.
North Platte NE 69101
(308) 532-4224
(800) 848-8888
pets with permission
Room rates from $34

Motel 6
1520 S. Jeffers St.
North Platte NE 69101
(308) 534-6200
1 small pet per room
Reservations (505) 891-6161
Room rates $29-30

Holiday Inn
US 83
North Platte NE 69101
(308) 532-9090
(800) 465-4329
Room rates $50-65

OGALLALA
Super 8 Motel
500 East "A" South
Ogallala NE 69153
(308) 284-2076
(800) 848-8888
pets with permission
Room rates from $34

OMAHA
Hampton Inn
10728 L St.
Omaha NE 68127
(402) 593-2380
(800) 426-7866
Room rates $49-52

Days Inn
7101 Grover
Omaha NE 68106
(402) 391-5757
(800) 325-2525
Room rates $41-56

Motel 6
10708 M St.
Omaha NE 68127
(402) 331-3161
1 small pet per room
Reservations (505) 891-6161
Room rates $29-30

Embassy Suites
7270 Cedar St.
Omaha NE 68124
(402) 397-5141
(800) 362-2779
$25 charge
Room rates $90-100

Howard Johnson
3650 72nd St.
Omaha NE 68124
(402) 397-3700
(800) 654-2000
Room rates $40-75

SIDNEY
Super 8 Motel
2115 W. Illinois St.
Sidney NE 69162
(308) 254-2081
(800) 848-8888
pets with permission
Room rates from $31

YORK
Super 8 Motel
I-80 & US 81
York NE 68467
(402) 362-3388
(800) 848-8888
pets with permission
Room rates from $33

Comfort Inn
I-80 & US 81
York NE 68467402
(402) 362-6661
(800) 228-5150
Room rates $33-45

 Always Call Ahead!

NEVADA
CARSON CITY
Motel 6
2749 S. Carson St.
Carson City NV 89701
(702) 885-7710
1 small pet per room
Reservations (505) 891-6161
Room rates $29-34

Best Western Trailside Inn
1300 Carson St.
Carson City NV 89701
(702) 883-7300
(800) 528-1234
ask mgr
Room rates $35-45

ELKO
Motel 6
3021 Idaho St.
Elko NV 89801
(702) 738-4337
1 small pet per room
Reservations (505) 891-6161
Room rates $29-34

Red Lion Inn & Casino
2065 Idaho St.
Elko NV 89801
(702) 738-2111
Room rates $60-90

ELY
Motel 6
7th & Avenue O
Ely NV 89301
(702) 289-6671
1 small pet per room
Reservations (505) 891-6161
Room rates $29-34

FALLON
Days Inn
60 S. Allen Rd.
Fallon NV 89406
(702) 423-7021
(800) 325-2525
Room rates $45-75

Econo Lodge
70 E. Williams Ave.
Fallon, NV 89406
(702) 423-2194
(800) 446-6900
$32-50

LAS VEGAS
Super 8 Motel
4250 Koval Lane
Las Vegas NV 89109
(702) 794-0888
(800) 848-8888
pets with permission
Room rates from $40

Friendship Inn
1150 Las Vegas Blvd.
Las Vegas, NV 89104
(702) 382-6001
(800) 453-4511
$35-85

Days Inn
3265 Las Vegas Blvd.
Las Vegas NV 89109
(702) 735-5102
(800) 325-2525
$15 pet charge & $50 deposit
Room rates $50-80

Travelodge
2028 East Fremont St.
Las Vegas NV 89101
(702) 384-7540
(800) 255-3050
Room rates from $37

Travelodge
3735 Las Vegas Blvd
Las Vegas NV 89109
(702) 736-3443
(800) 255-3050
Room rates $35-45

Motel 6
195 E. Tropicana Ave.
Las Vegas NV 89109
(702) 798-0728
1 small pet per room
Reservations (505) 891-6161
Room rates $29-34

LAUGHLIN
Best Western Riverside Resort
South of Davis Dam
Laughlin NV 89029
(702) 298-2535
(800) 528-1234
Room rates $30-60

PAHRUMP
Days Inn
Hwy 160 N. from Las Vegas
Pahrump NV 89041
(702) 727-5100
(800) 325-2525
$3/pets
Room rates $29-49

RENO
Days Inn
701 E. 7th
Reno NV 89512
(702) 786-4070
(800) 325-2525
$10 charge
Room rates $31-75

Motel 6
866 N. Wells
Reno NV 89512
(702) 786-9852
1 small pet per room
Reservations (505) 891-6161
Room rates $29-34

Motel 6
1901 S. Virginia
Reno NV 89502
(702) 827-0255
1 small pet per room
Reservations (505) 891-6161
Room rates $29-34

Motel 6
1400 Stardust St.
Reno NV 89503
(702) 747-7390
1 small pet per room
Reservations (505) 891-6161
Room rates $29-34

Harrah's
2nd & Center Streets
Reno NV 89512
(702) 786-3232
in kennels
Room rates $45-100

Holiday Inn
5851 Virginia St.
Reno NV 89502
(702) 825-2940
(800) 465-4329
Room rates $40-55

Holiday Inn
1000 6th St. E.
Reno NV 89512
(702) 786-5151
(800) 465-4329
Room rates $60-70

SPARKS
Motel 6
2405 B St.
Sparks NV 89431
(702) 358-1080
1 small pet per room
Reservations (505) 891-6161
Room rates $29-34

WELLS
Motel 6
I-80/US 40 & US 93
Wells NV 89835
(702) 752-2116
1 small pet per room
Reservations (505) 891-6161
Room rates $29-34

WINNEMUCCA
Motel 6
1600 Winnemucca Blvd.
Winnemucca NV 89445
(702) 623-1180
1 small pet per room
Reservations (505) 891-6161
Room rates $29-34

NEW HAMPSHIRE
CONCORD
Ramada Inn
172 N. Main St.
Concord NH 03301
(603) 224-9534
(800) 228-2828
Room rates $88-119

Comfort Inn
71 Hall St.
Concord NH 03301
(603) 226-4100
(800) 228-5150
Room rates $59-95

CONWAY
White Deer Motel
SR 16 & US 302
Conway NH 03818
(603) 447-5366
Room rates $40-70

The Hitching Post
Rt. 16
Conway NH 03818
(603) 447-3858
Room rates $40-90

DOVER
Friendship Inn
181 Silver St.
Dover NH 03820
(603) 742-4100
(800) 553-2666
Room rates $50-70

EXETER
Exeter Inn
90 Front St.
Exeter NH 03833
(603) 772-5901
Room rates $70-100

GORHAM
Gorham Inn
324 Main St.
Gorham NH 03581
(603) 466-3381
Room rates $35-60

KEENE
Ramada Inn
401 Winchester St.
Keene NH 03431
(603) 357-3038
(800) 228-2828
Room rates $59-85

Days Inn
175 Key Rd.
Keene NH 03431
(603) 352-7616
(800) 325-2525
small pets allowed $10 deposit
Room rates $59-76

HoJo Inn
379 West St.
Keene, NH 03431
(603) 352-7350
(800) 654-2000
$30-80

LACONIA
Days Inn
480 Main St.
Laconia NH 03246
(603) 524-8000
(800) 325-2525
$6/pets
Room rates $62-82

MANCHESTER
Days Hotel
55 John E. Devine Dr.
Manchester NH 03103
(603) 668-6110
(800) 325-2525
Room rates $60-95

Howard Johnson
298 Queen City Ave.
Manchester NH 03102
(603) 668-2600
(800) 654-2000
Room rates $63-83

NASHUA
Holiday Inn
9 Northwestern Blvd.
Nashua NH 03602
(603) 888-1551
(800) 465-4329
Room rates $70-125

Red Roof Inn
77 Spitbrook Rd.
Nashua NH 03063
(603) 888-1893
(800) 843-7663
Room rates $45-55

PLYMOUTH
Days Inn
I-93
Plymouth NH 03264
(603) 536-3520
(800) 325-2525
Room rates $49-80

PORTSMOUTH
The Port Motor Inn
US 1 Bypass & Portsmouth
Circle
Portsmouth NH 03801
(603) 436-4378
Room rates $35-100

ROCHESTER
Anchorage Inn
SR 125
Rochester NH 03867
(603) 332-3350
Room rates $40-65

SALEM
Red Roof Inn
15 Red Roof Lane
Salem NH 03079
(603) 898-6422
(800) 843-7663
small pets only
Room rates $45-55

SUNAPEE
Dexter's Inn
Winn Hill Rd.
Sunapee NH 03782
(603) 763-5571
in annex area only
Room rates $50-150

TWIN MOUNTAIN
Charlmont Inn
Rt. 3
Twin Mountain NH 03595
(603) 846-5549
$5 charge
Room rates $30-60

NEW JERSEY
ATLANTIC CITY
Howard Johnson Hotel
539 Abescon Blvd.
Atlantic City, NJ 08201
(609) 641-7272
(800) 654-2000
$48-200

CLIFTON
Howard Johnson
680 SR 3 West
Clifton NJ 07013
(201) 471-3800
(800) 654-2000
small pets only
Room rates $85-110

CRANFORD
Days Inn
Exit 136 Garden State Pkwy
Cranford NJ 07016
(201) 272-4700
(800) 325-2525
Room rates $55-99

**Always
Call
Ahead!**

88

EAST BRUNSWICK
Sheraton
195 SR 18
East Brunswick NJ 08816
(201) 828-6900
(800) 325-3535
Room rates $70-110

EAST HANOVER
Ramada Inn
130 Rte 10 W.
East Hanover NJ 07936
(201) 386-5622
(800) 228-2828
Room rates $99-135

EDISON
Ramada Inn
3050 Woodbridge Ave.
Edison NJ 08837
(201) 494-2000
(800) 228-2828
Room rates $85-90

Red Roof Inn
860 New Durham Rd.
Edison NJ 08817
(201) 248-9300
(800) 843-7663
Room rates $50-60

FAIRFIELD
Ramada Inn
Two Bridges Rd.
Fairfield NJ 07006
(201) 575-1742
(800) 228-2828
Room rates $100-129

KENILWORTH
Holiday Inn
Garden State Pkwy. & 31st St.
Kenilworth NJ 07033
(201) 241-4100
(800) 465-4329
Room rates $65-80

LAKEWOOD
Days Inn
1000 Madison Ave.
Lakewood NJ 08701
(908) 364-2020
(800) 325-2525
Room rates $55-65

LAWRENCEVILLE
Red Roof Inn
3203 Brunswick Pike
Lawrenceville NJ 08540
(609) 896-3388
(800) 843-7663
under 25 lbs.
Room rates $45-55

MAHWAH
Ramada Inn
180 Rte 17 S.
Mahwah NJ 07430
(201) 529-5880
(800) 228-2828
Room rates $90-120

MOUNT HOLLY
Best Wetern Motor Inn
1138 Burlington-Mt. Holly Rd.
Mount Holly NJ 08016
(609) 261-3800
Room rates $50-70

MOUNT LAUREL
Red Roof Inn
603 Fellowship Rd.
Mount Laurel NJ 08054
(609) 234-5589
(800) 843-7663
Room rates $45-55

NEWARK
Comfort Inn
50 Port St.
Newark NJ 07114
(201) 344-1500
(800) 228-5150
Room rates $64-84

Quality Inn
125 M. Main St.
Newark NJ 14513
(315) 331-9500
(800) 228-5151
Room rates $60-85
pet contract to sign

NORTH PLAINFIELD
Howard Johnson
US 22 & West End Avenue
North Plainfield NJ 07060
(201) 753-6500
(800) 654-2000
Room rates $55-65

PARAMUS
Howard Johnson
393 SR 17
Paramus NJ 07652
(201) 265-4200
(800) 654-2000
Room rates $55-75

PARSIPPANY
Days Inn
3159 US Rt. 46
Parsippany NJ 07054
(201) 335-0200
(800) 325-2525
Room rates $40-70

Howard Johnson
949 Rt. 46
Parsippany NJ 07054
(201) 335-5100
(800) 654-2000
Room rates $60-70

PHILLIPSBURG
Howard Johnson
I-78 & US 22
Phillipsburg NJ 08865
(201) 454-6461
(800) 654-2000
small pets only with deposit
Room rates $50-55

PISCATAWAY
Sheraton
Kingsbridge Rd.
Piscataway NJ 08854
(201) 469-5700
(800) 325-3535
small pets only
Room rates $50-85

**Always
Call
Ahead!**

89

RAMSEY
Wellesley Inn
946 Rt. 17 North
Ramsey NJ 07446
(201) 934-9250
$3 charge
Room rates $55-75

ROCHELLE PARK
Ramada Inn
375 W. Passaic St.
Rochelle Park NJ 07662
(201) 845-3400
(800) 228-2828
Room rates $110-138

ROCKAWAY
Howard Johnson
CR 513
Rockaway NJ 07866
(201) 625-1200
(800) 654-2000
Room rates $45-90

SADDLE BROOK
Clarion Inn
50 Kenney Pl.
Saddle Brook NJ 07662
(201) 843-0600
(800) 458-6262
Room rates $65-120

SOMERSET
Ramada Inn
Weston Canal Rd. & I-287
Somerset NJ 08873
(201) 560-9880
(800) 228-2828
Room rates $100-114

SOUTH PLAINFIELD
Holiday Inn
4701 Stenton Rd.
South Plainfield NJ 07080
(201) 753-5500
(800) 465-4329
Room rates $55-90

TRENTON
Howard Johnson
2991 Brunswick Pike
Trenton NJ 08648
(609) 896-1100
(800) 654-2000
Room rates $75-100

VINELAND
Ramada Inn
2216 W Landis Ave & Route 55
Vineland NJ 08360
(609) 696-3800
(800) 228-2828
Room rates $60-70

NEW MEXICO
ALAMOGORDO
Motel 6
251 Panorama Blvd.
Alamogordo NM 88310
(505) 434-5970
1 small pet per room
Reservations (505) 891-6161
Room rates $27-35

ALBUQUERQUE
Hampton Inn
7433 Pan American Fwy
Albuquerque NM 87109
(505) 344-1555
(800) 426-7866
Room rates $44-53

Super 8 Motel
2500 University Blvd. NE
Albuquerque NM 87107
(505) 888-4884
(800) 848-8888
pets with permission
Room rates from $39

Super 8 Motel
6030 Lliff NW
Albuquerque NM 87121
(505) 836-5560
(800) 848-8888
pets with permission
Room rates from $39

Ramada Inn
6815 Menaul NE
Albuquerque NM 87110
(505) 881-0000
(800) 228-2828
Room rates $82-98

Comfort Inn
2015 Menaul Blvd.
Albuquerque NM 87107
(505) 881-3210
(800) 228-5150
Room rates $44-55

Comfort Inn
13031 Central Ave. NE
Albuquerque NM 87123
(505) 294-1800
(800) 228-5150
Room rates $44-60

Days Inn
10321 Hotel Ave. NE
Albuquerque NM 87123
(505) 275-0599
(800) 325-2525
$5/pets
Room rates $38-58

Days Inn
13317 Central Ave. NE
Albuquerque NM 87123
(505) 294-3297
(800) 325-2525
$5/pets
Room rates $34-56

Travelodge
13139 Central Ave. N.E.
Albuquerque NM 87123
(505) 292-4878
(800) 255-3050
Room rates $36-42

Motel 6
13141 Central Ave. NE
Albuquerque NM 87123
(505) 294-4600
1 small pet per room
Reservations (505) 891-6161
Room rates $27-35

Motel 6
1701 University Blvd. NE
Albuquerque NM 87102
(505) 843-9228
1 small pet per room
Reservations (505) 891-6161
Room rates $27-35

Motel 6
6015 Lliff Rd. NW
Albuquerque NM 87105
(505) 831-3400
1 small pet per room
Reservations (505) 891-6161
Room rates $27-35

Doubletree Hotel
201 Marquette St. NW
Albuquerque NM 87103
(505) 247-3344
Room rates $45-95

Holiday Inn
2020 Menaul Blvd. NE
Albuquerque NM 87107
(505) 884-2511
(800) 465-4329
Room rates $50-75

CARLSBAD
Travelodge
3817 National Parks Hwy
Carlsbad NM 88220
(505) 887-8888
(800) 255-3050
Room rates $32-38

Motel 6
3824 National Parks Hwy.
Carlsbad NM 88220
(505) 885-0011
1 small pet per room
Reservations (505) 891-6161
Room rates $27-35

CLOVIS
Days Inn
1720 Mabry Dr.
Clovis NM 88101
(505) 762-2971
(800) 325-2525
$3/pets
Room rates $28-42

Motel 6
2620 Mabry Dr.
Clovis NM 88101
(505) 762-2995
1 small pet per room
Reservations (505) 891-6161
Room rates $27-35

DEMING
Motel 6
I-10 & Motel Dr.
Deming NM 88301
(505) 546-2623
1 small pet per room
Reservations (505) 891-6161
Room rates $27-35

FARMINGTON
Motel 6
1600 Bloomfield Hwy.
Farmington NM 87401
(505) 326-4501
1 small pet per room
Reservations (505) 891-6161
Room rates $27-35

Best Western
700 Scott Ave.
Farmington NM 87401
(505) 327-5221
(800) 528-1234
Room rates $50-65

GALLUP
Econolodge
I-40 & Exit 16
Gallup NM 87301
Room rates $42-52

Travelodge
1709 West 66th Ave.
Gallup NM 87301
(505) 863-9301
(800) 255-3050
Room rates $35-38

Motel 6
3306 W. 66
Gallup NM 87301
(505) 863-4462
1 small pet per room
Reservations (505) 891-6161
Room rates $27-35

GRANTS
Days Inn
1504 E. Santa Fe Ave. Box 29
Grants NM 87020
(505) 287-8883
(800) 325-2525
Room rates $45-57

Motel 6
1505 E. Santa Fe. Ave.
Grants NM 87020
(505) 285-4607
1 small pet per room
Reservations (505) 891-6161
Room rates $27-35

HOBBS
Motel 6
509 N. Marland Blvd.
Hobbs NM 88240
(505) 393-0221
1 small pet per room
Reservations (505) 891-6161
Room rates $27-35

LAS CRUCES
Hampton Inn
755 Avenida De Mesilla
Las Cruces NM 88005
(505) 526-8311
(800) 426-7866
Room rates $41-46

Days Inn
2600 S. Valley Dr.
Las Cruces NM 88001
(505) 526-4441
(800) 325-2525
Room rates $35-45

Motel 6
235 La Posada Lane
Las Cruces NM 88001
(505) 525-1010
1 small pet per room
Reservations (505) 891-6161
Room rates $27-35

MORIARTY
Days Inn
Rt. 66 W. exit 194
Moriarty NM 87035
(505) 832-4451
(800) 325-2525
charge & deposit
Room rates $37-45

RATON
Motel 6
1600 Cedar St.
Raton NM 87740
(505) 445-2777
1 small pet per room
Reservations (505) 891-6161
Room rates $27-35

ROSWELL
Comfort Inn
2803 W. 2nd St.
Roswell NM 88201
(505) 623-9440
(800) 228-5150
Room rates $39-45

SANTA FE
El Dorado Hotel
309 W. San Francisco St.
Santa Fe NM 87501
(505) 988-4455
(800) 458-6262
Room rates $125-215

NEW MEXICO, Santa Fe

Quality Inn
3011 Cerrillos Rd.
Santa Fe NM 87501
(505) 471-1211
(800) 228-5151
Room rates $48-77

Motel 6
3007 Cerillos Rd.
Santa Fe NM 87501
(505) 473-1380
1 small pet per room
Reservations (505) 891-6161
Room rates $27-35

SANTA ROSA
Motel 6
3400 Will Rogers Dr.
Santa Rosa NM 88435
(505) 472-3045
1 small pet per room
Reservations (505) 891-6161
Room rates $27-35

SOCORRO
Motel 6
807 S. US 85
Socorro NM 87801
(505) 835-4300
1 small pet per room
Reservations (505) 891-6161
Room rates $27-35

TAOS
Ramada Inn
Santa Fe Hwy & Frontier Rd
Taos NM 87571
(505) 758-2900
(800) 228-2828
Room rates $70-85

Quality Inn
1043 Camino Del Pueblo
Taos NM 87571
(505) 758-2200
(800) 228-5151
$25 deposit
Room rates $45-75

TUCUMCARI
Super 8 Motel
4001 E. Tucumcari Blvd.
Tucumcari NM 88401
(505) 461-4444
(800) 848-8888
pets with permission
Room rates from $35

Comfort Inn
1023 E. Tucumcari Blvd.
Tucumcari NM 88401
(505) 461-0360
(800) 228-5150
Room rates $47-53

Travelodge
1214 East Tucumcari Blvd
Tucumcari NM 88401
(505) 461-1401
(800) 255-3050
Room rates from $31

Motel 6
2900 E. Tucumcari Blvd.
Tucumcari NM 88401
(505) 461-4791
1 small pet per room
Reservations (505) 891-6161
Room rates $27-35

NEW YORK
ALBANY
Hampton Inn
981 New Loudon Rd
Albany NY 12110
(518) 785-0931
(800) 426-7866
Room rates $48-57

Hampton Inn
10 Ulenski Dr.
Albany NY 12205
(518) 438-2822
(800) 426-7866
Room rates from $62

Quality Inn
1-3 Watervilet Ave.
Albany NY 12206
(518) 438-8431
(800) 228-5151
Room rates $77-105

Travelodge
1230 Western Ave.
Albany NY 12203
(518) 489-4423
(800) 255-3050
Room rates from $51

Econo Lodge
1632 Central Ave.
Albany, NY 12205
(518) 456-8811
(800) 446-6900
$37-75

AMHERST
Red Roof Inn
42 Flint Rd.
Amherst NY 14226
(716) 689-7474
(800) 843-7663
small pets only
Room rates $40-50

ARMONK
Ramada Inn
I-684 Exit 3 South
Armonk NY 10504
(914) 273-9090
(800) 228-2828
Room rates $110-125

BATAVIA
Sheraton
8250 Park Rd.
Batavia NY 14020
(716) 344-2100
(800) 325-3535
Room rates $60-100

BATH
Days Inn
330 W. Morris St.
Bath NY 14810
(607) 776-7644
(800) 325-2525
Room rates $55-62

BINGHAMTON
Comfort Inn
1156 Front St.
Binghamton NY 13905
(607) 722-5353
(800) 228-5150
Room rates $52-74

Days Inn
1000 Front St.
Binghamton NY 13905
(607) 724-3297
(800) 325-2525
Room rates $61-66

**Always
Call
Ahead!**

92

Econo Lodge
196 E. Side Station
Binghamton, NY 13904
(607) 775-3443
(800) 446-6900
$45-60

BUFFALO
Howard Johnson Lodge
6700 Transit Rd.
Buffalo, NY 14221
(716) 634-7500
(800) 654-2000
$40-70

Hilton
120 Church St.
Buffalo NY 14202
(716) 845-5100
(800) 445-8667
$50 deposit
Room rates $90-125

Holiday Inn
620 Delaware Ave.
Buffalo NY 14202
(716) 886-2121
(800) 465-4329
Room rates $70-75

DANSVILLE
Daystop
I-390 @ exit 5 Commerce Dr.
Dansville NY 14437
(716) 335-6023
(800) 325-2525
$5/pets
Room rates $30-39

DUNKIRK
Quality Inn
Vineyard Dr.
Dunkirk NY 14048
(716) 366-4400
(800) 228-5151
Room rates $48-58

EAST SYRACUSE
Hampton Inn
6605 Old Collamer Rd
East Syracuse NY 13057
(315) 463-6443
(800) 426-7866
Room rates $51-55

ELMIRA
Holiday Inn
1 Holiday Plaza
Elmira NY 14901
(607) 734-4211
(800) 465-4329
Room rates $65-75

ELMSFORD
Ramada Inn
540 Saw Mill River Rd.
Elmsford NY 10523
(914) 592-3300
(800) 228-2828
Room rates $110-125

FREDONIA
Days Inn
10455 Bennett Rd.
Fredonia NY 14063
(716) 673-1351
(800) 325-2525
Room rates $53-70

GENEVA
Daystop
Exit 42 I-90
Geneva NY 14456
(315) 789-4510
(800) 325-2525
Room rates $37-40

GLEN FALLS
Ramada Inn
I-87 & Aviation Rd.
Glen Falls, NY 11788
(518) 793-7701
(800) 228-2828
$55-105

HAMBURG
Knights Inn
5245 Camp Rd.
Hamburg NY 14075
(716) 648-2000
(800) 722-7220
Room rates $35-40

HORSEHEADS
Best Western Marshall Manor
SR 14
Horseheads NY 14845
(607) 739-3891
(800) 528-1234
$4 charge
Room rates $35-55

Howard Johnson Lodge
Rts 17, 14 & 328
Horseheads, NY 14845
(607) 739-5636
(800) 654-2000
$42-65

ITHACA
Ramada Inn
222 S Cayuga St.
Ithaca NY 14850
(607) 272-1000
(800) 228-2828
Seasonal Rates
Room rates $69-95

Howard Johnson
2300 Triphammer Rd.
Ithaca NY 14850
(607) 257-1212
(800) 654-2000
$10 charge
Room rates $55-125

JAMESTOWN
Comfort Inn
2800 N. Main St.
Jamestown NY 14701
(716) 664-5920
(800) 228-5150
owner liable for damage
Room rates $49-70

KINGSTON
Ramada Inn
Exit 19 New York Thruway
Kingston NY 12401
(914) 339-3900
(800) 228-2828
Room rates $65-109

Always
Call
Ahead!

NEW YORK, Kingston

Holiday Inn
503 Washington Ave.
Kingston NY 12401
(914) 338-0400
(800) 465-4329
Room rates $72-110

LAKE GEORGE
Lake George Motel
431 Canada St.
Lake George NY 12845
(518) 668-2689
seasonal schedule, call ahead
Room rates $30-90

LAKE PLACID
Holiday Inn
1 Olympic Dr.
Lake Placid NY 12946
(518) 523-2556
(800) 465-4329
Room rates $45-130

LATHAM
Comfort Inn
866 Albany Shaker Rd.
Latham NY 12110
(518) 783-1216
(800) 228-5150
Room rates $56-68

Holiday Inn
946 New Louden Rd.
Latham NY 12110
(518) 783-6161
(800) 465-4329
Room rates $75-105

LONG ISLAND
Ramada Inn
1515 Veterans Mem. Hwy.
Long Island NY 11788
(516) 582-3600
(800) 228-2828
Room rates $69-119

MANHATTAN
Days Inn
440 W. 57th St.
Manhattan NY 10019
(212) 581-8100
(800) 325-2525
Room rates $134-164

MCGRAW
Econo Lodge
US 11
McGraw NY 13101
(607) 753-7594
(800) 553-2666
Room rates $35-45

MIDDLETOWN
Super 8 Motel
563 Rt. 211 E.
Middletown NY 10940
(914) 692-5828
(800) 848-8888
pets with permission
Room rates from $53

Daystop
Rt. 17M & 6
Middletown NY 10958
(914) 374-2411
(800) 325-2525
Room rates $48-60

MONTGOMERY
Super 8 Motel
207 Montgomery Rd.
Montgomery NY 12549
(914) 457-3143
(800) 848-8888
pets with permission
Room rates from $45

MOUNT KISCO
Holiday Inn
1 Holiday Dr.
Mount Kisco NY 10549
(914) 241-2600
(800) 465-4329
Room rates $100-110

NEW YORK
Travelodge
J.F.K. Int'l Airport
New York NY 11430
(718) 995-9000
(800) 255-3050
Room rates $125-150

Days Inn
440 West 57th St.
New York NY 10019
(212) 581-8100
(800) 325-2525
small pets only
Room rates $100-150

Marriott
1535 Broadway
New York NY 10036
(212) 398-1900
(800) 228-9290
small only
Room rates $125-525

Quality Inn
157 W. 47th St.
New York, NY 10036
(212) 768-3700
(800) 228-5151
$80-200

NEWBURGH
Howard Johnson
Rt. 17
Newburgh NY 12550
(914) 564-4000
(800) 654-2000
Room rates $60-100

NIAGARA FALLS
Ramada Inn
401 Buffalo Ave.
Niagara Falls NY 14303
(716) 285-2541
(800) 228-2828
Very Seasonal Rates
Room rates $69-126

Holiday Inn
114 Buffalo Ave.
Niagara Falls NY 14303
(716) 285-2521
(800) 465-4329
Room rates $65-150

OGDENSBURG
Quality Inn
SR 37
Ogdensburg NY 13669
(315) 393-4550
(800) 228-5151
Room rates $61-76

PLATTSBURGH
Super 8 Motel
Rt. 9 N.
Plattsburgh NY 12901
(518) 562-8888
(800) 848-8888
pets with permission
Room rates from $44

Howard Johnson
I-87
Plattsburgh NY 12901
(518) 561-7750
(800) 654-2000
Room rates $40-80

POUGHKEEPSIE
Econo Lodge
418 South Rd.
Poughkeepsie, NY 12601
(914) 452-6600
(800) 446-6900
$50-65

ROCHESTER
Hampton Inn
717 E. Henrietta Rd.
Rochester NY 14623
(716) 272-7800
(800) 426-7866
Room rates from $60

Comfort Inn
395 Buell Rd.
Rochester NY 14624
(716) 436-4400
(800) 228-5150
Room rates $44-53

Comfort Inn
1501 W. Ridge Rd.
Rochester NY 14615
(716) 621-5700
(800) 228-5150
Room rates $51-71

Econo Lodge
940 Jefferson Rd.
Rochester, NY 14623
(716) 427-2700
(800) 446-6900
$40-85

Holiday Inn
911 Brooks Ave.
Rochester NY 14624
(716) 328-6000
(800) 465-4329
Room rates $110-130

ROCK HILL
Holiday Mountain Lodge
Box 469
Rock Hill NY 12775
(914) 796-3000
Room rates $50-65

ROME
Park Inn
Erie Blvd. & S. James St.
Rome NY 13440
(315) 336-4300
Room rates $60-65

SARATOGA SPRINGS
Holiday Inn
Broadway & Circular St.
Saratoga Springs NY 12866
(518) 584-4550
(800) 465-4329
Room rates $65-190

SYRACUSE
Quality Inn
930 S. 1st St.
Syracuse NY 13069
(315) 593-2444
(800) 228-5151
Room rates $67-79

Inn at the Circle
Carrier Circle
Syracuse NY 13206
(315) 463-6601
Room rates $50-60

Days Inn
6609 Thompson Rd.
Syracuse NY 13206
(315) 437-5998
(800) 325-2525
$4/pet
Room rates $41-46

Holiday Inn
Farrell Rd. & State Fair Blvd.
Syracuse NY 13209
(315) 457-8700
(800) 465-4329
Room rates $60-70

Holiday Inn
701 Genesee St.
Syracuse NY 13210
(315) 474-7251
(800) 465-4329
Room rates $65-75

Sheraton
7th North St. & Electronics Pkwy.
Syracuse NY 13088
(315) 457-1122
(800) 325-3535
Room rates $60-70

UTICA
Red Roof Inn
20 Weaver St.
Utica NY 13502
(315) 724-7128
(800) 843-7663
Room rates $40-50

WATERTOWN
Quality Inn
1190 Arsenal St.
Watertown NY 13601
(315) 788-6800
(800) 228-5151
Room rates $60-72

NORTH CAROLINA
State law prohibits pets from staying in hotel or motel rooms. We suggest that you plan ahead for a reputable kennel near your lodging while in North Carolina.

NORTH DAKOTA
BEULAH
Super 8 Motel
720 Hwy 49 N.
Beulah ND 58523
(701) 873-2850
(800) 848-8888
pets with permission
Room rates from $25

BISMARCK
Comfort Inn
1030 Interstate Ave.
Bismarck ND 58501
(701) 223-1911
(800) 228-5150
Room rates $38-47

Always Call Ahead!

NORTH DAKOTA, Bismarck

Days Inn
1300 Capitol Ave.
Bismarck ND 58501
(701) 223-9151
(800) 325-2525
small pets allowed
Room rates $37-47

Motel 6
2433 State St.
Bismarck ND 58501
(701) 255-6878
1 small pet per room
Reservations (505) 891-6161
Room rates $28-29

BOWMAN
Super 8 Motel
Hwys 12 & 85
Bowman ND 58623
(701) 523-5613
(800) 848-8888
Room rates from $32

DEVILS LAKE
Super 8 Motel
Hwy 2 E.
Devils Lake ND 58301
(701) 662-8656
(800) 848-8888
pets with permission
Room rates from $29

DICKINSON
Super 8 Motel
637 12th St. W.
Dickinson ND 58601
(701) 227-1215
(800) 848-8888
pets with permission
Room rates from $27

Comfort Inn
493 Elk Dr.
Dickinson ND 58601
(701) 264-7300
(800) 228-5150
Room rates $31-37

FARGO
Super 8 Motel
3518 Interstate Blvd.
Fargo ND 58103
(701) 232-9202
(800) 848-8888
pets with permission
Room rates from $32

Comfort Suites
1415 35th St
Fargo ND 58103
(701) 237-5911
(800) 228-5150
Room rates $48-75

Comfort Inn
1407 35th St. S.
Fargo ND 58103
(701) 280-9666
(800) 228-5150
Room rates $39-50

Comfort Inn
3825 9th Ave. SW
Fargo ND 58103
(701) 282-9596
(800) 228-5150
Room rates $38-48

Motel 6
2202 S. University Dr.
Fargo ND 58103
(701) 235-0570
1 small pet per room
Reservations (505) 891-6161
Room rates $28-29

Econo Lodge
1401 35th St.
Fargo, ND 58103
(701) 232-3412
(800) 446-6900
$29-45

GRAND FORKS
Econo Lodge
900 N. 43rd St.
Grand Forks, ND 58201
(701) 746-6666
(800) 446-6900
$30-55

Ramada Inn
1205 N. 43rd St.
Grand Forks ND 58203
(701) 775-3951
(800) 228-2828
Room rates $56-70

Comfort Inn
3251 30th Ave. S.
Grand Forks ND 58201
(701) 775-7503
(800) 228-5150
Room rates $39-50

Days Inn
3101 34th St. S.
Grand Forks ND 58201
(701) 775-0060
(800) 325-2525
pets with permission
Room rates $40-50

MANDAN
Days Inn
2630 Old Red Trial
Mandan ND 58554
(701) 663-0001
(800) 325-2525
$6/pets
Room rates $30-41

MINOT
Comfort Inn
1515 22nd Ave. SW
Minot ND 58701
(701) 852-2201
(800) 228-5150
Room rates $40-55

Days Inn
1200 4th St. SW
Minot ND 58701
(701) 852-3646
(800) 325-2525
small pets allowed
Room rates $34-44

Holiday Inn
2315 Broadway
Minot ND 58702
(701) 852-4161
(800) 465-4329
Room rates $55-65

VALLEY CITY
Super 8 Motel
I-94
Valley City ND 58072
(701) 845-1140
(800) 848-8888
pets with permission
Room rates from $28

Wahpeton, NORTH DAKOTA

WAHPETON
Comfort Inn
209 13th St. S.
Wahpeton ND 58075
(701) 642-1115
(800) 228-5150
Room rates $38-50

WEST FARGO
Super 8 Motel
825 Main Ave.
West Fargo ND 58078
(701) 282-7121
(800) 848-8888
pets with permission
Room rates from $30

WILLISTON
Super 8 Motel
2324 2nd Ave. W.
Williston ND 58801
(701) 572-8371
(800) 848-8888
pets with permission
Room rates from $29

Select Inn
213 35th St. W.
Williston ND 58801
(701) 572-4242
Room rates $25-30

OHIO
AKRON
Days Inn
3150 Market St.
Akron OH 44313
(216) 869-9000
(800) 325-2525
$15 deposit
Room rates $39-45

Holiday Inn
5 Cascade Plaza
Akron OH 44308
(216) 762-0661
(800) 465-4329
Room rates $65-85

Knights Inn
3237 Arlington Rd.
Akron OH 44312
(216) 644-1204
(800) 722-7220
Room rates $35-40

ALLIANCE
Comfort Inn
2500 W. State St.
Alliance OH 44601
(216) 821-5555
(800) 228-5150
Room rates $52-65

AMHERST
Motel 6
704 N. Leavitt Rd.
Amherst OH 44001
(216) 988-3266
1 small pet per room
Reservations (505) 891-6161
Room rates $30-33

AUSTINBURG
Travelodge
SR-45 & I-90
Austinburg OH 44010
(216) 275-2011
(800) 255-3050
Room rates $45-48

BELLEFONTAINE
Comfort Inn
260 Northview
Bellefontaine OH 43311
(513) 599-6666
(800) 228-5150
Room rates $44-75

BOWLING GREEN
Holiday Inn
1550 Wooster St.
Bowling Green OH 43402
(419) 352-5211
(800) 465-4329
Room rates $55-70

BROOKVILLE
Days Inn
200 Parkview Dr.
Brookville OH 45309
(513) 833-4003
(800) 325-2525
Room rates $35-40

BUCYRUS
Days Inn
1515 N. Sandusky St.
Bucyrus OH 44820
(419) 562-3737
(800) 325-2525
Room rates $50-52

CANTON
Hampton Inn
5335 Broadmoor Circle
Canton OH 44709
(216) 492-0151
(800) 426-7866
Room rates $45-55

CELINA
Comfort Inn
1421 SR 703 E.
Celina OH 45822
(419) 586-4656
(800) 228-5150
Room rates $50-75

CHILLICOTHE
Holiday Inn
1250 Bridge St.
Chillicothe OH 45601
(614) 775-7000
(800) 465-4329
Room rates $45-55

CINCINNATI
Rodeway Inn
400 Glensprings Dr.
Cincinnati, OH 45246
(513) 825-3129
(800) 424-4777
$36-65

Clarion Hotel
141 W. 6th St.
Cincinnati, OH 45202
(513) 352-2100
(800) 228-5152
$77-150

Quality Hotel
666 5th St.
Cincinnati OH 41011
(606) 491-1200
(800) 228-5151
Room rates $64-76

Quality Inn
5589 Kings Mills Rd.
Cincinnati OH 45034-0425
(513) 398-8075
(800) 228-5151
Room rates $35-99

Quality Hotel
4747 Montgomery Rd.
Cincinnati OH 45212
(513) 351-6000
(800) 228-5151
Room rates from $67

97

OHIO, Cincinnati

Days Inn
I-275 & US 42
Cincinnati OH 45241
(513) 554-1400
(800) 325-2525
Room rates $40-50

Days Inn
4056 Mt. Carmel-Tobasco Rd.
Cincinnati OH 45255
(513) 528-3800
(800) 325-2525
Room rates $36-49

Holiday Inn
800 8th St.
Cincinnati OH 45203
(513) 241-8660
(800) 465-4329
Room rates $65-75

Marriott
11320 Chester Rd.
Cincinnati OH 45246
(513) 772-1720
(800) 228-9290
owner responsible
Room rates $75-115

CLEVELAND
Hampton Inn
29690 Detroit Rd.
Cleveland OH 44145
(216) 892-0333
(800) 426-7866
Room rates $56-51

Hampton Inn
25105 Country Club Blvd
Cleveland OH 44070
(216) 734-4477
(800) 426-7866
Room rates $51-56

Comfort Inn
6191 Quarry Ln.
Cleveland OH 44131
(216) 328-7777
(800) 228-5150
Room rates $56-76

Travelodge
7701 Reynolds Rd.
Cleveland, OH 44060
(216) 951-7333
(800) 255-3050
from 30

Ramada Inn
27981 Euclid Ave.
Cleveland, OH 44132
(216) 731-5800
(800) 228-2828
$52-70

Days Hotel
4600 Northfield Rd.
Cleveland OH 44128
(216) 663-4100
(800) 325-2525
Room rates $58-68

COLUMBUS
Ramada Inn
4601 W. Broad St.
Columbus OH 43228
(614) 878-5301
(800) 228-2828
Room rates $54-59

Quality Inn
4801 E. Broad St.
Columbus OH 43213
(614) 861-0321
(800) 228-5151
Room rates $55-61

Econo Lodge
920 Wilson Rd.
Columbus, OH 43204
(614) 274-8581
(800) 446-6900
$31-46

Comfort Suites
1001 Schrock Rd.
Columbus, OH 43229
(614) 431-0208
(800) 228-5150
$65-100

Days Inn
3232 Olentangy River Rd.
Columbus OH 43202
(614) 261-7141
(800) 325-2525
Room rates $38-44

Days Inn
1700 Clara St
Columbus OH 43211
(614) 299-4300
(800) 325-2525
Room rates $39-65

Days Inn
5930 Scarborough Rd.
Columbus OH 43232
(614) 868-9290
(800) 325-2525
small pets allowed
Room rates $32-37

Motel 6
5910 Scarborough Blvd.
Columbus OH 43232
(614) 755-2250
1 small pet per room
Reservations (505) 891-6161
Room rates $30-33

Motel 6
1289 E. Dublin-Granville Rd.
Columbus OH 43229
(614) 846-9860
1 small pet per room
Reservations (505) 891-6161
Room rates $30-33

Radisson Hotel
4900 Sinclair Rd.
Columbus OH 43229
(614) 846-0300
(800) 333-3333
$20 deposit
Room rates $55-90

DAYTON
Days Inn
7470 Miller Lane
Dayton OH 45414
(513) 898-4946
(800) 325-2525
Room rates $33-37

Motel 6
7130 Miller lane
Dayton OH 45414
(513) 898-3606
1 small pet per room
Reservations (505) 891-6161
Room rates $30-33

Rodeway Inn
7575 Poe Ave.
Dayton, OH 45414
(513) 454-0550
(800) 424-4777
$35-50

Radisson Inn
2401 Needmore Rd.
Dayton OH 45414
(513) 278-5711
(800) 333-3333
$25 fee
Room rates $70-80

Rodeway Inn
7575 Poe Ave.
Dayton, OH 45414
(513) 454-0550
(800) 424-4777
$35-50

Red Roof Inn
7370 Miller Lane
Dayton OH 45414
(513) 898-1054
(800) 843-7663
Room rates $35-40

DELAWARE
LK Motel
1001 US 23 North
Delaware OH 43015
(614) 369-4421
Room rates $35-45

ELYRIA
Holiday Inn
1825 Lorain Blvd.
Elyria OH 44035
(216) 324-5411
(800) 465-4329
Room rates $75-100

Knights Inn
325 Griswold Rd.
Elyria OH 44035
(216) 324-3911
(800) 722-7220
Room rates $35-45

FINDLAY
Super 8 Motel
1600 Fox St.
Findlay OH 45840
(419) 422-8863
(800) 848-8888
pets with permission
Room rates from $34

Econolodge
316 Emma st.
Findlay, OH 45840
(419) 422-0154
$27-35

FREMONT
Holiday Inn
3422 Port Clinton Rd.
Fremont OH 43420
(419) 334-2682
(800) 465-4329
Room rates $65-110

GIRARD
Motel 6
1600 Motor Inn Dr.
Girard OH 44420
(216) 759-7833
1 small pet per room
Reservations (505) 891-6161
Room rates $30-33

GROVE CITY
Ramada Inn
1879 Stringtown Road
Grove City OH 43123
(614) 871-2990
(800) 228-2828
Room rates $46-59

JACKSON
Comfort Inn
605 E. Main ST.
Jackson OH 45640
(614) 286-7581
(800) 228-5150
Room rates $52-72

LANCASTER
Holiday Inn
1858 Memorial Dr.
Lancaster OH 43130
(614) 653-3040
(800) 465-4329
Room rates $50-60

LIMA
Ramada Inn
1210 Neubrecht Rd.
Lima OH 45801
(419) 228-4251
(800) 228-2828
Room rates from $50

Quality Inn
1201 Neubrecht Rd.
Lima OH 45801
(419) 222-0596
(800) 228-5151
Room rates $45-49

Motel 6
1800 Harding Hwy
Lima OH 45804
(419) 228-0456
1 small pet per room
Reservations (505) 891-6161
Room rates $30-33

MACEDONIA
Travelodge
275 Highland Rd
Macedonia OH 44056
(216) 467-1516
(800) 255-3050
Room rates from $44

Motel 6
311 E. Highland Rd.
Macedonia OH 44056
(216) 468-1670
1 small pet per room
Reservations (505) 891-6161
Room rates $30-33

MANSFIELD
Super 8 Motel
2425 Interstate Circle
Mansfield OH 44903
(419) 756-8875
(800) 848-8888
pets with permission
Room rates from $41

Travelodge
555 N. Trimble Rd.
Mansfield OH 44906
(419) 529-2100
(800) 255-3050
Room rates $33-39

Travelodge
RR 11
Mansfield OH 44903
(419) 589-3938
(800) 255-3050
Room rates from $37

**Always
Call
Ahead!**

OHIO, Mansfield

Travelodge
90 Hanley Rd.
Mansfield OH 44903
(419) 756-7600
(800) 255-3050
Room rates from $41

MARIETTA
Super 8 Motel
46 Acme St. Wash. Center
Marietta OH 45750
(614) 374-8888
(800) 848-8888
pets with permission
Room rates from $36

Econo Lodge
702 Pike St.
Marietta, OH 45750
(614) 374-8481
(800) 446-6900
$30-50

MARION
Travelodge
1952 Marion-Mt. Gilead Rd.
Marion OH 43302
(614) 389-4671
(800) 255-3050
Room rates from $42

LK Motel
1838 Marion-Mt. Gilead Rd.
Marion OH 43302
(614) 389-4651
$5 charge
Room rates $35-40

MASON
Days Inn
9735 Mason/Montgomery Rd.
Mason OH 45040
(513) 398-3297
(800) 325-2525
small dogs only
Room rates $2-70

MASSILLON
Super 8 Motel
242 Lincoln Way W.
Massillon OH 44646
(216) 837-8880
(800) 848-8888
pets with permission
Room rates from $39

MENTOR
Super 8 Motel
7325 Palisades Pkwy
Mentor OH 44060
(216) 951-8558
(800) 848-8888
pets with permission
Room rates from $36

MIAMISBURG
Motel 6
8101 Springsboro Pike
Miamisburg OH 45342
(513) 434-8750
1 small pet per room
Reservations (505) 891-6161
Room rates $30-33

MIDDLEBURG HEIGHTS
Motel 6
7219 Engle Rd.
Middleburg Heights OH 44130
(216) 234-0990
1 small pet per room
Reservations (505) 891-6161
Room rates $30-33

MIDDLETOWN
Econo Lodge
4385 2nd St.
Middletown OH 45005
(513) 746-3627
(800) 553-2666
Room rates $30-40

MONROE
Days Inn
150 Garver Rd.
Monroe OH 45050
(513) 539-9221
(800) 325-2525
Room rates $29-43

NELSONVILLE
Quality Inn
US 33 & SR 691
Nelsonville OH 45764
(614) 753-3531
(800) 228-5151
Room rates $42-48

NEW PHILADELPHIA
Motel 6
181 Bluebell Dr. SW
New Philadelphia OH 44663
(216) 339-6446
1 small pet per room
Reservations (505) 891-6161
Room rates $30-33

NEWARK
Holiday Inn
733 Hebron Rd.
Newark OH 43055
(614) 522-1165
(800) 465-4329
Room rates $50-60

NILES
Park Inn
1225 Youngstown-Warren Rd.
Niles OH 44446
(216) 652-1761
Room rates $32-55

OREGON
Comfort Inn
2930 Navarre Ave.
Oregon OH 43616
(419) 691-8911
(800) 228-5150
Room rates $48-67

PERRYSBURG
Days Inn
10667 Fremont Pike
Perrysburg OH 43551
(419) 874-8771
(800) 325-2525
Room rates $39-49

PIQUA
Comfort Inn
987 Ash St. Miami Valley Center
Piqua OH 45356
(513) 778-8100
(800) 228-5150
Room rates $45-56

PORT CLINTON
Travelodge
1811 Harbor Rd.
Port Clinton OH 43452
(419) 732-2111
(800) 255-3050
Room rates $39-71

Always Call Ahead!

PORTSMOUTH
Holiday Inn
US 23
Portsmouth OH 45662
(614) 354-2851
(800) 465-4329
Room rates $50-65

REYNOLDSBURG
Ramada Inn
2100 Brice Road
Reynoldsburg OH 43068
(614) 864-1280
(800) 228-2828
Room rates $57-72

SANDUSKY
Friendship Inn
3309 Milan Rd.
Sandusky, OH 44870
(419) 626-8720
(800) 453-4511
$28-100

SHARONVILLE
Motel 6
2000 E. Kemper
Sharonville OH 45241
(513) 772-5944
1 small pet per room
Reservations (505) 891-6161
Room rates $30-33

SIDNEY
Days Inn
420 Folkerth Ave.
Sidney OH 45365
(513) 492-1104
(800) 325-2525
Room rates $37-50

SPRINGDALE
Sheraton
11911 Sheraton Ave.
Springdale OH 45246
(513) 671-6600
(800) 325-3535
charge
Room rates $70-170

SPRINGFIELD
Drake Motel
3200 Main St.
Springfield OH 45505
(513) 325-7334
$5 charge
Room rates $28-35

ST. CLAIRSVILLE
Days Inn
52601 Holiday Dr.
St. Clairsville OH 43950
(614) 695-0100
(800) 325-2525
Room rates $44-47

STEUBENVILLE
Holiday Inn
1300 University Blvd.
Steubenville OH 43952
(614) 282-0901
(800) 465-4329
Room rates $50-60

SIDNEY
Comfort Inn
I-75 & SR 47
Sidney OH 45365
(513) 492-3001
(800) 228-5150
Room rates $44-75

TOLEDO
Hampton Inn
1409 Reynolds Rd.
Toledo OH 43537
(419) 893-1004
(800) 426-7866
Room rates from $51

Ramada Inn
2340 S Reynolds Road
Toledo OH 43614
(419) 865-1361
(800) 228-2828
Room rates $65-79

Comfort Inn
445 E. Alexis Rd.
Toledo OH 43612
(419) 476-0170
(800) 228-5150
Room rates $50-60

Days Inn
1821 E. Manhattan Blvd.
Toledo OH 43608
(419) 729-3901
(800) 325-2525
$6/pets
Room rates $38-54

Motel 6
5335 Heatherdowns Rd.
Toledo OH 43614
(419) 865-2308
1 small pet per room
Reservations (505) 891-6161
Room rates $30-33

Marriott
2 Seagate
Toledo OH 43604
(419) 241-1411
(800) 228-9290
Room rates $125-140

TROY
Travelodge
1330 Archer Rd.
Troy OH 45373
(513) 335-0071
(800) 255-3050
Room rates from $38

TWINSBURG
Super 8 Motel
8848 Twin Hills Dr.
Twinsburg OH 44087
(216) 425-2889
(800) 848-8888
pets with permission
Room rates from $36

WADSWORTH
Knights Inn
810 High St.
Wadsworth OH 44281
(216) 336-6671
(800) 722-7220
Room rates $35-40

WAPAKONETA
Days Inn
1659 Wapak Fisher Rd.
Wapakoneta OH 45895
(419) 738-2184
(800) 325-2525
Room rates from $38

WOOSTER
LK Motel
969 Timken Rd.
Wooster OH 44691
(216) 264-9222
Room rates $40-50

YOUNGSTOWN
Super 8 Motel
5280 76th Dr.
Youngstown OH 44515
(216) 793-7788
(800) 848-8888
pets with permission
Room rates from $35

Quality Inn
1051 N. Canfield-Niles Rd.
Youngstown OH 44515
(216) 793-9851
(800) 228-5151
Room rates $45-61

ZANESVILLE
Super 8 Motel
2440 National Rd.
Zanesville OH 43701
(614) 455-3124
(800) 848-8888
pets with permission
Room rates from $36

Holiday Inn
4645 Pike
Zanesville OH 43701
(614) 453-0771
(800) 465-4329
Room rates $50-70

OKLAHOMA
ALTUS
Econo Lodge
3202 N. Main St.
Altus, OK 73521
(405) 477-2300
(800) 446-6900
$25-35

Ramada Inn
2515 E Broadway
Altus OK 73521
(405) 477-3000
(800) 228-2828
Room rates $48-60

ARDMORE
Ramada Inn
I-35 & Hwy 199
Ardmore OK 73401
(405) 226-1250
(800) 228-2828
Room rates $43-47

Motel 6
120 Holiday Dr.
Ardmore OK 73401
(405) 226-7666
1 small pet per room
Reservations (505) 891-6161
Room rates $25-30

Holiday Inn
2705 Holiday Dr.
Ardmore OK 73401
(405) 223-7130
(800) 465-4329
Room rates $40-50

BARTLESVILLE
Park Inn
222 Washington Blvd.
Bartlesville OK 74006
(918) 333-2100
Room rates $40-45

BROKEN ARROW
Econo Lodge
1401 N. Elm Place
Broken Arrow, OK 74012
(918) 258-6617
(800) 446-6900
$30-40

DUNCAN
Travelodge
2535 North US-81 Hwy
Duncan OK 73533
(405) 252-0810
(800) 255-3050
Room rates from $35

DURANT
Quality Inn
2121 W. Main St.
Durant OK 74701
(405) 924-5432
(800) 228-5151
Room rates $34-38

ELK CITY
Days Inn
1100 Hwy 34
Elk City OK 73644
(405) 225-9210
(800) 325-2525
Room rates $26-29

Travelodge
301 Sleepy Hollow Ct.
Elk City OK 73648
(405) 243-0150
(800) 255-3050
Room rates from $34

Motel 6
2500 E. Hwy 66
Elk City OK 73644
(405) 225-6661
1 small pet per room
Reservations (505) 891-6161
Room rates $25-30

Econo Lodge
108 Meadow Ridge
Elk City, OK 73644
(405) 225-5120
(800) 446-6900
$25-35

LAWTON
Ramada Inn
601 N 2nd
Lawton OK 73507
(405) 355-7155
(800) 228-2828
$10 charge
Room rates $42-48

Hospitality Inn
202 Lee Blvd.
Lawton OK 73502
(405) 355-9765
$25 deposit
Room rates $35-40

Park Inn
3110 Cache Rd.
Lawton OK 73505
(405) 353-3104
Room rates $40-50

MCALESTER
Comfort Inn
1215 George Nigh Expwy
McAlester OK 74502
(918) 426-0115
(800) 228-5150
Room rates $36-40

McAlester, OKLAHOMA

Days Inn
1217 S. George High Expwy
McAlester OK 74501
(918) 426-5050
(800) 325-2525
Room rates $44-46

MIDWEST CITY
Motel 6
6166 Tinker Diagonal
Midwest City OK 73110
(405) 737-6676
1 small pet per room
Reservations (505) 891-6161
Room rates $25-30

MOORE
Motel 6
1417 N. Moore Ave.
Moore OK 73160
(405) 799-6606
1 small pet per room
Reservations (505) 891-6161
Room rates $25-30

MUSKOGEE
Quality Inn
2300 E. Shawnee Ave. (US 62)
Muskogee OK 74403
(918) 638-6551
(800) 228-5151
Room rates $41-46

Days Inn
900 S. 32nd St.
Muskogee OK 74401
(918) 683-3911
(800) 325-2525
Room rates $41-46

Motel 6
903 S. 32nd St.
Muskogee OK 74401
(918) 683-8369
1 small pet per room
Reservations (505) 891-6161
Room rates $25-30

NORMAN
Sheraton
1000 Interstate Dr.
Norman OK 73072
(405) 364-2882
(800) 325-3535
under 45 lbs.
Room rates $55-90

OKLAHOMA CITY
Comfort Inn
4017 NW 39th Expwy
Oklahoma City OK 73112
(405) 947-0038
(800) 228-5150
Room rates $41-45

Days Inn
4712 W. I-40
Oklahoma City OK 73128
(405) 947-8721
(800) 325-2525
$5/pets
Room rates $25-30

Days Inn
2616 S. I-35
Oklahoma City OK 73129
(405) 677-0521
(800) 325-2525
$15 charge
Room rates $31-41

Motel 6
820 S. Meridian Ave.
Oklahoma City OK 73108
(405) 946-6662
1 small pet per room
Reservations (505) 891-6161
Room rates $25-30

Motel 6
11900 NE Expwy
Oklahoma City OK 73131
(405) 478-8666
1 small pet per room
Reservations (505) 891-6161
Room rates $25-30

Motel 6
4200 W. Interstate 40
Oklahoma City OK 73108
(405) 947-6550
1 small pet per room
Reservations (505) 891-6161
Room rates $25-30

SHAWNEE
Best Western Holiday Harbor
Rt. 2
Shawnee OK 74801
(405) 273-6231
(800) 528-1234
Room rates $30-40

STILLWATER
Motel 6
5122 W. 6th Ave.
Stillwater OK 74074
(405) 624-0433
1 small pet per room
Reservations (505) 891-6161
Room rates $25-30

SULPHER
Super 8 Motel
2110 W. Broadway
Sulpher OK 73086
(405) 622-6500
(800) 848-8888
pets with permission
Room rates from $30

TULSA
Super 8 Motel
6616 E. Archer St.
Tulsa OK 74115
(918) 836-1981
(800) 848-8888
pets with permission
Room rates from $33

Ramada Inn
11521 East Skelly Drive
Tulsa OK 74128
(918) 438-7700
(800) 228-2828
Room rates $46-50

Quality Inn
14831 S. Casper St.
Tulsa OK 74033
(918) 322-5201
(800) 228-5151
Room rates $38-44

Days Inn
1016 N. Garnett Rd.
Tulsa OK 74116
(918) 438-5050
(800) 325-2525
small pets allowed, $5
Room rates $26-30

 Always Call Ahead!

OKLAHOMA, Tulsa

Motel 6
5828 W. Skelly Dr.
Tulsa OK 74107
(918) 445-0223
1 small pet per room
Reservations (505) 891-6161
Room rates $25-30

Motel 6
1011 S. Garnett Rd.
Tulsa OK 74128
(918) 234-6200
1 small pet per room
Reservations (505) 891-6161
Room rates $25-30

Embassy Suites Hotel
3332 79th Ave.
Tulsa OK 74145
(918) 622-4000
(800) 362-2779
$25 charge
Room rates $60-85

La Quinta
10829 41st St. South
Tulsa OK 74146
(918) 665-0220
small pets
Room rates $35-60

YUKON
Comfort Inn
321 N. Mustang Rd.
Yukon OK 73099
(405) 324-1000
(800) 228-5150
Room rates $38-60

OREGON
ALBANY
Comfort Inn
251 Airport Rd. SE
Albany OR 97321
(503) 928-0921
(800) 228-5150
Room rates $53-60

ASHLAND
Quality Inn
2520 Ashland St.
Ashland OR 97520
(503) 488-2330
(800) 228-5151
Room rates $55-99

BEND
Hampton Inn
15 NE Butler Rd.
Bend OR 97701
(503) 388-4114
(800) 426-7866
Room rates $46-54

Comfort Inn
61200 S. US 97
Bend OR 97702
(503) 388-2227
(800) 228-5150
Room rates $49-120

BURNS
Motel 6
997 Oregon Ave.
Burns OR 97720
(503) 573-3013
1 small pet per room
Reservations (505) 891-6161
Room rates $28-33

COOS BAY
Edgewater Inn
275 Johnson St.
Coos Bay OR 97420
(503) 267-0423
$3 charge
Room rates $50-60

CORVALLIS
Motel Orleans
935 Garfield NW
Corvallis OR 97339
(503) 758-9125
Room rates $30-35

EUGENE
Motel 6
3690 Glenwood Dr.
Eugene OR 97403
(503) 687-2395
1 small pet per room
Reservations (505) 891-6161
Room rates $28-33

Red Lion Inn
205 Coburg Rd.
Eugene OR 97401
(503) 342-5201
Room rates $65-85

GOLD BEACH
River Bridge Inn
1010 Jerry's Flat Rd.
Gold Beach OR 97444
(503) 247-4533
Room rates $35-70

GRANTS PASS
Travelodge
748 Southeast 7th St.
Grants Pass OR 97526
(503) 476-7793
(800) 255-3050
Room rates $37-42

Motel 6
1800 NE 7th
Grants Pass OR 97526
(503) 474-1331
1 small pet per room
Reservations (505) 891-6161
Room rates $28-33

GRESHAM
Travelodge
23705 Sandy Blvd.
Gresham OR 97060
(503) 666-6623
(800) 255-3050
$5 charge
Room rates $35-40

HILLSBORO
Best Western Hallmark Inn
3500 Cornell Rd.
Hillsboro OR 97124
(503) 648-3500
(800) 528-1234
$10 deposit
Room rates $55-65

Always
Call
Ahead!

HOOD RIVER
Columbia Gorge Hotel
4000 W. Cliff Drive
Hood River OR 97031
(503) 386-5566
Room rates $125-155

KLAMATH FALLS
Motel 6
5136 S. 6th St.
Klamath Falls OR 97603
(503) 884-2110
1 small pet per room
Reservations (505) 891-6161
Room rates $28-33

MEDFORD
Motel 6
2400 Biddle Rd.
Medford OR 97504
(503) 779-0550
1 small pet per room
Reservations (505) 891-6161
Room rates $28-33

Motel 6
950 Alba Dr.
Medford OR 97504
(503) 773-4290
1 small pet per room
Reservations (505) 891-6161
Room rates $28-33

NEWPORT
Orca Motel
531 Fall St.
Newport OR 97365
(503) 265-6203
$50 deposit
Room rates $55-60

ONTARIO
Motel 6
275 Butler St.
Ontario OR 97914
(503) 889-6617
1 small pet per room
Reservations (505) 891-6161
Room rates $28-33

PENDLETON
Motel 6
325 SE Nye Ave.
Pendleton OR 97801
(503) 276-3160
1 small pet per room
Reservations (505) 891-6161
Room rates $28-33

PORTLAND
Comfort Inn
431 NE Multnomah
Portland OR 97232
(503) 233-7933
(800) 228-5150
Room rates $62-82

Travelodge
949 East Burnside St.
Portland OR 97214
(503) 234-8411
(800) 255-3050
Room rates from $43

Motel 6
3104 SE Powell Blvd.
Portland OR 97202
(503) 238-0600
1 small pet per room
Reservations (505) 891-6161
Room rates $28-33

Marriott
1401 Front Ave.
Portland OR 97201
(503) 226-7600
(800) 228-9290
sign damage waiver
Room rates $85-150

Holiday Inn
8439 Columbia Blvd.
Portland OR 97220
(503) 256-5000
(800) 465-4329
$50 deposit
Room rates $75-90

ROSEBURG
Motel Orleans
427 Garden Valley Blvd.
Roseburg OR 97470
(503) 673-5561
$3 charge
Room rates $30-45

Always Call Ahead!

SALEM
Motel 6
2250 Mission St. SE
Salem OR 97302
(503) 588-7197
1 small pet per room
Reservations (505) 891-6161
Room rates $28-33

Motel Orleans
1875 Fisher Rd.
Salem OR 97305
(503) 588-5423
$5 charge
Room rates $34-40

SEASIDE
Huntley Inn
441 2nd Ave.
Seaside OR 97138
(503) 738-9581
$15 charge, under 15 lbs
Room rates $55-70

SPRINGFIELD
Motel 6
3752 International Ct.
Springfield OR 97477
(503) 741-1105
1 small pet per room
Reservations (505) 891-6161
Room rates $28-33

TIGARD
Motel 6
17950 SW McEwan Rd.
Tigard OR 97224
(503) 620-2066
1 small pet per room
Reservations (505) 891-6161
Room rates $28-33

TROUTDALE
Travelodge
23705 N.E. Sandy Blvd
Troutdale OR 97060
(503) 666-6623
(800) 255-3050
Room rates $38-41

Motel 6
1610 NW Frontage Rd.
Troutdale OR 97060
(503) 665-2254
1 small pet per room
Reservations (505) 891-6161
Room rates $28-33

OREGON, Wilsonville

WILSONVILLE
Holiday Inn
25425 Boones Ferry Rd.
Wilsonville OR 97070
(503) 682-2211
(800) 465-4329
Room rates $50-60

WOODBURN
Comfort Inn
120 NE Arney Rd.
Woodburn OR 97071
(503) 982-1727
(800) 228-5150
Room rates $49-60

PENNSYLVANIA
ALLENTOWN
Days Inn
Rt. 22 & 15th St.
Allentown PA 18104
(215) 435-7880
(800) 325-2525
$3/pets
Room rates $48-56

Comfort Inn
7625 Imperial Way
Allentown, PA 18106
(215) 391-0344
(800) 228-5150
$48-70

Days Inn
1151 Bulldog Dr.
Allentown PA 18104
(215) 395-3731
(800) 325-2525
Room rates $44-66

ALTOONA
Super 8 Motel
3535 Fairway Dr.
Altoona PA 16602
(814) 942-5350
(800) 848-8888
pets with permission
Room rates from $41

Holiday Inn
2915 Pleasant Valley Blvd.
Altoona PA 16602
(814) 944-4581
(800) 465-4329
Room rates $50-60

BARTONSVILLE
Comfort Inn
SR 611
Bartonsville PA 18321
(717) 476-1500
(800) 228-5150
Room rates $59-162

BEAVER FALLS
Holiday Inn
SR 18
Beaver Falls PA 15010
(412) 846-3700
(800) 465-4329
Room rates $70-85

BEDFORD
Quality Inn
US 220 & I-70/76
Bedford PA 15522
(814) 623-5188
(800) 228-5151
Room rates $50-63

BETHLEHEM
Comfort Inn
3191 Highfield Dr.
Bethlehem PA 18017
(215) 865-6300
(800) 228-5150
Room rates $53-68

Hotel Bethlehem
437 Main St.
Bethlehem PA 18017
(215) 867-3711
Room rates $50-150

BLOOMSBURG
Quality Inn
1 Buckhorn Rd.
Bloomsburg PA 17815
(717) 784-5300
(800) 228-5151
Room rates $50-69

BROOKVILLE
Super 8 Motel
I-80
Brookville PA 15825
(814) 849-8840
(800) 848-8888
pets with permission
Room rates from $35

Days Inn
Rt. 36 & I-80
Brookville PA 15825
(814) 849-8001
(800) 325-2525
Room rates $35-55

BUTLER
Super 8 Motel
128 Pittsburgh Rd.
Butler PA 16001
(412) 287-8888
(800) 848-8888
pets with permission
Room rates from $41

Days Inn
139 Pittsburgh Rd.
Butler PA 16001
(412) 287-6761
(800) 325-2525
Room rates $39-80

CARLISLE
Super 8 Motel
100 Alexander Spring Rd.
Carlisle PA 17013
(717) 245-9898
(800) 848-8888
pets with permission
Room rates from $41

Holiday Inn
1450 Harrisburg Pike
Carlisle PA 17013
(717) 245-2400
(800) 465-4329
Room rates $55-65

CHAMBERSBURG
Travelodge
565 Lincoln Way East
Chambersburg PA 17201
(717) 264-2446
(800) 255-3050
Room rates $47-49

Always Call Ahead!

CHARLESTON
Super 8 Motel
2311 Ashley Phosphate Rd.
Charleston PA 29418
(803) 572-2228
(800) 848-8888
pets with permission
Room rates from $37

CLARION
Days Inn
Rt. 68 & I-80
Clarion PA 16214
(814) 226-8682
(800) 325-2525
Room rates $40-55

CORAOPOLIS
Hampton Inn
1420 Beers School Rd.
Coraopolis PA 15108
(412) 264-0020
(800) 426-7866
Room rates $62-64

Super 8 Motel
1455 Beers School Rd.
Coraopolis PA 15108
(412) 264-7888
(800) 848-8888
pets with permission
Room rates from $41

Ramada Inn
1412 Beers School Road
Coraopolis PA 15108
(412) 264-8950
(800) 228-2828
Room rates $80-95

Comfort Inn
1170 Thorn Run Rd.
Coraopolis PA 15108
(412) 269-0990
(800) 228-5150
mgr approval needed
Room rates $56-61

DANVILLE
Days Inn
RD 2
Danville PA 17821
(717) 275-5510
(800) 325-2525
Room rates $35-55

 Always Call Ahead!

DOWNINGTOWN
Hampton Inn
Intersection of Rtes 100 & 113
Downingtown PA 19341
(215) 363-5555
(800) 426-7866
Room rates $59-67

DU BOIS
Ramada Inn
I-80 Exit 17 & Route 255
Du Bois PA 15801
(814) 371-7070
(800) 228-2828
Room rates $57-67

DUNMORE
Days Inn
1100 O'Neil Hwy
Dunmore PA 18512
(717) 348-6101
(800) 325-2525
$3/pets
Room rates $51-60

EAST STROUDSBURG
Super 8 Motel
340 Green Tree Dr.
East Stroudsburg PA 18301
(717) 424-7411
(800) 848-8888
pets with permission
Room rates from $43

EASTON
Days Inn
25th St. Shopping Center
Easton PA 18042
(215) 253-0546
(800) 325-2525
$3 charge
Room rates $48-60

ERIE
Holiday Inn
18 - 18th St.
Erie PA 16501
(814) 456-2961
(800) 465-4329
Room rates $65-80

Knights Inn
7455 Schultz Rd.
Erie PA 16509
(814) 868-0879
(800) 722-7220
Room rates $35-40

Howard Johnson Lodge
7575 Peach St.
Erie, PA 16509
(814) 864-4811
(800) 654-2000
$55-110

EXTON
Comfort Inn
5 N. Pottstown Pike
Exton PA 19341
(215) 524-8811
(800) 228-5150
Room rates $54-67

GETTYSBURG
Howard Johnson Lodge
301 Steinwehr Ave.
Gettysburg, PA 17325
(717) 334-1188
(800) 654-2000
$35-70

Quality Inn
380 Steinwehr Ave.
Gettysburg PA 17325
(717) 334-1103
(800) 228-5151
Room rates $64-98

GREENSBURG
Knights Inn
1215 Main St.
Greensburg PA 15601
(412) 836-7100
(800) 722-7220
Room rates $35-40

GREENTREE
Hampton Inn
555 Trumbull Dr.
Greentree PA 15205
(412) 922-0100
(800) 426-7866
Room rates $60-66

HAMLIN
Comfort Inn
I-84 & SR 11
Hamlin PA 18436
(717) 689-4148
(800) 228-5150
Room rates $48-134

PENNSYLVANIA, Harrisburg

HARRISBURG
Hampton Inn
4950 Ritter Rd.
Harrisburg PA 17055
(717) 691-1300
(800) 426-7866
Room rates from $64

Comfort Inn
4021 Union Deposit Rd.
Harrisburg PA 17109
(717) 561-8100
(800) 228-5150
Room rates $66-69

Embers Convention Center
1700 Harrisburg Pike
Harrisburg PA 17013
(717) 243-1717
Room rates $52-67

Travelodge
525 S. Front St.
Harrisburg PA 17104
(717) 233-1611
(800) 255-3050
Room rates from $50

HAZLETON
Hazleton Motor Inn
615 Broad St.
Hazleton PA 18201
(717) 459-0731
Room rates $35-45

JOHNSTOWN
Super 8 Motel
1440 Scalp Ave.
Johnstown PA 15904
(814) 266-8789
(800) 848-8888
Room rates from $43

Comfort Inn
455 Theatre Dr.
Johnstown PA 15904
(814) 266-3678
(800) 228-5150
Room rates $50-61

Days Inn
1540 Scalp Ave.
Johnstown PA 15904
(814) 269-3366
(800) 325-2525
small pets allowed
Room rates from $44

KING OF PRUSSIA
Holiday Inn
260 Goddard Blvd.
King of Prussia PA 19406
(215) 265-7500
(800) 465-4329
$10 charge
Room rates $90-110

LAKE HARMONY
Days Inn
I-80 exit 42
Lake Harmony PA 18661
(717) 443-0391
(800) 325-2525
Room rates $47-130

LAMAR
Comfort Inn
I-80 & SR 64
Lamar, PA 16848
(717) 726-4901
(800) 228-5150
$40-100

LOCK HAVEN
Days Inn
101 E. Walnut St.
Lock Haven PA 17745
(717) 748-3297
(800) 325-2525
$3/pets
Room rates $45-50

MARS
Motel 6
Rt. 19
Mars PA 16046
(412) 776-4333
1 small pet per room
Reservations (505) 891-6161
Room rates $30-31

MEADVILLE
Super 8 Motel
845 Conneaut Lake Rd.
Meadville PA 16335
(814) 333-8883
(800) 848-8888
pets with permission
Room rates from $43

Days Inn
240 Conneaut Lake Rd.
Meadville PA 16335
(814) 337-4264
(800) 325-2525
$5/pets
Room rates $45-65

MOOSIC
Travelodge
4130 Briney Ave.
Moosic PA 18507
(717) 457-6713
(800) 255-3050
Room rates $45-55

NEW CASTLE
Comfort Inn
1740 New Butler Rd.
New Castle, PA 16101
(412) 658-7700
(800) 228-5150
$45-110

Super 8 Motel
1699 Butler Rd.
New Castle PA 16101
(412) 658-8849
(800) 848-8888
pets with permission
Room rates from $40

Comfort Inn
1740 New Butler Rd.
New Castle PA 16101
(412) 658-7700
(800) 228-5150
Room rates $46-93

NEW COLUMBIA
Comfort Inn
I-80 & US 15
New Columbia PA 17856
(717) 568-8000
(800) 228-5150
Room rates $48-65

NEW CUMBERLAND
Days Inn
353 Lewisberry Rd.
New Cumberland PA 17070
(717) 774-4156
(800) 325-2525
Room rates $51-55

**Always
Call
Ahead!**

New Cumberland, PENNSYLVANIA

Motel 6
200 Commerce Dr.
New Cumberland PA 17070
(717) 774-8910
1 small pet per room
Reservations (505) 891-6161
Room rates $30-31

NEW STATION
Super 8 Motel
103 Bair Blvd.
New Station PA 15672
(412) 925-8915
(800) 848-8888
pets with permission
Room rates from $38

PENN STATE
Days Inn
240 S. Pugh St.
Penn State PA 16801
(814) 238-8454
(800) 325-2525
$7/pets
Room rates $63-89

PHILADELPHIA
Comfort Inn
3660 Street Rd.
Philadelphia PA 19020
(215) 245-0100
(800) 228-5150
Room rates $57-89

Comfort Inn
51 Industrial Hwy
Philadelphia PA 19029
(215) 521-9800
(800) 228-5150
Room rates $68-85

Comfort Inn
6401 Bristol Pk
Philadelphia PA 19057
(215) 547-5000
(800) 228-5150
Room rates $55-65

Ramada Hotel
2015 Penrose Ave.
Philadelphia, PA 19145
(215) 755-6500
(800) 228-2828
$45-100

Quality Inn
1010 Race St.
Philadelphia PA 19107
(215) 922-1730
(800) 228-5151
Room rates $79-109

Howard Johnson Hotel
1300 Providence Rd.
Philadelphia, PA 19013
(215) 876-7211
(800) 654-2000
$60-80

Days Hotel
530 Pennsylvannia Ave.
Philadelphia PA 19034
(215) 643-1111
(800) 325-2525
Room rates $59-89

PITTSBURGH
Days Inn
300 Tarentum Bridge Rd.
Pittsburgh PA 15068
(412) 335-9171
(800) 325-2525
Room rates $45-62

Days Inn
2727 Mosside Blvd.
Pittsburgh PA 15146
(412) 856-1610
(800) 325-2525
Room rates $46-49

Motel 6
211 Beecham Dr.
Pittsburgh PA 15205
(412) 922-9400
1 small pet per room
Reservations (505) 891-6161
Room rates $30-31

Holiday Inn
4859 McKnight Rd.
Pittsburgh PA 15237
(412) 366-5200
(800) 465-4329
with advance reservation
Room rates $90-100

POTTSTOWN
Comfort Inn
99 Robinson St.
Pottstown PA 19464
(215) 326-5000
(800) 228-5150
Room rates $58-73

READING
Econo Lodge
422E Papermill Rd.
Reading PA 19610
(215) 378-5105
(800) 553-2666
$3 charge
Room rates $48-55

Wellesley Inn
910 Woodland Ave.
Reading PA 19610
(215) 374-1500
$3 charge
Room rates $35-55

SCRANTON
Days Inn
Rt. 6 & 11 Clarks Summit
Scranton PA 18411
(717) 586-9100
(800) 325-2525
$3 charge
Room rates $50-60

Howard Johnson
307 Rt. 315
Scranton PA 18640
(717) 654-3301
(800) 654-2000
Room rates $50-75

Summit Inn
Rt. 6 & 11
Scranton PA 18411
(717) 586-1211
$3 charge
Room rates $35-48

SOMERSET
Days Inn
I-70/76
Somerset PA 15501
(814) 445-9200
(800) 325-2525
Room rates from $57

**Always
Call
Ahead!**

STATE COLLEGE
Hampton Inn
1101 E. College Ave
State College PA 16801
(814) 231-1590
(800) 426-7866
Room rates $49-63

STROUDSBURG
Sheraton
1220 Main St.
Stroudsburg PA 18360
(717) 424-1930
(800) 325-3535
Room rates $90-110

WARREN
Super 8 Motel
204 Struthers St.
Warren PA 16365
(814) 723-8881
(800) 848-8888
pets with permission
Room rates from $41

Hampton Inn
210 Executive Dr.
Warrendale PA 16046
(412) 776-1000
(800) 426-7866
Room rates $52-58

WARWICK
Comfort Inn
1940 Post Rd.
Warwick PA 02886
(401) 732-0470
(800) 228-5150
Room rates $74-105

WASHINGTON
Knights Inn
125 Knights Inn Dr.
Washington PA 15301
(412) 223-8040
(800) 722-7220
Room rates $35-40

WAYNESBURG
Super 8 Motel
80 Miller Lane
Waynesburg PA 15370
(412) 627-8880
(800) 848-8888
pets with permission
Room rates from $39

WEST COLUMBIA
Super 8 Motel
2516 Augusta Hwy.
West Columbia PA 29169
(803) 796-4833
(800) 848-8888
Room rates from $32

WEST HAZELTON
Comfort Inn
SR 93 & Kiwanis Blvd.
West Hazelton PA 18201
(717) 455-9300
(800) 228-5150
Room rates $61-77

WEST MIDDLESEX
Comfort Inn
SR 18 & Wilson Rd.
West Middlesex PA 16159
(412) 342-7200
(800) 228-5150
Room rates $55-85

WILKES-BARRE
Friendship Inn
497 Kidder St.
Wilkes-Barre, PA 18702
(717) 823-8881
(800) 453-4511
$35-45

HoJo Inn
500 Kidder St.
Wilkes-Barre PA 18702
(717) 824-2411
Room rates $48-52

Days Inn
760 Kidder St.
Wilkes-Barre PA 18702
(717) 826-0111
(800) 325-2525
Room rates $46-55

YORK
Ramada Inn
US 30 & I-83
York PA 17402
(717) 846-4940
(800) 228-2828
Room rates $55-75

Holiday Inn
2600 Market St.
York PA 17402
(717) 755-1966
(800) 465-4329
Room rates $70-100

RHODE ISLAND
MIDDLETOWN
Comfort Inn
936 W. Main Rd.
Middletown RI 02840
(401) 846-7600
(800) 228-5150
$8/pets
Room rates $50-105

NEWPORT
Treadway Newport Resort
49 America's Cup Ave.
Newport RI 02840
(401) 847-9000
Room rates $85-200

PROVIDENCE
Econo Lodge
2138 Post Rd.
Providence, RI 02886
(401) 737-7400
(800) 446-6900
$55-75

SOUTH KINGSTOWN
Quality Inn
US 1 & SR 138 W
South Kingstown RI 02874
(401) 789-1051
(800) 228-5151
Room rates $55-105

SOUTH CAROLINA
AIKEN
Comfort Suites
3608 Richland Ave. W.
Aiken SC 29801
(803) 641-1100
(800) 228-5150
Room rates $49-125

ANDERSON
Quality Inn
3509 Clemson Blvd.
Anderson SC 29621
(803) 226-1000
(800) 228-5151
Room rates $62-69

CHARLESTON
Hampton Inn
4701 Arco Lane
Charleston SC 29418
(803) 554-7154
(800) 426-7866
Room rates $41-48

Quality Inn
125 Calhoun St.
Charleston SC 29401
(803) 722-3391
(800) 228-5151
Room rates $49-84

Econo Lodge
2237 Savannah Hwy.
Charleston, SC 29414
(803) 571-1880
(800) 446-6900
$30-45

HoJo Inn
3640 Dorchester Rd.
Charleston, SC 29405
(803) 554-4140
(800) 654-2000
$25-75

Comfort Inn
310 US 17 Bypass
Charleston SC 29464
(803) 884-5853
(800) 228-5150
Room rates $46-63

Days Inn
2998 W. Montague Ave.
Charleston SC 29405
(803) 747-4101
(800) 325-2525
$4/pets
Room rates $37-47

Motel 6
2551 Ashley Phosphate Rd.
Charleston SC 29418
(803) 572-6590
1 small pet per room
Reservations (505) 891-6161
Room rates $27-34

Motel 6
2058 Savannah Hwy
Charleston SC 29407
(803) 556-5144
1 small pet per room
Reservations (505) 891-6161
Room rates $27-34

CLEMSON
Ramada Inn
US 76 & 123
Clemson SC 29631
(803) 654-7501
(800) 228-2828
Room rates $49-65

COLUMBIA
Hampton Inn
1094 Chris Dr.
Columbia SC 29169
(803) 791-8940
(800) 426-7866
Room rates $41-48

Econo Lodge
494 Beltline Blvd.
Columbia, SC 29205
(803) 738-1642
(800) 446-6900
$30-35

Quality Inn
1029 Briargate Circle
Columbia SC 29212
(803) 772-0270
(800) 228-5151
Room rates $41-67

Quality Inn
1539 Horseshoe Dr.
Columbia SC 29223
(803) 736-1600
(800) 228-5151
Room rates $44-64

Days Inn
827 Bush River Rd.
Columbia SC 29210
(803) 772-9672
(800) 325-2525
Room rates $29-36

Econolodge
494 Piney Grove Rd.
Columbia SC 29210
(803) 731-4060
Room rates from $34

Motel 6
1144 Bush River Rd.
Columbia SC 29210
(803) 772-4910
1 small pet per room
Reservations (505) 891-6161
Room rates $27-34

CROMWELL
Super 8 Motel
1 Industrial Park Rd.
Cromwell SC 06416
(203) 632-8888
(800) 848-8888
pets with permission
Room rates $50-54

DILLON
Days Inn
I-95 & SC 9
Dillon SC 29536
(803) 774-6041
(800) 325-2525
$4/pets
Room rates $29-45

EASLEY
Days Inn
US Hwy 123 & SC 93
Easley SC 29640
(803) 859-9902
(800) 325-2525
$5/pets under 35 lbs.
Room rates $36-42

FLORENCE
Hampton Inn
1826 West Lucas St.
Florence SC 29501
(803) 662-7000
(800) 426-7866
Room rates $49-55

Ramada Inn
I-95 & US 52
Florence SC 29501
(803) 669-4241
(800) 228-2828
Room rates $48-58

Quality Inn
I-95 & TV Rd.
Florence SC 29503
(803) 669-1715
(800) 228-5151
Room rates $40-60

Days Inn
I-95 & US Hwy 76
Florence SC 29502
(803) 665-8550
(800) 325-2525
$4/pets
Room rates $29-37

GAFFNEY
Comfort Inn
I-85 & SR 11
Gaffney SC 29340
(803) 487-4200
(800) 228-5150
Room rates $42-60

GREENVILLE
Ramada Inn
1001 S. Church St.
Greenville SC 29601
(803) 232-7666
(800) 228-2828
Room rates $46-64

Days Inn
3905 Augusta Rd.
Greenville SC 29605
(803) 277-4010
(800) 325-2525
$5/pets
Room rates $32-36

Travelodge
850 Congaree Rd.
Greenville SC 29607
(803) 288-6221
(800) 255-3050
Room rates $52-56

Motel 6
224 Bruce Rd.
Greenville SC 29605
(803) 277-8630
1 small pet per room
Reservations (505) 891-6161
Room rates $27-34

HARDEEVILLE
Days Inn
I-95 & US 17
Hardeeville SC 29927
(803) 784-2221
(800) 325-2525
$2/pets
Room rates $35-48

LUGOFF
Days Inn
529 Hwy 601
Lugoff SC 29078
(803) 438-6990
(800) 325-2525
$5/day pet fee
Room rates $35-45

MANNING
Comfort Inn
I-95 @ SR 261
Manning SC 29102
(803) 473-7550
(800) 228-5150
Room rates $40-45

Days Inn
I-95 & US 301
Manning SC 29102
(803) 473-2596
(800) 325-2525
Room rates $30-50

MT. PLEASANT
Days Inn
261 Hwy 17 Bypass
Mt. Pleasant SC 29464
(803) 881-1800
(800) 325-2525
$4/pets
Room rates $39-48

NEWBERRY
Comfort Inn
1147 Wilson Rd.
Newberry SC 29108
(803) 276-1600
(800) 228-5150
Room rates $36-60

Daystop
Jct I-26 @ Hwy 34
Newberry SC 29108
(803) 276-2294
(800) 325-2525
$4/pets
Room rates $33-39

POINT SOUTH
Days Inn
Jct. I-95 & US 17
Point South SC 29945
(803) 726-8156
(800) 325-2525
$3/pets
Room rates $42-50

ROCK HILL
Holiday Inn
I-77 & US 21 North
Rock Hill SC 29730
(803) 329-1122
Room rates $53-62

Howard Johnson Lodge
2625 Cherry Rd.
Rock Hill, SC 29731
(803) 329-3121
(800) 654-2000
$45-60

SANTEE
Ramada Inn
I-95 & Rt. 6
Santee SC 29142
(803) 854-2191
(800) 228-2828
Room rates $48-58

Quality Inn
I-95 & SR 6
Santee SC 29142
(803) 854-2141
(800) 228-5151
Room rates $25-50

Days Inn
I-95 & SC 6
Santee SC 29142
(803) 845-2175
(800) 325-2525
$4/pets
Room rates $35-42

SIMPSONVILLE
Comfort Inn
I-385 @ Fairfield Rd.
Simpsonville SC 29681
(803) 963-2777
(800) 228-5150
Room rates $45-65

SPARTANBURG
Hampton Inn
4930 College Dr
Spartanburg SC 29301
(803) 576-6080
(800) 426-7866
Room rates $41-48

Ramada Inn
1000 Hearon Circle
Spartanburg SC 29303
(803) 578-7170
(800) 228-2828
Room rates $40-67

Always Call Ahead!

Quality Inn
578 N. Church St.
Spartanburg SC 29305
(803) 585-4311
(800) 228-5151
Room rates $42-48

Days Inn
1355 Boiling Springs Rd.
Spartanburg SC 29303
(803) 585-2413
(800) 325-2525
Room rates $39-43

Motel 6
105 Jones Rd.
Spartanburg SC 29303
(803) 573-6383
1 small pet per room
Reservations (505) 891-6161
Room rates $27-34

WALTERBORO
Comfort Inn
1109 Sniders Hwy
Walterboro SC 29488
(803) 538-5403
(800) 228-5150
Room rates $47-53

SOUTH DAKOTA
ABERDEEN
Super 8 Motel
2405 SE 6th Ave
Aberdeen SD 57401
(605) 229-5005
(800) 848-8888
pets with permission
Room rates from $36

BADLANDS NATIONAL PARK
Badlands Inn
SR 377
Badlands National Park SD 57750
(605) 433-5401
Room rates $28-38

CUSTER
Dakota Cowboy
208 Mt. Rushmore Rd.
Custer SD 57730
(605) 673-4659
$5 charge
Room rates $27-58

HILL CITY
Super 8 Motel
201 Main St.
Hill City SD 57745
(605) 574-4141
(800) 848-8888
pets with permission
Room rates from $31

HOT SPRINGS
Super 8 Motel
800 Mammoth St.
Hot Springs SD 57747
(605) 745-3888
(800) 848-8888
pets with deposit
Room rates from $35

HURON
Super 8 Motel
Dakota & 22nd St.
Huron SD 57350
(605) 352-0740
(800) 848-8888
pets with permission
Room rates from $34

LEMMON
Super 8 Motel
Hwy 12
Lemmon SD 57938
(605) 374-3711
(800) 848-8888
Room rates from $30

MADISON
Super 8 Motel
Jct. Hwy 34 & 81
Madison SD 57042
(605) 256-6931
(800) 848-8888
pets with permission
Room rates from $30

Always
Call
Ahead!

MILBANK
Super 8 Motel
E. Hwy 12
Milbank SD 57252
(605) 432-9288
(800) 848-8888
pets with permission
Room rates from $31

MILLER
Super 8 Motel
Hwys 14W. & 45N
Miller SD 57362
(605) 853-2721
(800) 848-8888
pets with permission
Room rates from $27

MITCHELL
Motel 6
1309 S. Ohlman St.
Mitchell SD 57301
(605) 996-0530
1 small pet per room
Reservations (505) 891-6161
Room rates $25-29

MOBRIDGE
Super 8 Motel
Hwy 12 W.
Mobridge SD 57601
(605) 845-7215
(800) 848-8888
pets with permission
Room rates from $29

MURDO
Super 8 Motel
604 E. 5th
Murdo SD 57559
(605) 669-2437
(800) 848-8888
pets with permission
Room rates from $27

N. SIOUX CITY
Super 8 Motel
1300 River Dr.
N. Sioux City SD 57049
(605) 232-4716
(800) 848-8888
pets with permission
Room rates from $35

SOUTH DAKOTA, Oacoma

OACOMA
Comfort Inn
I-90 &SR 16
Oacoma SD 57365
(605) 734-5593
(800) 228-5150
Room rates $33-71

PIERRE
Super 8 Motel
320 W. Sioux
Pierre SD 57501
(605) 224-1617
(800) 848-8888
pets with permission
Room rates from $35

RAPID CITY
Super 8 Motel
2124 LaCrosse St.
Rapid City SD 57701
(605) 348-8070
(800) 848-8888
pets with permission
Room rates from $31

Ramada Inn
1721 Lacrosse St.
Rapid City SD 57701
(605) 342-1300
(800) 228-2828
Very Seasonal Rates
Room rates $39-150

Quality Inn
2208 Mt. Rushmore Rd.
Rapid City SD 57709
(605) 342-3322
(800) 228-5151
Room rates $25-99

Comfort Inn
1550 N. LaCrosse
Rapid City SD 57701
(605) 348-2221
(800) 228-5150
Room rates $24-99

Motel 6
620 E. Latrobe St.
Rapid City SD 57701
(605) 343-3687
1 small pet per room
Reservations (505) 891-6161
Room rates $25-29

SIOUX FALLS
Super 8 Motel
4808 N. Cliff
Sioux Falls SD 57104
(605) 339-9212
(800) 848-8888
pets with permission
Room rates from $37

Comfort Inn
3216 S. Carolyn Ave
Sioux Falls SD 57106
(605) 361-2822
(800) 228-5150
Room rates $40-51

Travelodge
809 West Ave. North
Sioux Falls SD 57104
(605) 336-0230
(800) 255-3050
Room rates from $36

Motel 6
3009 W. Russell St.
Sioux Falls SD 57107
(605) 336-7800
1 small pet per room
Reservations (505) 891-6161
Room rates $25-29

Holiday Inn
100 8th St.
Sioux Falls SD 57102
(605) 339-2000
(800) 465-4329
Room rates $48-58

STURGIS
Super 8 Motel
I-90
Sturgis SD 57785
(605) 347-4447
(800) 848-8888
pets with permission
Room rates from $32

VERMILLION
Super 8 Motel
1208 E. Cherry St.
Vermillion SD 57069
(605) 642-8005
(800) 848-8888
pets with permission
Room rates from $37

WEBSTER
Super 8 Motel
W. Hwy 12
Webster SD 57274
(605) 345-4701
(800) 848-8888
pets with permission
Room rates from $27

WINNER
Super 8 Motel
902 E. Hwy 44
Winner SD 57580
(605) 842-0991
(800) 848-8888
pets with permission
Room rates from $30

YANKTON
Super 8 Motel
Hwy 50 E.
Yankton SD 57078
(605) 665-6510
(800) 848-8888
pets with permission
Room rates from $33

TENNESSEE

ALCOA
Ramada Inn
Hwy 129
Alcoa TN 37701
(615) 970-3060
(800) 228-2828
Room rates $44-54

ATHENS
Homestead Inn
Rt. 1
Athens TN 37303
(615) 744-9002
$2 charge
Room rates $30-35

Always
Call
Ahead!

BRISTOL
Quality Inn
I-81 & US 11 W. exit 74A
Bristol TN 37621
(615) 968-9119
(800) 228-5151
Room rates $46-58

HoJo Inn
975 Volunteer Pkwy
Bristol, TN 37620
(615) 968-9474
(800) 654-2000
$30-45

BROWNSVILLE
Daystop
2530 Anderson Ave.
Brownsville TN 38012
(901) 772-2676
(800) 325-2525
$3/pets
Room rates $34-37

CHATTANOOGA
Quality Inn
2100 S. Market St.
Chattanooga TN 37402
(615) 265-0551
(800) 228-5151
small pets
Room rates $39 & up

Comfort Inn
7717 Lee Hwy
Chattanooga TN 37421
(615) 894-5454
(800) 228-5150
Room rates $40-60

Comfort Hotel
407 Chestnut St.
Chattanooga TN 37402
(615) 756-5150
(800) 228-5150
Room rates $45-54

HoJo Inn
6616 Ringgold Rd.
Chattanooga, TN 37412
(615) 499-4432
(800) 654-2000
$25-35

Days Inn
101 E. 20th St.
Chattanooga TN 37408
(615) 267-9761
(800) 325-2525
Room rates $38-42

Travelodge
7725 Lee Hwy
Chattanooga TN 37421
(615) 899-2288
(800) 255-3050
Room rates from $36

Motel 6
7707 Lee Hwy.
Chattanooga TN 37421
(615) 892-7707
1 small pet per room
Reservations (505) 891-6161
Room rates $25-31

CLARKSVILLE
Ramada Inn
50 College St.
Clarksville TN 37040
(615) 552-3331
(800) 228-2828
Room rates $48-56

Comfort Inn
1112 SR 76
Clarksville TN 37043
(615) 358-2020
(800) 228-5150
Room rates $38-46

Days Inn
3065 Guthrie Hwy
Clarksville TN 37040
(615) 552-1155
(800) 325-2525
Room rates $36-40

Motel 6
881 Kraft St.
Clarksville TN 37040
(615) 552-0045
1 small pet per room
Reservations (505) 891-6161
Room rates $25-31

CLEVELAND
Quality Inn
2595 Georgetown Rd.
Cleveland TN 37311
(615) 476-8511
(800) 228-5151
Room rates $45-47

Days Inn
2550 Georgetown Rd.
Cleveland TN 37311
(615) 476-2112
(800) 325-2525
$5/pet
Room rates $40-45

COOKEVILLE
Howard Johnson
2021 Spring St.
Cookeville TN 38501
(615) 526-3333
(800) 654-2000
Room rates $30-45

CROSSVILLE
Ramada Inn
I-40 & SR 127
Crossville TN 38555
(615) 484-7581
(800) 228-2828
Room rates $41-49

DICKSON
Days Inn
Hwy 46 & I-40
Dickson TN 37055
(615) 446-7561
(800) 325-2525
$5/pets
Room rates $34-45

EAST RIDGE
Days Inn
1401 Mack Smith Rd.
East Ridge TN 37412
(615) 894-7480
(800) 325-2525
$4/pet
Room rates $35-45

Always
Call
Ahead!

ELIZABETHON
Comfort Inn
1515 US 19 E. Bypass
Elizabethon TN 37643
(615) 542-4466
(800) 228-5150
Room rates $41-85

GATLINBURG
Ramada Inn
756 Parkway
Gatlinburg TN 37738
(615) 436-7881
(800) 228-2828
Room rates $46-96

GOODLETTSVILLE
Motel 6
323 Cartwright St.
Goodlettsville TN 37072
(615) 859-9674
1 small pet per room
Reservations (505) 891-6161
Room rates $25-31

HURRICANE MILLS
Days Inn
Exit 143 on I-40
Hurricane Mills TN 37078
(615) 296-7647
(800) 325-2525
Room rates $39-55

JACKSON
Ramada Inn
1849 Hwy 45 Bypass
Jackson TN 38305
(901) 668-4222
(800) 228-2828
Room rates $45-56

Days Inn
1919 Hwy 45 Bypass
Jackson TN 38305
(901) 668-3444
(800) 325-2525
Room rates $32-38

JELLICO
Days Inn
I-75 & 25 W.
Jellico TN 37762
(615) 784-7281
(800) 325-2525
$4/pets
Room rates $28-38

JOHNSON CITY
Holiday Inn
2406 Roan St.
Johnson City TN 37601
(615) 282-2161
(800) 465-4329
Room rates $50-65

KINGSPORT
Comfort Inn
100 Indian Center Ct.
Kingsport TN 37660
(615) 378-4418
(800) 228-5150
$8/pets
Room rates $53-72

KINGSTON
Days Inn
I-40 & Gallaher Rd.
Kingston TN 37763
(615) 376-2069
(800) 325-2525
$5/pets
Room rates $38-48

KNOXVILLE
Hampton Inn
119 Cedar Ln
Knoxville TN 37912
(615) 689-1011
(800) 426-7866
Room rates $51-54

Hampton Inn
9128 Executive Park Blvd
Knoxville TN 37923
(615) 693-1101
(800) 426-7866
Room rates $52-55

Quality Inn
2306 Airport Hwy.
Knoxville TN 37701
(615) 970-3140
(800) 228-5151
Room rates $44-65

Quality Inn
7621 Kingston Pike
Knoxville TN 37919
(615) 693-8111
(800) 228-5151
Room rates $55-67

Comfort Inn
11748 Snyder Rd.
Knoxville TN 37922
(615) 675-5556
(800) 228-5150
Room rates $45-55

Comfort Inn
5334 Central Ave. Pike
Knoxville TN 37912
(615) 688-1010
(800) 228-5150
Room rates $40-72

Days Inn
206 S. Illinois
Knoxville TN 37830
(615) 483-5615
(800) 325-2525
$4/pets
Room rates $47-49

Days Inn
5423 Asheville Hwy @ I-40
Knoxville TN 37914
(615) 637-3511
(800) 325-2525
$5/day
Room rates $44-64

Days Inn
200 Lovell Rd. NW
Knoxville TN 37922
(615) 966-5801
(800) 325-2525
$4/pets
Room rates $36-43

Motel 6
10115 Watkins Blvd.
Knoxville TN 37922
(615) 675-5700
1 small pet per room
Reservations (505) 891-6161
Room rates $25-31

Holiday Inn
1315 Kirby Rd.
Knoxville TN 37909
(615) 584-3911
(800) 465-4329
Room rates $65-80

LEBANON
Comfort Inn
829 S. Cumberland St.
Lebanon TN 37087
(615) 444-1001
Room rates $30-55

MANCHESTER
Comfort Inn
I-24 & US 41
Manchester TN 37355
(615) 728-0800
(800) 228-5150
Room rates $35-37

MEMPHIS
Ramada Inn
2490 Mt. Moriah at I-240
Memphis TN 38115
(901) 362-8010
(800) 228-2828
Room rates $55-79

Comfort Inn
1581 Brooks Rd.
Memphis TN 38116
(901) 345-3344
(800) 228-5150
Room rates $40-60

Days Inn
5877 Poplar Ave.
Memphis TN 38119
(901) 767-6300
(800) 325-2525
Room rates $30-38

Days Inn
2949 Airways Blvd.
Memphis TN 38116
(901) 345-1250
(800) 325-2525
Room rates $37-42

Motel 6
1321 E. Brooks Rd.
Memphis TN 38116
(901) 346-0992
1 small pet per room
Reservations (505) 891-6161
Room rates $25-31

HoJo Inn
3265 Elvis Presley Blvd.
Memphis, TN 38116
(901) 398-9999
(800) 654-2000
$38-50

Sheraton
2411 Winchester Rd.
Memphis TN 38116
(901) 332-2370
(800) 325-3535
Room rates $49-75

MONTEAGLE
Days Inn
102 College St.
Monteagle TN 37356
(615) 924-2900
(800) 325-2525
small pets
Room rates $32-42

MURFREESBORO
Hampton Inn
2230 Old Fort Parkway
Murfreesboro TN 37130
(615) 896-1172
(800) 426-7866
Room rates $41-43

Comfort Inn
118 Westgate Blvd.
Murfreesboro TN 37130
(615) 896-5450
(800) 228-5150
Room rates $34-38

Days Inn
1855 S. Church St.
Murfreesboro TN 37130
(615) 896-5080
(800) 325-2525
Room rates $36-51

Motel 6
114 Chaffin Place
Murfreesboro TN 37129
(605) 890-8524
1 small pet per room
Reservations (505) 891-6161
Room rates $25-31

NASHVILLE
Hampton Inn
2407 Brick Church Pike
Nashville TN 37207
(615) 226-3300
(800) 426-7866
Room rates $41-49

Super 8 Motel
412 Robertson Ave.
Nashville TN 37209
(615) 356-0888
(800) 848-8888
pets with permission
Room rates from $39

Howard Johnson Lodge
2401 Brick Church Pike
Nashville, TN 37207
(615) 226-4600
(800) 654-2000
$40-70

Quality Inn
1407 Division St.
Nashville TN 37203
(615) 242-1631
(800) 228-5151
Room rates $52-62

Econo Lodge
1400 Brick Church pike
Nashville, TN 37207
(615) 228-5977
(800) 446-6900
$26-80

Quality Inn
1 International Plaza
Nashville TN 37217
(615) 361-7666
(800) 228-5151
Room rates $57-72

Comfort Inn
97 Wallace Rd.
Nashville TN 37211
(615) 833-6860
(800) 228-5150
Room rates $35-50

Holiday Inn
2516 Music Valley Dr.
Nashville TN 37214
(615) 889-0086
Room rates $38-65

Days Inn
I-65 & W. Trinity Lane
Nashville TN 37207
(615) 226-4500
(800) 325-2525
$4/pets
Room rates $38-44

Days Inn
I-24 & Bell Rd. exit 59
Nashville TN 37013
(615) 731-7800
(800) 325-2525
$4/pets
Room rates $29-49

TENNESSEE, Nashville

Days Inn
1300 Plaza Dr.
Nashville TN 37167
(615) 355-6161
(800) 325-2525
$5/pets
Room rates $43-64

Econo Lodge
1400 Brick Church pike
Nashville, TN 37207
(615) 228-5977
(800) 446-6900
$26-80

Motel 6
311 W. Trinity Lane
Nashville TN 37207
(615) 227-9696
1 small pet per room
Reservations (505) 891-6161
Room rates $25-31

Motel 6
95 Wallace Rd.
Nashville TN 37211
(615) 333-9933
1 small pet per room
Reservations (505) 891-6161
Room rates $25-31

Stouffer Hotel
611 Commerce St.
Nashville TN 37203
(615) 255-8400
small pets only
Room rates $140-180

Holiday Inn
2613 W. End Ave.
Nashville TN 37203
(615) 327-4707
(800) 465-4329
Room rates $55-60

OAK RIDGE
Comfort Inn
433 S. Rutgers Ave.
Oak Ridge TN 37830
(615) 481-8200
(800) 228-5150
Room rates $56-72

PIGEON FORGE
Econo Lodge
1165 Parkway
Pigeon Forge TN 37863
(615) 428-1231
(800) 553-2666
small pets only
Room rates $35-85

SWEETWATER
Quality Inn
I-75 & SR 68
Sweetwater TN 37874
(615) 337-3541
(800) 228-5151
Room rates $36-40

Comfort Inn
803 S. Main
Sweetwater TN 37874
(615) 337-6646
(800) 228-5150
Room rates $34-40

Daystop
I-75 & Hwy 68
Sweetwater TN 37874
(615) 337-4200
(800) 325-2525
Room rates $29-32

TEXAS
ABILENE
Econo Lodge
1633 W. Stamford
Abilene, TX 79601
(915) 673-5424
(800) 446-6900
$25-40

Quality Inn
505 Pine St.
Abilene TX 79604
(915) 676-0222
(800) 228-5151
Room rates $46-49

Econolodge
1633 W. Stamford St.
Abilene TX 79605
(915) 673-5424
Room rates $25-39

Days Inn
840 E. Hwy 80
Abilene TX 79601
(915) 677-8100
(800) 325-2525
small pets
Room rates $35-44

Motel 6
4951 W. Stamford St.
Abilene TX 79603
(915) 672-8462
1 small pet per room
Reservations (505) 891-6161
Room rates $25-37

ADDISON
Motel 6
4325 Beltline Rd.
Addison TX 75244
(214) 386-4577
1 small pet per room
Reservations (505) 891-6161
Room rates $25-37

ALICE
Days Inn
555 N. Johnson
Alice TX 78332
(512) 664-6616
(800) 325-2525
small pets
Room rates $40-45

AMARILLO
Hampton Inn
1700 I-40 East
Amarillo TX 79103
(806) 372-1425
(800) 426-7866
Room rates from $36

Travelodge
2801 I-40 W.
Amarillo TX 79106
(806) 355-9171
Room rates $40-56

Comfort Inn
1515 I-40 E.
Amarillo TX 79102
(806) 376-9993
(800) 228-5150
Room rates $40-57

Travelodge
3205 I-40 East
Amarillo TX 79104
(806) 372-8171
(800) 255-3050
Room rates $32-34

Travelodge
2035 Paramount Blvd
Amarillo TX 79109
(806) 353-3541
(800) 255-3050
Room rates from $30

Motel 6
2032 Paramount Blvd.
Amarillo TX 79109
(806) 355-6554
1 small pet per room
Reservations (505) 891-6161
Room rates $25-37

Motel 6
3930 I-40 E.
Amarillo TX 79103
(806) 374-6444
1 small pet per room
Reservations (505) 891-6161
Room rates $25-37

ARLINGTON
Days Inn
1195 N. Watson Rd.
Arlington TX 76011
(817) 649-8881
(800) 325-2525
$5/pets
Room rates $29-45

Days Inn
Hwy 157 @ Randol Mill
Arlington TX 76011
(817) 261-8444
(800) 325-2525
$5/pets
Room rates $32-42

Motel 6
2626 Randol Mill Rd. E.
Arlington TX 76011
(817) 649-0147
1 small pet per room
Reservations (505) 891-6161
Room rates $25-37

Ramada
700 Lamar Blvd.
Arlington TX 76011
(817) 265-7711
(800) 228-2828
must be quiet
Room rates $45-65

AUSTIN
Quality Inn
2200 S. Interregional
Austin TX 78704
(512) 444-0561
(800) 228-5151
Room rates $51-59

Comfort Inn
7928 Gessner Dr.
Austin TX 78753
(512) 339-7311
(800) 228-5150
Room rates $39-68

Days Inn
8210 N. I-35
Austin TX 78753
(512) 835-2200
(800) 325-2525
$5/small pets
Room rates $39-45

Motel 6
9420 N. Interstate 35
Austin TX 78753
(512) 339-6161
1 small pet per room
Reservations (505) 891-6161
Room rates $25-37

Motel 6
2707 Interregional Hwy. S.
Austin TX 78741
(512) 444-5882
1 small pet per room
Reservations (505) 891-6161
Room rates $25-37

Hilton - Airport
6000 Middle Fiskville Rd.
Austin TX 78752
(512) 451-5757
(800) 445-8667
$25 deposit
Room rates $70-100

Holiday Inn
8901 Business Park Dr.
Austin TX 78759
(512) 343-0888
(800) 465-4329
Room rates $60-65

BAYTOWN
La Quinta
4911 I-10 East
Baytown TX 77521
(713) 421-5566
(800) 531-5900
small pets only
Room rates $40-50

BEAUMONT
Daystop
4085 I-10 S.
Beaumont TX 77705
(409) 842-9341
(800) 325-2525
$5/pets
Room rates $32-37

Motel 6
2640 Interstate 10E
Beaumont TX 77703
(409) 898-7190
1 small pet per room
Reservations (505) 891-6161
Room rates $25-37

Hilton
2355 I-10 South
Beaumont TX 77705
(409) 842-3600
(800) 445-8667
$50 deposit
Room rates $65-110

Rodeway Inn
30 I-10 & Rusk St.
Beaumont, TX 77702
(409) 838-0581
(800) 424-4777
$25-40

Econo Lodge
1155 I-10 S.
Beaumont, TX 77701
(409) 835-5913
(800) 446-6900
$30-40

Always Call Ahead!

BELLMEAD
Motel 6
1509 Hogan Lane
Bellmead TX 76705
(817) 799-4957
1 small pet per room
Reservations (505) 891-6161
Room rates $25-37

BIG BEND NATIONAL PARK
Chisos Mountain Lodge
Basin Station
Big Bend National Park TX
79834-9801
(915) 477-2291
Room rates $50-65

BIG SPRING
Days Inn
300 Tulane Ave.
Big Spring TX 79720
(915) 263-7621
(800) 325-2525
Room rates $48-54

Motel 6
600 W. I-20
Big Springs TX 79720
(915) 267-1695
1 small pet per room
Reservations (505) 891-6161
Room rates $25-37

BROWNSVILLE
Motel 6
2255 N. Expwy
Brownsville TX 78521
(512) 546-4699
1 small pet per room
Reservations (505) 891-6161
Room rates $25-37

Holiday Inn
1945 Expwy North
Brownsville TX 78520
(512) 546-4591
(800) 465-4329
Room rates $50-60

BROWNWOOD
Comfort Inn
410 E. Commerce St.
Brownwood TX 76801
(915) 646-3511
(800) 228-5150
Room rates $40-49

BURLESON
Days Inn
329 S. Burleson Blvd.
Burleson TX 76028
(817) 447-1111
(800) 325-2525
$10 pet deposit
Room rates $32-36

CANTON
Days Inn
Hwy 19
Canton TX 75103
(214) 567-6588
(800) 325-2525
$5/pets
Room rates $35-40

CARROLLTON
Days Inn
1735 S. I-35
Carrolton TX 75006
(214) 242-6431
(800) 325-2525
Room rates $42-45

CLUTE
Motel 6
1000 Hwy 332
Clute TX 77531
(409) 265-4764
1 small pet per room
Reservations (505) 891-6161
Room rates $25-37

COLLEGE STATION
Ramada Inn
1502 Texas Ave.
College Station TX 77840
(409) 693-9891
(800) 228-2828
Room rates $44-60

Comfort Inn
104 Texas Ave. S.
College Station TX 77840
(409) 846-7333
(800) 228-5150
$5/pets
Room rates $45-60

Motel 6
2327 Texas Ave.
College Station TX 77840
(409) 696-3379
1 small pet per room
Reservations (505) 891-6161
Room rates $25-37

CONROE
Motel 6
820 I-45 S.
Conroe TX 77304
(409) 760-4003
1 small pet per room
Reservations (505) 891-6161
Room rates $25-37

CORPUS CHRISTI
Comfort Inn
6301 I-37
Corpus Christi TX 78409
(512) 289-6925
(800) 228-5150
$25 deposit
Room rates $34-52

Days Inn
I-37 & 901 Navigation Blvd.
Corpus Christi TX 78408
(512) 888-8599
(800) 325-2525
$6/pets
Room rates $34-62

Motel 6
8202 S. Padre Island Dr.
Corpus Christi TX 78412
(512) 991-8858
1 small pet per room
Reservations (505) 891-6161
Room rates $25-37

Motel 6
845 Lantana St.
Corpus Christi TX 78408
(512) 289-9397
1 small pet per room
Reservations (505) 891-6161
Room rates $25-37

Holiday Inn
1102 Shoreline Dr.
Corpus Christi TX 78401
(512) 883-5731
(800) 465-4329
Room rates $60-85

DALHART
Super 8 Motel
Jct of Hwys 87 & 385
Dalhart TX 79022
(806) 249-8526
(800) 848-8888
pets with permission
Room rates from $30

DALLAS
Ramada Inn
3232 W Mockingbird Ln.
Dallas TX 75235
(214) 357-5601
(800) 228-2828
Room rates $53-72

Comfort Inn
1601 E. Division
Dallas TX 76011
(817) 261-2300
(800) 228-5150
Room rates $44-54

Econo Lodge
4213 South Fwy.
Dallas, TX 76115
(817) 923-1987
(800) 446-6900
$30-50

Ramada Inn
13700 LBJ Fwy
Dallas TX 75041
(214) 279-6751
Room rates $48-56

Royal Hotel
1401 S. Stemmons
Dallas TX 75067
(214) 436-0080
$25 fee
Room rates $34-42

Days Inn
1575 Regal Row
Dallas TX 75247
(214) 638-6100
(800) 325-2525
Room rates $60-74

Ramada Inn
1011 S. Akard St.
Dallas TX 75215
(214) 421-1083
small only
Room rates $55-135

Travelodge
4500 Harry Hines Blvd
Dallas TX 75219
(214) 522-6650
(800) 255-3050
Room rates $47-79

Motel 6
2753 Forest Lane
Dallas TX 75234
(214) 620-2828
1 small pet per room
Reservations (505) 891-6161
Room rates $25-37

Motel 6
4610 S. R.L. Thornton Fwy
Dallas TX 75224
(214) 372-5924
1 small pet per room
Reservations (505) 891-6161
Room rates $25-37

Motel 6
9626 C.F. Hawn Fwy
Dallas TX 75217
(214) 286-7952
1 small pet per room
Reservations (505) 891-6161
Room rates $25-37

Embassy Suites
2727 Stemmons Fwy.
Dallas TX 75207
(214) 630-5332
(800) 362-2779
$25 charge
Room rates $100-125

DEL RIO
Motel 6
2115 F Avenue
Del Rio TX 78840
(512) 774-2115
1 small pet per room
Reservations (505) 891-6161
Room rates $25-37

DENTON
Excel Inn
4211 I-35E North
Denton TX 76201
(817) 383-1471
Room rates $31-35

Motel 6
4125 I-35 N.
Denton TX 76201
(817) 566-4798
1 small pet per room
Reservations (505) 891-6161
Room rates $25-37

EAGLE PASS
Eagle Pass Inn
2150 Hwy. 277 North
Eagle Pass TX 78852
(512) 773-9531
Room rates $30-40

EL PASO
Ramada Inn
113 W. Missouri
El Paso TX 79901
(915) 544-3300
(800) 228-2828
Room rates $45-125

Comfort Inn
900 Yarbrough Dr.
El Paso TX 79915
(915) 594-9111
(800) 228-5150
$25 deposit
Room rates $44-75

Motel 6
7840 N. Mesa St.
El Paso TX 79932
(915) 584-2129
1 small pet per room
Reservations (505) 891-6161
Room rates $25-37

Motel 6
11049 Gateway Blvd. W.
El Paso TX 79935
(915) 594-8533
1 small pet per room
Reservations (505) 891-6161
Room rates $25-37

Marriott
1600 Airway Blvd.
El Paso TX 79925
(915) 779-3300
(800) 228-9290
Room rates $55-110

FOREST LANE
Motel 6
2660 Forest Lane
Forest Lane TX 75234
(214) 484-9111
1 small pet per room
Reservations (505) 891-6161
Room rates $25-37

FREDRICKSBURG
Comfort Inn
908 S. Adams St.
Fredricksburg TX 78624
(512) 997-9811
(800) 228-5150
Room rates from $49

FT. STOCKTON
Motel 6
3001 W. Dickinson Blvd.
Ft. Stockton TX 79735
(915) 336-9737
1 small pet per room
Reservations (505) 891-6161
Room rates $25-37

Days Inn
8709 Airport Freeway
Ft. Worth TX 76180
(817) 656-8881
(800) 325-2525
Room rates $39-55

FT. WORTH
Great Western Inn
913 E. Northside Dr.
Ft. Worth TX 76102
(817) 332-9693
Room rates $31-34

Days Inn
8500 I-30 & Las Vegas Trail
Ft. Worth TX 76108
(817) 246-4961
(800) 325-2525
pets with $5 deposit
Room rates $34-38

Econo Lodge
9386 LBJ Fwy.
Ft. Worth, TX 75243
(214) 690-1220
(800) 446-6900
$40-50

Motel 6
3271 I-35 W.
Ft. Worth TX 76106
(817) 625-4359
1 small pet per room
Reservations (505) 891-6161
Room rates $25-37

Motel 6
6600 S. Fwy
Ft. Worth TX 76134
(817) 293-8595
1 small pet per room
Reservations (505) 891-6161
Room rates $25-37

Motel 6
4433 S. Fwy
Ft. Worth TX 76115
(817) 921-4900
1 small pet per room
Reservations (505) 891-6161
Room rates $25-37

Motel 6
8701 I-20 W.
Ft. Worth TX 76116
(817) 244-9740
1 small pet per room
Reservations (505) 891-6161
Room rates $25-37

Ramada Midtown
1401 University Dr.
Ft. Worth TX 76107
(817) 336-9311
Room rates $55-65

GALVESTON
Motel 6
7404 Avenue J
Galveston TX 77554
(409) 740-3794
1 small pet per room
Reservations (505) 891-6161
Room rates $25-37

La Quinta
1402 Seawall Blvd.
Galveston TX 77550
(409) 763-1224
(800) 531-5900
Room rates $45-75

Best Western
5914 Seawall Blvd.
Galveston Island TX 77551
(409) 740-1261
Seasonal Rates
Room rates $40-80

GARLAND
Days Inn
6222 Beltline Rd.
Garland TX 75043
(214) 226-7621
(800) 325-2525
Room rates $35-38

Motel 6
436 W I-30 & Beltline Rd.
Garland TX 75043
(214) 226-7140
1 small pet per room
Reservations (505) 891-6161
Room rates $25-37

GEORGETOWN
Ramada Inn
333 N I-35
Georgetown TX 78628
(512) 869-2541
(800) 228-2828
Room rates $47-55

Comfort Inn
1005 Leander Rd.
Georgetown TX 78628
(512) 863-7504
(800) 228-5150
Room rates $40-50

GRAND PRAIRIE
Motel 6
406 E. Safari Blvd.
Grand Prairie TX 75050
(214) 642-9424
1 small pet per room
Reservations (505) 891-6161
Room rates $25-37

GREENVILLE
Motel 6
5109 I-30
Greenville TX 75401
(214) 455-0515
1 small pet per room
Reservations (505) 891-6161
Room rates $25-37

GROVES
Motel 6
5201 E. Parkway
Groves TX 77619
(409) 962-2211
1 small pet per room
Reservations (505) 891-6161
Room rates $25-37

HALTOM CITY
Great Western Inn
5050 Northeast Loop 820
Haltom City TX 76117
(817) 485-9828
small only
Room rates $32-35

Motel 6
6401 Airport Fwy
Haltom City TX 76117
(817) 834-7136
1 small pet per room
Reservations (505) 891-6161
Room rates $25-37

HARLINGEN
Motel 6
224 S. US Expwy 77
Harlingen TX 78550
(512) 421-4200
1 small pet per room
Reservations (505) 891-6161
Room rates $25-37

HENDERSON
Days Inn
1500 US 259 S.
Henderson TX 75652
(903) 657-9561
(800) 325-2525
Room rates $35-42

HILLSBORO
Ramada Inn
I-35 & Hwy. 22
Hillsboro TX 76645
(817) 582-3493
(800) 228-2828
Room rates $38-44

HOUSTON
Super 8 Motel
15350 JFK Blvd.
Houston TX 77032
(713) 442-1830
(800) 848-8888
pets with permission
Room rates from $37

Rodeway Inn
3135 Southwest Fwy.
Houston, TX 77098
(713) 526-1071
(800) 424-4777
$35-50

Ramada Inn
7787 Katy Freeway @ I-10
Houston TX 77024
(713) 681-5000
(800) 228-2828
Room rates $39-69

Ramada Inn
12801 NW Fwy
Houston TX 77040
(713) 462-9977
(800) 228-2828
Room rates $69-79

Ramada Inn
4225 N Freeway
Houston TX 77022
(713) 695-6011
(800) 228-2828
Room rates $48-58

Ramada Inn
1301 NASA Road One
Houston TX 77058
(713) 488-0220
(800) 228-2828
Room rates $60-64

Motel 6
8911 SR 146
Houston TX 77520
(713) 576-5777
1 small pet
Room rates $40-80

Quality Inn
6115 Will Clayton Pkwy
Houston TX 77205
(713) 446-9131
(800) 228-5151
Room rates $59-67

Motel 6
16884 Northwest Fwy
Houston TX 77040
(713) 937-7056
1 small pet per room
Room rates $36-42

Days Inn
17607 Eastex Fwy
Houston TX 77396
(713) 446-4611
(800) 325-2525
$10 charge
Room rates $43-47

Travelodge
2828 Southwest Frwy
Houston TX 77098
(713) 526-4571
(800) 255-3050
Room rates $48-58

Travelodge
4204 North Hwy 6
Houston TX 77084
(713) 859-2233
(800) 255-3050
small + $5/day
Room rates from $38

Motel 6
3223 S. Loop W.
Houston TX 29303
(713) 664-6425
1 small pet per room
Reservations (505) 891-6161
Room rates $25-37

Motel 6
9638 Plainfield Rd.
Houston TX 77036
(713) 778-0008
1 small pet per room
Reservations (505) 891-6161
Room rates $25-37

Econo Lodge
10525 Eastex Fwy.
Houston, TX 77093
(713) 692-4000
(800) 446-6900
$32-50

Econo Lodge
7905 S. Main St.
Houston, TX 77025
(713) 667-8200
(800) 446-6900
$25-45

Always Call Ahead!

Texas, Houston

Hyatt Regency
1200 Louisianna St.
Houston TX 77002
(713) 654-1234
(800) 233-1234
$50 charge
Room rates $120-160

Marriott
5150 Westheimer Rd.
Houston TX 77056
(713) 961-1500
(800) 228-9290
$50 deposit
Room rates $100-145

Holiday Inn
6701 Main St.
Houston TX 77030
(713) 797-1110
(800) 465-4329
under 25 lbs
Room rates $70-90

Marriott
255 Beltway North
Houston TX 77060
(713) 875-4000
(800) 228-9290
Room rates $60-152

Holiday Inn
3702 Sam Houston Pkwy N
Houston TX 77032
(713) 449-2311
(800) 465-4329
Room rates $60-90

HUNTSVILLE
Motel 6
1607 I-45
Huntsville TX 77340
(409) 291-6927
1 small pet per room
Reservations (505) 891-6161
Room rates $25-37

HURST
Ramada Inn
Loop 820 & Hwy 183
Hurst TX 76053
(817) 284-9461
(800) 228-2828
Room rates $54-66

IRVING
Holiday Inn
4441 Hwy 114
Irving TX 75063
(214) 929-8181
(800) 465-4329
under 50 lbs
Room rates $75-100

La Quinta
4105 Airport Fwy.
Irving TX 75062
(214) 252-6546
(800) 531-5900
Room rates $40-55

JASPER
Ramada Inn
239 E Gibson
Jasper TX 75951
(409) 384-9021
(800) 228-2828
Room rates $47-57

JUNCTION
Days Inn
111 S. Martinez St.
Junction TX 76849
(915) 446-3730
(800) 325-2525
$4/pets
Room rates $39-49

KILGORE
Ramada Inn
3501 Hwy 259 N
Kilgore TX 75662
(214) 983-3456
(800) 228-2828
Room rates $46-52

KILLEEN
Howard Johnson Lodge
404 Hwy 440
Killeen, TX 76541
(817) 526-4632
(800) 654-2000
$35-45

KINGSVILLE
Motel 6
101 N. US 77
Kingsville TX 78363
(512) 592-5106
1 small pet per room
Reservations (505) 891-6161
Room rates $25-37

LAREDO
Motel 6
5920 San Bernardo Ave.
Laredo TX 78041
(512) 722-8133
1 small pet per room
Reservations (505) 891-6161
Room rates $25-37

Motel 6
5310 San Bernardo Ave.
Laredo TX 78041
(512) 725-8187
1 small pet per room
Reservations (505) 891-6161
Room rates $25-37

Howard Johnson
1 - Main Ave.
Laredo TX 78040
(512) 722-2411
(800) 654-2000
Room rates $50-75

LONGVIEW
Comfort Inn
203 N. Spur 63
Longview TX 75601
(903) 757-7858
(800) 228-5150
Room rates $38-42

Motel 6
110 W. Access Rd.
Longview TX 75603
(903) 758-5256
1 small pet per room
Reservations (505) 891-6161
Room rates $25-37

La Quinta
502 Access Rd.
Longview TX 75602
(903) 757-3663
(800) 531-5900
Room rates $40-50

LUBBOCK
Days Inn
2401 4th St.
Lubbock TX 79415
(806) 747-7111
(800) 325-2525
Room rates $40-50

Motel 6
909 66th St.
Lubbock TX 79412
(806) 745-5541
1 small pet per room
Reservations (505) 891-6161
Room rates $25-37

Holiday Inn
801 Q Ave.
Lubbock TX 79401
(806) 763-1200
(800) 465-4329
Room rates $70-85

LUFKIN
Days Inn
2130 S. 1st
Lufkin TX 75901
(409) 639-3301
(800) 325-2525
Room rates $42-47

Motel 6
1110 S. Timberland
Lufkin TX 75901
(409) 637-7850
1 small pet per room
Reservations (505) 891-6161
Room rates $25-37

Park Inn
4601 Medford Dr.
Lufkin TX 75901
(409) 634-2201
Room rates $30-40

MARSHALL
Days Inn
100 I-20 W. & Hwy 59
Marshall TX 75670
(214) 935-7923
(800) 325-2525
Room rates $37-42

Motel 6
300 I-20 E.
Marshall TX 75670
(214) 935-4393
1 small pet per room
Reservations (505) 891-6161
Room rates $25-37

MCALLEN
Motel 6
700 US 83 Expwy
McAllen TX 78501
(512) 687-3700
1 small pet per room
Reservations (505) 891-6161
Room rates $25-37

Sheraton
2105 10th St.
McAllen TX 78503
(512) 682-2445
(800) 325-3535
Room rates $60-110

MCKINNEY
Comfort Inn
2104 N. Central Expwy
McKinney TX 75070
(214) 548-8888
(800) 228-5150
Room rates $42-50

MESQUITE
Days Inn
3601 Hwy 80
Mesquite TX 75150
(214) 279-6561
(800) 325-2525
Room rates $40-48

Motel 6
3629 Hwy 80
Mesquite TX 75150
(214) 613-1662
1 small pet per room
Reservations (505) 891-6161
Room rates $25-37

MIDLAND
Ramada Inn
3100 West Wall St.
Midland TX 79701
(915) 699-4144
(800) 228-2828
$50 deposit
Room rates $48-52

Motel 6
1000 S. Midkiff
Midland TX 79701
(915) 697-3197
1 small pet per room
Reservations (505) 891-6161
Room rates $25-37

La Quinta
4130 Wall St.
Midland TX 79703
(915) 697-9900
(800) 531-5900
Room rates $40-50

MT. PLEASANT
Days Inn
2401 N. Ferguson Rd.
Mt. Pleasant TX 75455
(214) 572-1771
(800) 325-2525
Room rates $34-40

NACOGDOCHES
La Quinta
3215 South St.
Nacogdoches TX 75961
(409) 560-5453
(800) 531-5900
Room rates $35-40

ODEM
Daystop
Hwy 77 South
Odem TX 78370
(512) 368-2166
(800) 325-2525
$3/pets + mgr approval
Room rates $33-38

ODESSA
Motel 6
2925 E. Hwy 80
Odessa TX 79761
(915) 332-2600
1 small pet per room
Reservations (505) 891-6161
Room rates $25-37

Motel 6
200 E I-20 Service Rd.
Odessa TX 79766
(915) 333-4025
1 small pet per room
Reservations (505) 891-6161
Room rates $25-37

Lexington Hotel
3031 Hwy 80 East
Odessa TX 79761
(915) 333-9678
Room rates $35-40

TEXAS, Orange

ORANGE
Ramada Inn
2610 I-10
Orange TX 77630
(409) 883-0231
(800) 228-2828
Room rates $50-52

Days Inn
2900 I-10
Orange TX 77630
(409) 883-9981
(800) 325-2525
Room rates $39-41

Motel 6
4407 27th St.
Orange TX 77630
(409) 883-4891
1 small pet per room
Reservations (505) 891-6161
Room rates $25-37

OZONA
Daystop
820 Loop 466
Ozona TX 76943
(915) 392-2631
(800) 325-2525
Room rates $28-30

PALESTINE
Days Inn
100 E. Palestine Ave.
Palestine TX 75801
(214) 729-3151
(800) 325-2525
Room rates $39-43

PECOS
Motel 6
3002 S. Cedar
Pecos TX 79772
(915) 445-9034
1 small pet per room
Reservations (505) 891-6161
Room rates $25-37

PLAINVIEW
Holiday Inn
4005 Olton Rd.
Plainview TX 79072
(806) 293-4181
(800) 465-4329
Room rates $40-50

PLANO
Motel 6
2550 N. Central Expwy
Plano TX 75074
(214) 578-1626
1 small pet per room
Reservations (505) 891-6161
Room rates $25-37

Holiday Inn
700 Central Pkwy East
Plano TX 75074
(214) 881-1881
(800) 465-4329
Room rates $40-55

PORT ARTHUR
Ramada Inn
3801 Hwy 73
Port Arthur TX 77642
(409) 962-9858
(800) 228-2828
Room rates $56-71

Econo Lodge
2811 Memorial Blvd.
Port Arthur, TX 77640
(409) 985-9316
(800) 446-6900
$25-35

PORT LAVACA
Days Inn
2100 North Hwy 35 Bypass
Port Lavaca TX 77979
(512) 552-4511
(800) 325-2525
Room rates $41-66

ROCKPORT
Days Inn
1212 Laurel
Rockport TX 78382
(512) 729-6379
(800) 325-2525
Room rates $43-48

SAN ANGELO
Inn of the Conchos
2021 N. Bryant Blvd.
San Angelo TX 76903
(915) 658-2811
limited pet rooms
Room rates $42-46

Riverview Inn
333 Rio Concho Dr.
San Angelo TX 76903
(915) 655-8151
small pets, limited rooms
Room rates from $45

Motel 6
311 N. Bryant
San Angelo TX 76903
(915) 658-8061
1 small pet per room
Reservations (505) 891-6161
Room rates $25-37

SAN ANTONIO
Hampton Inn
4803 Manitou Dr.
San Antonio TX 78228
(512) 684-9966
(800) 426-7866
Room rates $48-54

Rodeway Inn
6804 I-10 W.
San Antonio, TX 78201
(512) 734-7111
(800) 424-4777
$36-55

Ramada Inn
1111 NE Loop 410
San Antonio TX 78209
(512) 828-9031
(800) 228-2828
Seasonal Rates
Room rates $48-95

Ramada Inn
1131 Austin Hwy
San Antonio TX 78209
(512) 824-1441
(800) 228-2828
Room rates $34-52

**Always
Call
Ahead!**

Rodeway Inn
900 N. Main Ave.
San Antonio, TX 78233
(512) 223-2951
(800) 424-4777
$40-90

Days Inn
3443 I-35 North
San Antonio TX 78219
(512) 225-4521
(800) 325-2525
Room rates $44-64

Days Inn
I-10 & 4039 E. Houston St.
San Antonio TX 78220
(512) 337-6753
(800) 325-2525
Room rates $44-64

Travelodge
405 Broadway
San Antonio TX 78205
(512) 222-9401
(800) 255-3050
Room rates $45-55

Motel 6
211 N. Pecos St.
San Antonio TX 78207
(512) 225-1111
1 small pet per room
Reservations (505) 891-6161
Room rates $25-37

Motel 6
138 N. W. White Rd.
San Antonio TX 78219
(512) 333-1850
1 small pet per room
Reservations (505) 891-6161
Room rates $25-37

Motel 6
9503 Interstate Hwy 35N.
San Antonio TX 78233
(512) 650-4419
1 small pet per room
Reservations (505) 891-6161
Room rates $25-37

Motel 6
9400 Wurzbach Rd.
San Antonio TX 78240
(512) 690-8000
1 small pet per room
Reservations (505) 891-6161
Room rates $25-37

Motel 6
2185 SW Loop 410
San Antonio TX 78227
(512) 673-9020
1 small pet per room
Reservations (505) 891-6161
Room rates $25-37

Marriott
711 Riverwalk
San Antonio TX 78205
(512) 224-4555
(800) 228-9290
$150 deposit
Room rates $140-170

Embassy Suites
10110 Hwy. 281 North
San Antonio TX 78216
(512) 525-9999
(800) 362-2779
$25 charge
Room rates $99-110

Holiday Inn
3855 Pan Am Hwy.
San Antonio TX 78219
(512) 226-4361
(800) 465-4329
Room rates $50-65

SAN MARCOS
Motel 6
1321 I-35 N.
San Marcos TX 78666
(512) 396-8705
1 small pet per room
Reservations (505) 891-6161
Room rates $25-37

SHERMAN
Super 8 Motel
111 E. Hwy 1417
Sherman TX 75090
(214) 868-9325
(800) 848-8888
pets with permission
Room rates from $30

SOUTH PADRE ISLAND
Best Western
5701 Padre Blvd.
South Padre Island TX 78597
(512) 761-4913
(800) 528-1234
$25 deposit, small pets
Room rates $45-110

SWEETWATER
Motel 6
510 NW Georgia
Sweetwater TX 79556
(915) 235-4387
1 small pet per room
Reservations (505) 891-6161
Room rates $25-37

TEMPLE
Ramada Inn
400 SW Dodgen Loop 363
Temple TX 76501
(817) 773-1515
(800) 228-2828
Room rates $44-51

Days Inn
5505 S. General Bruce Dr.
Temple TX 76502
(817) 778-0962
(800) 325-2525
Room rates $34-40

Motel 6
1100 N. General Bruce Dr.
Temple TX 76504
(817) 778-0272
1 small pet per room
Reservations (505) 891-6161
Room rates $25-37

Econo Lodge
1001 N. General Bruce Dr.
Temple, TX 76504
(817) 771-1688
(800) 446-6900
$26-40

TEXARKANA
Ramada Inn
I-30 @ Summerhill Road
Texarkana TX 75503
(214) 794-3131
(800) 228-2828
Room rates $45-51

Always
Call
Ahead!

TEXAS, Texarkana

Motel 6
1924 Hampton Rd
Texarkana TX 75503
(214) 793-1413
1 small pet per room
Reservations (505) 891-6161
Room rates $25-37

Holiday Inn
5100 State Line Ave.
Texarkana TX 75502
(501) 774-3521
(800) 465-4329
Room rates $55-75

TYLER
Travelodge
2616 Loop 323 North
Tyler TX 75702
(903) 593-8361
pets under 35 lbs.
Room rates $37-47

Days Inn
3300 Mineola Hwy
Tyler TX 75702
(214) 595-2451
(800) 325-2525
Room rates $35-55

Motel 6
3236 Brady Gentry Pkwy
Tyler TX 77901
(512) 573-1273
1 small pet per room
Reservations (505) 891-6161
Room rates $25-37

UNIVERSAL CITY
Comfort Inn
200 Palisades
Universal City TX 78148
(512) 659-5851
(800) 228-5150
Room rates $38-52

VAN HORN
Comfort Inn
1601 W. Broadway St.
Van Horn TX 79855
(915) 283-2211
(800) 228-5150
Room rates $40-44

Days Inn
600 East Broadway
Van Horn TX 79855
(915) 283-2401
(800) 325-2525
$5/pets
Room rates $40-50

VICTORIA
La Quinta
7603 Navarro St.
Victoria TX 77904
(512) 572-3585
(800) 531-5900
Room rates $35-45

Holiday Inn
2705 Houston Hwy.
Victoria TX 77901
(512) 575-0251
(800) 465-4329
Room rates $40-50

WACO
Ramada Inn
4201 Franklin Ave.
Waco TX 76710
(817) 772-9440
(800) 228-2828
Room rates $44-51

Days Inn
1504 W. I-35 N.
Waco TX 76705
(817) 799-8585
(800) 325-2525
$5/pets
Room rates from $40

Holiday Inn
1001 Lake Brazos Dr.
Waco TX 76704
(817) 753-0261
(800) 465-4329
Room rates $55-65

WEBSTER
Motel 6
1001 W. NASA Rd. 1
Webster TX 77598
(713) 332-4581
1 small pet per room
Reservations (505) 891-6161
Room rates $25-37

WICHITA FALLS
Hampton Inn
1317 Kenley Ave.
Wichita Falls TX 76305
(817) 766-3300
(800) 426-7866
Room rates $41-48

Days Inn
1211 Central Expwy
Wichita Falls TX 76305
(817) 723-5541
(800) 325-2525
$5/pets
Room rates $42-48

WITCHITA FALLS
Motel 6
1812 Maurine St.
Witchita Falls TX 76304
(817) 322-8817
1 small pet per room
Reservations (505) 891-6161
Room rates $25-37

UTAH
BEAVER
Beaver Lodge
355 Main St.
Beaver UT 84713
(801) 438-2462
Room rates $24-30

CEDAR CITY
Quality Inn
18 S. Main St
Cedar City UT 84720
(801) 586-2433
(800) 228-5151
Room rates $38-68

Rodeway Inn
281 Main St.
Cedar City UT 84720
(801) 586-9916
(800) 228-2000
Room rates $30-60

FARMINGTON
Country Creek Inn
1100 US 89
Farmington UT 84037
(801) 544-3439
$5 deposit
Room rates $25-40

Always Call Ahead!

128

Green River, UTAH

GREEN RIVER
Motel 6
964 E. Main
Green River UT 84525
(801) 564-3436
1 small pet per room
Reservations (505) 891-6161
Room rates $27-33

LOGAN
Super 8 Motel
865 Hwy 89-91 S.
Logan UT 84321
(801) 753-8883
(800) 848-8888
pets with permission
Room rates from $32

MIDVALE
Motel 6
496 N. Catalpa
Midvale UT 801561
(801) 561-0058
1 small pet per room
Reservations (505) 891-6161
Room rates $27-33

MOAB
Ramada Inn
182 S. Main Street
Moab UT 84532
(801) 259-7141
(800) 228-2828
Room rates $39-68

MONUMENT VALLEY
Goulding's Trading Post
US 163 @ Goulding's Jct.
Monument Valley UT 84536
(801) 727-3231
Room rates $50-70

OGDEN
Super 8 Motel
1508 W. 2100 S.
Ogden UT 84401
(801) 731-7100
(800) 848-8888
pets with permission
Room rates from $37

Quality Inn
1500 W. Riverdale Rd.
Ogden UT 84405
(801) 627-2880
(800) 228-5151
Room rates $58-69

Motel 6
1455 Washington Blvd.
Ogden UT 84404
(801) 627-4560
1 small pet per room
Reservations (505) 891-6161
Room rates $27-33

Best Western
247 24th St.
Ogden UT 84401
(801) 627-1190
$25 fee
Room rates $70-100

PAYSON
Comfort Inn
830 N. Main St.
Payson UT 84651
(801) 465-4861
(800) 228-5150
Room rates $52-60

PRICE
Days Inn
838 Westwood Blvd.
Price UT 84501
(801) 637-8880
(800) 325-2525
Room rates $42-51

PROVO
Comfort Inn
1555 Canyon Rd.
Provo UT 84604
(801) 374-6020
(800) 228-5150
Room rates $54-70

Days Inn
1675 N. 200 West
Provo UT 84604
(801) 375-8600
(800) 325-2525
Room rates $43-48

Travelodge
124 South University Ave.
Provo UT 84601
(801) 373-1974
(800) 255-3050
Room rates $32-34

Motel 6
1600 S. University Ave.
Provo UT 84601
(801) 375-5064
1 small pet per room
Reservations (505) 891-6161
Room rates $27-33

SALT LAKE CITY
Quality Inn
4465 Century Dr.
Salt Lake City UT 84123
(801) 268-2533
(800) 228-5151
Room rates $42-80

Quality Inn
154 W. 600 South
Salt Lake City UT 84101
(801) 521-2930
(800) 228-5151
Room rates $61-84

Econo Lodge
715 North Temple
Salt Lake City, UT 84116
(801) 363-0062
(800) 446-6900
$38-60

Comfort Inn
200 N. Admiral Byrd Rd.
Salt Lake City UT 84116
(801) 537-7444
(800) 228-5150
Room rates $54-90

Days Inn
1900 West North Temple
Salt Lake City UT 84116
(801) 539-8538
(800) 325-2525
Room rates $36-50

Travelodge
144 West North Temple St.
Salt Lake City UT 84103
(801) 533-8200
(800) 255-3050
Room rates from $40

Always Call Ahead!

UTAH, Salt Lake City

Howard Johnson Hotel
122 South Temple
Salt Lake City, UT 84101
(801) 521-0130
(800) 654-2000
$50-100

Motel 6
176 W. 6th South St.
Salt Lake City UT 84101
(801) 531-1252
1 small pet per room
Reservations (505) 891-6161
Room rates $27-33

Motel 6
1990 W. North Temple St.
Salt Lake City UT 84116
(801) 364-1053
1 small pet per room
Reservations (505) 891-6161
Room rates $27-33

Hilton
5151 Wiley Post Way
Salt Lake City UT 84116
(801) 539-1515
(800) 445-8667
$50 deposit
Room rates $50-55

ST. GEORGE
Super 8 Motel
915 S. Bluff St.
St. George UT 84770
(801) 628-4251
(800) 848-8888
pets with permission
Room rates from $38

Days Inn
747 E. St. George Blvd.
St. George UT 84770
(801) 673-6111
(800) 325-2525
Room rates $39-44

Travelodge
175 North 1000th East
St. George UT 84770
(801) 673-4621
(800) 255-3050
no large pets
Room rates $35-36

Motel 6
205 N. 1000 E. St.
St. George UT 84770
(801) 628-7979
1 small pet per room
Reservations (505) 891-6161
Room rates $27-33

VERNAL
Econo Lodge
311 Main St.
Vernal, UT 84078
(801) 789-2000
(800) 446-6900
$28-45

WELLINGTON
Comfort Inn
50 S. 700 St. E.
Wellington UT 84542
(801) 637-7980
(800) 228-5150
Room rates $38-55

WENDOVER
Motel 6
561 E. Wendover Blvd.
Wendover UT 84083
(801) 665-2267
1 small pet per room
Reservations (505) 891-6161
Room rates $27-33

VERMONT
BENNINGTON
Ramada Inn
Rte 7 & Kocher Dr.
Bennington VT 05201
(802) 442-8145
(800) 228-2828
Room rates $69-85

BRATTLEBORO
Quality Inn
Putney Rd.
Brattleboro VT 05301
(802) 254-8701
(800) 228-5151
Room rates $60-95

BURLINGTON
Econo Lodge
1076 Williston Rd.
Burlington, VT 05403
(802) 863-1125
(800) 446-6900
$50-80

Howard Johnson
US 2
Burlington VT 05402
(802) 863-5541
(800) 654-2000
Room rates $55-85

COLCHESTER
Maple Ridge Motel
23 College Pkwy.
Colchester VT 05446
(802) 655-0900
$50 charge
Room rates $50-85

KILLINGTON
Val Roc Motel
US 4
Killington VT 05751
(802) 422-3881
Room rates $35-99

MANCHESTER
Captain's Quarters
Rt. 7A
Manchester VT 05254
(802) 362-1033
Room rates $40-65

MIDDLEBURY
Middlebury Inn
US 7
Middlebury VT 05753
(802) 388-4961
$6 charge
Room rates $85-120

**Always
Call
Ahead!**

MONTPELIER
Days Inn
100 State St.
Montpelier VT 05602
(802) 223-5252
(800) 325-2525
$6/pets
Room rates $63-73

NEWPORT
Top of the Hills Inn
Jct. I-95 & US 5
Newport VT 05855
(802) 334-6748
Room rates $45-50

NORTH SPRINGFIELD
Abby Lynn Motel
Rt. 1
North Springfield VT 05150
(802) 886-2223
Room rates $30-60

QUECHEE
Friendship Inn
US 4
Quechee VT 05059
(802) 295-7600
(800) 553-2666
Room rates $50-80

RUTLAND
Edelweiss Motel
Jct. US 7 & US 4
Rutland VT 05701
(802) 775-5577
dogs only
Room rates $30-100

Holiday Inn
Main St.
Rutland VT 05701
(802) 775-1911
(800) 465-4329
Room rates $90-235

SHELBURNE
Red Carpet Inn
1961 Shelburne Rd.
Shelburne VT 05482
(802) 985-3377
$5 charge
Room rates $40-105

SOUTH WOODSTOCK
Kedron Valley Inn
Rt. 106
South Woodstock VT 05071
(802) 457-1473
Room rates $115-200

SPRINGFIELD
Hartiness House
30 Orchard St.
Springfield VT 05156
(802) 885-2115
Room rates $75-80

Howard Johnson
818 Charlestown Rd.
Springfield VT 05156
(802) 885-4516
(800) 654-2000
small pets only
Room rates $55-90

STOWE
Country Squire Inn
SR 100
Stowe VT 05672
(802) 253-4207
Room rates $35-89

Green Mountain Inn
Main St.
Stowe VT 05672
(802) 253-7301
Room rates $60-125

Notch Brook Resort
Notch Brook Rd.
Stowe VT 05672
(802) 253-4882
Room rates from $60

The Salzburg Inn
SR 108 Mountain Rd.
Stowe VT 05672
(802) 253-8541
Room rates $50-150

WATERBURY
Holiday Inn
SR 100
Waterbury VT 05676
(802) 244-7822
(800) 465-4329
$30 deposit
Room rates $60-130

WHITE RIVER JUNCTION
Howard Johnson
US 5 @ Jct. I-89 & I-91
White River Junction VT 05001
(802) 295-3015
(800) 654-2000
Room rates $60-90

VIRGINIA
ALEXANDRIA
Ramada Inn
4641 Kenmore Ave.
Alexandria VA 22304
(703) 751-4510
(800) 228-2828
small pets only
Room rates $90-114

Days Inn
110 S. Bragg St.
Alexandria VA 22312
(703) 354-4950
(800) 325-2525
$5/pets
Room rates $48-56

Sheraton
Old Fellows Rd.
Alexandria VA 24501
(804) 847-9041
(800) 325-3535
Room rates $45-60

ARLINGTON
Ramada Inn
950 N. Stafford St.
Arlington VA 22203
(703) 528-6000
(800) 228-2828
Room rates $108-140

Holiday Inn
1850 Ft. Myers Dr.
Arlington VA 22209
(703) 522-0400
(800) 465-4329
Room rates $60-125

 Always Call Ahead!

VIRGINIA, Arlington

Marriott
1700 Jefferson Davis Hwy.
Arlington VA 22202
(703) 920-3230
(800) 228-9290
must sign pet waiver
Room rates $150-200

ASHLAND
Comfort Inn
101 Cottage Greene Dr.
Ashland VA 23005
(804) 752-7777
(800) 228-5150
Room rates $47-60

BELLINGHAM
Motel 6
3701 Bryon Ave.
Bellingham VA 98225
(206) 671-4494
1 small pet per room
Reservations (505) 891-6161
Room rates $28-31

BLACKSBURG
Comfort Inn
3705 S. Main St.
Blacksburg VA 24060
(703) 951-1500
(800) 228-5150
Room rates $56-75

Holiday Inn
3505 Main
Blacksburg VA 24060
(703) 951-1330
(800) 465-4329
Room rates $45-65

CARMEL CHURCH
Comfort Inn
I-95 & US 207
Carmel Church VA 22546
(804) 448-2828
(800) 228-5150
Room rates $44-78

CHARLOTTESVILLE
Comfort Inn
1807 Emmet St.
Charlottesville VA 22901
(804) 293-6188
(800) 228-5150
Room rates $48-58

Holiday Inn
I-64 & 5th St.
Charlottesville VA 22901
(804) 977-5100
(800) 465-4329
Room rates $65-75

Econo Lodge
400 Emmet St.
Charlottesville VA 22903
(804) 296-2104
(800) 553-2666
Room rates $40-50

CHESAPEAKE
Super 8 Motel
100 Red Cedar Court
Chesapeake VA 23320
(804) 547-8880
(800) 848-8888
pets with permission
Room rates from $39

Red Roof Inn
724 Woodlake Dr.
Chesapeake VA 23320
(804) 523-0123
(800) 843-7663
Room rates $40-50

CHESTER
Comfort Inn
2100 W. Hundred Rd.
Chester VA 23831
(804) 751-0000
(800) 228-5150
Room rates $52-60

Days Inn
I-95 & VA 10
Chester VA 23831
(804) 748-5871
(800) 325-2525
$4/pets
Room rates $38-45

CHRISTIANSBURG
Days Inn
I-80 & US 11
Christiansburg VA 24073
(703) 382-0261
(800) 325-2525
$4/pets
Room rates $45-55

Econo Lodge
2430 Roanoke St.
Christiansburg VA 24073
(703) 382-6161
(800) 553-2666
Room rates $30-40

COLONIAL HEIGHTS
Days Inn
2310 Indian Hill Rd.
Colonial Heights VA 23834
(804) 520-1010
(800) 325-2525
$5/pets
Room rates $35-55

COVINGTON
Comfort Inn
SR 5
Covington VA 24426
(703) 962-2141
(800) 228-5150
Room rates $51-63

DUMFRIES
Quality Inn
17133 Dumfries Rd.
Dumfries VA 22026
(703) 221-1141
(800) 228-5151
Room rates $55-72

EMPORIA
Hampton Inn
1207 W. Atlantic St.
Emporia VA 23847
(804) 634-9200
(800) 426-7866
Room rates $46-52

**Always
Call
Ahead!**

Comfort Inn
I-95 & US 301
Emporia VA 23847
(804) 348-3282
(800) 228-5150
Room rates $39-41

Travelodge
Rt. 2
Emporia VA 23847
(804) 535-8535
(800) 255-3050
Room rates from $30

FAIRFAX
Holiday Inn
3535 Chain Bridge Rd.
Fairfax VA 22030
(703) 591-5500
(800) 465-4329
Room rates $55-100

Wellesley Inn
16327 Lee Hwy.
Fairfax VA 22030
(703) 359-2888
$3 charge
Room rates $45-55

FALLS CHURCH
Ramada Inn
7801 Leesburg Pike
Falls Church VA 22043
(703) 893-1340
(800) 228-2828
small pets only
Room rates $100-200

FARMVILLE
Super 8 Motel
Hwy 15 S. & US 460 Bypass
Farmville VA 23901
(804) 392-8196
(800) 848-8888
pets with permission
Room rates from $42

FRANKLIN
Super 8 Motel
1599 Armory Dr.
Franklin VA 23851
(804) 562-2888
(800) 848-8888
Room rates from $38

FREDERICKSBURG
Days Inn
5316 Jefferson Davis Hwy
Fredericksburg VA 22401
(703) 898-6800
(800) 325-2525
$5/pets
Room rates $37-47

Motel 6
400 Warrenton Rd.
Fredericksburg VA 22405
(703) 371-5443
1 small pet per room
Reservations (505) 891-6161
Room rates $28-31

Holiday Inn
564 Warrenton Rd.
Fredericksburg VA 22405
(703) 371-5550
(800) 465-4329
Room rates $55-75

FT. LEE
Days Inn
S. on I-95
Ft. Lee VA 23805
(804) 733-4400
(800) 325-2525
$5/pets
Room rates $40-50

HAMPTON
Hampton Inn
1813 West Mercury Blvd
Hampton VA 23666
(804) 838-8484
(800) 426-7866
Room rates $45-51

Super 8 Motel
1330 Thomas St.
Hampton VA 23669
(804) 723-2888
(800) 848-8888
pets with permission
Room rates from $39

Days Inn
1918 Coliseum Dr.
Hampton VA 23666
(804) 826-4810
(800) 325-2525
$4/pets
Room rates $35-40

Emporia, VIRGINIA

Radisson Hotel
700 Settlers Landing Rd.
Hampton VA 23669
(804) 727-9700
(800) 333-3333
Room rates $65-110

HARRISONBURG
Comfort Inn
1440 E. Market St.
Harrisonburg VA 22801
(703) 433-6066
(800) 228-5150
Room rates $53-58

Days Inn
1131 Forest Hill Rd.
Harrisonburg VA 22801
(703) 433-9353
(800) 325-2525
Room rates $41-46

Howard Johnson
605 Port Republic Rd.
Harrisonburg VA 22801
(703) 434-6771
(800) 654-2000
Room rates $35-50

Sheraton
1400 Market St.
Harrisonburg VA 22801
(703) 433-2521
(800) 325-3535
Room rates $65-80

LEESBURG
Days Inn
721 E. Market St.
Leesburg VA 22075
(703) 777-6622
(800) 325-2525
Room rates $55-60

LEXINGTON
Comfort Inn
I-64 & US 11
Lexington VA 24450
(703) 463-7311
(800) 228-5150
Room rates $41-62

Days Inn
I-80 & US 11
Lexington VA 24450
(703) 463-9131
(800) 325-2525
$4/pets
Room rates $40-50

133

VIRGINIA, Lexington

Holiday Inn
US 11
Lexington VA 24450
(703) 463-7351
(800) 465-4329
under 30 lbs only
Room rates $45-75

Howard Johnson
Jct I-64 & 81
Lexington VA 24450
(703) 463-9181
(800) 654-2000
Room rates $45-65

LYNCHBURG
Holiday Inn
Odd Fellows Rd.
Lynchburg VA 24506
(804) 847-4424
(800) 465-4329
Room rates $55-65

MANASSAS
Red Roof Inn
10610 Automotive Dr.
Manassas VA 22110
(703) 335-9333
(800) 843-7663
Room rates $45-55

MARTINSVILLE
Econo Lodge
800 Virginia Ave.
Martinsville VA 24078
(703) 647-3941
(800) 553-2666
$20 deposit
Room rates $35-40

NEWPORT NEWS
Super 8 Motel
945 J. Clyde Morris Blvd.
Newport News VA 23601
(804) 595-8888
(800) 848-8888
pets with permission
Room rates from $40

Super 8 Motel
6105 Jefferson Ave.
Newport News VA 23605
(804) 825-1422
(800) 848-8888
pets with permission
Room rates from $40

Comfort Inn
12330 Jefferson Ave.
Newport News VA 23602
(804) 249-0200
(800) 228-5150
Room rates $48-61

NORFOLK
Quality Inn
6280 Northampton Blvd.
Norfolk VA 23502
(804) 461-6251
(800) 228-5151
Room rates $55-70

Quality Inn
719 E. Oceanview Ave.
Norfolk VA 23503
(804) 583-5211
(800) 228-5151
Room rates $40-75

Comfort Inn
930 Virginia Bch Blvd.
Norfolk VA 23504
(804) 623-5700
(800) 228-5150
Room rates $45-70

Days Inn
1631 Bayville St.
Norfolk VA 23503
(804) 583-4521
(800) 325-2525
$50 pet deposit required
Room rates $42-48

Days Inn
5701 Chambers St.
Norfolk VA 23502
(804) 461-0100
(800) 325-2525
$4/pets
Room rates $38-50

Holiday Inn
700 Monticello Ave.
Norfolk VA 23501
(804) 627-5555
(800) 465-4329
small pets only
Room rates $70-85

OYSTER POINT
Days Inn
11829 Fishing Point Dr.
Oyster Point VA 23606
(804) 873-6700
(800) 325-2525
Room rates $40-57

PETERSBURG
Super 8 Motel
555 Wythe St. E.
Petersburg VA 23803
(804) 861-0793
(800) 848-8888
pets with permission
Room rates from $36

Quality Inn
16600 Sunnybrook Rd.
Petersburg VA 23805
(804) 733-1152
(800) 228-5151
Room rates $45-50

Quality Inn
I-95 & US 301
Petersburg VA 23805
(804) 733-0600
(800) 228-5151
Room rates $40-50

Comfort Inn
12002 S. Crater Rd.
Petersburg VA 23805
(804) 732-2000
(800) 228-5150
Room rates $41-55

PORTSMOUTH
Super 8 Motel
925 London Blvd.
Portsmouth VA 23704
(804) 398-0612
(800) 848-8888
Room rates from $40

Econo Lodge
1031 London Blvd.
Portsmouth VA 23704
(804) 399-4414
(800) 553-2666
Room rates $35-50

Holiday Inn
8 Crawford Pkwy.
Portsmouth VA 23704
(804) 393-2573
(800) 465-4329
Room rates $70-85

RICHMOND
Super 8 Motel
5110 Williamsburg Rd.
Richmond VA 23231
(804) 222-8008
(800) 848-8888
pets with permission
Room rates from $41

Days Inn
2100 Dickens Rd.
Richmond VA 28230
(804) 282-3300
(800) 325-2525
$5/pets
Room rates $42-52

Days Inn
1600 Robin Hood Rd.
Richmond VA 23220
(804) 353-1287
(800) 325-2525
$2/pets
Room rates from $45

Travelodge
5701 Chamberlayne Rd.
Richmond VA 23227
(804) 266-7616
(800) 255-3050
Room rates $37-46

Motel 6
5704 US Hwy 60
Richmond VA 23150
(804) 222-7600
1 small pet per room
Reservations (505) 891-6161
Room rates $28-31

Holiday Inn
301 Franklin St.
Richmond VA 23220
(804) 644-9871
(800) 465-4329
under 30 lbs.
Room rates $60-75

Marriott
500 Broad St.
Richmond VA 23219
(804) 643-3400
(800) 228-9290
sign liability contract
Room rates $80-140

ROANOKE
Friendship Inn
526 Orange Ave.
Roanoke, VA 24016
(703) 981-9341
(800) 453-4511
$29-45

Motel 6
6520 Thirlane Rd.
Roanoke VA 24019
(703) 563-2871
1 small pet per room
Reservations (505) 891-6161
Room rates $28-31

Holiday Inn
6626 Thirlane Rd.
Roanoke VA 24019
(703) 366-8861
(800) 465-4329
Room rates $60-85

Holiday Inn
1927 Franklin Rd.
Roanoke VA 24014
(703) 343-0121
(800) 465-4329
Room rates $50-80

SALEM
Quality Inn
179 Sheraton Dr.
Salem VA 24153
(703) 562-1912
(800) 228-5151
Room rates $45-58

SANDSTON
Hampton Inn
5300 Airport Sq. Lane
Sandston VA 23150
(804) 222-8200
(800) 426-7866
Room rates $52-58

Econo Lodge
5408 Williamsburg Rd.
Sandston, VA 23150
(804) 222-1020
(800) 446-6900
$33-45

STAFFORD
Days Inn
2868 Jefferson Davis Hwy
Stafford VA 22554
(703) 659-0022
(800) 325-2525
Room rates $41-51

STAUNTON
Comfort Inn
1302 Richmond Ave.
Staunton VA 24401
(703) 886-5000
(800) 228-5150
Room rates $52-76

Days Inn
I-81 & VA 654
Staunton VA 24401
(703) 337-3031
(800) 325-2525
$4/pets
Room rates $40-50

Econo Lodge
1031 Richmond Ave.
Staunton, VA 24401
(703) 885-5158
(800) 446-6900
$30-50

STERLING
Hampton Inn
45440 Holiday Dr.
Sterling VA 22170
(703) 471-8300
(800) 426-7866
Room rates $63-66

SUFFOLK
Econo Lodge
1017 Main St.
Suffolk VA 23434
(804) 539-3451
(800) 553-2666
small pets only
Room rates $30-40

TAPPAHANNOCK
Super 8 Motel
Rt. 17
Tappahannock VA 22560
(804) 443-3888
(800) 848-8888
pets with permission
Room rates from $40

TROUTVILLE
Comfort Inn
2654 Lee Hwy.
Troutville VA 24175
(703) 992-5600
(800) 228-5150
Room rates $45-59

VIRGINIA BEACH
Holiday Inn
5725 Northampton Blvd.
Virginia Beach VA 23455
(804) 464-9351
(800) 465-4329
Room rates $60-80

Travelodge
4600 Bonney Rd.
Virginia Beach VA 23462
(804) 473-9745
Room rates $40-55

Econo Lodge
5819 Northhampton Blvd.
Virginia Beach, VA 23455
(804) 464-9306
(800) 446-6900
$38-65

La Quinta
192 Newtown Rd.
Virginia Beach VA 23462
(804) 497-6620
(800) 531-5900
Room rates $48-60

WAYNESBORO
Comfort Inn
640 W. Broad St.
Waynesboro VA 22980
(703) 942-1171
(800) 228-5150
Room rates $48-55

WILLIAMSBURG
Motel 6
3030 US Hwy 60
Williamsburg VA 23185
(804) 565-3433
1 small pet per room
Reservations (505) 891-6161
Room rates $28-31

Holiday Inn
3032 Richmond Rd.
Williamsburg VA 23185
(804) 565-2600
(800) 465-4329
$50 deposit
Room rates $45-100

Ramada Inn
351 York St.
Williamsburg VA 23185
(804) 229-4100
(800) 228-2828
small pets only
Room rates $45-100

Friendship Inn
1413 Richmond Rd.
Williamsburg, VA 23185
(804) 229-8551
(800) 453-4511
$25-50

WINCHESTER
Super 8 Motel
1116 Millwood Pike
Winchester VA 22601
(703) 665-4450
(800) 848-8888
pets with permission
Room rates $37-42

Quality Inn
603 Millwood Ave
Winchester VA 22601
(703) 667-2250
(800) 228-5151
Room rates $41-70

Quality Inn
2649 Valley Ave.
Winchester VA 22601
(703) 662-2521
(800) 228-5151
Room rates $43-63

WYTHEVILLE
Ramada Inn
955 Pepper's Ferry Rd.
Wytheville VA 24382
(703) 228-6000
(800) 228-2828
Room rates $44-57

Days Inn
150 Malin Dr.
Wytheville VA 24382
(703) 228-5500
(800) 325-2525
$5/pets
Room rates $40-49

WASHINGTON
ABERDEEN
Red Lion Motel
521 Wishkah
Aberdeen WA 98520
(206) 532-5210
small pets only
Room rates $55-60

ANACORTES
Anacortes Inn
3006 Commerical Ave.
Anacortes WA 98221
(206) 293-3153
Room rates $40-55

BELLEVUE
Holiday Inn
11211 Main St.
Bellevue WA 98004
(206) 455-5240
(800) 465-4329
$30 fee
Room rates $85-95

BELLINGHAM
Coachman Inn
120 Samish Way
Bellingham WA 98225
(206) 671-9000
$5 charge
Room rates $40-50

BOTHELL
Windom Gardens
19333 N. Creek Pkwy.
Bothell WA 98011
(206) 485-5557
(800) 228-2828
$30 fee
Room rates from $78

BREMERTON
Super 8 Motel
5068 Kitsap Way
Bremerton WA 98310
(206) 377-8881
(800) 848-8888
pets with deposit
Room rates from $39

Bremerton, WASHINGTON

Quality Inn
5640 Kitsap Way
Bremerton WA 98312
(206) 373-7349
(800) 228-5151
pets with deposit
Room rates $50-65

CENTRALIA
Motel 6
1310 Belmont Ave.
Centralia WA 98531
(206) 330-2057
1 small pet per room
Reservations (505) 891-6161
Room rates $28-34

ELLENSBURG
Super 8 Motel
1500 Canyon Rd.
Ellensburg WA 98926
(509) 962-6888
(800) 848-8888
pets with deposit
Room rates from $40

EVERETT
Motel 6
10006 Evergreen Way
Everett WA 98204
(206) 347-2060
1 small pet per room
Reservations (505) 891-6161
Room rates $28-34

Quality Inn
101 128th St. SW
Everett WA 98204
(206) 745-2555
$25 fee
Room rates $55-65

Nendel's Inn
2800 Pacific Ave.
Everett WA 98201
(206) 258-4141
$25 deposit
Room rates $55-70

Always
Call
Ahead!

FEDERAL WAY
Super 8 Motel
1688 S. 348th St.
Federal Way WA 98063
(206) 838-8808
(800) 848-8888
$25 deposit
Room rates from $42

FIFE
Motel 6
5201 20th St. E
Fife WA 98424
(206) 922-1270
1 small pet per room
Reservations (505) 891-6161
Room rates $28-34

ISSAQUAH
Motel 6
1885 15th Place NW
Issaquah WA 98027
(206) 392-8405
1 small pet per room
Reservations (505) 891-6161
Room rates $28-34

KELSO
Motel 6
106 Minor Rd.
Kelso WA 98626
(206) 425-3229
1 small pet per room
Reservations (505) 891-6161
Room rates $28-34

KENNEWICK
Tapadera Budget Inn
300 Ely
Kennewick WA 99336
(509) 783-6191
Room rates $25-40

KENT
Best Western Pony Soldier Inn
1233 Central
Kent WA 98032
(206) 852-7224
(800) 528-1234
$20 deposit, small only
Room rates $55-65

KIRKLAND
Motel 6
12010 120th Place NE
Kirkland WA 98034
(206) 821-5618
1 small pet per room
Reservations (505) 891-6161
Room rates $28-34

La Quinta
10530 Northup Way
Kirkland WA 98033
(206) 828-6585
(800) 531-5900
25 lb max
Room rates $60-65

LACEY
Super 8 Motel
4615 Martin Way
Lacey WA 98503
(206) 459-8888
(800) 848-8888
pets with deposit
Room rates from $44

LEAVENWORTH
Obertal Inn
922 Commerical St.
Leavenworth WA 98826
(509) 548-5204
$7 charge
Room rates $35-70

LONG BEACH
Nendel Inn
409 10th ST.
Long Beach WA 98631
(206) 642-2311
on 1st floor
Room rates $45-65

LONGVIEW
Town Chalet Motel
1822 Washington Way
Longview WA 98632
(206) 423-2020
1 small pet
Room rates $30-40

MOSES LAKE
Super 8 Motel
449 Melva Lane
Moses Lake WA 98837
(509) 765-8886
(800) 848-8888
pets with deposit
Room rates from $38

WASHINGTON, Moses Lake

Motel 6
2822 Wapato Dr.
Moses Lake WA 98837
(509) 766-0250
1 small pet per room
Reservations (505) 891-6161
Room rates $28-34

Lake Shore Motel
3206 Lakeshore Dr.
Moses Lake WA 98837
(509) 765-9201
Room rates $30-40

MOUNT VERNON
Travelodge
1910 Freeway Dr.
Mount Vernon WA 98273
(206) 428-7020
(800) 255-3050
$20 deposit
Room rates $40-55

OAK HARBOR
Acorn Motor Inn
8066 80th NW
Oak Harbor WA 98277
(206) 675-6646
$5 charge
Room rates $40-45

OCEAN PARK RESORT
Ocean Park Resort
Hwy. 259 & R Street
Ocean Park Resort WA 98640
(206) 665-4585
$5 charge
Room rates $35-45

OCEAN SHORES
Polynesian Condo Resort
291 Ocean Shores Blvd.
Ocean Shores WA 98569
(206) 289-3361
$10 charge
Room rates $40-90

OLYMPIA
Westwater Inn
2300 Evergreen Park Dr.
Olympia WA 98502
(206) 943-4000
$10 charge
Room rates $55-65

PASCO
Motel 6
1520 N. Oregon St.
Pasco WA 99301
(509) 546-2010
1 small pet per room
Reservations (505) 891-6161
Room rates $28-34

PORT ANGELES
Super 8 Motel
2104 E. 1st St.
Port Angeles WA 98362
(206) 452-8401
(800) 848-8888
$25 deposit, closed oct-may
Room rates from $39

Lake Crescent Lodge
HC 62
Port Angeles WA 98362
(206) 928-3211
$4 charge, closed oct-may
Room rates $45-90

PULLMAN
Quality Inn
S.E. 1050 Johnson Ave.
Pullman WA 99163
(509) 332-0500
(800) 228-5151
Room rates $60-85

PUYALLUP
Northwest Motor Inn
1409 Meridian
Puyallup WA 98371
(206) 841-2600
$5 charge
Room rates $35-45

RICHLAND
Nendel's Inn
615 Jadwin
Richland WA 99352
(509) 943-4611
$5 charge
Room rates $25-35

Shilo Inn
50 Comstock St.
Richland WA 99352
(509) 946-4661
$6 charge
Room rates $45-50

RITZVILLE
Best Western
1405 Smitty's Blvd.
Ritzville WA 99169
(509) 659-1007
only smoking rooms
Room rates $49-58

S. SEATTLE
Motel 6
20651 Military Rd.
S. Seattle WA 98188
(206) 824-9902
1 small pet per room
Reservations (505) 891-6161
Room rates $28-34

SEATTLE
Super 8 Motel
3100 S. 192nd
Seattle WA 98168
(206) 433-8188
(800) 848-8888
pets with deposit
Room rates from $57

Ramada Inn
2140 N. Northgate Way
Seattle WA 98133
(206) 365-0700
(800) 228-2828
Seasonal Rates
Room rates $90-120

Quality Inn
2224 - 8th Ave.
Seattle WA 98121
(206) 624-6820
(800) 228-5151
Room rates $71-85

Days Inn
2205 7th Ave.
Seattle WA 98121
(206) 448-3434
(800) 325-2525
$3/pets
Room rates $64-71

**Always
Call
Ahead!**

Days Inn
1711 West Meeker St.
Seattle WA 98032
(206) 854-1950
(800) 325-2525
Room rates $45-65

Travelodge
200 6th Ave.
Seattle WA 98109
(206) 441-7878
(800) 255-3050
Room rates $62-72

Motel 6
18900 47th Ave. S.
Seattle WA 98188
(206) 241-1648
1 small pet per room
Reservations (505) 891-6161
Room rates $28-34

Howard Johnson Lodge
17108 Pacific Coast Hwy.
Seattle WA 98188
(206) 244-1230
$5 small pets
Room rates $45-90

Econo Lodge
325 Aurora Ave.
Seattle, WA 98109
(206) 441-0400
(800) 446-6900
$45-85

SHELTON
Super 8 Motel
6 Northview Circle
Shelton WA 98584
(206) 426-1654
(800) 848-8888
pets with deposit
Room rates from $38

SPOKANE
Super 8 Motel
W. 11102 Westbow Blvd.
Spokane WA 99204
(509) 838-8800
(800) 848-8888
Room rates from $41

Quality Inn
N.7919 Division St.
Spokane WA 99208
(509) 467-4900
(800) 228-5151
Room rates $56-74

Friednship Inn
4301 W. Sunset Hwy
Spokane WA 99204
(509) 838-1471
Room rates $55-66

Quality Inn
E.8923 Mission Ave.
Spokane WA 99212
(509) 928-5218
(800) 228-5151
Room rates $55-135

Comfort Inn
7111 N. Division
Spokane WA 99208
(509) 467-7111
(800) 228-5150
Room rates $54-63

Comfort Inn
6309 E. Broadway Ave.
Spokane WA 99212
(509) 535-7185
(800) 228-5150
Room rates $45-65

Quality Inn
905 N. Sullivan Rd.
Spokane WA 99037
(509) 924-3838
(800) 228-5151
Room rates $51-60

Motel 6
1508 S. Rustle St.
Spokane WA 99204
(509) 459-6120
1 small pet per room
Reservations (505) 891-6161
Room rates $28-34

Ramada Inn Int'l Airport
Box 19228
Spokane WA 99219
(509) 838-5211
(800) 228-2828
Room rates $55-75

TACOMA
Quality Inn
101 - 128th St. SE
Tacoma WA 98208
(206) 745-2555
(800) 228-5151
Room rates $81-99

Quality Hotel
2611 East E St.
Tacoma WA 98421
(206) 572-7272
(800) 228-5151
Room rates $71-150

Motel 6
1811 S. 76th St.
Tacoma WA 98408
(206) 473-7100
1 small pet per room
Reservations (505) 891-6161
Room rates $28-34

Best Western Executive Inn
5700 Pacific Coast Hwy.
Tacoma WA 98424
(206) 922-0080
(800) 528-1234
Room rates $55-65

Econo Lodge
3518 Pacific Hwy
Tacoma, WA 98424
(206) 922-0550
(800) 446-6900
$30-40

Motel 6
5201 20th St.
Tacoma, WA 98424
(206) 922-1270
(505) 891-6161
$28-36

Always
Call
Ahead!

TUMWATER
Motel 6
400 W. Lee St.
Tumwater WA 98501
(206) 754-7320
1 small pet per room
Reservations (505) 891-6161
Room rates $28-34

Tyee Hotel
500 Tyee Dr.
Tumwater WA 98502
(206) 352-0511
$25 deposit, $6 / night
Room rates $55-65

UNION GAP
Super 8 Motel
2605 Rudkin Rd.
Union Gap WA 98903
(509) 248-8880
(800) 848-8888
pets with deposit
Room rates from $42

VANCOUVER
Comfort Suites
4714 NE 94th Ave
Vancouver WA 98662
(206) 253-3100
(800) 228-5150
Room rates $54-59

Ferryman's Inn
7901 6th Ave. NE
Vancouver WA 98665
(206) 574-2151
$3 charge
Room rates $40-50

WALLA WALLA
Comfort Inn
520 N. 2nd Ave.
Walla Walla WA 99362
(509) 525-2522
(800) 228-5150
Room rates $51-63

Econo Lodge
305 2nd Ave.
Walla Walla WA 99362
(509) 529-4410
(800) 553-2666
small pets only
Room rates $30-35

WENATCHEE
Econo Lodge
700 N. Wenatchee Ave.
Wenatchee, WA 98801
(509) 663-8133
(800) 446-6900
$30-50

Red Lion Inn
1225 Wenatchee Ave.
Wenatchee WA 98801
(509) 663-0711
Room rates $65-75

YAKIMA
Days Inn
2408 Rudkin Rd.
Yakima WA 98903
(509) 248-9700
(800) 325-2525
Room rates $38-50

Motel 6
1104 N. 1st St.
Yakima WA 98901
(509) 454-0080
1 small pet per room
Reservations (505) 891-6161
Room rates $28-34

Holiday Inn
9 - 9th St.
Yakima WA 98801
(509) 452-6511
(800) 465-4329
Room rates $45-55

WEST VIRGINIA
BECKLEY
Super 8 Motel
2014 Harper Rd.
Beckley WV 25801
(304) 253-0802
(800) 848-8888
pets with permission
Room rates from $38

Hilton Hotel
1940 Harper Road
Beckley WV 25801
(304) 252-8661
Room rates $63-70

Comfort Inn
1909 Harper Rd.
Beckley WV 25801
(304) 255-2161
(800) 228-5150
$10 deposit
Room rates $40-55

BLUEFIELD
Holiday Inn
US 460 & 52
Bluefield WV 24701
(304) 325-6170
(800) 465-4329
Room rates $45-65

Park Inn
US 460 & 52
Bluefield WV 24701
(304) 325-5421
Room rates $40-45

CHARLESTON
Ramada Inn
2nd Ave & B St.
Charleston WV 25303
(304) 744-4641
(800) 228-2828
Room rates $54-73

Motel 6
6311 MacCorkle Ave. SE
Charleston WV 25304
(304) 925-0471
1 small pet per room
Reservations (505) 891-6161
Room rates $31-34

Holiday Inn
1000 Washington St.
Charleston WV 25301
(304) 343-4661
(800) 465-4329
Room rates $45-55

Knights Inn
6401 MacCorkle Ave. SE
Charleston WV 25304
(304) 925-0451
(800) 722-7220
Room rates $35-40

Motel 6
330 Goff Mountain Rd.
Charleston WV 25313
(304) 776-5911
Room rates $35-45

CLARKSBURG
Holiday Inn
100 Lodgeville Rd.
Clarksburg WV 26330
(304) 842-5411
(800) 465-4329
Room rates $40-60

Knights Inn
1235 Main St.
Clarksburg WV 26330
(304) 842-7115
(800) 722-7220
Room rates $30-40

ELKINS
Best Western
US 33 & SR 55
Elkins WV 26241
(304) 636-7711
(800) 528-1234
$5/day, small only
Room rates $40-50

Econo Lodge
US 33 East
Elkins WV 26241
(304) 636-5311
(800) 553-2666
Room rates $30-45

FAIRMONT
Holiday Inn
I-79 @ East Grafton Rd.
Fairmont WV 26554
(304) 366-5500
(800) 465-4329
Room rates $40-55

Red Roof Inn
Rt. 1
Fairmont WV 26554
(304) 366-6800
(800) 843-7663
Room rates $35-40

FAYETTEVILLE
Comfort Inn
UA 19 & Laurel Creek Rd.
Fayetteville WV 25840
(304) 574-3443
(800) 228-5150
small pets only
Room rates $38-58

HUNTINGTON
Econo Lodge
3325 Hwy. 60 East
Huntington WV 25705
(304) 529-1331
(800) 553-2666
Room rates $30-35

LEWISBURG
Budget Host Ft. Savannah Inn
204 Jefferson St.
Lewisburg WV 24901
(304) 645-3055
$3 charge
Room rates $35-55

MARTINSBURG
Arborgate Inn
1599 Edwin Miller Blvd.
Martinsburg WV 25401
(304) 267-2211
(800) 722-7220
Room rates $35-40

MORGANTOWN
Holiday Inn
1400 Saratoga Ave.
Morgantown WV 26505
(304) 599-1680
(800) 465-4329
Room rates $40-55

NEW MARTINSVILLE
Plaza Inn
291 SR 2 North
New Martinsville WV 26155
(304) 455-4490
$20 deposit
Room rates $35-50

PARKERSBURG
Red Roof Inn
3714 7th St.
Parkersburg WV 26101
(304) 485-1741
(800) 843-7663
small pets only
Room rates $35-40

The Stables Lodge
3604 7th St.
Parkersburg WV 26101
(304) 424-5100
Room rates $25-30

PRINCETON
Days Inn
I-77 & Rt. 460
Princeton WV 24740
(304) 425-8100
(800) 325-2525
$5/pets
Room rates $46-49

RIPLEY
Super 8 Motel
102 Duke Dr.
Ripley WV 25271
(304) 372-8880
(800) 848-8888
pets with permission
Room rates from $38

ST. ALBANS
Days Inn
6210 MacCorkle Ave.
St. Albans WV 25117
(304) 766-6231
(800) 325-2525
small pets $5
Room rates $32-40

TEAYS VALLEY
Days Inn
I-64 @ SR 34
Teays Valley WV 25569
(304) 757-8721
(800) 325-2525
Room rates $46-51

WESTON
Comfort Inn
I-79 & US 33 E.
Weston WV 26452
(304) 269-7000
(800) 228-5150
$5/pets
Room rates $40-44

WHEELING
Days Inn
I-10 & Dallas Pike
Wheeling WV 26059
(304) 547-0610
(800) 325-2525
Room rates $45-50

Comfort Inn
I-70 & Dallas Pike
Wheeling WV 26059
(304) 547-1380
$5 / night
Room rates $35-70

WISCONSIN, Antigo

WISCONSIN

ANTIGO
Super 8 Motel
535 century Ave.
Antigo WI 54914
(414) 731-0880
(800) 848-8888
pets with permission
Room rates from $40

APPLETON
Comfort Suites
3809 W. Wisconsin Ave.
Appleton WI 54911
(414) 730-3800
(800) 228-5150
Room rates $55-125

Budgetel Inn
3033 College Ave.
Appleton WI 54914
(414) 734-6070
(800) 428-3438
Room rates $30-40

BAILEYS HARBOR
Sands Resort
Ridges Rd.
Baileys Harbor WI 54202
(414) 839-2401
$5 charge
Room rates $50-100

BARABOO
Thunderbird Inn
1013 8th St.
Baraboo WI 53913
(608) 356-7757
Room rates $34-60

BEAVER DAM
Super 8 Motel
711 Park Ave.
Beaver Dam WI 53916
(414) 887-8880
(800) 848-8888
pets with deposit
Room rates from $40

BELOIT
Comfort Inn
2786 Milwaukee Rd.
Beloit WI 53511
(608) 362-2666
(800) 228-5150
Room rates $42-55

BROOKFIELD
Marriott
375 Moorland Rd.
Brookfield WI 53005
(414) 786-1100
(800) 228-9290
Room rates $65-110

DODGEVILLE
Super 8 Motel
1308 Johns St.
Dodgeville WI 53533
(608) 935-3888
(800) 848-8888
pets w/ permission & $50
refundable dep.
Room rates from $38

EAU CLAIRE
Super 8 Motel
6260 Texaco Dr.
Eau Claire WI 54703
(715) 874-6868
(800) 848-8888
pets with permission
Room rates from $37

Comfort Inn
3117 Craig Rd.
Eau Claire WI 54701
(715) 833-9798
(800) 228-5150
Room rates $42-50

Heartland Inn
4075 Commonwealth
Eau Claire WI 54701
(715) 839-7100
(800) 334-3277
Room rates $35-45

Howard Johnson Lodge
809 W. Clairemont Ave.
Eau Claire, WI 54701
(715) 834-6611
(800) 654-2000
$45-70

Holiday Inn
1202 Clairemont Ave.
Eau Claire WI 54701
(715) 834-3181
(800) 465-4329
Room rates $50-70

FOND DU LAC
Days Inn
107 N. Pioneer Rd.
Fond Du Lac WI 54935
(414) 923-6790
(800) 325-2525
small pets allowed $3 fee
Room rates $32-48

Motel 6
738 W. Johnston St.
Fond Du Lac WI 54935
(414) 923-0678
1 small pet per room
Reservations (505) 891-6161
Room rates $26-31

Holiday Inn
625 Rolling Meadows Dr.
Fond Du Lac WI 54935
(414) 923-1440
(800) 465-4329
Room rates $60-70

GERMANTOWN
Super 8 Motel
N. 96 W.
Germantown WI 53022
(414) 255-0880
(800) 848-8888
pets with deposit
Room rates from $39

GREEN BAY
Super 8 Motel
2868 S. Oneida
Green Bay WI 54304
(414) 494-2042
(800) 848-8888
pets with permission
Room rates from $42

Days Inn
406 N. Washington St.
Green Bay WI 54301
(414) 435-4484
(800) 325-2525
Room rates $52-66

Daystop
1978 Gross Ave.
Green Bay WI 54304
(414) 498-8088
(800) 325-2525
small pets allowed
Room rates $40-50

Motel 6
1614 Shawano Ave.
Green Bay WI 54303
(414) 494-6730
1 small pet per room
Reservations (505) 891-6161
Room rates $26-31

Holiday Inn
2580 Ashland Ave.
Green Bay WI 54304
(414) 499-5121
(800) 465-4329
Room rates $55-70

Holiday Inn
200 Main St.
Green Bay WI 54301
(414) 437-5900
(800) 465-4329
Room rates $50-70

HUDSON
Comfort Inn
811 Dominion Dr.
Hudson WI 54016
(715) 386-6355
(800) 228-5150
Room rates $44-68

JANESVILLE
Ramada Inn
3431 Milton Ave.
Janesville WI 53545
(608) 756-2341
(800) 228-2828
Room rates $51-59

Motel 6
2422 Fulton St.
Janesville WI 53545
(608) 756-1742
1 small pet per room
Reservations (505) 891-6161
Room rates $26-31

KENOSHA
Knights Inn
7221 122st Ave.
Kenosha WI 53142
(414) 857-2622
(800) 722-7220
Room rates $35-45

LA CROSSE
Days Inn
2325 Bainbridge St.
La Crosse WI 54603
(608) 785-0420
(800) 325-2525
$5/small pets
Room rates $54-49

Excel Inn
2150 Rose St.
La Crosse WI 54603
(608) 781-0400
Room rates $30-35

MADISON
Super 8 Motel
1602 W. Beltline Hwy
Madison WI 53713
(608) 258-8882
(800) 848-8888
pets with deposit
Room rates from $41

Quality Inn
4916 E. Broadway
Madison WI 53716
(608) 225-5501
(800) 228-5151
Room rates $59-62

Motel 6
6402 E. Broadway
Madison WI 53207
(414) 482-4414
1 small pet per room
Reservations (505) 891-6161
Room rates $26-31

Holiday Inn
4402 Washington Ave.
Madison WI 53704
(608) 244-4703
(800) 465-4329
Room rates $70-80

MARINETTE
Super 8 Motel
1508 Marinette Ave.
Marinette WI 54143
(715) 735-7887
(800) 848-8888
pets with permission
Room rates $37-40

MENOMONEE FALLS
Days Inn
14776 Main St.
Menomonee Falls WI 53051
(414) 255-1700
(800) 325-2525
Room rates $41-70

MILWAUKEE
Ramada Inn
6401 S 13th St.
Milwaukee WI 53221
(414) 764-5300
(800) 228-2828
Room rates $52-68

Marc Plaza
509 Wisconsin Ave.
Milwaukee WI 53203
(414) 271-7250
pets by prior arrangement
Room rates $90-190

**Always
Call
Ahead!**

Holiday Inn
201 Mayfair Rd.
Milwaukee WI 53226
(414) 771-4400
(800) 465-4329
Room rates $65-90

Holiday Inn
6331 13th St.
Milwaukee WI 53221
(414) 764-1500
(800) 465-4329
Room rates $65-90

OAK CREEK
Knights Inn
9420 20th St.
Oak Creek WI 53154
(414) 761-3807
(800) 722-7220
Room rates $35-45

ONALASKA
Comfort Inn
1223 Crossing Meadows Dr.
Onalaska WI 54650
(608) 781-7500
(800) 228-5150
Room rates $40-48

OSHKOSH
Super 8 Motel
1581 S. Park Ave.
Oshkosh WI 54901
(414) 426-2885
(800) 848-8888
pets with permission
Room rates from $37

Motel 6
1015 S. Washburn St.
Oshkosh WI 54901
(414) 235-0265
1 small pet per room
Reservations (505) 891-6161
Room rates $26-31

Always Call Ahead!

Holiday Inn
500 Koeller Rd.
Oshkosh WI 54901
(414) 233-1511
(800) 465-4329
Room rates $60-70

PLATTEVILLLE
Super 8 Motel
100 Hwy 80-81 S.
Plattevillle WI 53818
(608) 348-8800
(800) 848-8888
pets w/ permission & $10
charge
Room rates from $42

PLOVER
Daystop
Hwy 51 & 54
Plover WI 54467
(715) 341-7300
(800) 325-2525
Room rates $44-95

PRAIRIE DU CHIEN
Prairie Motel
1616 Marquette Rd.
Prairie Du Chien WI 53821
(608) 326-6461
Room rates $20-50

RACINE
Holiday Inn
3700 Northwestern Ave.
Racine WI 53405
(414) 637-9311
(800) 465-4329
Room rates $51-71

Knights Inn
1149 Oakes Rd.
Racine WI 53406
(414) 886-6667
(800) 722-7220
Room rates $42-50

RHINELANDER
Super 8 Motel
667 W. Kemp St.
Rhinelander WI 54501
(715) 369-5880
(800) 848-8888
pets with permission
Room rates from $36

Holiday Inn
US 8 @ SR 47
Rhinelander WI 54501
(715) 369-3600
(800) 465-4329
small pets only
Room rates $50-60

RICE LAKE
Red Carpet Inn
2401 Main St.
Rice Lake WI 54868
(715) 234-6956
$15 charge
Room rates $30-40

SHAWANO
Super 8 Motel
211 Waukechon St.
Shawano WI 54166
(715) 526-6688
(800) 848-8888
pets with permission
Room rates from $37

SHEBOYGAN
Super 8 Motel
3402 Wilgus Rd.
Sheboygan WI 53081
(414) 458-8080
(800) 848-8888
pets with permission
Room rates from $41

ST. CROIX FALLS
Dalles House
SR 35
St. Croix Falls WI 54024
(715) 483-3206
Room rates $35-70

STEVENS POINT
Holiday Inn
1501 Point Dr.
Stevens Point WI 54481
(715) 341-1340
(800) 465-4329
small pets only
Room rates $73-85

Point Motel
209 Division St.
Stevens Point WI 54481
(715) 344-8312
$2 charge
Room rates $32-36

STURGEON BAY
Chal A Motel
3910 Hwy 42 & 57
Sturgeon Bay WI 54235
(414) 743-6788
$5 charge
Room rates $25-35

SUPERIOR
Days Inn
110 2nd St.
Superior WI 54880
(715) 392-4783
(800) 325-2525
Room rates $45-90

TOMAH
Super 8 Motel
I-94 & Hwy 21
Tomah WI 54660
(608) 372-3901
(800) 848-8888
pets with permission
Room rates from $41

Comfort Inn
305 Wittig Rd.
Tomah WI 54660
(608) 372-6600
(800) 228-5150
Room rates $42-50

WAUKESHA
Motel 6
20300 W. Bluemound Rd.
Waukesha WI 53186
(414) 786-7337
1 small pet per room
Reservations (505) 891-6161
Room rates $26-31

Knights Inn
2501 Plaza Ct.
Waukesha WI 53186
(414) 785-1590
(800) 722-7220
Room rates $35-42

WAUSAU
Super 8 Motel
2006 W. Stewart Ave.
Wausau WI 54401
(715) 848-2888
(800) 848-8888
pets with deposit
Room rates from $40

Holiday Inn
201 17th Ave.
Wausau WI 54401
(715) 845-4341
(800) 465-4329
Room rates $50-66

WISCONSIN DELLS
Super 8 Motel
800 County Hwy
Wisconsin Dells WI 53965
(608) 254-6464
(800) 848-8888
pets with permission
Room rates from $38

Holiday Inn
I-90 & I-94
Wisconsin Dells WI 53965
(608) 254-8306
(800) 465-4329
Room rates $50-90

New Concord Inn
411 Wisconsin Dells Pkwy
Wisconsin Dells WI 53965
(608) 254-4338
open April-October
Room rates $50-85

WISCONSIN RAPIDS
Chalet Motel
3300 8th St.
Wisconsin Rapids WI 54494
(715) 423-7000
$25 deposit
Room rates $30-35

WYOMING
AFTON
Mountain Inn
US 89
Afton WY 83110
(307) 886-3156
Room rates $40-50

BUFFALO
Super 8 Motel
655 Hart St.
Buffalo WY 82834
(307) 684-2531
(800) 848-8888
$2/pets
Room rates from $32

Best Western Cross Roads Inn
US 16
Buffalo WY 82834
(307) 684-2256
(800) 528-1234
$1 charge, small
Room rates $35-50

CASPER
Super 8 Motel
3838 Cy Ave.
Casper WY 82604
(307) 266-3480
(800) 848-8888
pets with permission
Room rates from $31

Days Inn
400 Frontier Ave.
Casper WY 82601
(307) 235-6668
(800) 325-2525
$6/pets
Room rates $31-57

Motel 6
1150 Wilkins Circle
Casper WY 82601
(307) 234-3903
1 small pet per room
Reservations (505) 891-6161
Room rates $25-32

Holiday Inn
300 F Street
Casper WY 82602
(307) 235-2531
(800) 465-4329
Room rates $55-65

Super 8 Motel
1900 W. Lincolnway
Cheyenne WY 82001
(307) 635-8741
(800) 848-8888
pets with permission
Room rates from $35

CHEYENNE
Motel 6
1735 Westland Rd.
Cheyenne WY 82001
(307) 635-6806
1 small pet per room
Reservations (505) 891-6161
Room rates $25-32

WYOMING, Cheyenne

La Quinta
2410 Lincolnway
Cheyenne WY 82001
(307) 632-7117
(800) 531-5900
Room rates $45-50

Rodeway Inn
3839 Lincolnway
Cheyenne WY 82001
(307) 634-2171
(800) 228-2000
$4 charge
Room rates $35-45

CODY
Holiday Inn
1701 Sheridan Ave.
Cody WY 82414
(307) 587-5555
(800) 465-4329
Room rates $50-90

Shoshone Lodge
349 Yellowstone Hwy.
Cody WY 82414
(307) 587-4044
open May - October
Room rates $35-55

DOUGLAS
Super 8 Motel
314 Russell Ave.
Douglas WY 82633
(307) 358-6800
(800) 848-8888
pets with permission
Room rates from $33

Holiday Inn
1450 Riverbend Dr.
Douglas WY 82633
(307) 358-9790
(800) 465-4329
Room rates $50-60

DUBOIS
Black Bear Inn
US 26 & 287
Dubois WY 82513
(307) 455-2344
Room rates $25-35

EVANSTON
Super 8 Motel
70 Bear River Dr.
Evanston WY 82930
(307) 789-7510
(800) 848-8888
pets with permission
Room rates from $29

GILLETTE
Super 8 Motel
208 S. Decker Court
Gillette WY 82716
(307) 682-8078
(800) 848-8888
pets with permission
Room rates from $28

Days Inn
910 E. Boxelder Rd.
Gillette WY 82716
(307) 682-3999
(800) 325-2525
Small pets allowed
Room rates $34-38

GREEN RIVER
Super 8 Motel
280 W. Flaming Gorge
Green River WY 82935
(307) 875-9330
(800) 848-8888
pets with permission
Room rates $30-33

JACKSON
Motel 6
1370 W. Broadway
Jackson WY 83001
(307) 733-1620
1 small pet per room
Reservations (505) 891-6161
Room rates $25-32

Virginian Lodge
750 Broadway
Jackson WY 83001
(307) 733-2792
Room rates $35-65

LANDER
Holiday Inn
210 McFarlane Dr.
Lander WY 82520
(307) 332-2511
(800) 465-4329
$2 charge
Room rates $30-45

LARAMIE
Motel 6
621 Plaza Lane
Laramie WY 82070
(307) 742-2307
1 small pet per room
Reservations (505) 891-6161
Room rates $25-32

Holiday Inn
2313 Soldier Springs
Laramie WY 82070
(307) 742-6611
(800) 465-4329
Room rates $55-70

LOVELL
Super 8 Motel
595 E. Main
Lovell WY 82431
(307) 548-2725
(800) 848-8888
pets with permission
Room rates from $31

RAWLINS
Days Inn
2222 E. Cedar
Rawlins WY 82301
(307) 324-6615
(800) 325-2525
$4/pets
Room rates $32-49

RIVERTON
Holiday Inn
Federal Blvd. @ Sunset
Riverton WY 82501
(307) 856-8100
(800) 465-4329
Room rates $35-55

ROCK SPRINGS
Comfort Inn
1670 Sunset Dr.
Rock Springs WY 82901
(307) 382-9490
(800) 228-5150
Room rates $39-50

Motel 6
2645 Commercial Way
Rock Springs WY 82901
(307) 362-1850
1 small pet per room
Reservations (505) 891-6161
Room rates $25-32

**Always
Call
Ahead!**

146

Holiday Inn
1675 Sunset Dr.
Rock Springs WY 82901
(307) 382-9200
(800) 465-4329
Room rates $55-65

SHERIDAN
Super 8 Motel
2435 N. Main St.
Sheridan WY 82801
(307) 672-9725
(800) 848-8888
pets with permission
Room rates $28-34

Holiday Inn
1809 Sugarland Dr.
Sheridan WY 82801
(307) 672-8931
(800) 465-4329
Room rates $50-75

TETON VILLAGE
Crystal Springs Inn
SR 390
Teton Village WY 83025
(307) 733-4423
Room rates $40-80

THERMOPOLIS
Holiday Inn
Hot Springs State Park
Thermopolis WY 82443
(307) 864-3131
(800) 465-4329
Room rates $40-70

TORRINGTON
Maverick Motel
US 26 & 85
Torrington WY 82240
(307) 532-4064
Room rates $25-30

YELLOWSTONE PARK
Canyon Lodge
Canyon Junction
Yellowstone Park WY 82190
(307) 344-7311
Room rates $45-65

Lake Lodge
Lake Junction
Yellowstone Park WY 82190
(307) 344-7311
open June - August
Room rates $40-65

Mammoth Hot Springs Hotel
Mammoth Hot Springs
Yellowstone Park WY 82190
(307) 344-7311
open June - September
Room rates $30-130

**Always
Call
Ahead!**

ZIP INDEX
An easy way to locate more hotels and motels along your way

To help your use our directory more effectively while traveling, we have provided a **ZIP INDEX**, a listing of all cities in this directory by the first 3 digits of their zip code. We did this so that you can quickly locate cities near your destination without having to spend alot of time looking at maps! Here's how to use the **ZIP INDEX:**

1. Find the zip code of your destination

2. Locate the first 3 digits of your destination's zip code in ZIP INDEX (Be sure to look under the correct state name!)

3. Since similar zip codes are located geographically close together, cities with the same first 3 zip code digits will probably be within easy driving distance.

For example, if you were going to visit Minneapolis, MN (Zip Code 55410), you would find the following in the ZIP INDEX around 554 MN Minneapolis entry:

553 MN Rogers
554 MN Bloomington
554 MN Minneapolis
554 MN Richfield
556 MN Grand Marias

If you can't find accomdations in Minneapolis, try Bloomington or Richfield. If that still doesn't work, try 553 & 556 zip codes for even more choices!

It couldn't be easier! Just find your destination's zip, look it up in the ZIP INDEX, and quickly find more accomodations where
Pets R Permitted!

ZIP INDEX

ALASKA - CALIFORNIA

ALASKA
995 AK Anchorage
997 AK Fairbanks
998 AK Juneau
998 AK Sitka
999 AK Ketchikan

ALABAMA
336 AL Tillmans Corner
350 AL Bessemer
350 AL Cullman
350 AL Fultondale
352 AL Birmingham
352 AL Hoover
352 AL Mountain Brook
354 AL Tuscaloosa
356 AL Decatur
356 AL Athens
356 AL Florence
356 AL Sheffield
356 AL Muscle Shoals
357 AL Madison
357 AL Scottsboro
358 AL Huntsville
358 AL Mobile
359 AL Gadsden
359 AL Attalla
359 AL Boaz
360 AL Greenville
360 AL Prattville
360 AL Shorter
361 AL Montgomery
362 AL Oxford
362 AL Anniston
363 AL Dothan
363 AL Enterprise
365 AL Gulf Shores
365 AL Orange Beach
368 AL Opelika
368 AL West Point

ARKANSAS
716 AR Crossett
717 AR El Dorado
718 AR Prescott
719 AR Hot Springs
719 AR Arkadelphia
720 AR Conway
720 AR Jacksonville
721 AR Newport
721 AR N. Little Rock
722 AR Little Rock
723 AR W. Memphis
723 AR Blytheville
724 AR Jonesboro
726 AR Harrison
726 AR Mountain Home
727 AR Fayetteville
727 AR Bentonville

728 AR Russellville
728 AR Clarksville
729 AR Fort Smith
729 AR Van Buren
755 AR Texarkana

ARIZONA
720 AZ Brinkley
727 AZ Bentonville
850 AZ Phoenix
852 AZ Mesa
852 AZ Apache Junction
852 AZ Scottsdale
852 AZ Tempe
853 AZ Youngtown
853 AZ Yuma
856 AZ Douglas
856 AZ Green Valley
856 AZ Nogales
856 AZ Sierra Vista
856 AZ Willcox
857 AZ Tucson
860 AZ Flagstaff
860 AZ Grand Canyon
860 AZ Holbrook
860 AZ Williams
860 AZ Winslow
863 AZ Prescott
864 AZ Kingman
864 AZ Lake Havasu City
864 AZ Laughlin-Bullhead City
864 AZ Bullhead City

CALIFORNIA
900 CA Hollywood
900 CA Commerce
902 CA Culver City
903 CA Los Angeles
904 CA Santa Monica
906 CA Whittier
906 CA Buena Park
906 CA Cypress
906 CA Montebello
906 CA Stanton
907 CA Bellflower
907 CA Harbor City
907 CA Carson
908 CA Long Beach
910 CA Arcadia
911 CA Pasadena
913 CA San Fernando
913 CA Canoga Park
913 CA Newbury Park
913 CA Thousand Oaks
913 CA Sylmar
913 CA Castaic
915 CA Burbank

917 CA Baldwin Park
917 CA Chino
917 CA Claremont
917 CA Corona
917 CA El Monte
917 CA Rowland Heights
917 CA Ontario
917 CA Rosemead
917 CA San Dimas
917 CA West Covina
920 CA Carlsbad
920 CA Chula Vista
920 CA El Cajon
920 CA Escondido
920 CA Fallbrook
920 CA La Jolla
920 CA Oceanside
920 CA San Ysidro
921 CA San Diego
922 CA Indio
922 CA Bermuda Dunes
922 CA Banning
922 CA Blythe
922 CA Desert Hot Springs
922 CA El Centro
922 CA Palm Springs
922 CA Yucca Valley
923 CA Barstow
923 CA Big Bear Lake
923 CA Colton
923 CA Fontana **Always**
923 CA Hemet **Call**
923 CA Needles **Ahead!**
923 CA Redlands
923 CA Moreno Valley
923 CA Rancho California
923 CA Victorville
924 CA San Bernardino
925 CA Riverside
926 CA Newport Beach
926 CA Costa Mesa
926 CA Hunington Harbor
926 CA Orange
926 CA Westminister
926 CA Mission Viejo
927 CA Santa Ana
928 CA Anaheim
930 CA Ventura
930 CA Camarillo
930 CA Carpinteria
930 CA Ojai
930 CA Oxnard
930 CA Simi Valley
931 CA Santa Barbara
932 CA Buttonwillow
932 CA Coalinga
932 CA Big Bear
932 CA Lost Hills

Always Call Ahead!

ILLINOIS - MASSACHUSETTS ZIP INDEX

609 IL Kankakee
610 IL Dixon
610 IL Freeport
610 IL Galena
611 IL Rockford
612 IL Moline
613 IL Mendota
613 IL Peru
614 IL Galesburg
614 IL Macomb
616 IL Peoria
617 IL Bloomington
617 IL Normal
617 IL Pontiac
618 IL Urbana
618 IL Champaign
618 IL Danville
619 IL Mattoon
619 IL Tuscola
620 IL Alton
620 IL Litchfield
622 IL Fairview Heights
622 IL Collinsville
622 IL O'Fallon
623 IL Quincy
624 IL Effingham
624 IL Effinham
624 IL Vandalia
625 IL Decatur
625 IL Forsyth
626 IL Jacksonville
627 IL Springfield
628 IL Benton
628 IL Mt. Vernon
628 IL Salem
629 IL Carbondale
629 IL Marion

INDIANA
460 IN Anderson
460 IN Daleville
461 IN Franklin
461 IN Shelbyville
462 IN Indianapolis
462 IN Speedway
463 IN Hammond
463 IN Michigan City
463 IN Portage
463 IN Valpraiso
464 IN Merrillville
465 IN Elkhart
465 IN Plymouth
465 IN Warsaw
466 IN South Bend
468 IN Ft. Wayne
469 IN Kokomo
471 IN Jeffersonville
471 IN Clarksville
472 IN Columbus

472 IN Seymour
473 IN Muncie
473 IN Richmond
474 IN Bloomington
475 IN Jasper
475 IN Tell City
475 IN Vincennes
477 IN Evansville
478 IN Terre Haute
478 IN Sullivan
479 IN Lafayette
479 IN Crawfordsville
479 IN Remington

KANSAS
660 KS Atchinson
660 KS Lawrence
660 KS Leavenworth
660 KS Olathe
661 KS Kansas City
662 KS Overland Park
662 KS Lenexa
664 KS Junction City
665 KS Manhattan
666 KS Topeka
668 KS Emporia
671 KS Newton
672 KS Witchita
672 KS Wichita
673 KS Coffeyville
674 KS Salina
674 KS Abilene
674 KS McPherson
675 KS Hutchinson
675 KS Great Bend
676 KS Hays
677 KS Colby
677 KS Goodland
678 KS Dodge City
678 KS Garden City
679 KS Liberal

KENTUCKY
400 KY Bardstown
401 KY Radcliff
401 KY Shepherdsville
402 KY Louisville
403 KY Georgetown
403 KY Mt. Sterling
404 KY Berea
404 KY Richmond
405 KY Lexington
406 KY Frankfort
407 KY Corbin
407 KY London
410 KY Carrollton
410 KY Ft. Wright
410 KY Covington
410 KY Erlanger

410 KY Florence
410 KY Walton
410 KY Williamstown
411 KY Ashland
420 KY Paducah
421 KY Bowling Green
421 KY Cave City
421 KY Franklin
422 KY Hopkinsville
423 KY Owensboro
424 KY Fulton
424 KY Henderson
424 KY Madisonville
427 KY Elizabethtown

LOUISIANA
700 LA New Orleans
700 LA Harvey
700 LA Kenner
703 LA Thibodaux
703 LA Houma
704 LA Covington
704 LA Slidell
705 LA Lafayette
705 LA Jennings
706 LA Lake Charles
707 LA Port Allen
708 LA Baton Rouge
711 LA Shreveport
711 LA Bossier City
712 LA Monroe
713 LA Alexandria
714 LA Natchitoches

MASSACHUSETTS
010 MA Amherst
010 MA Chicopee
010 MA Hadley
010 MA Springfield
013 MA Greenfield
013 MA South Deerfield
014 MA Leominster
015 MA Sturbridge
015 MA Westborough
016 MA Worcester
017 MA Boston
017 MA Framingham
017 MA Concord
018 MA Andover
018 MA Haverhill
018 MA Lawrence
018 MA Lowell
019 MA Danvers
020 MA Mansfield
021 MA Braintree
023 MA Middleboro
024 MA Brockton
025 MA Edgartown

025 MA Cape Cod
025 MA Falmouth
026 MA Hyannis
026 MA North Eastham
026 MA Provincetown
027 MA New Bedford
027 MA Fall River
027 MA Westport

MARYLAND
206 MD Waldorf
206 MD La Plata
207 MD Beltsville
207 MD Lankam
207 MD Laurel
207 MD Capitol Heights
207 MD Oxon Hill
207 MD Camp Springs
208 MD Bethesda
208 MD Rockville
210 MD Aberdeen
210 MD Hunt Valley
210 MD Columbia
210 MD Havre De Grace
210 MD Baltimore
211 MD Westminster
212 MD Towson
214 MD Annapolis
215 MD Frostburg
215 MD Grantsville
216 MD Easton
216 MD Cambridge
217 MD Frederick
217 MD Hagerstown
217 MD Williamsport
218 MD Salisbury
218 MD Ocean City
218 MD Pocomoke
219 MD Elkton

MAINE
039 ME Kittery
040 ME Freeport
040 ME Sanford
040 ME Kennebunk
041 ME Portland
041 ME South Portland
042 ME Auburn
042 ME Rumford
043 ME Augusta
044 ME Bangor
044 ME Greenville
046 ME Ellsworth
046 ME Bar Harbor
048 ME Glen Cove
049 ME Waterville
049 ME Farmington
049 ME Searsport

MICHIGAN
480 MI Bloomfield Hills
480 MI Clawson
480 MI Farmington
480 MI Hazel Park
480 MI Southfield
480 MI New Baltimore
480 MI Novi
480 MI Auburn Hills
480 MI Port Huron
480 MI Roseville
480 MI Madison Heights
480 MI Troy
480 MI Warren
481 MI Ann Arbor
481 MI Belleville
481 MI Dearborn
481 MI Livonia
481 MI Detroit
481 MI Monroe
481 MI Nothville
481 MI Romulus
481 MI Taylor
481 MI Westhaven
481 MI Canton
483 MI Sterling Heights
484 MI Clio
484 MI Grand Blanc
484 MI Imlay City
485 MI Flint
486 MI Saginaw
486 MI Houghton Lake
486 MI Midland
487 MI Bay City
488 MI Mt. Pleasant
488 MI Okemos
489 MI Lansing
490 MI Kalamazoo
490 MI Battle Creek
490 MI Benton Harbor
490 MI Coldwater
490 MI Plainwell
491 MI New Buffalo
492 MI Jackson
494 MI Ludington
495 MI Walker
495 MI Grand Rapids
496 MI Traverse City
497 MI Mackinaw City
497 MI Alpena
497 MI Cheboygan
497 MI Gaylord
497 MI Petoskey
497 MI St. Ignace
498 MI Escanaba
498 MI Manistique
498 MI Marquette
498 MI Munising
499 MI Baraga

499 MI Ironwood

MINNESOTA
550 MN Chisago City
550 MN Faribault
550 MN Hastings
550 MN Lakeville
550 MN Owatonna
551 MN St. Paul
551 MN Maplewood
551 MN Roseville
553 MN Anoka
553 MN Buffalo
553 MN Chanhassen
553 MN Chaska
553 MN Glencoe
553 MN Burnsville
553 MN S. Burnsville
553 MN Monticello
553 MN Rogers
554 MN Bloomington
554 MN Minneapolis
554 MN Richfield
556 MN Grand Marais
557 MN Eveleth
557 MN Grand Rapids
557 MN Hibbing
558 MN Duluth   **Always**
559 MN Rochester **Call**
559 MN Austin   **Ahead!**
559 MN Winona
559 MN Zumbrota
560 MN Mankato
560 MN Albert Lea
560 MN Blue Earth
560 MN New Ulm
561 MN Worthington
562 MN Willmar
562 MN Marshall
563 MN St. Cloud
563 MN Alexandria
563 MN St. Joseph
564 MN Brainerd
564 MN Baxter
565 MN Detroit Lakes
565 MN Moorhead
566 MN Bemidji
566 MN International Falls

MISSOURI
620 MO Edwarsville
630 MO Eureka
630 MO Bridgeton
630 MO Sullivan
631 MO St. Louis
633 MO St. Charles
633 MO Wentzville
634 MO Hannibal

635 MO Kirksville
637 MO Cape Girardeau
638 MO Sikeston
638 MO Hayti
640 MO Blue Springs
640 MO Higginsville
640 MO Independence
640 MO Platte City
640 MO Warrensburg
641 MO N. Kansas City
641 MO Kansas City
644 MO Maryville
645 MO St. Joseph
647 MO Nevada
648 MO Joplin
650 MO Osage Beach
651 MO Jefferson
652 MO Columbia
652 MO Boonville
653 MO Sedalia
654 MO Rolla
655 MO Lebanon
655 MO Waynesville
656 MO Branson
657 MO Ozark
657 MO West Plains
658 MO Springfield

MISSISSIPPI
386 MS Batesville
386 MS Clarksdale
386 MS Southhaven
387 MS Greenville
388 MS Tupelo
389 MS Greenwood
391 MS Natchez
392 MS Jackson
393 MS Meridian
393 MS Newton
394 MS Hattiesburg
394 MS Laurel
395 MS Gulfport
395 MS Biloxi
395 MS Escatawpa
396 MS McCombs
397 MS Columbus

MONTANA
590 MT Columbus
590 MT Gardiner
590 MT Livingston
590 MT Red Lodge
591 MT Billings
593 MT Miles City
593 MT Glendive
594 MT Great Falls
594 MT Conrad
594 MT East Glacier Park
595 MT Havre

596 MT Helena
597 MT Butte
597 MT Belgrade
597 MT Bozeman
597 MT Deer Lodge
597 MT Dillon
597 MT W. Yellowstone
598 MT Missoula
598 MT Polson
598 MT St. Regis
599 MT Kalispell
599 MT Libby
599 MT Whitefish

NORTH DAKOTA
580 ND Valley City
580 ND Wahpeton
580 ND West Fargo
581 ND Fargo
582 ND Grand Forks
582 ND Grafton
583 ND Devils Lake
585 ND Bismarck
585 ND Beulah
585 ND Mandan
586 ND Dickinson
586 ND Bowman
587 ND Minot
588 ND Williston

NEBRASKA
680 NE Bellevue **Always**
681 NE Omaha **Call**
684 NE York
685 NE Lincoln **Ahead!**
686 NE Columbus
687 NE Norfolk
688 NE Grand Island
688 NE Kearney
689 NE Hastings
690 NE McCook
691 NE North Platte
691 NE Kimball
691 NE Ogallala
691 NE Sidney
692 NE Ainsworth
693 NE Alliance
693 NE Chadron

NEW HAMPSHIRE
030 NH Salem
031 NH Bedford
031 NH Manchester
032 NH Laconia
032 NH Plymouth
033 NH Concord
034 NH Keene
035 NH Gorham
035 NH Twin Mountain

036 NH Nashua
037 NH Sunapee
038 NH Portsmouth
038 NH Conway
038 NH Dover
038 NH Exeter
038 NH Hampton
038 NH Rochester

NEW JERSEY
070 NJ Fairfield
070 NJ Clifton
070 NJ Cranford
070 NJ Kenilworth
070 NJ Parsippany
070 NJ North Plainfield
070 NJ Clark
070 NJ South Plainfield
071 NJ Newark
074 NJ Mahwah
074 NJ Ramsey
076 NJ Paramus
076 NJ Rochelle Park
076 NJ Saddle Brook
078 NJ Rockaway
079 NJ East Hanover
080 NJ Mount Holly
080 NJ Mt. Laurel
080 NJ Mount Laurel
083 NJ Vineland
085 NJ Princeton
085 NJ Lawrenceville
086 NJ Trenton
087 NJ Lakewood
088 NJ East Brunswick
088 NJ Edison
088 NJ Piscataway
088 NJ Phillipsburg
088 NJ Somerset

NEW MEXICO
870 NM Grants
870 NM Moriarty
871 NM Albuquerque
873 NM Gallup
874 NM Farmington
875 NM Santa Fe
875 NM Taos
877 NM Raton
878 NM Socorro
880 NM Las Cruces
881 NM Clovis
882 NM Roswell
882 NM Carlsbad
882 NM Hobbs
883 NM Deming
883 NM Alamogordo
884 NM Tucumcari
884 NM Santa Rosa

Always Call Ahead!

155

Always
Call
Ahead!

ZIP INDEX

TEXAS - WASHINGTON

759 TX Jasper
759 TX Nacogdoches
760 TX Arlington
760 TX Bedford
760 TX Burleson
760 TX Hurst
761 TX Ft. Worth
761 TX Haltom City
762 TX Denton
763 TX Witchita Falls
763 TX Wichita Falls
765 TX Temple
765 TX Killeen
766 TX Hillsboro
767 TX Bellmead
767 TX Waco
768 TX Brownwood
768 TX Junction
769 TX San Angelo
769 TX Ozona
770 TX Houston
773 TX Conroe
773 TX Huntsville
773 TX Spring
775 TX Baytown
775 TX Clute
775 TX Galveston
775 TX Webster
776 TX Groves
776 TX Orange
776 TX Port Arthur
777 TX Beaumont
778 TX College Station
779 TX Victoria
779 TX Port Lavaca
780 TX Laredo
781 TX Universal City
782 TX San Antonio
783 TX Alice
783 TX Kingsville
783 TX Odem
783 TX Rockport
784 TX Corpus Christi
785 TX McAllen
785 TX Brownsville
785 TX Harlingen
785 TX South Padre Island
786 TX Fredricksburg
786 TX Georgetown
786 TX San Marcos
787 TX Austin
788 TX Del Rio
788 TX Eagle Pass
790 TX Dalhart
790 TX Plainview
791 TX Amarillo
794 TX Lubbock
795 TX Sweetwater
796 TX Abilene

797 TX Midland
797 TX Big Spring
797 TX Ft. Stockton
797 TX Odessa
797 TX Pecos
798 TX Big Bend National Park
798 TX Van Horn
799 TX El Paso

UTAH
801 UT Midvale
840 UT Farmington
840 UT Wendover
841 UT Salt Lake City
843 UT Logan
844 UT Ogden
845 UT Price
845 UT Green River
845 UT Moab
845 UT Monument Valley
845 UT Wellington
846 UT Provo
846 UT Payson
847 UT Beaver
847 UT Cedar City
847 UT St. George

VIRGINIA
220 VA Dumfries
220 VA Fairfax
220 VA Falls Church
220 VA Leesburg
221 VA Manassas
221 VA Springfield
221 VA Sterling
222 VA Arlington
223 VA Alexandria
224 VA Fredericksburg
225 VA Carmel Church
225 VA Stafford
225 VA Tappahannock
226 VA Winchester
226 VA Stephens City
228 VA Harrisonburg
229 VA Charlottesville
229 VA Waynesboro
230 VA Ashland
231 VA Sandston
231 VA Williamsburg
232 VA Richmond
233 VA Chesapeake
234 VA Suffolk
234 VA Virginia Beach
235 VA Norfolk
236 VA Newport News
236 VA Oyster Point
236 VA Hampton
237 VA Portsmouth
238 VA Petersburg

238 VA Ft. Lee
238 VA Chester
238 VA Colonial Heights
238 VA Emporia
238 VA Franklin
239 VA Farmville
240 VA Roanoke
240 VA Blacksburg
240 VA Christiansburg
240 VA Martinsville
240 VA Dublin
241 VA Salem
241 VA Troutville
243 VA Wytheville
244 VA Staunton
244 VA Covington
244 VA Lexington
245 VA Lynchburg
982 VA Bellingham

VERMONT
050 VT White River Junction
050 VT Quechee
050 VT South Woodstock
051 VT North Springfield
051 VT Springfield
052 VT Bennington
052 VT Manchester
053 VT Brattleboro
054 VT Burlington
054 VT Colchester
054 VT Shelburne
056 VT Montpelier **Always**
056 VT Stowe **Call**
056 VT Waterbury **Ahead!**
057 VT Rutland
057 VT Killington
057 VT Middlebury
058 VT Newport

WASHINGTON
980 WA Bellevue
980 WA Bothell
980 WA Issaquah
980 WA Kent
980 WA Kirkland
980 WA Federal Way
981 WA Seattle
981 WA Tukwira
981 WA S. Seattle
982 WA Everett
982 WA Tacoma
982 WA Anacortes
982 WA Bellingham
982 WA Mount Vernon
982 WA Oak Harbor
983 WA Bremerton
983 WA Packwood
983 WA Port Angeles

983 WA Puyallup
984 WA Fife
985 WA Tumwater
985 WA Olympia
985 WA Lacey
985 WA Aberdeen
985 WA Centralia
985 WA Ocean Shores
985 WA Shelton
986 WA Kelso
986 WA Long Beach
986 WA Longview
986 WA Ocean Park Resort
986 WA Vancouver
988 WA Wenatchee
988 WA Leavenworth
988 WA Moses Lake
989 WA Union Gap
989 WA Yakima
989 WA Ellensburg
991 WA Pullman
991 WA Ritzville
992 WA Spokane
993 WA Pasco
993 WA Kennewick
993 WA Richland
993 WA Walla Walla
994 WA Clarkston

WISCONSIN
530 WI Brookfield
530 WI Germantown
530 WI Menomonee Falls
530 WI Sheboygan
531 WI Kenosha
531 WI Oak Creek
531 WI Waukesha
532 WI Milwaukee
534 WI Racine
535 WI Beloit
535 WI Dodgeville
535 WI Janesville
537 WI Madison
538 WI Plattevillle
538 WI Prairie Du Chien
539 WI Baraboo
539 WI Beaver Dam
539 WI Wisconsin Dells
540 WI Hudson
540 WI St. Croix Falls
541 WI Marinette
541 WI Shawano
542 WI Baileys Harbor
542 WI Manitowoc
542 WI Sturgeon Bay
543 WI Green Bay
544 WI Wausau
544 WI Antigo
544 WI Plover

544 WI Stevens Point
544 WI Wisconsin Rapids
545 WI Rhinelander
546 WI La Crosse
546 WI Onalaska
546 WI Tomah
547 WI Eau Claire
548 WI Rice Lake
548 WI Superior
549 WI Oshkosh
549 WI Appleton
549 WI Fond Du Lac

WEST VIRGINIA
247 WV Bluefield
247 WV Princeton
249 WV Lewisburg
251 WV St. Albans
252 WV Ripley
253 WV Charleston
254 WV Martinsburg
255 WV Teays Valley
257 WV Huntington
258 WV Beckley
258 WV Fayetteville
260 WV Wheeling
261 WV Parkersburg
261 WV New Martinsville
262 WV Elkins
263 WV Clarksburg
264 WV Weston
265 WV Morgantown
265 WV Fairmont

WYOMING
820 WY Cheyenne
820 WY Laramie
821 WY Yellowstone Park
822 WY Torrington
823 WY Rawlins
824 WY Cody
824 WY Lovell
824 WY Thermopolis
825 WY Riverton
825 WY Dubois
825 WY Lander
826 WY Casper
826 WY Douglas
827 WY Gillette
828 WY Sheridan
828 WY Buffalo
829 WY Rock Springs
829 WY Evanston
829 WY Green River
830 WY Jackson
830 WY Teton Village
831 WY Afton

Always
Call
Ahead!

APPENDICES

APPENDIX A
PERSONAL TRAVELER'S GUIDE OF TELEPHONE NUMBERS

NOTICE about the personal traveler's guide of telephone numbers. Although these numbers were in effect at press time, Pets-R-Permitted cannot be responsible should the numbers change. They are provided for your general information. In cases where toll-free numbers were not available, area code + local numbers were provided.

1. STATE TOURIST BUREAUS
State tourist bureaus are happy to answer your questions and can supply you with helpful information and details about the destinations you plan to visit. They can tell you about particular points of interest such as, parks, historical locations, tourist attractions, campgrounds and so forth which are located within their state. When available, we have included toll free phone numbers.

AL	1-800-ALABAMA	LA	1-800-334-8626	OK	1-405-521-2409
AK	1-800-465-2010	ME	1-207-289-2423	OR	1-800-547-7842
AZ	1-602-542-TOUR	MD	1-800-543-1036	PA	1-800-VISTA-PA
AR	1-800-643-8383	MA	1-617-727-3201	RI	1-401-277-2601
CA	1-800-TO-CALIF	MI	1-800-5432-YES	SC	1-803-734-0237
CO	1-800-433-2656	MN	1-800-328-1461	SD	1-800-843-1930
CT	1-800-CT-BOUND	MO	1-314-751-4122	TN	1-615-741-2158
DC	1-202-789-7000	MS	1-800-647-2290	TX	1-512-462-9191
DE	1-800-441-8846	MT	1-800-541-1447	UT	1-801-538-1030
FL	1-904-487-1462	NE	1-800-228-4307	VT	1-802-828-3236
GA	1-404-656-3590	NH	1-603-271-2666	VA	1-804-786-4484
HI	1-808-923-1811	NJ	1-800-JERSEY-7	WA	1-800-544-1800
ID	1-800-635-7820	NM	1-800-545-2040	WV	1-800-CALL-WVA
IL	1-800-223-0121	NY	1-800-CALL-NYS	WI	1-608-266-2161
IN	1-800-2-WANDER	NC	1-800-VISIT-NC	WY	1-800-CALL-WYO
IA	1-800-345-IOWA	ND	1-800-437-2077		
KS	1-913-296-2009	NV	1-800-NEVADA-8		
KY	1-800-225-TRIP	OH	1-800-BUCKEYE		

2. STATE ROAD CONDITIONS

Listed below are state road condition numbers. These numbers can provide information about a state's road conditions, road construction, detours and so forth.

AL	205-261-4378	LA	504-342-8196	ND	701-224-2545
AZ	602-262-8011	ME	207-289-3427	OH	614-466-2660
AR	501-371-2157	MD	301-268-3101	OK	405-424-4011
CA	916-445-7623	MA	617-237-5210	OR	503-378-6532
CO	303-639-1111	MI	517-332-2521	PA	717-939-9871
CT	203-566-4880	MN	612-296-3076	RI	401-647-3311
DE	302-736-4313	MS	601-982-1212	SD	605-773-3536
DC	202-789-7000	MO	314-636-5171	TN	615-741-2060
FL	904-488-8676	MT	406-444-6339	TX	512-475-3661
GA	404-656-5267	NE	402-471-4545	VT	802-244-8727
ID	208-336-6600	NV	702-792-1313	VA	804-323-2000
IL	217-782-5730	NH	603-225-5191	WA	206-464-6897
IN	317-232-8250	NJ	609-292-3033	WV	304-746-2222
IA	515-288-1047	NM	505-841-8066	WI	800-762-3947
KS	913-296-3102	NY	518-449-1293	WY	307-635-9966
KY	502-564-3579	NC	919-733-3861	UT	801-964-6000

3. US AUTO CLUBS

Listed below are several major US auto clubs.

All State Motor Club	1-800-ALL-CLUB
Chevron Travel Club	1-800-222-0585
Sears Discount Travel Club	1-800-331-0257
Shell Motor Club	1-800-621-8663

4. RENTAL CAR TOLLFREE NUMBERS

Pets-R-Permitted is pleased to provide the toll-free numbers of most major car rental firms nationwide.

Alamo Rent A Car	1-800-GO-ALAMO	Hertz Rent A Car	1-800-654-3131
Avis Rent A Car	1-800-331-1212	National Car Rental	1-800-227-7398
Agency Rent-A-Car	1-800-362-1794	Payless Car Rental	1-800-PAY-LESS
Ajax Rent-A-Car	1-800-367-2529	Rent-A-Wreck	1-800-535-1391
American Internat'l	1-800-527-0202	Thrifty Car Rental	1-800-FOR-CARS
Budget Rent a Car	1-800-527-0700	U-Save	1-800-426-5299
Dollar Rent A Car	1-800-421-6868	Value	1-800-327-2501

5. HOTEL & MOTEL CHAIN TOLLFREE NUMBERS

This list is a handy guide of hotel & motel toll free reservation numbers. Save time and money by using these numbers in the continental United States. NOTE: This is a comprehensive listing of accomodations, not just those that permit pets.

Adam's Mark Hotels	1-800-231-5858	Loews Hotels	1-800-223-0888
AMFAC Hotels	1-800-227-1117	Marriott Hotels & Resorts	1-800-228-9290
Best Value Inns	1-800-322-8029	Master Hosts	1-800-251-1962
Best Western Int'l	1-800-528-1234	Meridien	1-800-543-4300
Budgetel Inns	1-800-428-3438	Omni Dunfey Hotels	1-800-843-6664
Choice Hotels	1-800-221-2222	Quality Inns	1-800-228-5151
Clarion Hotels	1-800-228-5152	Radisson Hotels	1-800-333-3333
Comfort Inns	1-800-228-5150	Ramada Inns	1-800-228-2828
Compri Hotels	1-800-4-COMPRI	Red Carpet	1-800-251-1962
Courtyards by Marriott	1-800-321-2211	Red Lion	1-800-547-8010
Days Inn	1-800-325-2525	Red Roof Inns	1-800-843-7663
Dillon Inns	1-800-253-7503	Regal Inns	1-800-851-8888
Doubletree	1-800-258-0444	Residence Inn by Marriott	1-800-331-3131
Drury Inn	1-800-325-8300	Rodeway Inns	1-800-228-2000
Econo Lodges	1-800-446-6900	Rodeway, Friendship & Econo	1-800-424-4777
Embassy Suites	1-800-362-2779	Scottish Inns	1-800-251-1962
Exel Inns	1-800-356-8013	Sheraton	1-800-325-3535
Fairfield Inns	1-800-527-4724	Sonesta Hotels	1-800-343-7170
Friendship Inns	1-800-453-4511	Stouffer Hotels & Inns	1-800-468-3571
Guest Quarters	1-800-424-2900	Super 8 Motels	1-800-843-1991
Hampton Inns	1-800-HAMPTON	Susse Chalet Motor Lodges	1-800-258-1980
Hilton Hotels	1-800-HILTONS	Thunderbird Motor Inns	1-800-547-8010
Holiday Inns	1-800-HOLIDAY	Travelodge	1-800-255-3050
Hospitality Int'l	1-800-251-1962	Treadway Inns	1-800-873-2392
Howard Johnson's Motor Lodges	1-800-654-2000	Trusthouse Forte Hotels	1-800-225-5843
Hyatt Hotels	1-800-233-1234	Vagabond Inns	1-800-522-1555
Imperial 400 Motor Inns	1-800-368-4400	Viscount Hotels	1-800-255-3050
Inter-Continental Hotels	1-800-327-0200	West Coast Hotels & Inns	1-800-426-0670
L-K Motels & Country Hearth	1-800-848-5767	Western Host Motor Hotels	1-800-648-6440
La Quinta Motor Inns	1-800-531-5900	Westin Motels & Resorts	1-800-228-3000

6. MAJOR US AIRLINES

This list is a handy guide of major US airline toll free reservation numbers. Save time and money by using these numbers in the continental United States.

America West	1-800-247-5692	Northwest Airlines	1-800-225-2525
American Airlines	1-800-433-7300	Pan Am	1-800-221-1111
Delta Air Lines	1-800-221-1212	TWA	1-800-221-2000
Great Lakes Airlines	1-800-554-5111	United Airlines	1-800-241-6522
Midway Airlines	1-800-621-5700	USAir	1-800-428-4322
Midwest Express Airlines	1-800-452-2022		

APPENDIX B
MAJOR THEME PARKS AND PET DAY CARE INFORMATION

You shouldn't have any problem with Pet Care at many of the tourist attractions across the nation. Many have on-site kennels or have made arrangments with nearby kennels to ascommodate their visitors' pets. However during busy times, when possible, you will want to call ahead to reserve space.

Always remember to bring your pet's health certificate. Reputable kennels will not board a pet without one. To avoid exposure to contagious conditions, you will not want to board your pet in a kennel that does not require a health certificate, even if you're only going to leave them there for a little while.

Listed below in alphabetical state order are the attractions that either have on-site kennels or kennels nearby. This information was supplied by the parks and is subject to change. Always call ahead to avoid disappointment. And remember to bring your own pet food!

Dogpatch USA, Box 20, Dogpatch, AR 72648 (501) 741-3343
Pets are permittted in the park, leashed at all times. No on-site kennel.

Grand Canyon National Park, South Rim Village, Grand Canyon National Park, AZ 86023 (602) 638-2631
Pets are permitted in the park but are not permitted on the trails below the rim. Pets can be kenneled in the South Rim Village for a daily fee.

Disneyland 1313 Harbor Blvd. Anaheim, CA 92803 (714) 999-4565
For a daily fee, an on site pet care center available.

~~Great America 2401 Agnew Rd., Santa Clara, CA 95052 (408) 988-1776~~
~~Pet Pourri kennel available for a fee.~~   **PET POURRI CLOSED**

Knott's Berry Farm 8039 Beach Blvd., Box 5002, Buena Park, CA 90620 (714) 827-1776
No on-site pet care available but they will send you a list of nearby kennels.

Marineland, Department of Guest Relations, Box 937, Rancho Palos Verdes, CA 90274 (707) 644-4000
No on-site pet care but they will send information on nearby kennels.

San Diego Zoo, Zoological Society of San Diego, Box 551, San Diego, CA, 92112
Pets are not permitted in the zoo but you can write for a list of nearby kennels.

Sea World, 1720 S. Shores Rd., San Diego, CA 92109 (619) 222-6363
Pets are not permitted but they will send you a list of nearby kennels.

Six Flags Magic Mountain, Box 5500, Valencia, CA, 91355 (805) 255-4100
Your pet can stay free in the on-site kennel.

Busch Gardens, 3605 Bougainvillea, Tampa FL, 33674, (813) 988-5171
For a fee your pet can stay in the on-site kennel.

Cypress Gardens, Winter Haven, FL, 34787 (813) 324-2111
For a fee your pet can stay in the on-site kennel.

Kennedy Space Center, Cape Canaveral, FL 32920
On-site kennel available at no charge.

Walt Disney World, Box 10000, Lake Buena Vista, FL 32830-1000, (407) 824-2222
For a daily fee, an on site pet care center is available.

Six Flags over Georgia, 7561 Six Flags Pkwy, Mapleton, GA 30378 (404) 739-3400
A fee is charged at their Park-a-Pet Kennel.

Six Flags Great America, Grand Ave., Gurnee, IL 60031 (708) 249-1776
A fee is charged at the kennel.

Six Flags Over Mid-America, I-44 & Allenton, Eureka, MO 63025 (314) 938-5300
Free kennels are available on-site.

Worlds of Fun, 4545 Worlds of Fun Ave., Kansas City, MO 64161, (816) 454-4545
Free kennels are available on-site.

Six Flags Great Adventure, Box 120, Route 537, Jackson, NJ 08527 (908) 928-2000
Free kennels are available on-site.

Carowinds, Box 410289, Carowinds Blvd., Charlotte, NC 28241 (704) 588-6568
No charge to use on-site kennels. Check in at Guest Relations desk.

Carlsbad Caverns National Park, 31 Carlsbad Hwy., White City, NM 88268 (505) 785-2291
or 1- (800) CAVERNS
A fee is charged to stay in their facilities.

Cedar Point, Sandusky, OH 44871-8006 (419) 626-0830
$4 charge for your pet to stay at Pet Check.

Kings Island, 6300 Kings Island Dr., Kings Island, OH 45034 (513) 241-5600
Free on-site pet care available.

Sea World of Ohio, 1100 Sea World Dr., Aurora, OH 44202 (216) 562-8101
No on-site kennel. Nearby kennel's number is (216) 562-7011

Herseypark, 100 W. Herseypark Dr., Hersey, PA 17033 (717) 534-3900
On-site kennels available for $3/day.

Dollywood, 700 Dollywood Lane, Pidgeon Forge, TN 37863 (615) 428-9400
Pets are permitted in the park if they are leashed. Because the park is all paved however,
their paws may get hot. Dollywood has an arrangement with a kennel that's half a mile
away. The "Loving Care Kennels" will come to the gate to pick up your pet.

Opryland USA, 2802 Opryland Dr., Nashville, TN, 37214 (615) 889-6700
A fee is charged at the kennel.

Six Flags Over Texas, 2201 Road to Six Flags, Arlington, TX 76010 (817) 640-8900
Your pet can stay in their kennel free of charge.

Kings Dominion, I-95 & Route 30, Doswell, VA 23047 (804) 876-5000
A $1 fee is charged for your pet to stay in their on-site kennels.

APPENDIX C

MAJOR CITY MILEAGE TABLE

INSTRUCTIONS To find the distance between two cities, find the numbers of the cities in the table below, then look on the chart for the smaller number->larger number. For example, New York (14) to Seattle (23) is (14->23) 3025 miles. All mileages are common routes.

1->Atlanta, GA	7->Detroit, MI	13->New Orleans, LA	19->St. Louis, MO
2->Boston, MA	8->Houston, TX	14->New York, NY	20->Salt Lake City, UT
3->Chicago, IL	9->Kansas City, MO	15->Omaha, NE	21->San Diego, CA
4->Cleveland, OH	10->Los Angeles, CA	16->Philadelphia, PA	22->San Francisco, CA
5->Dallas, TX	11->Miami, FL	17->Portland, OR	23->Seattle, WA
6->Denver, CO	12->Minneapolis, MN	18->Reno, NV	24->Washington, DC

1->2 1085	2->15 1455	4->8 1360	5->24 1415
1->3 715	2->16 310	4->9 800	
1->4 730	2->17 3225	4->10 2490	6->7 1305
1->5 830	2->18 2955	4->11 1365	6->8 1040
1->6 1520	2->19 1190	4->12 770	6->9 604
1->7 740	2->20 2431	4->13 1135	6->10 1190
1->8 875	2->21 3290	4->14 500	6->11 2125
1->9 880	2->22 3200	4->15 820	6->12 875
1->10 2250	2->23 3165	4->16 425	6->13 1295
1->11 660	2->24 445	4->17 2600	6->14 1855
1->12 1140		4->18 2310	6->15 540
1->13 520	3->4 345	4->19 550	6->16 1770
1->14 865	3->5 940	4->20 1800	6->17 1350
1->15 1027	3->6 1020	4->21 2625	6->18 1040
1->16 780	3->7 280	4->22 2565	6->19 860
1->17 2875	3->8 1075	4->23 2540	6->20 540
1->18 2615	3->9 510	4->24 360	6->21 1245
1->19 585	3->10 2190		6->22 1270
1->20 1960	3->11 1390	5->6 800	6->23 1430
1->21 2230	3->12 420	5->7 1195	6->24 1710
1->22 2555	3->13 940	5->8 245	
1->23 2955	3->14 820	5->9 505	7->8 1330
1->24 645	3->15 480	5->10 1430	7->9 750
	3->16 770	5->11 1400	7->10 2450
2->3 980	3->17 2250	5->12 940	7->11 1400
2->4 645	3->18 1980	5->13 500	7->12 695
2->5 1870	3->19 300	5->14 1650	7->13 1145
2->6 2010	3->20 1415	5->15 685	7->14 635
2->7 710	3->21 2280	5->16 1570	7->15 750
2->8 1965	3->22 2235	5->17 2145	7->16 590
2->9 1442	3->23 2185	5->18 1695	7->17 2525
2->10 3130	3->24 700	5->19 645	7->18 2240
2->11 1550		5->20 1240	7->19 515
2->12 1400	4->5 1225	5->21 1430	7->20 1725
2->13 1625	4->6 1375	5->22 1795	7->21 2550
2->14 215	4->7 165	5->23 2225	7->22 2495

7->23 2460
7->24 525

8->9 715
8->10 1565
8->11 1310
8->12 1185
8->13 365
8->14 1750
8->15 935
8->16 1650
8->17 2365
8->18 1975
8->19 780
8->20 1505
8->21 1580
8->22 1985
8->23 2445
8->24 1505

9->10 1635
9->11 1485
9->12 440
9->13 810
9->14 1225
9->15 185
9->16 1145
9->17 1955
9->18 1655
9->19 255
9->20 1105
9->21 1650
9->22 1900
9->23 1985
9->24 1065

10->11 2885
10->12 2035
10->13 1950

10->14 2910
10->15 1670
10->16 2829
10->17 1015
10->18 500
10->19 1940
10->20 710
10->21 125
10->22 420
10->23 1195
10->24 2755

11->12 1785
11->13 885
11->14 1325
11->15 1685
11->16 1230
11->17 3440
11->18 3220
11->19 1235
11->20 2625
11->21 2880
11->22 3240
11->23 3470
11->24 1100

12->13 1230
12->14 1265
12->15 375
12->16 1180
12->17 1830
12->18 1780
12->19 555
12->20 1310
12->21 2085
12->22 2080
12->23 1695
12->24 1120

13->14 1405
13->15 995
13->16 1315
13->17 2655
13->18 2350
13->19 690
13->20 1735
13->21 1935
13->22 2300
13->23 2735
13->24 1165

14->15 1295
14->16 90
14->17 3090
14->18 2790
14->19 970
14->20 2275
14->21 2850
14->22 3085
14->23 3025
14->24 235

15->16 1215
15->17 1750
15->18 1520
15->19 440
15->20 940
15->21 1760
15->22 1730
15->23 1825
15->24 1150

16->17 3005
16->18 2710
16->19 890
16->20 2195
16->21 2780
16->22 2960

16->23 2945
16->24 140

17->18 665
17->19 2210
17->20 770
17->21 1140
17->22 610
17->23 175
17->24 2945

18->19 1905
18->20 520
18->21 585
18->22 220
18->23 860
18->24 2645

19->20 1360
19->21 1910
19->22 2160
19->23 2240
19->24 920

20->21 815
20->22 730
20->23 925
20->24 2130

21->22 525
21->23 1315
21->24 2705

22->23 785
22->24 2895

23->24 2880

1->Atlanta, GA	7->Detroit, MI	13->New Orleans, LA	19->St. Louis, MO
2->Boston, MA	8->Houston, TX	14->New York, NY	20->Salt Lake City, UT
3->Chicago, IL	9->Kansas City, MO	15->Omaha, NE	21->San Diego, CA
4->Cleveland, OH	10->Los Angeles, CA	16->Philadelphia, PA	22->San Francisco, CA
5->Dallas, TX	11->Miami, FL	17->Portland, OR	23->Seattle, WA
6->Denver, CO	12->Minneapolis, MN	18->Reno, NV	24->Washington, DC

APPENDIX D
TIPS FOR BOARDING S.U.C.C.E.S.S.

There is no reason to fear kenneling your pet, BUT, you must make the time to plan and prepare for Boarding **S.U.C.C.E.S.S.**

Remember to make your reservations early! Before you commit to a particular kennel, be sure that you have time for an inspection visit. When talking with a kennel, take in a list of things you want to talk about, such as their boarding rates, policies, agreements or contracts, and hours-of-operation. The following points will help you make your list about your pet's needs.

Safety/Security
The kennel must be well-maintained with sturdy fencing to prevent pets from escaping. Be sure to let the kennel know if your pet has a tendency toward jumping, climbing, or digging its way out of confined situations so extra precautions can be taken.

not Unhealthy
Determine whether the kennel requires "proof of immunization" or a "health certificate" before admitting pets. To be on the safe side, it is wise to board your pet at kennels that require such proof. Otherwise you run the risk of boarding your pet with other animals who are not immunized. Also find out if the kennel has a method for controlling fleas and ticks, such as a pre-entry exam.

Also find out about the kennels access to veterinary service. Some have on-site veterinary service, others will use your pet's regular vet. If your pet needs medication, inform the kennel regarding the nature of the problem and the frequency with which the medication will need to be administered. Some kennels may not take in pets who require a lot of medication and special attention.

Cuisine
Check to make sure each pet has its own container of clean drinking water which is changed frequently throughout the day. Ask the kennel what their policy is on supplying food. Some provide food, others require that your bring your pet's food. If you pet is choosey, be sure to provide food.

Clean/Comfortable

The kennels should look and smell neat and clean. Fecal debris and dirt should be cleaned up regularly and there should be a set schedule of chemical disinfection to combat parasites and odors.

Be sure the kennel can maintain a temperature that will be comfortable for your pet and that is has a good ventilation system. Good ventilation helps to cut down on the spread of bacteria and viruses. Air conditioning is a must in some areas.

Exercise

If you are boarding a dog, make sure it has space to run and that the exercise area has protection from the wind, rain, snow and sun. Also, find out how frequently your dog will be exercised to determine if it will be adequate for your dog's needs.

While cats don't need "exercise areas" per se, be sure your cat's enclosure is roomy enough to permit movement, stretching and a regularly cleaned litter box.

Supervision

Find out how many times your pet will be checked throughout the day. Be sure the personnel are well trained in handling pets and are able to spot signs of distress and able to determine when pets need veterinary attention.

Sleeping

Be sure cages are large enough to move around in comfortably. Determine whether the kennel provides bedding or if you'll need to bring your own, and whether they restrict what you can bring.

If you have additional questions about choosing the right boarding kennel for your pet, you can call or write:

Amercian Boarding Kennel Association
4575 Galley Road, Suite 400A
Colorado Springs, CO 80915
(719) 591-1113

ALASKA

Arcy's Rabbit Creek Kennel
Barbara Potterf
14950 Snowshoe Lane
Anchorage AK 99516
(907) 345-1152

Citadel K-9 Kennels
Cathy Harman
PO Box 8315
Nikiski AK 99635
(907) 776-8029

ALABAMA

Dog Gone Hotel & Cat House
Robert E. Pitman, DVM
1701 Hwy 72 East
Athens AL 35611
(205) 233-1515

Oporto Pet Hotel
Dr. T.C. Branch
6912 Oporto Madrid Blvd S
Birmingham AL 35206
(205) 836-5229

Pet Lodge
Mark D. Kidd, D.V.M.
2509 Rocky Ridge Road
Birmingham AL 35243
(205) 823-5473

Riverview Animal Clinic/P.C.
Dr. Arthur Serwitz
4640 Highway 280 East
Birmingham AL 35242
(205) 991-9580

Kountry K-9 Kennels
Bev Mackall-Jacobs
105 Terry Taylor Dr.
Hope Hull AL 36043
(205) 288-6933

Copeland's Pet Motel&Grmg Inc
Kathy M. Copeland
4457 Halls Mill Rd.
Mobile AL 36693
(205) 661-5021

Animal Health Care
Dr P Simms/Dr P Baxter
217 W. Grand Ave.
Rainbow City AL 35901
(205) 442-2967

Canine Country Club Inc.
Maurice R. Bell
6560 McDonald Rd.
Theodore AL 36582
(205) 653-8926

PSP America, Inc.
Leah Ann M. Sexton
4918 McWright Ferry Rd
Tuscaloosa AL 35406
(205) 759-4614

ARKANSAS

Waggin'Tails&Wheel's Pet Care
Darleen S. Wheelington
1825 Fairview Rd.
Camden AR 71701
(501) 836-7297

Eureka Springs Pet Care Center
Ray & Gayle Benge, CKO's
Route 5 Box 172
Eureka Springs AR 72632
(501) 253-9426

Wee Pals Inc.
William McQuade
1021 Carthage
Ft. Smith AR 72901
(501) 782-0471

Pet Stop Inc
James Croker/M.E. Croker DVM
Rt 1 Box 235B
Heber Springs AR 72543
(501) 728-3222

Meadowlands Kennels
Robin L. Anderson
Rt 9 Box 58-B
Jonesboro AR 72401
(501) 972-5822

Fairview Kennels
Joan M. Walker
11523 Fairview Road
Little Rock AR 72212
(501) 225-1391

Nell's Pet Resort
Woodie & Nell Conkling
820 Hwy 201 North
Mountain Home AR 72653
(501) 425-0604

Timberlane Pet Motel
Don & Jean Douglas
Rt 1 Box 373
Mtn Home AR 72653
(501) 425-3227

ARIZONA

Kennel Care
Debra Warren
6277 W. Chandler Blvd
Chandler AZ 85226
(602) 940-0066

Cinder Hills Brdg Kennel
Denise & Steve Goodwin
Route 8, Box 245
Flagstaff AZ 86001
(602) 526-3812

Kingsmark Kennel
John & Patricia Kavanagh
8311 Koch Field Rd.
Flagstaff AZ 86004
(602) 526-2222

Fred Harvey Kennel
Tom J. Doerr
P.O. Box 699
Grand Canyon AZ 86023
(602) 638-2631

Scales' Arizona Boarding/Trng
Stacy Speer/K. Zmudzinski
PO Box 210 / Foudy Rd
Hereford AZ 85615
(602) 366-5675

Tails' End
Dr. R.G. Litchfield, DVM
1968 Mesquite Ave.
Lake Havasu City AZ 86403
(602) 855-5252

Canine Country Club
Gordon L. & Norma G. Bennett
2332 E. Washington Street
Phoenix AZ 85034
(602) 244-8171

McCormick Ranch Pet Cntr
A.R. Rubano DVM
10370 N. Hayden Road
Scottsdale AZ 85258
(602) 483-6245

Sun City Boarding Kennels
Joseph Kiss
10026 Santa Fe Drive
Sun City AZ 85351
(602) 933-9011

A-Dobe Dog Training Cntr Inc.
Paul Blaushild
3825 E. 40th St.
Tucson AZ 85713
(602) 790-4450

Coy's Pet Resort
David & Linda Coy
6030 S Camino Verde
Tucson AZ 85746
(602) 578-2977

Williams Kanine Kennels
Gary Williams
PO Box 57118 / 4701 S Irving
Tucson AZ 85732
(602) 750-1501

CALIFORNIA
Baseline Animal Resort
Paul Newman
9350-A Baseline Road
Alta Loma CA 91701
(714) 989-8900

My Little Cat House
Pamela Cooper/Betty
Lockwood
261 Appy Way
Arroyo Grande CA 93420
(805) 481-0238

Accipiter Kennels
P Anderson/J Kiseskey
5801 S Fairfax/Rt 6 Bx 534E
Bakersfield CA 93307
(805) 845-3329

Blue J Kennels
Diana Geerling
700 E 4TH
Beaumont CA 92223
(714) 845-3361

McManus Kennel
Linda Fish, Mgr.
1683 Old Country Rd.
Belmont CA 94002
(415) 591-7458

Bonita Boarding Kennel
Moe & Cynthia Miyagawa
5775 Quarry Rd.
Bonita CA 92002
(619) 475-3850

Dhubhne Kennels
Elizabeth Campbell
PO Box 336/5806 Sweetwater Rd
Bonita CA 91908
(619) 479-8670

The Kitty Hotel
Tami Anthony
2020 S. Bascom Ave Ste B
Campbell CA 95008
(408) 377-7745

Carley's Pet Center
Jason E. Gross
7333 Canoga Ave.
Canoga Park CA 91303
(818) 348-6882

Seacrest Kennels
Kathryn Leider, Owner
7250 Ponto Drive
Carlsbad CA 92009
(619) 438-2469

Kenar Pet Resort, Inc.
Kenneth & Arlene Eldredge
3633 Garfield Ave.
Carmichael CA 95608
(916) 489-3628

K-9 Dog Ranch
Bernard & Judith C. Jones
3495 Foothill Road
Carpinteria CA 93013
(805) 684-3223

The Canine Spa
Gary & Lilo Klein
68-766 Perez Road
Cathedral City CA 92234
(714) 328-0876

The Country Cattery
Tricia T. Timmons
P.O. Box 1629
Cedar Ridge CA 95924
(916) 477-1003

Circle City Animal Resort
Paul Newman, DVM
1302 E. 6th St.
Corona CA 91719
(714) 735-2441

Breton's School For Dogs
Judy Breton Fulop, CKO
1455 Lawrence Road
Danville CA 94506
(415) 736-6231

Glennroe Kennels, Inc.
Zona S. & Glenn Grupe
183 Love Lane
Danville CA 94526
(415) 837-4077

Montwood Kennels
Vic & Angie Monteleon
9821 Dunbar Lane
El Cajon CA 92021
(619) 443-8944

Airport Kennel Inn
Jack Baldelli
235 East Franklin
El Segundo CA 90245
(213) 322-6506

Klassic Tails Inn
Ada V. Curtis
90010 Knight Rd
Elmira CA 97437
(503) 935-1180

Alcala Pet Care
L. J. Lockwood, PhD.
1273 Crest Dr.
Encinitas CA 92024
(714) 436-6619

Amy's Pet Care
Amy Burger
659 Camino El Dorado
Encinitas CA 92024
(619) 942-0714

Falconmoor Kennels
L. Jas. Lockwood/J. Perkins
1273 Crest Dr.
Encinitas CA 92024
(619) 745-2759

Holiday Pet Hotel/Cats
Pajamas
Jennifer Perkins, CKO
551 Union Street
Encinitas CA 92024
(619) 753-6754

ABKA Kennels

Green Valley Kennels
Diane Wegmann/Perus Taylor
380 Green Valley Rd.
Folsom CA 95630
(916) 933-1780

Regency Pet Hotel
Jim & Ann Bowers
10917 Cherry Ave.
Fontana CA 92335
(714) 829-0626

Alluvial Pet Center
Francis Testoni
445 N. Abby
Fresno CA 93701
(209) 442-1127

Elaines' Animal Inn
Elaine Nestell
3912 N. Barton
Fresno CA 93726
(209) 227-5959

Rambelane Knls & Vet Hospital
Gerald Everett
3436 North First Street
Fresno CA 93726
(209) 222-5291

Aanimal Inns of America
Leslie S. Malo
10852 Garden Grove Blvd.
Garden Grove CA 92643
(714) 636-4455

Pet Set Inn/Cozy Pet Inn
Leon & Marilyn Lewison
14423 Crenshaw
Gardena CA 90249
(213) 644-2938

Homeland Pet Hotel
Bob & Kay Goeschl
24750 Juniper Flats Rd
Homeland CA 92348
(714) 926-1549

Waiterock Kennels
Candence Harper
1010 Pine Lane
Lafayette CA 94549
(415) 284-4729

Canine Country Club
W. Bruce Coates
42116 4th St. E.
Lancaster CA 93535
(805) 942-4251

Livermore Ranch Kennels
Robert & Pamela Dal Porto
4964 Tesla Rd
Livermore CA 94550
(415) 447-1729

Camp Best Friends
Ron Swallow/Cathi Helfer
1819 Pontius Ave.
Los Angeles CA 90025
(213) 473-8585

Malibu Animal Hospital
Nancy Smith DVM
23431 Pac. Coast Hwy
Malibu CA 90265
(213) 456-6441

Farrington Kennels
Sheila Farrington-Polk
170 Nardi Lane
Martinez CA 94553
(415) 288-3069

Midway Kennel
Joyce E. Shelp
15201 Jackson
Midway City CA 92655
(714) 893-5549

The Pet Bazaar
Jan Holder
15102 Jackson St.
Midway City CA 92655
(714) 892-5008

Country Place Kennels
W.L. Renno
10538 - 54th St.
Mira Loma CA 91752
(714) 685-2561

Country View Kennels
Christopher & Debbie Lamke
3900 Sylvan Ave
Modesto CA 95355
(209) 551-5070

Nat'l Institute of Dog Trng.
Jay Collins
1839 Potrero Grande Dr.
Monterey Park CA 91754
(213) 283-4242

American Canine Inst & Knl
Robert J. Vance
894 Independence Ave.
Mountain View CA 94043
(415) 964-4422

Crestfield Kennel
Herb & Martha Fielder
1199 Cuttings Wharf Road
Napa CA 94559
(707) 252-7877

Silverado Boarding Center
Peter Morse, DVM/Karen Morse
2035 Silverado Trail
Napa CA 94558
(707) 224-7970

Hollywood Dog Training School
Richard & Judy Karl
10805 Vanowen
North Hollywood CA 91605
(818) 762-1262

Windsor House Kennels
Sheila & Bill Gordon
13100 Saticoy Street
North Hollywood CA 91605
(213) 765-5592

Porter Pet Hospital
Ronald Newman
18224 Parthenia
Northridge CA 91325
(818) 349-8387

Bridewell Hilltop Kennels
June Lohmeyer
325 Sunset Trail
Novato CA 94947
(415) 897-5471

The Animal Keeper
Norm Costello, DVM
3532 College Blvd.
Oceanside CA 92056
(619) 941-3221

Lu Meyer's Obedience Adacemy
Lu Meyer & Thomas Griffin
464 "E" St.
Olivenhain CA 92024-9797
(619) 436-3571

Canine Care Castle, Inc.
Denise L. Rehder
618 West Collins Ave.
Orange CA 92667
(714) 633-0955

Pet Care Centers of Amer. Inc
Felix Lapuz
809-813 E. Katella Ave
Orange CA 92667
(714) 771-3870

Inglis Pet Hotel
Debbie Inglis
3889 N. Southbank
Oxnard CA 93030
(805) 647-1990

Buff's Pets N' More
R.L.(Buff) Benson, MSC
75-100 Merle Dr.
Palm Desert CA 92260
(619) 346-8511

The Cats Pajamas
Renee Strouse
2400 E. Foothill Blvd
Pasadena CA 91107
(818) 449-1717

Ken Neill Kennels
Eileen Neill
4304 W. Ave. N
Quartz Hill CA 93536
(805) 943-3434

Buckwood Boarding Kennel
Susan Buck/Wiliam Buck Jr.
1410 Ramona St.
Ramona CA 92065
(619) 442-1121

Desert View Pet Resort
M.S. Jackson, DVM
71-075 Hwy 111
Rancho Mirage CA 92270
(619) 346-6103

Country-Aire Kennels
Barbara Butcher-Cross
6400 Hwy 299 East
Redding CA 96003
(916) 549-3335

Fun Fair Pet Care
Nancy M. Mulica
732 S. Acacia Ave.
Rialto CA 92376
(714) 874-1221

Salinas Boarding Kennel
Linda M. Hoff
1072 El Camino Real North
Salinas CA 93907
(408) 663-3601

Peninsula Pet Resort
Wanda Adams
851-B Old County Rd
San Carlos CA 94070
(415) 592-2441

Animal Care Ctr. of San Diego
Terry Roberts, D.V.M.
8020 Ronson Rd.
San Diego CA 92111
(619) 565-8455

Fon Jon Kennels
Mark Jacobson/Kim Jacobson
CKO
5050 Santa Fe Street
San Diego CA 92109
(619) 273-2266

Pet Express
Victoria S. Weatherbee
1000 Iowa Street
San Francisco CA 94107
(415) 821-7111

Orchard Plaza Pet Center
Rick Watson, DVM
6992 Burnside Dr
San Jose CA 95120
(408) 227-9110

Aspen Glen Kennels
Thomas Stanley
1190 E. San Martin Ave.
San Martin CA 95046
(408) 683-2163

Cambria Kennels
Rebec Riggs
1451 E. McFadden Ave.
Santa Ana CA 92705
(714) 542-2285

Je Neill Kennels
J. O'Neill
1205 Laurelwood Road
Santa Clara CA 95050
(408) 988-3118

Capitola Kennels
Kathleen M Gale
3720 Capitola Road
Santa Cruz CA 95062
(408) 462-0784

Country Club Kennels
Todd Harris
2341 17 Ave
Santa Cruz CA 95062
(408) 475-1580

Sea Breeze Kennels
Cheryl Crabtree
681 E. Newlove
Santa Maria CA 93454
(805) 925-2825

Santa Monica Kennels
Ira & Mary Meisler
2116 Main Street
Santa Monica CA 90405
(213) 396-2088

Canine Knls & Dog Laundry
Sue Costello
6065 Old Redwood Hwy.
Santa Rosa CA 95403
(707) 542-3647

Olivet Knl & Dog Trng Resort
Sapir Weiss/Robert Sisemore
1404 Olivet Road
Santa Rosa CA 94952
(707) 542-2066

Shiloh Kennels
Marie Millick
4305 Langner Ave.
Santa Rosa CA 95407
(707) 584-9115

The Pet Connection
Debbie Levine, Mgr.
4340 Occidental Rd.
Santa Rosa CA 95401
(707) 546-4364

Springdale Kennels
Ellen Prandi
20878 Jacks Road
Saratoga CA 95070
(408) 281-1965

West Valley Pet Lodge & Grmg
Sallie Ditto
15050 Oriole Rd.
Saratoga CA 95070
(408) 379-6820

The Pet Resort
Dr. Ted J. Adler
16915 Roscoe Blvd
Sepulveda CA 91343
(818) 891-4472

Becky's Pet Hotel & Grmg
Laura Pastor
3800 Durock Rd.
Shingle Springs CA 95682
(916) 677-9192

Aberglen Kennels
Mark & Sally George
1755 Napa Rd.
Sonoma CA 95476
(707) 928-2657

Kamlo Kennels
S. Kelly / D. Ortwein
3350 Westach Way
Sonoma CA 95476
(707) 996-9472

Ronakers Kennels
Ron & Dixie Akers
22071 Bonness Road
Sonoma CA 95476
(707) 938-1173

Monoway Pet Center
Lewis & Barbara Bergstrom
2895 Monoway
Sonora CA 95370
(209) 532-1939

Spring Creek Knl & Cattery
Karen Pechacek/Patrick Murphy
9279 Campo Rd
Spring Valley CA 91977
(619) 463-1722

Mission Gate Kennels
Patricia & Terry Perkins
7142 Kermore Lane
Stanton CA 90680
(714) 527-0422

Club Pet, Inc.
Arthur A. Bousquet
3464 East Cherokee Road
Stockton CA 95205
(209) 465-2400

Truckee Sierra Boarding Kennel
Larry McCurry
PO Box 8398 / 10040 Alder Crk
Truckee CA 95737
(916) 587-2678

Gln-Be's Cockers & Pet Motel
Betty Mae Ashby
HC01-Box 690, 68854 29 Palms
Twentynine Palms CA 92277
(619) 362-5154

Eden Kennels
Mr & Mrs Loftsgaard
30644 Dyer Street
Union City CA 94587
(415) 471-0573

Van Nuys Pet Hotel
A.B. Thomas/Sharon Mortensen
7004 Hayvenhurst Ave.
Van Nuys CA 91406
(818) 787-7232

CeCe Belle Pet Hotel
Sharon R. Campbell-Black
29920 Margale Lane
Vista CA 92084
(619) 758-7322

Elenbusch Kennels, Reg.
Mary K. Karat
814 Crestview Road
Vista CA 92083
(619) 726-2068

Wunderbar's Pet Hotel
Roberta Semjenow
695-North Gate Road
Walnut Creek CA 94598
(415) 930-9767

Westlake Pet Motel
John C. Mills
800 E. Carlisle Road
Westlake Village CA 91361
(805) 497-8669

Canyon Hills Animal Clinic
Dr. M.E. Turano
23259 Lapalma Ave.
Yorba Linda CA 92687-3801
(714) 692-8232

John's Knl "Camp Best Friends"
Cathi Helfer
4691 Valley View Ave.
Yorba Linda CA 92686
(714) 528-8188

Vinjon's Kennel
Vince & Judy Jones
17651 Imperial Hwy.
Yorba Linda CA 92686
(714) 528-8734

Hi Dez Kennels
Kay Baker
56460 Paseo Los Ninas
Yucca Valley CA 92284
(619) 365-3111

CANADA

Terramara Kennels Reg'd
Terry & Ray Bagley
Box 426 Grand Centre
Alberta CD T0A 1T0
(403) 639-3477

A Very Important Pet Care Ctr
Shane Gullacher
4311 Glenmore Trail S.E.
Calgary CD T2C 2R8
(403) 297-2273

Calgary's Pet Hotel
Marlene Brooks
624 147th Ave SW
Calgary Alb. CD T2Y 2E7
(403) 256-4433

Country Clubs Pet Resort
Marlene Brooks
624 147th Ave SW
Calgary Alb. CD T2Y 2E7
(403) 256-4775

Dalmeny Farm Kennel
Peter & Jane Gibson
1400 Freeman Rd. RR 3
Cobble Hill CD V0R 1L0
(604) 743-2338

Centre Canin Dorval Inc.
Nicole MacDuff
175 Jenkins
Dorval, Quebec CD H9P 2W6
(514) 636-8316

Forrestdale Boarding Kennels
Brian & Janet Forrest
RR#1
Freelton CD L0R 1K0
(416) 659-1520

Terra Glen Total Pet Care Inc
Dr. Nancy Tarzwell
RR #4
Georgetown CD L7G 4S7
(416) 873-0431

Valley East Pet World
R.E. Rowell
1639 Radar Road
Hanmer CD P0M 1Y0
(705) 969-5490

Del Norte Kennels
R. Bruce Maclean/D. Hayden
7491 Lantzville Road
Lantzville CD V0R 2H0
(604) 390-3289

Aarondare Kennels
Doug & Jo Ann Belter
6534-46 A St (Box 3601)
Ledue CD T9E 6M4
(403) 986-9802

Molly Bay Kennels
John & Siegrid Edworthy
2621 Powerline Rd. W./RR2
Lynden Ontario CD L0R 1T0
(519) 647-3073

Cawlar Enterprises Inc
Wm. Caw/Diana Lariviere-Caw
RR #2
Maberly Ontario CD K0H 2B0
(613) 268-2520

Seneca Knls-A Place For Pets
Greg & Bette Holtman, CKO's
Box 37 GR13 SS1 Winnipeg
Manitoba CD R3C 2E8
(204) 633-6114

Cat & Dog Hotel
Bill & Wendy Waters
861-17th Street S.W.
Medicine Hat Alb. CD T1A 4X9
(403) 527-2865

Harphill Kennels, Reg'd
Mrs. Helene J. Proudfoot
P.O. Box 84 Goulds
Newfoundland CD A1S 1G3
(709) 745-5373

Li Ming's Pet Resort
Dawn Cutforth
PO Box 299
Nobleford CD T0L 1S0
(403) 757-2476

Cape Breton Brdg Knl Sls/Svc
Keith Clarke
RR # 1 Glace Bay
Nova Scotia CD B1A 5T9
(902) 737-2281

Pussy Pause Motel
Barbara J. Corbin
Site 28 Box 14-RR 1 Tantallon
Nova Scotia CD B0J 3J0
(902) 823-2501

Dennison Boarding Kennels
Lilias Dennison
RR# Martintown
Ontario CD K0C 1S0
(613) 528-4929

Brighton Kennels
T. Touzel/M. Edwards
Bx30 Montee InterProvincale
Pointe Fortune CD J0P 1N0
(514) 451-5112

Aberdeen Kennels
7300 #5 Road
Richmond CD V6Y 2V2
(604) 273-3022

The Paw Shoppe Ltd.
Bertha Little
662 Gondola Point Rd.
Rothesay CD E2E 1L7
(506) 847-8812

Puppy Love Pet Care Centre
Martin James & James Angus
2918 Lamont Road
Saanichton CD V0S 1M0
(604) 652-6255

Spruce Haven Kennels
Helen & Kenneth Marshall
2016 3rd Line West
Sault St Marie CD P6A 6K4
(705) 254-7423

Nobleton Boarding Kennels
Ellis Greenstein
RR 3
Schomberg CD L0G 1T0
(416) 859-3922

Country Kennels
Ron & Marie Glover
RR#1
Smithville CD L0R 2A0
(416) 945-4021

Berrydown Pet Boarding
Barbara Bird
4181 - 152nd Street
Surrey CD V3S 4N7
(604) 576-6248

Barala Kennels
Stewart Gerrior
Station A Box 237
Winnipeg CD R3K 2A1
(204) 633-2629

COLORADO

Academy Acres Kennels
Chuck & Barbara Grote
16501 E. Arapahoe Rd.
Aurora CO 80016
(303) 690-1188

Stonebridge Country Kennels
Barbara J. Holloway
1205 S. Lima St.
Aurora CO 80012
(303) 755-1888

Cottonwood Kennels
Penny Vardell
7275 Valmont Road
Boulder CO 80301
(303) 442-2602

D n R Kennels
Doug and Renate Pearson
PO Box 4029 /0115 Gateway
Dr
Breckenridge CO 80424
(303) 453-6708

Mid-Valley Kennel
Beth Acker
16478 Hwy 82
Carbondale CO 81623
(303) 963-2744

Cedar Ridge Animal Hospital
Dr. John Sudduth
757 Garden of the Gods Rd.
Colo. Springs CO 80907
(719) 593-9592

Countryside Kennel
Ann Roache
7945 Maverick Road
Colorado Springs CO 80908
(719) 495-3678

Pinehurst Animal Center
Judy and Robert Thiel
6500 W. Hampden Ave.
Denver CO 80227
(303) 985-1845

Southeast Area Vet. Med. Cntr
Karen Slocum, Mgr.
9801 E. Iliff Ave.
Denver CO 80231
(303) 751-4954

Trails End Kennels
Ms. Deane C. Newman
3293 E. Hwy 40, Box 106
Dinosaur CO 81610
(303) 374-2201

Wingate Kennels
Sam Mersfelder, DVM
9464 E. Coley Ave.
Englewood CO 80111
(303) 771-8620

K-Fel Boarding Kennel
Susan Andelt
3200 E. Mulberry
Fort Collins CO 80524
(303) 224-2908

Country Squire Kennels
Shaun & Donna Jordan
3320 N. Shields St.
Ft. Collins CO 80524
(303) 484-3082

Country Aire Brdg Knl
Hildegarde S. Morgan
808 S. Country Road E
Loveland CO 80537
(303) 669-2084

Blue River Kennel
Koma Murray
PO Box 10000 / 26454 Hwy 9
Silverthorne CO 80498
(303) 468-2761

Steamboat Veterinary Hospital
Nancy A. Nelson, Knl Mgr.
Box 775267
Steamboat Springs CO 80477
(303) 879-1049

Pet Village Boarding Kennel
Jeff & Catherine McLaury
11440 W. 44th Ave.
Wheat Ridge CO 80033
(303) 422-2055

CONNECTICUT
Keystone Kennels
Mark Levine, CKO
Route 42 Cheshire Road
Bethany CT 06525
(203) 393-3126

MacDonald Veterinary Hosp, Inc
Jeff G. Will DVM
267 Cottage Grove Road
Bloomfield CT 06002
(203) 242-5506

Shoreline Pet Lodge
Dennis Butler
PO Box 43
Branford CT 06405
(203) 488-9660

Roaring Brook Kennels
Peter D. Berk, DVM
PO Box 330
Canton CT 06019
(203) 693-0603

Cromwell Kennels
Robert F. Efron DVM
547 Main Street
Cromwell CT 06416
(203) 635-2984

Oronoque Kennel
Glenn Grover
1 Krakow Street
Derby CT 06148
(203) 735-3624

Nevatel Kennels
Stewart Warren
Rt. 79, Madison Road
Durham CT 06422
(203) 349-8493

Wes-Mar
Joan & Norman Girard
119 Goodwin St.
East Hartford CT 06108
(203) 289-7585

Harlan Ridge Kennel
Sharon Griswold
PO Box 243 (Old Colony Rd)
Eastford CT 06242
(203) 974-0256

Engelberg-Kristy Animal Hosp.
John T. Kristy, VMD
181 Kings Hwy
Fairfield CT 06430
(203) 367-4475

Sand Road Animal Hospital
Cindy Sandefer
136 Sand Road
Falls Village CT 06031
(203) 824-5223

Balmoral Canine Summer Camp
Allen C. Ade II
Rt 7 PO Box 154
Gaylordsville CT 06755
(203) 354-3433

Candlewick Kennels
Dennis M. Roy
2811 Hebron Ave.
Glastonbury CT 06033
(203) 633-6878

Lone Pine Kennel
Mrs. Paul Roitsch
39 John Street
Greenwich CT 06831
(203) 661-4739

Bar-Mike Kennel
Bill Arnold
25 Briscoe Road
Lakeville CT 06039
(203) 531-1061

Sterling Pet Lodge
Dan & Lucia Spendolini
193 Porter Pond Rd
Moosup CT 06354
(203) 564-4310

Merryall Kennels
Edward & Josette Miller
83 Merryall Road
New Milford CT 06776
(203) 355-2732

Connecticut K-9 Ed Cntr
Robert C. Schatz
239 Maple Hill Ave
Newington CT 06111
(203) 666-4646

Canine Country Kennel
Patti Clark
227 Hattertown Road
Newtown CT 06470
(203) 426-6535

Cassio Kennels
Joy S. Brewster
173 Mt. Pleasant Rd.
Newtown CT 06470
(203) 426-2881

Red Rock Kennels
Fred R. Olson
Box 129, Boom Bridge Rd.
North Stomington CT 06359
(203) 599-3977

Silver Trails Animal Inn
William Bernard
454 Providence New London
Tnpk
North Stonington CT 06359
(203) 599-1784

Norwichtown Brdg Kennels
E. Joyce Luft
763 Scotland Road
Norwich CT 06360
(203) 822-6342

Hemlock Trails Brdg Cattery
Barbara & Howard McKee
157-1 Mile Creek Rd.
Old Lyme CT 06371
(203) 434-2771

Severn Kennels
Fred & Carol Vogel
31 Jericho Rd.
Pomfret Center CT 06259
(203) 928-3978

Wayfarer Kennel
Lloyd and Eileen Erskine
46 Jobs Pond Road
Portland CT 06480
(203) 342-1067

The Boarding House
Dr. Donald W. Hartrick
726 Connecticut Ave.
So. Norwalk CT 06854
(203) 838-8421

Baywood Kennels
Gail Pivar
10 Moose Meadow Road
West Willington CT 06279
(203) 429-5533

Silver Trails The Animal Inn
Lillian & George Bernard, CKOs
706 Horse Hill Road
Westbrook CT 06498
(203) 399-7673

Town House For Dogs
Mel & Sandra Goldman
1040 Post Road East
Westport CT 06880
(203) 227-3276

Sundial Kennels
37 Liberty Street
Wilton CT 06897
(203) 762-7147

Day Hill Kennels
Roger P. Ball
136 Addison Rd.
Windsor CT 06095
(203) 688-2370

Camelot Kennels, Inc.
Amanda A. Albert
45 Porter Road
Wolcott CT 06716
(203) 879-4280

Wolcott Veterinary Clinic P.C.
Jeffrey Miller
400 Center St.
Wolcott CT 06716
(203) 879-4641

DELAWARE
Home Away From Home
Denise J. Irwin
RD 5, Box 223 A
Lewes DE 19958
(302) 684-8576

Never Never Land Knl & Cattery
D. Quillen
RD #3 Box 261 A
Lewes DE 19958
(302) 645-6140

Branch Oaks Kennel
Agnes M Stevenson
RD 1 Box 76
Rehoboth Beach DE 19971
(302) 227-8268

Heavenly Hound Hotel
Janice K. Gohl
Rt 1 Box 57
Selbyville DE 19975
(302) 436-2926

Animal Inn Inc
Gayle Warren
912 S. Dupont Hwy
Smyrna DE 19977
(302) 653-5560

FLORIDA
Greenbrier Kennel
Barry Grimm
3703 W. Kelly Park Rd.
Apopka FL 32712
(407) 886-2620

K-9, Inc.
Robert & Helen Gailey
15020 County Road 48
Astatula FL 34705
(904) 742-3427

Spanish River Dog & Cat Brdg
Dr. J.E. Phillips
180 W. Spanish River Blvd
Boca Raton FL 33431
(407) 368-0583

Chateau du Chien
Scott Holloway
5006 34th Ave East
Bradenton FL 34208
(813) 746-5060

Pooch's Pet Lodge Inc.
Bob & Pooch Tubbert
2105 64th St. Court East
Bradenton FL 34208
(813) 747-6199

For Fours Acres
Sue Finter
4444 Raines Road
Brooksville FL 34609
(904) 796-2441

Haus Sirius Kennel
Martha H. Sadler
19123 Yontz Road
Brooksville FL 34601
(904) 796-4715

Sweet 'N Lo Pet Motel
W. E. Watson
24392 Lanark Rd.
Brooksville FL 34601
(904) 796-7788

Bow Meow Grmg & Brdg Corp
Inc
Teresa Lombardo
349 N. Orlando Ave
Cocoa Beach FL 32931
(407) 783-7684

Coral Spgrs Animal Hosp
Lloyd S. Meisels, DVM
1730 University Dr.
Coral Springs FL 33071
(305) 345-6000

Hush Puppy Knls & Pet Cem. Inc
Dennis & Diane Thomas
3629 Hwy 92
Daytona Beach FL 32124
(904) 258-3591

Palmieri's V.I.P. Kennels
Margaret M. Palmieri
6222 Airport Rd.
Daytona Beach FL 32124
(904) 756-2313

Part of The Family Knls,East
Don or Judy Hester
10202 McIntosh Rd.
Dover FL 33527
(813) 986-4646

Bobbi's World Kennels
Rene Russo, CKO - Jack Russo
1040 NW 53rd St
Ft. Lauderdale FL 33309
(305) 491-8189

Hill's Home Boarding For Dogs
J. Nelson
1724 NE 58 St
Ft. Lauderdale FL 33334
(305) 733-8454

Holly Acres Kennel
Kelley Rose
10701 Stirling Rd.
Ft. Lauderdale FL 33328
(305) 434-1535

The Animal House
Carol Stinson, CKO
912 Denton Blvd.
Ft. Walton Beach FL 32548
(904) 863-1333

Suburban Animal Hospital
Mark W. Coleman, D.V.M.
3831 Newberry Road
Gainesville FL 32607
(904) 377-3361

Sun Kiva Farm Kennel
Marie (Toni) Thompson
Rt 1 Box 361F
Hawthorne FL 32640
(904) 481-3082

Wolff's Kennel Inc.
Fidel Acosta
2530 West 2nd Ave.
Hialeah FL 33010
(305) 885-3623

El Saba Kennels, Inc.
Mrs. S.J. Monett/D.L. Bloom
21255 SW 312th St.
Homestead FL 33030
(305) 248-8013

Cypress Springs Kennels
Carrie Christain
PO Box 2931
Homosassa Springs FL 32647
(904) 628-6174

Lakeside Kennels
John & Janet Carroll
5999 Turner Camp Rd.
Inverness FL 32650
(904) 726-5591

Southside Boarding Kennel
Dr. Thomas O. Kennard, D.V.M.
11459 Beach Blvd.
Jacksonville FL 32216
(904) 641-2230

Creature Comforts Pet Resort
Pati Hatfield
5534 Park Street
Jacksonville FL 32205
(904) 389-9008

Hideaway Knls/Camelot Poodles
Paula S. & Gareld B. Smith
4549 U.S. Alt. 27, N.
Lake Wales FL 33853
(813) 676-1987

The Pet Motel
Putt Boucher
313 Hickory Hammock Road
Lake Wales FL 33853
(813) 676-5736

Cleveland Hts Animal Clinic
Willie H. Tucker
3710 Cleveland Hghts Blvd.
Lakeland FL 33813
(813) 646-2995

Animal House
Nancy J. Saxe DVM
3530 Lantana Rd
Lantana FL 33462
(407) 439-2246

Paradise Pet Motel
Alice Mandelker
1641 West Bay Drive
Largo FL 34640
(813) 581-6831

Driftwood Boarding Kennels
Fred Figg, CKO & Rita Figg
P.O. Box 668
Laurel FL 34272
(813) 485-6672

J D P Kennel
Richard & Janet Yant, CKO's
4865 W. Gulf to Lake Hwy
Lecanto FL 32661
(904) 746-3302

Country Club Pet World
Ken Dobmeier
PO Box 1370
Longwood FL 32750
(407) 767-6428

A Country Cat House
JoAnn Roberts, CKO
12006 S.W. 64 St
Miami FL 33183
(305) 279-9770

Kritter Kennels Inc.
Vera Brown
507 John Sims Parkway
Niceville FL 32578
(904) 678-6121

Ormond Kennel & Pet Center
Gary & Debbie Bessette
1211 Golf Ave.
Ormond Beach FL 32174
(904) 673-8041

Canine Estates Inc.
Barbara & Blayne Doyle
1808 Hardin Lane, NE
Palm Bay FL 32905
(305) 723-3703

"Just Like Home Kennel" Inc
Jill Davies
7925 SW 48th Ave.
Palm City FL 34990
(407) 220-2239

Parkway Pet Hotel
Dr. K. Duesenberg
739 S. Tyndall Parkway
Panama City FL 32404
(904) 763-8387

Acacia Animal Clinic
Dr. Theodore J. Leif
4771 North Federal Highway
Pompano Beach FL 33064
(305) 942-5955

The Dog House
Elliott Federman
3541 Northwest 14th Ave.
Pompano Beach FL 33064
(305) 941-9391

The Total Pet Complex
Jay A. Shapiro, DVM
880 State Rd. A1A
Ponte Vedra Beach FL 32082
(904) 285-7684

Bryn Kennels, Inc.
Jacqueline Long
834 Taylor Road
Port Orange FL 32019
(904) 761-3647

All Pets Motel
Thomas Riva/Ronald Riva
9725 Fruitville Rd.
Sarasota FL 34240
(813) 371-1200

Colkim Kennel Inc.
Laurel & Betty Colgate
7518 Churchill Downs Rd.
Sarasota FL 34241
(813) 922-8476

Windsong Acres Brdg Knls/
Stbls
Judy Ciampi
701 Thunderbird Hill Rd.
Sebring FL 33872
(813) 385-5245

Oakhurst Kennels, Inc.
Drs David Tollon CKO/ T. Krall
7785 Oakhurst Rd.
Seminole FL 34646
(813) 397-8844

Four Paws Boarding &
Grooming
Virginia & Alfred Makuc
P.O. Box 5010
Spring Hill FL 34606
(904) 596-5607

All Pets Inn
Carole Ann Larson
5340 66th Street N.
St. Petersburg FL 33709
(813) 546-1108

Lafayette Boarding Kennels
Richard Bevis
1120 March Rd.
Tallahassee FL 32301
(904) 656-2856

Air Animal/Woolf Animal Hosp.
Walter M. Woolf, V.M.D.
4120 West Cypress Street
Tampa FL 33607
(813) 879-3210

Holiday Pet Inn
Pete Keeney
3907 Henderson Blvd.
Tampa FL 33629
(813) 289-9214

Part Of The Family, Inc.
S. LaDue / S. Rodriguez
3820 W. Humphrey
Tampa FL 33614
(813) 932-3232

Village Animal Lodge/Pet Care
Sheila Shaw
13221 N. Dale Mabry
Tampa FL 33618
(813) 961-6699

Animal Inn
Michael Pyles
39564 US 19 N
Tarpon Springs FL 34689
(813) 942-3691

Windsong Kennels
Sharon Carr
12540 U.S. Hwy 301 N.
Thonotosassa FL 33592
(813) 986-5699

Ed's Pet Motel
Edward E. Snead
205 Ave "T" NW
Winter Haven FL 33881
(813) 293-0295

GEORGIA

Pet Lodge, Inc.
Kitty Cathey
3456 Bethany Rd.
Alpharetta GA 30201
(404) 475-8554

Animal Med Clinic Pet Care
Maxwell R. Sidner, DVM
1785 Hwy. 29 N.
Athens GA 30601
(404) 548-9207

Pet's Retreat
Lynda S. Grant
145 Sandy Springs Rd.
Athens GA 30601
(404) 354-8944

The Alpha Academy of Dog
Trng.
Bob & Diane Moorefield
710 Ponce De Leon Ave NE
Atlanta GA 30306
(404) 874-5224

Back Acre Kennels
Bill & Becky Cole, CKO's
Rt 2 Box 245
Boston GA 31626
(912) 498-7321

Canine/Cattery Country Club
Henri C. Woodman
Rt. 2, Box 90
Brunswick GA 31520
(912) 264-9060

Rockdale Kennels
Gary & Nancy Gschwind
3006 Highway 20 SE
Conyers GA 30208
(404) 483-3918

Professional Grmg & Brdg Knl
B J Darnell & Judy Pratt CKOs
1813 Old Lafayette Road
Ft. Oglethorpe GA 30742
(404) 866-8228

Reigning Cats & Dogs
Walter Britt Schaffeld
563 Battlefield Pkwy
Ft. Oglethorpe GA 30742
(404) 858-0362

Mountain View Pet Lodge
Joyce DeLay
Rt 3 Box 130-D
Jasper GA 30143
(404) 692-6604

Camden Kennels
Sam & Cheryll Pierce
1177 Oldstill Road
Kingsland, GA 31548
(912) 729-9000

Brookside Kennel Inc.
Bunny Sherman
769 Grayson-New Hope Road
Lawrenceville GA 30245
(404) 962-1117

Bay Creek Kennels
Pamela DeHetre
3149 Georgia Hwy 81 SW
Loganville GA 30249
(404) 466-8944

The Dog House Knl & Grmg Inc
Grace A. Woodford
22 Jefferson Place
Newnan GA 30263
(404) 253-7234

Indian Shoals Pet Resort
Kenneth & Angela Peevy
3560 Indian Shoals Road
Pacula GA 30211
(404) 995-9123

Clanton Vet Hosp/Pet Motel
Kathy NeSmith
PO Box 547
Thomasville GA 31799
(912) 226-1914

Bar-King Dog Kennel
James & Sarah Scanlon
P.O. Box 1184
Keaau HI 96749
(808) 966-8733

IOWA
Countryside Boarding Kennel
Tim & Sheryl Martin
8940 N.E. 29th Street
Ankeny IA 50021
(515) 964-1180

Mississippi Ridge Brdg Kennels
Jim and Nancy Kettmann
RR2 Box 88
Bellevue IA 52031
(319) 872-3735

Hilltop Kennels
John and Sharon Pease
1403 Wilson Ave SW
Cedar Rapids IA 52404
(319) 363-1054

Avondale Animal Hospital,P.C.
Dennis O. Woodruff DVM
4318 S.E. Army Road
Des Moines IA 50320
(515) 262-6111

Vista Kennels
R.F. & Harriet Anderson, CKO
4400 NE 46th Street
Des Moines IA 50317
(515) 262-0309

A+ Boarding Kennel
Garry & Barbara Mishler
201 S. 16th Ave.
Eldridge IA 52748
(319) 285-9977

Mite-Win-Kennels
Marie Hollinger
Rt 1
Mason City IA 50401
(515) 423-4851

IDAHO
ADA Boarding Kennel
Dr. Virgil Pennell
8250 W. Victory Rd.
Boise ID 83709
(208) 362-5288

Teton Kennels
Karleen Janssen
1947 East 65th North
Idaho Falls ID 83401
(208) 353-9387

Gem Crest Kennels
Mona Allison
4140 Goldenrod
Meridian ID 83642
(208) 375-4398

ILLINOIS
Apolda Kennels
John & Carol Magill
2380 E. New York St.
Aurora IL 60504
(708) 898-2947

Barrington Brdg Kennels, Inc.
Dan & Barb Jelinek
10 Hillside Drive
Barrington IL 60010
(708) 381-6009

Meyer's Kennel
Brian Meyer
5390 Irene Rd.
Belvidere IL 61008
(815) 547-5778

Scott's Boarding Kennel
David Kruger, DVM
2005 Beich Road
Bloomington IL 61701
(309) 829-5023

Rowens Kennels
Pat (CKO) & Robert Owens Sr.
Rt I Box 10A, Brown Road
Brighton IL 62012
(618) 372-3837

Indian Creek Kennel
Marilyn Bouhl
R# 1 Box 331
Carbondale IL 62901
(618) 529-4700

Erickson's Brdg & Grmg Kennel
Jack T. Erickson
8711 Ridgefield Rd.
Crystal Lake IL 60014
(815) 459-9580

Countryside Pet Motel
Paul & Carolyn Leifheit
3117 S. Waterman Road
Dekalb IL 60115
(815) 758-3074

Aboretum View Animal Hosp
Thomas Lassiter, DVM
2551 Warrenville Rd
Downers Grove IL 60515
(708) 963-0424

Cedar Lane Kennels
Peter & Susan Gabor
6901 Dunham Road
Downers Grove IL 60516
(312) 969-1198

Brewster Creek Kennels, Inc.
Sandra G. Roberts
7N337 Route 25
Elgin IL 60120
(708) 697-1525

Country Lane Pet Lodge
Deborah Held
4948 W. Stephenson St. Rd
Freeport IL 61032
(815) 232-3915

Timber Hill Kennel
Donna Werkheiser
682 N. Van Buren
Freeport IL 61032
(815) 235-8999

Casey Road Pet Motel
Oscar Calanca, CKO
18753 West Casey Road
Grayslake IL 60030
(708) 362-3567

Kountry Kennels
Judi Roberts
12 N 911 Rt 20
Hampshire IL 60140
(708) 741-5434

Canine Inn Ltd
Rhea & Marvin Yanow
454 Green Bay Rd.
Highwood IL 60040
(312) 432-0771

Bark 'N' Town Kennels
Sherry Linning, CKO
27607 W. Brandenburg Rd.
Ingleside IL 60041
(815) 385-0632

Lake Forest Boarding Kennel
810 W. Everett Rd.
Lake Forest IL 60045
(312) 234-3120

Sunny Acres Kennel, Inc.
Timothy Harris B.S., D.V.M.
27848 N. Bradley Rd
Libertyville IL 60048
(708) 362-0390

Topono Boarding Kennel
Timothy & Patricia Olmstead
RR#1 - Box 628
Momence IL 60954
(815) 472-6836

Prospect Boarding Kennel
Charles Esser
P.O. Box 127
Mt. Prospect IL 60056
(708) 253-8389

Countryside Animal Spa/Small's
David W. Small
29278 Rt 83
Mundelein IL 60060
(312) 566-4650

Pampered Paws
Susan M. Koutny
Box 236 / Highway 45
Mundelein IL 60060
(312) 816-6494

Natl Dog & Cat Hotel, Inc.
William E. Taylor
3375 North Milwaukee Ave.
Northbrook IL 60062
(708) 824-4455

Preiser Animal Hospital
H.W. Preiser, DVM
2975 N. Milwaukee
Northbrook IL 60062
(708) 827-5200

Preiser Boarding Kennel
Herbert W. Preiser, DVM
2975 N. Milwaukee
Northbrook IL 60062
(708) 827-5200

Green Meadow Kennels
Denise Monaco
3110 Meyers Rd
Oak Brook IL 60521
(708) 968-3343

Airport Pet Lodge
Dr. D. R. Stephenson
1213 Lockheed Lane
Rockford IL 61109
(815) 397-4597

Country Lane Kennels
Richard Theyerl
8000 E. Riverside
Rockford IL 61111
(815) 398-7387

Illiana Brdg. & Grmg. Inc.
Bob Beezie
16249 Van Dam Road
S. Holland IL 60473
(312) 339-4424

Dal Acres Boarding Kennel
Glen Hudspeth
3528 E. Cook St.
Springfield IL 62703
(217) 522-1047

Doggone Grooming &
Boarding
Geri & Greg Wessel
RR #1 Box 180A
St. Jacob IL 62281
(618) 644-5823

Poochi's
Pauline W. Eldred
3412 Kings Rd.
Steger IL 60475
(312) 747-7074

Sumar Kennel
Sue & Marv Meyer
Rt 1 Box 218
Trivoli IL 61569
(309) 362-2321

Oakview Kennel & Cattery
Cassie Inman
27645 Case Rd
Wauconda IL 60084
(708) 526-1288

Paw Print Kennel
Thomas Blosser/Pat Blosser
27 W 150 North Ave.
West Chicago IL 60185
(708) 231-1117

INDIANA
Spring Valley Kennels Inc.
P.J. Shubert
6149 W Country Ln
Anderson IN 46011
(317) 643-8444

Wayport Kennels, Inc.
Geoff & Sandy Harlan, CKO's
7657 N. Hwy 37
Bloomington IN 47404
(812) 876-2098

Bittersweet Kennels
Ray W. Weaver
19341 C.R. 16
Bristol IN 46507
(219) 848-5210

Carmel Pet Inn
Sue Veroneau
376 Gradle Drive
Carmel IN 46032
(317) 848-7387

Village Park Animal Center
Dr. Michael P. Graves
15018 Greyhound Court
Carmel IN 46032
(317) 848-1898

Belmar Farms Kennels, Inc.
Billie J. & Elmer D. Marlin
5841 N. 500 West
Columbus IN 47201
(812) 372-0561

Windsong Pet Care Center
Phyllis & Richard Dixon
52677 CR 11
Elkhart IN 46514
(219) 264-0396

East Side Animal Hospital
Scott L. Thompson, DVM
4125 East Morgan Ave.
Evansville IN 47715
(812) 477-3826

Alpine Kennels, Inc.
Daniel Den Uyl
6358 St. Joe Center Rd.
Fort Wayne IN 46835
(219) 485-3512

Shady Oaks Farm
Ron & Annie Jureziz
12631 Alexander Drive
Granger IN 46530
(219) 272-1533

Sleepy Hollow Pet Ranch
Teresa Black
147 W. Tri Sab Ln.
Indianapolis IN 46217
(317) 787-8040

Petsburgh by Paw Prints
Dr. John F. Griese, DVM
2506 State Road 25 North
Lafayette IN 47905
(317) 423-5500

Pet Pals, Inc.
Julie Getz / Peggy Swain
10388 West 400 North
Michigan City IN 46360
(219) 879-2898

Hurstacres Kennel
Mrs. Pat Hurst
2910 N. Nebo Rd.
Muncie IN 47304
(317) 284-0903

Bay Creek Pet Care Centre
Bruce & Kathy Shand
30750 Inwood Road, RR #1
North Liberty IN 46554
(219) 232-7314

Hickory Acres Boarding Kennel
Edward Peter Huser
RR#3, Box 261
Sheridan IN 46069
(317) 769-4296

Southlane Veterinary Hospital
Dr C J Keeley - Dr R J Jones
1259 Sturdy Road
Valparaiso IN 46383
(219) 462-4114

Klondike Kennels Inc
Lisa B Banker/John Blair,DVM's
3663 North 250 West
West Lafayette IN 47906
(317) 463-1603

KANSAS
High Halo Kennels Inc.
Mel & Milli Dold-Pat Pile
15901 West Hwy 54
Goddard KS 67052
(316) 794-2203

Morning Star Kennels
James M. Middleton
Rt. 4, Box 215
Lawrence KS 66044
(913) 842-9979

Somsen's
Marge & Warne Somsen
8550 E. Hwy 24
Manhattan KS 66502
(913) 776-9686

Denly Kennels
Dennis and Emily Snyder
1817 East 22nd Street
Topeka KS 66605
(913) 233-8368

Holly Lane Kennels
Eileen McClintock
1731 N.W. Menoken Rd.
Topeka KS 66618
(913) 233-6612

Bed & Bisquit Pet Center
Jim Halsig
5 Central Pkwy
Wichita KS 67206
(316) 681-1411

KENTUCKY
Robinwood Kennel
Ann C. Robinson
102 Robin Lane
Cold Spring KY 41076
(606) 781-2352

Shady Grove Kennel
Julia Worthington
Rt #5 - 2479 Airport Rd
Danville KY 40422
(606) 236-0624

Sundance Kennels, Inc.
Deana J. Ucinski
5088 Oliver Rd. Box 709
Independence KY 41051
(606) 356-7900

Village Kennels
Mary Kastner, CKO
501 S. 1st St.
La Grange KY 40031
(502) 222-7000

Keshlyn Kennels
Kevin & Carolyn Hamlin
3566 Walnut Hill Road
Lexington KY 40503
(606) 272-4412

Dogwood Kennels
Charles & Joyce Thompson
15811 Shelbyville Road
Louisville KY 40245
(502) 245-9740

Minirosa Kennels
Gary & Hilda Ellis
5225 Bardstown Road
Louisville KY 40291
(502) 499-1910

Royalton Kennels
Harold & Maydene Ellen Kapen
8620 Bardstown Road
Louisville KY 40291
(502) 239-0827

Vine Crest Kennels
Ellen T. Leslie
7924 Vine Crest Ave.
Louisville KY 40222
(502) 425-5145

Waggin Tail Kennels
Beverly & Ronald Tucker
2105 Lexington Road
Louisville KY 40206
(502) 583-2498

Bluegrass Kennel & Cattery
Joel Duchin
Box 137D Burger Road
Melbourne KY 41059
(606) 635-7534

All Creatures' Inn
Lindley P. Wemmer
1989 Catnip Hill Rd.
Nicholasville KY 40356
(606) 233-9000

Woodford Vet. Clinic/Kennel
Jacqueline Nielsen, Mgr
PO Box 108 (Lexington Rd)
Versailles KY 40383
(606) 873-1595

LOUISIANA

Alexandria Pet Inn
Angie Townley
56 Heyman Lane
Alexandria LA 71303
(318) 473-2070

Pine Hill Boarding Kennels
Elizabeth Grobe
Rt 7 Bx 198-9 (Peach Orch. Rd)
Bastrop LA 71220
(318) 281-2963

Animal Care Unlimited
Janice K. Breaux
61734 Shady Pine Road
Lacombe LA 70445
(504) 882-5601

All Creatures Cntry Club
Bill & Shari Karanas
23098 Hwy 1088
Mandeville LA 70448-9806
(504) 626-9664

Good Going Pet Resort
Henry & Ann Minton
4436 N. LA Hwy 169
Mooringsport LA 71060
(318) 929-2435

Moonbeam Kennels
Debbi LeClere
HC 69 Box 620-E
St. Francisville LA 70775
(504) 766-4620

MASSACHUSETTS

Belchertown Boarding Kennel
Diane Villemaire
176 Ware Road
Belchertown MA 01007
(413) 323-7641

Puddlebank Farm
Carrie Barrett
12 Cranberry Meadow Road
Bellingham MA 02019
(508) 883-4663

Petcetera Kennels
Randall Feld D.V.M.
820 A Pleasant St.
Belmont MA 02178
(617) 484-6133

Country Time Pet Retreat
Joseph A. & Mary M. Rein
51 Elm Street
Berkley MA 02780
(617) 823-1903

Skipton Kennel
Steve H. Carlin
123 Terrace St.
Boston MA 02120
(617) 442-0747

Weloset Kennels & Shop
Robert Hughes, CKO
Route 97
Boxford MA 01921
(508) 887-5760

Holiday Kennels
Norman Sebell
1014 Pearl Street
Brockton MA 02401
(508) 583-8555

Sutter Creek Kennel Inc.
Beth Freeman/Larry Breakell
114 N Worcester St-PO Box
387
Chartley MA 02712
(508) 222-4752

Wignall Animal Hospital
David McGrath DVM
1837 Bridge St
Dracut MA 01826
(508) 454-8272

Greengate Farm & Kennels
Inc.
Jean Mason
881 Congress St.
Duxbury MA 02332
(617) 837-5125

Palmer's Kennels Inc.
Warner Cross
141 Porter Rd.
East Longmeadow MA 10128
(413) 525-3532

Kilduff Kennels
Maribeth McMahon
140 Brookfield Road
Fiskdale MA 01518
(508) 347-7701

Stacy Kennels
Carol A. Stacy
High Rock Rd
Fitchburg MA 01420
(508) 345-1001

Animal Inn Inc.
A.M. Bernstein D.V.M.
Route 130
Forestdale MA 02644
(508) 477-0990

ABKA Kennels

Harvard Kennels
Donna Kelleher
259 Ayer Rd.
Harvard MA 01451
(617) 772-4242

Canine College
Bruce D. Billings, Jr.
White Rock Spring Road
Holbrook MA 02343
(617) 767-3908

Blue Moon Kennel
Leslie Taft
RD 1 Box 76F / Rt 183
Housatonic MA 01236
(413) 274-6674

Kamelot Knl of Mendon Inc
Gene Milbier
97 Millville Rd.
Mendon MA 01756
(508) 478-6390

Tee Emm's Kennels, Inc.
Frederic W. Meisner
202 Tyler Street
Methuen MA 01844
(617) 683-5795

Rufco Kennels
Bertie & George Royal
154 Riverlin St.
Millbury MA 01527
(617) 791-2145

Bed And Biscuit Kennels
Kathleen Barry
RR 1 Box 196 -Beers Plain Rd
Northfield MA 01360
(413) 498-4311

Lake Farm Boarding Kennels
Bette P. Nale
53 Finlay Rd., P.O. Box 1721
Orleans MA 02653
(508) 255-7214

Starwood...a pet resort
Gale Studeny
RR 1 Federal Hill Road
Oxford MA 01540
(508) 987-0077

Animal Inn
Sally O. Kellogg
120 Hubbard Avenue
Pittsfield MA 01201
(413) 442-3472

Muddy Creek Animal Care Cntr
John K. Prentiss DVM
993 Haverhill St.
Rowley MA 01969
(508) 948-2345

Wintergreen Kennels
Judith Miller Conlin
Douglas Road
Southampton MA 01073
(413) 562-9478

Southboro Kennels Inc
Rebecca A. Moore
47 Oregon Rd.
Southboro MA 01772
(508) 485-5136

Briarhill Kennel
Susan W. Crowley
64 Taft St
Upton MA 01568
(508) 529-3580

Fairlawn Kennels
Ralph Bornstein
15 Main Street
Wakefield MA 01880
(617) 245-1237

Ven-Elger Pet Care Center
Ellen Ventura
855 Main Road
Westport MA 02790
(508) 636-8143

Meadowbrook Kennels
Robert & Patricia Nowosielski
25 Wright St
Woburn MA 01801
(617) 933-1237

Countryside Kennels
J. Richard Redmond
90 Ellery St.
Wrentham MA 02093
(508) 384-3484

MARYLAND
Anchors, Inc.
Norman & Marilyn Randall
17810 Indian Head Highway
Accokeek MD 20607
(301) 283-2626

Oak Park Kennels
Marion, Dee, Stephen
2133 Monumental Road
Baltimore MD 21227
(301) 242-8735

Pleasant View Kennels
Barbara Lundell
2825 Cub Hill Road
Baltimore MD 21234
(301) 665-6011

Rivermist Kennels Inc.
Barry Goodman
19515 New Hampshire Ave
Brinklow MD 20862
(301) 774-3100

Buckeystown Vet Hosp
Dr K Miller/S Sewell
3820 Buckeystown Pk POB 5
Buckeystown MD 21717-0005
(301) 698-9930

Happy Run Kennel
Lois Hunt
RD 1 Box 600AB
Chestertown MD 21620
(301) 778-5158

Kontinental Kennel
Valerie Fox
11209 Tippett Rd.
Clinton MD 20735
(301) 297-9244

Captain's Quarters For Pets
Barbara & Wayne Hambleton
175 Deaver Road
Elkton MD 21921
(301) 398-8320

Faraway Kennels
Robert & Lisa Barrett
4622 Lower Beckleysville Rd.
Hampstead MD 21074
(301) 239-8266

Riviera Boarding Kennels
Arlene Dodson/Linda Javorski
PO Box 429
Hughesville MD 20637
(301) 274-4456

Hunt Valley Kennels
Allan A. Frank, D.V.M.
11206 York Road
Hunt Valley MD 21030
(301) 527-1119

Bowag Kennels
O'Neill & Beverly Wagner
1501 Singer Road
Joppa MD 21085
(301) 679-3333

Cherry Lane Kennels Inc.
C C Sine, R M Sine, CKO
7218 Cherry Lane
Laurel MD 20707
(301) 776-6093

The Pet Salon
Deborah Wood
204 Obrecht Road
Millersville MD 21108
(301) 647-3505

Belquest Kennels
Michael & Vicky Creamer
18745 Penn Shop Rd.
Mt. Airy MD 21771
(301) 831-7507

Country Kennel, Inc.
Lawrence E. Cunnick
5718 Ridge Road
Mt. Airy MD 21771
(301) 831-7766

Countryside Kennels
Dennis Davidson
Box 36, Boyd's Turn Rd.
Owings MD 20736
(301) 855-8308

Deer Park Kennels
Stuart & Suzanne Berney
4815 Wards Chapel Road
Owings Mills MD 21117
(301) 655-8330

Tricrown Kennels
John & Polly Hanes
Box 27563 Rt 1
Oxford MD 21654
(301) 822-1921

Fieldstone Kennel
George & Mary Ann Alston
PO Box 96 (174 Obrecht Rd)
Pasadena MD 21122
(301) 647-6516

El Taro Kennels
Linda Wallaesa
18511 Darnestown Road
Poolesville MD 20837
(301) 428-8091

Lipsitt Training Services
Mark Lipsitt
14710 Sugarland Rd
Poolesville MD 20837
(301) 428-8300

Wonmore Kennel
Ms. Deane Lee Gutman
1404 Tome Hwy
Port Deposit MD 21904
(301) 658-4919

Reisterstown Boarding Knl Inc
Velma Gakenheimer
14454 Old Hanover Rd.
Reisterstown MD 21136
(301) 833-2090

Debendale Kennels
Deborah Smart
2332 Emory Road
Reistertown MD 21136
(301) 833-4762

Animal Inn
Jon R. Martin
15820 Red Land Rd.
Rockville MD 20855
(301) 926-9000

Carol's Pet Grooming & Brdg
Carol Graham
14650 Southlawn Lane
Rockville MD 20850
(301) 340-2547

Rockville Pet Hotel
Linda Leigh Buel
609 S. Stonestreet
Rockville MD 20850
(301) 340-3376

The Doghouse
Janet E. Messick
Rt 4 Box 276
Salisbury MD 21801
(301) 543-2525

Columbia Knls/Pet Ctr Inc
Sam & Elaine Milligan
9455 Lanham-Severn Road
Seabrook MD 20706
(301) 577-1090

Country Comfort Kennels
Patricia A. Weiskopf
2102 Mt. Horeb Rd.
Street MD 21154
(301) 692-5055

Pinewood Kennels
Ronald & Julia Bonar
Rt 1 Box 123A
Sudlersville MD 21668
(301) 758-2942

Dog & Cat Hotel Inc.
Gary Hauptmann DVM
714 1/2 North York Road
Towson MD 21204
(301) 825-8880

Groom & Board Kennel
Donald S. Armstrong
1030 1/2 York Rd.
Towson MD 21204
(301) 296-0484

Precious Pup Kennels
Norm & Jackie Weber
4705 Largo Road
Upper Marlboro MD 20772
(301) 952-0318

Queen Anne Kennels
George Saymon/Shirley Hobbs
17705 Queen Anne Road
Upper Marlborough MD 20772
(301) 249-1210

Amberlyn Kennel
Joseph/Deborah Simoldoni
10508 Daysville Rd.
Walkersville MD 21793
(301) 898-3106

Happy Hollow
Louise B. Pascal
1114 Fridinger Mill Rd.
Westminster MD 21157
(301) 876-1235

Woodland Farm's Knl &
Cattery
Carol Wallace
259A Burnt Mill Road
Willards MD 21874
(301) 835-3559

Shady Spring Boarding
Kennels
Don Farb/Charlotte Katz,
CKO's
P.O. Box 156
Woodbine MD 21797
(301) 795-1957

MAINE

Green Acres Kennel - Shop
Charles & Mary Jones
1653 Union St.
Bangor ME 04401
(207) 945-6841

Groom N' Board Kennels
Jessi MacGregor
1410 Essex St.
Bangor ME 04401
(207) 941-9825

Happy Hunter Kennels
Michael P. Gale
RR 2 Box 337
Belfast ME 04915
(207) 338-5483

Bear Pond Kennels Inc
Sibylle Perry
Bear Pond Rd / RFD 2 Box 2548
Buckfield ME 04220
(207) 224-7092

Creature Comforts
Dr Scott Moffat/K Fleming
RR2, Box 41
Kittery ME 03904
(207) 439-6674

Haggett Hill Kennels
Joan Goodwin
RR1 Box 1074 Dodge Rd
No. Edgecomb ME 04556
(207) 882-6709

Goose River Kennels
Linda Blazonis
Box 422 Cross St.
Rockport ME 04856
(207) 236-9753

Suntar's Kennel
Cliff & Sharon Plourd
POB# 444 / 750 Portland Rd
Saco ME 04072
(207) 282-1948

Avant-Garde Pet Care/Trng Ctr
Stella Russell
301 Roosevelt Trail
Windham ME 04062
(207) 892-8388

Pride and Joy Kennel
Frank & Donna Pride
59 Nash Rd.
Windham ME 04062
(207) 892-6883

York Country Kennels
N & W Perkins & S & J Ouprie
PO Box 334
York ME 03909
(207) 363-7950

MICHIGAN

Arbor Hills Pet Care/Trng Ctr
3290 Rentz Rd.
Ann Arbor MI 48103
(313) 475-2296

Wingford Kennel
Julie Nicholson
5220 Glyshaw Rd.
Avoca MI 48006
(313) 385-5335

"Paws 'N Claws" Pet Brdg Inn
Carol A. Nielsen
8780 Krupp Road
Bellding MI 48809
(616) 794-3641

Donto Kennels
Donna Wojan
05133 Barnard Rd.
Charlevoix MI 49720
(616) 547-6866

Pet Club, Inc.
Teri Kreple
05844 Pincherry Road
Charlevoix MI 49720
(616) 582-6800

Touchstone Kennels
Carol E. Hein
8314 Spicerville Hwy
Eaton Rapids MI 48827
(517) 663-2158

Pampered Pet Petel
Nora L. Wilkerson-Betts
7190 Dixie Hwy/Sterns Rd.
Erie MI 48133
(313) 848-8186

Brooknelle Kennels
Mr/Mrs Kenneth Nelson
4600 Knapp NE
Grand Rapids MI 49505
(616) 363-0619

The Animal Inn
Tracee & John Horn
Co Rd NF Box 545
Gwinn MI 49841
(906) 346-5945

Bay Pines Boarding & Grmg
Joan G. McDonald
8769 M-119
Harbor Springs MI 49740
(616) 347-1383

Caraway Kennels
Mary Beukemg
714 Gulick Rd.
Hasleh MI 48840
(517) 655-4178

Hill's Kennels
Fanny S. Hill
North 11405 Junet Road
Ironwood MI 49938
(906) 932-5810

Hallas Doghouse Acres
Don & Cindy Hallas
1700 Lindsey Road
Jackson MI 49201
(517) 529-9305

Woodland Veterinary Cntr P.C.
Dr. Edward Farnham
3012 Shaffer SE
Kentwood MI 49508
(616) 942-6780

Orion Kennel Club
Annette M. Battaglia
PO Box 788 / 75 Waldon Rd.
Lake Orion MI 48035
(313) 391-4200

Darling Dogs
Mary & David Darling
217 N. Fairview Avenue
Lansing MI 48912
(517) 484-7221

Wag'n Tails Pet Motel
Dina Perry
2408 East Mt. Hope
Lansing MI 48910
(517) 482-7799

Belle Creek Kennels
Katherine Lucy
29625 Munger
Livonia MI 48154
(313) 421-1144

Perky's Kennel
Herman Pyrkosz
37629 Lyndon
Livonia MI 48154
(313) 464-0232

Springfield Pet Resort/Trng
Dave D'Hulster
5200 Beard Road
North Street MI 48049
(313) 385-7007

Char Mur Kennels
Barbara L. Goodwin
48300 12 Mile Rd.
Novi MI 48050
(313) 349-2017

Burney's Ark Inc.
Ann Burney/Sallie Harroun
POB 269 (3100 Granger Rd)
Ortonville MI 48462
(313) 627-2929

Green Acres Boarding Kennels
Harold & Pat Sears
7100 West Samaria Road
Otawa Lake MI 49267
(313) 856-5735

Eves' Groom 'N' Room
Eva Pokryfke
37792 Paw Paw Road
Paw Paw MI 49079
(616) 657-3463

Blue Water Boarding Kennels
Cyril Grobbel/Maureen Healey
4209 Griswold Rd
Port Huron MI 48060
( ) -

Holiday Kennels
Brian & Cheryle Tuel
10950 Northland Drive
Rockford MI 49341
(616) 866-2294

Pine Hill Kennels
James Rypkema
8347 10 Mile Road
Rockford MI 49341
(616) 874-8459

Bill Wells Kennels, Ltd
Robert Turner
32283 Ecorse Road
Romulus MI 48174
(313) 721-2329

Arion Greenwillow Brdg Knl
Robert & Patricia Pellow
25430 W 9 Mile
Southfield MI 48034
(313) 356-3394

Kamber Kennels
Dr. R. E. Berman, CKO
33711 Harper Ave.
St. Clair Shores MI 48082
(313) 792-3000

Shores Kennels
Regina M. Vesco
33633 Harper
St. Clair Shores MI 48082
(313) 293-1429

AAA Dog & Cat Motel
Maryellen Darin
25280 Pennsylvania
Taylor MI 48180
(313) 946-5555

Rexpointe Kennels Inc.
Joel J. Smiler D.V.M.
6765 Rochester Rd.
Troy MI 48098
(313) 879-0940

Union Lake Pet Services
Robert I. Redisch, D.V.M.
6547 Cooley Lake Road
Union Lake MI 48387
(313) 363-6262

Pinehill Farm Pet Care
Richard & Gail Pellegrom
17063 Lake Mich. Dr.
West Olive MI 49460
(616) 842-7426

Acme Creek Kennel
Carol & Thomas Finch
5311 Bunker Hill
Williamsburg MI 49690
(616) 938-9518

MINNESOTA

Pet Watchers' Boarding Kennel
Rondell C. Peck
Rt # 2 Box 204
Austin MN 55912
(507) 433-4950

Northern Kennels
Gordon & Patricia Day
8633 Bemidji Rd NE
Bemidji MN 56601
(218) 751-5280

Pine Shadows Inc
M. Bronczyk/S. & M. Haglin
1313 3 Mile Rd. NE B
Brainerd MN 56401
(218) 829-4736

Derrickson Kennel
Richard & Robin Derrickson
RT 4 Box 181
Buffalo MN 55313
(612) 682-5539

Canine Comfort & Care
Jack Ignatowicz
33 Water Street
Excelsior MN 55331
(612) 474-3338

Oak Crest Kennels
Marilyn F. Brust
1450 - 50th St. E.
Inver Grove Heights MN 55077
(612) 451-7687

Animal Inn Boarding Kennel
Don & Joan Tauer
P.O.Box D/ 8633 34th St. N.
Lake Elmo MN 55042
(612) 777-0255

Doggie Daycare Kennel
Terry and Jana Demars
6360-233rd Ave NE
Linwood MN 55079
(612) 462-5789

Madison Avenue Pet Grooming
Jim Theuninck
501 Madison Ave
Mankato MN 56001
(507) 387-5894

Oak Ridge Kennels
Marilyn M. Swanson
1640 Game Farm Rd No
Mound MN 55364
(612) 472-3702

Lake Shady Kennels
Randy & Susan Bartz
1225 W. Center St.
Oronoco MN 55960
(507) 367-4782

Plymouth Heights Pet Hospital
Pierce Fleming DVM
3401 N. Hwy 169
Plymouth MN 55441
(612) 544-4141

Animal Friends
Kathy Schroeder/Rita Bee
28 7th St. N.E.
Rochester MN 55904
(507) 280-9572

K-9 Kennels Inc.
Kevin, Mike, Dan, Williams
5330 Hwy 14 East
Rochester MN 55904
(507) 289-2470

TLC For Pets
Don Orke
1205 7th St. NW
Rochester MN 55901
(507) 281-2944

Pensinger's Bluff High
Gerald Jack Pensinger
8260 McColl Drive West
Savage MN 55378
(612) 890-6010

Jan's Doghouse Inc.
Jan Ritsche
1692 St. Hwy 23 N.E
St. Cloud MN 56301
(612) 253-7555

Animal Ark
Marlene Foote, Pres.
PO Box 4444
St. Paul MN 55104
(612) 739-8512

Goldwood Kennels
Frank & Peggy Hilton
9500 Dellwood Road, North
White Bear Lake MN 55110
(612) 429-0648

Lone Lake Kennels Inc.
Colleen Griffis
6655 Bailey Road
Woodbury MN 55125
(612) 459-2234

Camp Comfort Kennel
Alan C. Seaton
7280 - 260th St.
Wyoming MN 55092
(612) 462-4614

MISSOURI
Dogwood Kennels
Joseph &Pamela Bonchonsky
Rt 1 Box 334
Centertown MO 65023
(314) 584-9305

Petropolis
Dr. Paul Schifano
16830 Chesterfield Airport Rd.
Chesterfield MO 63005-1404
(314) 537-2322

Ann Gafke's Teacher's Pet
Ann & Roger Gafke
325 East Dripping Springs Rd
Columbia MO 65202
(314) 443-0716

Fenwick Kennel
A. Clark Pennypacker
1105 W. Gleason Rd.
Columbia MO 65203
(314) 657-6100

The Pet Fair
Stephanie Kemp
1706 I-70 Dr. S.W.
Columbia MO 65203
(314) 445-7783

Sorenson Kennel
Tom Sorenson
1073 Hwy DD
Defiance MO 63341
(314) 828-5149

Baronwood Kennels
Gene & Donna Smith
17220 New Halls Ferry
Florissant MO 63034
(314) 838-2021

Hideaway Kennel
Mary Utter, CKO
RR 3 Box 392
Harrisonville MO 64701
(816) 884-5387

Dog House Inc.
Tom & Holly Rose
6701 Antire Road
High Ridge MO 63049
(314) 677-3131

Nancy Crane Kennel & Cattery
E R & Nancy Crane Davison
4216 Wilderness Lane
High Ridge MO 63049
(314) 343-2182

Honey Creek Pet Boarding
Elana & Kim McCoy
1714 Honey Creek Rd.
Jefferson City MO 65101
(314) 496-3138

Country Kennels
Caroline Crouthers
10014 E. 47th Street
Kansas City MO 64133
(816) 353-5675

Hecker Animal Clinic
Drs. Daniel Hecker/Ward Brown
7240 Wornall Rd.
Kansas City MO 64114
(816) 333-4330

Red Bridge Hideaway Kennel
Debby Smith, CKO
11135 Locust
Kansas City MO 64131
(816) 942-6800

Williams Elkhound Ranch
David J. Williams
9205 N. Brooklyn RR 29
Kansas City MO 64155
(816) 734-2526

Country Acres Kennels
Robert/Deborah Spitler-CKO
739 Weidman Road
Manchester MO 63011
(314) 227-1919

Wiliamsburg Kennels
Ed Rowley
13998 Manchester
Manchester MO 63011
(314) 227-5764

Bold Monarch Kennels
Halsey/Cornelia Tichenor,CKO
6101 Ozark Way
St. Charles MO 63303
(314) 441-1350

Kennelwood Village Inc.
D. Danforth Jr/Alan Jones, CKO
2008 Kratky Road
St. Louis MO 63114
(314) 872-7007

Silver Maple Farm
Paul Schifano,DVM
2014 N. Ballas Road
St. Louis MO 63131
(314) 965-1630

Innisfree Kennels
Gregory & Susan Lister
290 Hwy C
St. Peters MO 63376
(314) 278-3323

MISSISSIPPI
Lamay's Kennel
Wm. G. & Linda A. Lamay
10118 Choctaw Dr.
Bay St. Louis MS 39520
(601) 467-5281

Butler's Boarding Kennel
Oscar & David Butler
2030 Pass Road
Biloxi MS 39531
(601) 388-4093

Okatoma All Breed Brdg.
Kennel
Patricia Lambert
Route 1, Box 825
Hattiesburg MS 39401
(601) 582-4153

MONTANA
Heath Veterinary Hospital
Jean Allbright
1321 N. 27th St.
Billings MT 59101
(406) 245-4772

Guardian Kennels
J.M. Zednick
710 Jackson Creek
Clancy MT 59634
(406) 443-1117

Carol's Kennels & Dog Grmg
Carol Pierce, CKO
HC 68 Box 8154
Glendive MT 59330
(406) 687-3745

F & L Pet Resort, Corp.
Phyllis Fennel/Nancy Loendorf
1700 14th Ave. So.
Great Falls MT 59405
(406) 452-6828

Kanine Kondo
Judith Fenton
390 Norris Road
Helena MT 59601
(406) 458-5670

Ron's Rascal Ranch
Ron Hines
200 Kelly Rd.
Kalispell MT 59901
(406) 752-3647

AnimaLodge
Don Woerner, DVM
1310 Allendale Rd
Laurel MT 59044
(406) 628-4683

NORTH CAROLINA
North Carolina law prohibits pets
from staying in the room with
their owners at hotels, motels,
and other lodging. Be sure to
arrange for kennel space well
ahead of your trip to North
Carolina.

Apex Animal Care Center
Rebecca Stirewalt
1600 E. Williams St
Apex NC 27502
(919) 362-1123

Greenlevel Kennels
Deanna Haseltine
1401 Old Ivey Road
Apex NC 27502
(919) 362-7877

Avery Creek Kennel
Carol Powell
Rt 1 Box 112A
Arden NC 28704
(704) 684-2161

Greenwood Pet Motel
Susan Greene
Rt 1 Box 429
Bolivia NC 28422
(919) 253-6970

Cascade Valley Boarding Knls
Ruth A. Crowe
PO Box 1409 (Asheville Hwy)
Brevard NC 28712
(704) 883-3030

Tender Loving Care
Glenda Peterson
Town N Country Animal Hosp
204 S. Gurney St
Burlington NC 27215
(919) 227-9989

Tender Loving Care
Glenda Peterson
204 S. Gurney St
Burlington NC 27215
(919) 227-9989

Pet Manor
Sherry Pate
1217 E. Franklin St.
Chapel Hill NC 27514
(919) 942-5116

Blue Velvet Inn
Johnny Guthrie
5306 Poplar Springs Dr
Charlotte NC 28213
(704) 527-6671

Granbar Kennels
Peggy Giulini, CKO
6700 Orr Road
Charlotte NC 28213
(704) 596-8941

Horky's Paws Inn
Elizabeth Horky
5420 George St.
Charlotte NC 28208
(704) 399-1609

Durham Boarding Kennel, Inc.
Don W. Leathers
Rt 2 Box 576
Durham NC 27705
(919) 383-4238

Shady Grove Kennel
Don & Marty Koehler
Rt. 6, Box 236-A
Durham NC 27703
(919) 596-0235

Haus Schura Kennel
Irina S. Anderson
Rt. 12 Box 654
Fayetteville NC 28306
(919) 425-1774

Northgate Animal Hospital
Jack D. Brown
2921 Ramsey Street
Fayetteville NC 28311
(919) 822-3141

Hideaway Hills Kennel
Vicki Hope
225 Lane Rd
Flat Rock NC 28731
(704) 685-3149

Battle Branch Kennels
Jeff & Vicki Walker
181 Ellijoy Rd.
Franklin NC 28734
(704) 369-6726

Beechline Kennels
Marie & Bob Beech, CKO
3410 Spring Garden
Greensboro NC 27407
(919) 855-8292

Best Friends Bed/Biscuit
Melanie/Rick Schlaginhaufen
PO Box 13545
Greensboro NC 27415
(919) 282-8533

Nanhall Training Center
Frances W. Keyes
2206 Asheboro Street
Greensboro NC 27406
(919) 272-6584

Helens Grmg World & Pet Motel
Helen D. Bach
3198 E. 10th St.
Greenville NC 27858
(919) 758-6333

5 Star Kennel
Scott Lambert
PO Box 1209   (Hwy 64-70)
Hickory NC 28601
(704) 324-4372

Horse Shoe Kennel
Jeri J. Peterson
PO Box 84
Horse Shoe NC 28742
(704) 891-3705

Bar-B's Pampered Pooch
Barbara Walters
405 Center St.
Jacksonville NC 28540
(919) 577-7297

Four Seasons Pet Care
Robert M. Sheegog, Jr.D.V.M
10 Doris Avenue East
Jacksonville NC 28540
(919) 347-5298

Willow Run Boarding Kennels
Warren "Buddy" Weiss
1456 Oak Ridge Rd.
Kernersville NC 27284
(919) 993-3647

Salty Dog Grooming & Boarding
Justine O'Neal
Rt 1 Box 905K
Kill Devil Hills NC 27948
(919) 441-6501

Animal Kennel Care
Melanie Wallwork
10524 Idlewild Road
Matthews NC 28105
(704) 545-5192

Kustom Kare Kennel
Betty Ganung
PO Box 914
Morgantown NC 28655
(704) 438-4126

Wyndham Wood Kennel
Deborah K. Womble
Rt 1 box 41E
Nashville NC 27856
(919) 443-4868

The Pet Spa
Susan G. Ridgeway
1804 South Glenburnie Rd.
New Bern NC 28560
(919) 633-1204

Country Side Brdg Knl
Robert M. McBride, CKO
6280 Robinhood Rd
Pfafftown NC 27040
(919) 945-9321

Pineville Pet Quarters
Barry Davis
12716 Downs Circle
Pineville NC 28134
(704) 588-5800

Canine Country Club
Susan Schaler
1654 North Market Drive
Raleigh NC 27609
(919) 876-9538

Dr. Norman F. Manning
2200 Digby Ct
Raleigh NC 27613
(919) 870-5804

Pinebrook Kennel
JoAnn Luckwaldt
5332 Yates Pond Rd.
Raleigh NC 27606
(919) 851-1554

Pet's Companion Inn
Charles & Gwen Pharr, CKO
Rt 1 Box 11-K
Rougemont NC 27572
(919) 477-0618

Happy Hills Prof. Grmg & Brdg
Cheryl Routh
Rt 2 Box 364
Staley NC 27355
(919) 622-3620

Wildwood Kennels
Lynn & Blaine Garland
Rt. 1, Box 117 (Hwy 16)
Stanley NC 28164
(704) 822-6082

Dogwood Acres
Karen Clarke/Loretta Miller
Rt 2 Box 104A
Sylva NC 28779
(704) 586-6109

Cobble Hill Kennels Inc
Patty & Bill Pace
Chalks Rd P.O. Box 31
Wake Forest NC 27588
(919) 556-1177

Rahama Kennel and Cattery
Leslie Young/Don Denman
223 Underwood Rd.
Waynesville NC 28786
(704) 452-2176

Meadow Sweet Kennels
Judie & Eddie Inscoe
5523 Greenville Loop Rd
Wilmington NC 28409
(919) 791-6421

Sylvia's Pet Care Center
Sylvia C. Hall
26 New Bern Ave.
Wilmington NC 28405
(919) 799-2375

The Nature of Things Brdg Knl
Stan Johnson
5746-B Oleander Drive
Wilmington NC 28403
(919) 452-2225

Briarwood Kennel
Charlie P. Dedmon, Jr.
Rt 6 Box 230G
Winston Salem NC 27107
(919) 769-2649

Winston Brdg Knl & Grmg
Parlor
Nancy Sapp
5400 Indiana Ave.
Winston-Salem NC 27106
(919) 767-7320

Hoffman-Haus Kennels
Lu & Doreen Livermon
Rt 2 Box 320
Winterville NC 28590
(919) 355-4663

Wilkinson Animal Hospital
Dr. James Gill
PO Box 83 - 510 Wilkinson Blvd
Wolell NC 28098
(704) 824-9876

NORTH DAKOTA
West Dakota Vet. Clinic Inc
Kim Brummond, DVM
Rt 6 Box 136
Dickinson ND 58601
(701) 225-0240

Fargo Boarding & Grooming
Svc
David & Sally Harmon
4108 3 Ave. NW
Fargo ND 58102
(701) 282-0197

Dakota Hunting Club/Knl
George Newton
Box 1643
Grand Forks ND 58206-1643
(701) 775-2074

NEBRASKA
Kenl Inn
K.Q. Allen
10101 E. Old Cheney Rd.
Lincoln NE 68526-9306
(402) 488-8190

Clearview Boarding Kennels
Kenneth & Mary Johansen
15601 Maple
Omaha NE 68116
(402) 493-5151

Kar Sim Kennel, Inc
Dan Jensen
6777 "C" St
Omaha NE 68106-4218
(402) 397-6950

Midlands Kennels
J.E. & Lu DeVoll
9223 N. 72nd
Omaha NE 68122
(402) 571-8594

Tully's Kennel
Allen & Julie Tully
7777 "D" St.
Omaha NE 68124
(402) 391-2456

Cottonwood Kennels, Inc.
Larry & Janice Dvorak
R.R. 1, Box 188A
Waterloo NE 68069
(402) 359-4155

NEW HAMPSHIRE
Nottingham Kennel
Russell H. Goodwin
6 Ponemah Rd
Amherst NH 03031
(603) 673-2771

Auburn Groom & Board
Lee Gallagher
18 Old Candia Rd.
Auburn NH 03032
(603) 668-8551

Brentwood Lochness Kennel
Barbara E. Lutes
340 Rt 125
Brentwood NH 03042
(603) 679-8874

Village Kennels/Grmg by Karla
Karla Schwarz
PO Box 534
Conway NH 03818
(603) 447-3435

Country Road Kennels
Robert & Linda Caley
RFD 1
Exeter NH 03833
(603) 772-4049

Village Sentry Kennel
Patricia A. Ciampa
PO Box 37 (14 Proctor Hill Rd)
Hollis NH 03049
(603) 465-3368

Sendaishi Kennels
William & Joyce Matott
355 Straw Road
Manchester NH 03102
(603) 622-9684

Stateline Veterinary Hospital
Dr. Roland E. Huston
325 So. D.W. Hwy
Nashua NH 03060
(603) 888-2751

Upwind Farms
Elizabeth de Forest
Pig Pen Corner
New Durham NH 03855
(603) 859-4171

Marcoda-Chantur Pet Shop/Knl
Theodore & Eileen Turchan
PO Box 561/125 Lafayette Rd.
North Hampton NH 03862
(603) 964-8514

Bittersweet Kennels
Richard B. Capron
20 Squamscott Road
Stratham NH 03885
(603) 772-5453

NEW JERSEY
Northcliff Kennels
Chris Doyle/Kathy Doyle
Brighton Road
Andover NJ 07821
(201) 786-5250

Bernardsville Country Kennels
Stephen & Robin Forish
PO Box 869/570 Mine Brook
Rd
Bernardsville NJ 07924
(201) 766-3929

ABKA Kennels

Hope's Kennels
Judith H. Tighe
RD 4, Box 464
Blairstown NJ 07825
(201) 459-4354

Cedarview Kennel
Catherine Ayars
RD 3 Box 313/Marlboro Jericho
Bridgeton NJ 08302
(609) 451-0350

Hal Wheeler's School For Dogs
Michael V. Marchese
1126 Pompton Ave.
Cedar Grove NJ 07009
(201) 256-0694

T. Blumig Kennels Inc.
Gloria Blumig
645 Old Stage Road
East Brunswick NJ 08816
(908) 251-3210

Hi-Crest Kennels
Joseph Reno
2154 Oak Tree Rd.
Edison NJ 08820
(908) 561-7098

Pets & Their People
Charles F. Price
133 South Ave.
Fanwood NJ 07023
(201) 322-5111

Mansion House Kennels, Inc.
Jennifer E. Keller
46 Old Swartswood Sta. Rd.
Fredon NJ 07860
(201) 579-1476

Brookline Kennels
Mark & Cathy Engleman
RD 3, Elton Road
Freehold NJ 07728
(201) 462-1397

Forge Hill Farm
Marjorie Krauter
RR 3 Box 436
Glen Gardner NJ 08826
(201) 689-6046

Hay Hill Kennels
Richard Quackenbush
905 N. Washington Ave.
Green Brook NJ 08812
(201) 968-2265

Carriage House Kennel
Gale B. Armstrong
PO Box 2 - Kennedy Road
Greendell NJ 07839
(201) 383-5733

Highland Kennels
Lillian Knobloch
1424 Maxim Southard Road
Howell NJ 07731
(908) 364-4443

Sugar Pine Kennels
Betty Ryan
4023 Ridgeway Rd/Rt 1
Lakehurst NJ 08733
(201) 657-7818

Animal Inn Pet Hotel
Dr Stan Golub/Sally Smith CKOs
PO Box 425 (1901 Rte 46 W)
Ledgewood NJ 07852
(201) 691-2662

Bryans Country Kennel
Hank & Linda Bialous
2750 Egg Harbor Rd.
Lindenwold NJ 08021
(609) 784-4559

Falkenturn Kennels
Lois Theile/Carl Theile
20 Force Hill Rd.
Livingston NJ 07039
(201) 994-6194

Harvest House Kennels
Harry Stiles & Lee Walker
46I W. Mill Rd. Rt 513
Long Valley NJ 07853
(201) 832-2025

Holly Creek Kennels
Frank & Norma Hugo
RD 19 Taunton Road
Marlton NJ 08053
(609) 983-0460

Clover Mall Animal Hospital
Kathleen Stryeski, DVM
3100 Quakerbridge Rd
Mercerville NJ 08619
(609) 890-7844

Allen's Kennel Inc.
Dottie Allen
25 Beth Drive
Moorestown NJ 08057
(609) 235-0196

Morris Animal Inn, Inc.
Walter & Marianne Morris
Sand Spring Road
Morristown NJ 07960
(201) 539-0377

Pioneer Pet Care
Vincent J. Demasi Jr.
623 Amwell Road
Neshanic Station NJ 08853
(201) 369-3955

Stonehill Farm Kennel Inc
Judy Laureano
125 Union Valley Rd
Newfoundland NJ 07435
(201) 697-8480

Sandy Hill Kennels
Charles P. Lucas
RD #4 Box 409 Bank Bridge Rd
Sewell NJ 08080
(609) 468-5060

Somers Point Kennels
Dennis & Ann Minton
5 Holly Hills Dr
Somers Point NJ 08244
(609) 927-5118

Woodland Kennels, Inc.
Christina Dickson
RD 2 Box 161A
Sussex NJ 07461
(201) 875-3908

Purr 'N Pooch Inc.
Dick Palazzo
86 Gilbert Road West
Tinton Falls NJ 07724
(201) 528-8100

Applewood Kennels
Bruce & Susan Gregory
P.O. Box 344 / Rt. 94
Vernon NJ 07462
(201) 764-4691

Lotta Luv Animal Lodge
Gene & Kathy Mittnacht
2981 N. Delsea Dr.
Vineland NJ 08360
(609) 696-4965

Brookside Country Kennels
Edward & Ginger Buis
21 Brookside Drive
Warren NJ 07060
(201) 469-2633

Roxdane Kennels Inc.
Lenore & David Cooke, CKO
75 Stirling Road
Warren NJ 07060
(201) 755-0227

Kauffman Kennels Inc.
Raymond & June Kauffman
P.O. Box 353
Windsor NJ 08561
(609) 448-3114

NEW MEXICO
Academy Boarding Kennels
John & Carolee Douglas
6000 Brentwood Lane N.E.
Albuquerque NM 87109
(505) 884-7878

Acoma Pet Center, Inc.
Robert L. Spradley
321 Wyoming S.E.
Albuquerque NM 87123
(505) 268-3391

Canine Country Club
A.S.Wershaw
7327 4th Street NW
Albuquerque NM 87107
(505) 898-0725

New Mexican Kennels
Juxi & Dan Burr
4401 Yale, N.E.
Albuquerque NM 87107
(505) 344-0158

Black Mesa Boarding Kennel
Allen & Bernice Meddles
Rt 1 Box 393-BB
Espanola NM 87532
(505) 753-9530

Best Friends
Augusta Farley
Rt 2 Box 305F
Santa Fe NM 87505
(505) 471-6140

Paw Print Kennels
Phoebe Wershaw
Rt 14 Box 316/Racetrack Frg Rd
Santa Fe NM 87501
(505) 471-7194

Rice's Kennels
William E. Rice
Rt 2 Box 600
Santa Fe NM 87505
(505) 473-0925

Southwest Animal Care Complex
John and Lyn McKee
Box 88
Santa Teresa NM 88008
(505) 589-4417

NEVADA
Brebeau Kennel
Sharon Badger
PO Box 2041
Elko NV 89801
(702) 738-2108

Irrenhaus Boarding Kennels
Herb & Doris Estabrook
1931 Churchill Street
Gardnerville NV 89410
(702) 782-3664

Paws 'N Claws Animal Lodge
Terri Bounty
650-A W. Sunset Rd
Henderson NV 89015
(702) 565-7297

Animal Inn/Am Animal Svcs
John A. Schoumaker
3460 West Oquendo Rd.
Las Vegas NV 89118
(702) 736-0036

Pet Village Inc.
E. Lee Monthei
3161 S. Industrial Road
Las Vegas NV 89109
(702) 735-7160

Sierra View Kennel
Laurel Kawchack/Tammy Litka
3140 Hwy 395
Minden NV 89423
(702) 267-2251

NEW YORK
Alden Boarding & Trng Kennels
Marsha Whipple
100 Sullivan Rd.
Alden NY 14004
(716) 937-3331

Pinekroff Kennels, Inc.
Deborah & John Mohr
W. 5 Mile Box 402
Allegany NY 14706
(716) 372-0961

Betenbil Kennels
William J. Savoca
RD 2 Box 468/Brandle Rd.
Altamont NY 12009
(518) 861-8391

Chestnut Ridge Boarding Knls
Betty Farrell
RD 4 Box 349
Auburn NY 13021
(315) 252-8087

Windsong Farm
Don& Lisa DelloStritto
RD 4 Box 217
Auburn NY 13021
(315) 253-3185

Shield Crest Kennel
Robert & Sheila Monks
3340 Galway Rd.
Ballston Spa NY 12020
(518) 885-1738

Northwood Kennels Inc.
DBA Northwind Kennels
Route 22
Bedford NY 10506
(914) 234-3771

Cariblu's Country Club
Rita McHugh
RD 1 Box 213A Pierce Creek
Rd
Binghamton NY 13903
(607) 723-0229

Pennwoods TLC Resort
Kent Rosenbloom/G. Margaritis
1556 Morgan Road
Binghamton NY 13903
(607) 669-4277

Camillus Hills Pet Lodge
Sally Sherman
2744 West Genese Turnpike
Camillus NY 13031
(315) 672-5154

Maple Ridge Kennels
Styles Bridges
RD 4 Box 45/Pierrepont Rd.
Canton NY 13617
(315) 386-3796

Shannon Kennels
Andrea Derr/Mike Fusco
Box A
Carlisle NY 12031
(518) 234-7748

Carmel Country Kennels
Christopher & Eileen Gabriel
Richardsville Road
Carmel NY 10512
(914) 225-7717

Happy Day Kennel
Clifford W. Steele
111 Rt 6
Carmel NY 10512
(914) 225-2463

Wyeland Kennel
Jane E. Eckelman
RD.2 Box 145-Jackson 2 Rd.
Carthage NY 13619
(315) 493-1886

Blue Jay Kennels
Jay & Rusty Josephson
RD I Brown Hollow Road
Corning NY 14830
(607) 524-6603

Willow Pet Hotel
Marc Rosenzweig
1926 Deer Park Ave.
Deer Park NY 11729
(516) 667-8924

Kliffside Kennel
Lynn G. Sisson
Route 28, PO Box 255
Eagle Bay NY 13331
(315) 357-3607

Delta Pond Kennel
John & Mary DeFreest
RFD #1 Box 206
East Nassau NY 12062
(518) 766-5103

Malibu Pet Hotel
Michael Smith
107 Guy Lombardo Ave.
Freeport NY 11520
(516) 379-6040

We Kair Kennels
Jean E. Breen
RD 7 Box 666 Chase Rd.
Fulton NY 13069
(315) 592-9284

Black Forest Kennels Inc
Karl Kneis
2135 Jericho Tpke
Garden City Park NY 11040
(516) 746-1547

The Animal Inn, Inc.
Robert & Sandra Paddock
I Sea Cliff Ave.
Glen Cove NY 11542
(516) 759-2662

Whispering Pines Brdg Kennel
Janet L. Cook
RD 1 Box 482 (Pine Grove Rd)
Glenfield NY 13343
(315) 376-8349

Heatherstone Kennels
Carol C. Stone
2070 Grand Island Blvd.
Grand Island NY 14072
(716) 773-4296

Island Pet Services
Kevin & Valarie Wilson
1821 Grand Island Blvd.
Grand Island NY 14072
(716) 773-1595

Aegis Kennels, Inc.
Iris Almanza
H.C. 83 - Box 170
Harpersfield NY 13786
(607) 652-7654

Balmoral Kennels
Mary Ann Collins
590 Harrison Ave.
Harrison NY 10528
(914) 967-1721

Ludworth Knls of Westchester
Thomas J. Braig
Jackson Ave.
Hastings on Hudson NY 10706
(914) 478-1633

Grenadier Kennels
Sheila Marson
16191 Ridge Rd
Holley NY 14470
(716) 638-5608

Add-En-On Kennels, Inc.
Patty & Bruce Coates, CKO
112 Pond Rd.
Honeoye Falls NY 14472
(716) 624-1155

White Meadow Farm Inc.
Mayling Koval
PO Box 503
Hopewell Jct. NY 12533
(914) 221-2066

Country Acres Kennels
Andrea Russell
111 Whitson Road
Huntington Station NY 11746
(516) 427-6077

Country Club Kennels
Robert/Suzanne DalCortivo
Box 94 Cross Rd.
LaGrangeville NY 12540
(914) 223-3618

Club Pet
Kimberly Addesso
Rt 9W
Lake Katrine NY 12449
(914) 336-5893

Mahopac Joylymar Kennels Inc
Joyce Diamond/Margaret Nichols
RD 13 Box 303 Austin Rd
Mahopac NY 10541
(914) 628-4460

Quail Run Kennel Inc.
Donald & Mary Sterling
126 Peconic Ave.
Medford NY 11763
(516) 475-4573

Dakola Kennels & Cattery
Eileen Murphy
560 North Street
Middletown NY 10940
(914) 342-2005

Rock Ridge Kennels
Ellen & Eugene Nesin
PO Box 859 (Rock Ridge Dr.)
Monticello NY 12701
(914) 791-7444

Lohr's "Country" Boarding
Kathy Lohr
RD #2 Box 112
Munnsville NY 13409
(315) 495-5781

Capt Haggertys Scl for Dogs
Capt. A.J. Haggerty
222 Seaman Ave #8B
New York NY 10034-6101
(212) 220-7771

Manhattan Pet Hotel
Lorin Caputo
312 E. 95th St.
New York NY 10128
(212) 831-2900

Sutton Dog Parlour
Marcia Habib
1161 York Avenue
New York NY 10021
(212) 355-2850

We Kare Kennels Inc.
Jan Kornhauser
410 W. 220th Street
New York NY 10034
(212) 567-2100

Niagara Kennels
John & Joanne Schaal
7920 E. Britton Dr.
Niagara Falls NY 14304
(716) 297-0696

Schaffer Kennels
Michael S. Schaffer
3376 Niagara Falls Blvd.
North Tonawanda NY 14120
(716) 694-6070

Eagle Ridge Brdg Kennel, Inc.
Sally & Carolyn Cataldo
7081 Ellicott Road
Orchard Park NY 14127
(716) 662-5302

K-9 Grooming & Pet Motel
Marie C. Schadt
RD #7 Johnson Road
Oswego NY 13126
(315) 343-5158

Fawnacre Pet Care
Barbara D. Craig
6379 Valley Rd
Owego NY 13827
(607) 687-5271

Holiday Tyme Pet Hotel
Janet Hansen
P.O. Box 77
Patterson NY 12563
(914) 878-6655

Quimbanda Kennel
Gordon H. & Mary A. Link
Box 118, Banks Road
Pike NY 14130
(716) 567-2655

Central Kennels
F. Pilato/A. Pilato
1710 Hudson Ave.
Rochester NY 14617
(716) 342-3140

Rye Country Brdg Kennels Inc.
Stella & Sam DiEdwards
Nursery Lane
Rye NY 10580
(914) 967-4577

Briarpatch Farm & Kennel
Marianne Porter
RD 1 Gordon Rd
Sloansville NY 12160
(518) 868-2058

Country Estate Kennels
Kenneth McGowan/James Shea
4850 Authur Kill Rd
Staten Island NY 10309
(718) 356-3933

Baby Brown Kennels
Harriet Lynne Sage
PO Box 184
Stone Ridge NY 12484
(914) 687-7237

Colby Kennels
Linda & Alan Jobson
Box 655 Route 94
Vails Gate NY 12584
(914) 562-5275

New Hartford Anml Hospital
Frank Mondi V.M.D.
3947 Oneida St. Box 431
Washington Mills NY 13479
(315) 737-Pets

Supernal Pet Motel
Jacqueline & Donald Neddo
480 Hudson River Rd
Waterford NY 12188
(518) 235-2103

Hillside Kennels
Stanley Eldridge
RD2 6205 Hadcock Road
Watertown NY 13601
(315) 788-2844

Dolly Marshall Kennels
Sandra Betz-Savoca
PO Box 171 /Tanners Neck Ln
Westhampton NY 11977
(516) 288-3535

Eagle Hill Pet Care Center
Joyce Hill
P.O. Box 248, Graves Road
Westmoreland NY 13490
(315) 853-8523

Stonybrook Kennels
Michael Larizza
500 Lake Street
White Plains NY 10604
(914) 946-0961

OHIO

Hayden Run Kennels
Susan W. Osborn
7187 Hayden Run Road
Amlin OH 43002
(614) 876-7974

Mellett Grooming & Boarding
Shirley Fritz
4636 W. Tuscarawas St
Canton OH 44708
(216) 477-8808

Windcrest Kennels & Cattery
Cynthia Schwartz Hoskins
501 Meadowcrest Drive
Cincinnati OH 45231
(513) 771-6224

LaRoi's Kennels
LaRoi Susan Johnson
1145 Williams Road
Columbus OH 43207
(614) 491-0093

Fieldacre Kennel
Patricia J. Goodwin
3270 Sawmill Rd/PO Box 4019
Copley OH 44321
(216) 666-8334

DeBo Kennels
Emil & Ida Tolnar
2356 Howland-Wilson Rd.
Cortland OH 44410
(216) 637-8176

Balmorhea Kennels, Inc.
David E. Luken, Pres.
5285 Wagoner-Ford Rd.
Dayton OH 45414
(513) 233-2577

Jae-Mar Kennels
Winston L. Blythe
4040 Seybold Rd.
Dayton OH 45426
(513) 837-1563

Paws Inn Inc.
Raymond Fournier, D.V.M.
8926 Kingsridge Drive
Dayton OH 45458
(513) 435-1500

The Narrows
Kathleen Smith
6330 Frederick Pike
Dayton OH 45414
(513) 890-0574

Torok Kennels
Marilyn Sims
2016 Troy Street
Dayton OH 45404
(513) 233-6281

Findlay Animal Care Center
Kim Haggerty
1614 W. Main Cross
Findlay OH 45840
(419) 423-4445

Sweet Run Kennel
Treena Smith Mgr
8485 Dustin Rd
Galena OH 43021
(614) 965-1767

Dawn's T.L.C. Grmg & Brdg
Dawn Yoder
1704 Amity Rd.
Galloway OH 43119
(614) 878-0049

Calico Kennels
Judy M. Allie
6237 Kyles Station Rd.
Hamilton OH 45011
(513) 777-2027

Pine View Kennels
Robert & Tamara Conmay
PO Box 155
Hoytville OH 43529
(419) 278-7145

Tannenberg Kennels
Robert L. Becker
2625 E. Stroop Rd.
Kettering OH 45440
(513) 293-9233

Hocking Hills Kennel
Christine & Charles Parsons
Rt. 2, Box 199
Little Hocking OH 45742
(614) 989-2295

Animal Medical Clinic
Palmer J. Johnson, DVM
2450 Leavitt Road
Lorain OH 44053
(216) 282-3105

Mohican Kennels
Joni Studer
2656 Lexington Ave.
Mansfield OH 44904-1428
(419) 884-7387

Phil-Adore Kennels
Phyllis Simmons
1550 Harding Hwy. E
Marion OH 43302
(614) 387-0545

All Breed Kennels
David Robison/Denise Hurd
833 Illinois Ave.
Maumee OH 43537
(419) 893-7218

Chippewa Kennels & Grooming
John Zimmerly
5873 Lafayette Rd.
Medina OH 44256
(216) 725-8529

Mentor TLC Pet Lodge
George & Laraine Zivich
7430 Clover Avenue
Mentor OH 44060
(216) 975-9789

Colonial Acres Kennel Inc.
Laura Kling
5373 Cincinnatti/Dayton Rd.
Middletown OH 45044
(513) 777-2266

River Taw Kennels Inc.
Ron & Glenna Chidester
Box 159 (27681 Cummings Rd)
Millbury OH 43447
(419) 241-7387

Kittens & Canines Country Inn
Phillip Curry
18280 Hopewell Rd
Mt. Vernon OH 43050
(614) 392-1237

Promway Kennels, Inc.
Thomas A. Cassidy, Pres.
6451 Promway Ave. N.W.
North Canton OH 44720
(216) 494-8100

Kenilridge Kennel & Kattery
Carol & Roger Au, CKO
31882 Center Ridge
North Ridgeville OH 44039
(216) 327-8281

Braemar Kennels
Stephen C. & Deborah K. Smith
748 Zenobia Rd.
Norwalk OH 44857
(419) 668-4073

Joyce Widynski
6184 Darlene Circle
Painesville OH 44077
(216) 357-8846

Pinewood Pet Lodge
J. Plassard
661 Newell Street
Painesville OH 44077
(216) 354-4331

Paws Awhile Kennel & Grmg
Joseph & Angie Pavone
3430 Brush Rd.
Richfield OH 44286
(216) 659-9450

Big Times Kennel Inc.
Ronald & Harriet Buxton
10650 Clyo Road
Spring Valley OH 45370
(513) 885-3427

Karnik Inns Of America, Inc
Ray & Charon Bauman, CKO's
5411 Black Road
Waterville OH 43566
(419) 878-8888

OHIO

The Pet Cottage
Judy Edgecomb
8330 Rd 28
Zanesfield OH 43360
(513) 465-8590

The Pet Motel
Sue Patterson
3798 Chandlersville Rd
Zanesville OH 43701
(614) 455-3855

OKLAHOMA
Country Club Kennels
Harrell G & Nona L Harwell
24401 E. 97th St. S.
Broken Arrow OK 74014
(918) 251-1478

Hilltop Pet Hotel, Inc.
Virgil J. Reed
Rt 2 Box 135-3
Coweta OK 74429
(713) 495-8483

Moore Pet Center
Rick & Sharon Elkins
P.O. Box 1625/1317 N. 5th
Duncan OK 73534
(405) 255-6051

Delmar Smith Kennels, Inc.
Delmar Smith
Rt 3 Box 257
Edmond OK 73013
(405) 478-1171

Redwind Kennels
James J. Baum, CKO
Rt 1 Box 114-B
Norman OK 73072
(405) 329-9129

Westwood Veterinary Hospital
Dr. Don Biles
111 North Mercedes
Norman OK 73069
(405) 364-1100

Anne's Country Club for Pets
A. Lockney & M. Blackburn
4200 E. Britton Rd.
Oklahoma City OK 73131
(405) 478-2303

The Pet Resort
Larry J. Nieman, DVM
13517 Railway Dr.
Oklahoma City OK 73114
(405) 751-1944

Cottonwood Ctry Club/Pets
Clarence & Priscilla Wells
80 Sherwin Ave.
Ponca City OK 74604
(405) 762-7790

DeShane Kennels, Inc.
David E. Nickle
1115 S. 129th E.Ave.
Tulsa OK 74108
(918) 437-3343

Circle "C" Doggie Dude Ranch
Thomas & Gloria Cronin
PO Box 155
Vera OK 74082
(918) 371-4537

OREGON
Smokette Kennels
Harris & Nancy Kimble
1140 S.W. 185th
Aloha OR 97006
(503) 649-1367

Forest Glen Kennel Inc.
Leland & Winnifred Irwin
16645 S.W. Scholls Ferry Rd
Beaverton OR 97007
(503) 649-4962

Sunny-Butte Kennel
Madeleine Davis
66220 Barr Rd.
Bend OR 97701
(503) 389-1228

Don Logan Boarding Kennel
Don Logan
18651 S.E. Foster
Boring OR 97009
(503) 666-4800

Corvallis Kennels
Larry & Marlene McNeill
720 S.W. Wake Robin Ave.
Corvallis OR 97333
(503) 757-9089

The Shaggy Dog
Kim Schaecher
11975 Clow Corner Rd.
Dallas OR 97338
(503) 623-3883

Countryside Pet Spa
Terry & Cheryl McCamman
7769 Southeast 282
Gresham OR 97080
(503) 663-3370

Mountainview Boarding
Kennels
Lester & Theresa Jonak
24809-B S.E. Rugg Rd.
Gresham OR 97080
(503) 666-8118

Buttercreek Kennels
Carol L. McIntosh
Rt 4 Bx 4250 Buttercreek Hwy
Hermiston OR 97838
(503) 567-9663

Rock Creek Kennels
Darrell Lewis
Rt 1 Box 1013
Hillsboro OR 97124
(503) 645-2912

Fletcher's Boarding Kennels
John & Vicki Huber
12959 Southeast Powell Blvd.
Portland OR 97236
(503) 761-2091

Townhouse Pet Care Center
Lorlyn Anderson, CKO
2965 NE Sandy Blvd.
Portland OR 97232
(503) 230-9596

Weona Kennel, Inc.
M. Greenwood/Anne Belter
Mgr.
8427 SW 58th Ave.
Portland OR 97219
(406) 453-4946

Pet Village LTD.
Ray Reid
3185 Turner Rd. S.E.
Salem OR 97302
(503) 363-3647

Pommoregon Kennels
Alan Ivers
2670 Hollywood Dr. N.E.
Salem OR 97305
(503) 362-6263

Archer's Boarding Kennels
Darlene Morris
18750 S.W. Pacific Hwy.
Sherwood OR 97140
(503) 639-2343

Wilson River K-9 Lodge
Koko Laviolette
15780 Wilson River Hwy
Tillamook OR 97141
(503) 842-6930

PENNSYLVANIA
Groomingdale's Country
Kennels
Mary Beth Trout
2941 Hickory St.
Allison Park PA 15101
(412) 443-8989

Lay Dee Ayr Kennel
Dolores Leahy
RD 3 Box 507
Beaver Falls PA 15010
(412) 843-6083

Bucks County Pet Care
Karla Woodward
PO Box 917
Buckingham PA 18912
(215) 794-0423

Town and Country Dogs
Melissa S. Krane
R.D. #1 Box 111A
Canonsburg PA 15317
(412) 746-4052

Country-Aire Kennels
Doug Beattie/Robert Foltz
240 Shady Lane
Carlisle PA 17013
(717) 249-3809

Foxy Lady Kennels
Carole & Elaine Miller
404 Clay Rd.
Carlisle PA 17013
(717) 243-1020

The Funny Farm
Henry & Ruby Weeks
211 Echo Road
Carlisle PA 17013
(717) 249-5512

Steward Kennels, Inc.
Bill, Rita, & Mary Steward,CKO
3914 Pyle Road
Chadds Ford PA 19317
(215) 459-2724

Hickorybrook Farm Kennels
Pat Buerger
P.O. Box 304
Chalfont PA 18914
(215) 348-4454

Hickory Springs Farm Knls Ltd
Hartley Connett
Route 113
Chester Springs PA 19425
(814) 933-9584

Fifeshire's Pet Motel
Mary Sapovchak
1506 Gill Hall Road
Clairton PA 15025
(412) 655-3393

L.C. Smathers' Groom Room
Lenore Smathers
112 1/2 West Main Street
Clarion PA 16214
(814) 226-5524

Al-Rozzy Kennels
Alexander J. DesRosiers
92 Level Rd.
Collegeville PA 19426
(215) 489-2424

Country Road Kennel
Barbara Dempsey Alderman
Spring Run Road Ext.
Coraopolis PA 15108
(412) 264-5836

Parkway West Pet Care Center
Dorothy Sweeney
Box 90 RD 5 Gringo/Clinton Rd
Coraopolis PA 15108
(412) 262-2727

Pet Care Associates Inc.
Bill/Diane Haddle/S. Horn DVM
RD #1 Box 380
Dallas PA 18612
(717) 675-1621

All Breeds Grooming & Brdg
George Haldeman
4115 Swamp Rd.
Doylestown PA 18901
(215) 348-7605

Holiday House Pet Resort
Ted K. Herrmann
380 Shady Retreat Rd.
Doylestown PA 18901
(215) 345-6960

Bolingbroke Kennels
Vernon W. Vogel
Box 24-5850 Gibson Hill Rd.
Edinboro PA 16412
(814) 734-5255

Brizes Boarding Kennel
Barbara Brizes, CKO
Box 91B, Rd. 3
Elizabeth PA 15037
(412) 384-6445

Northcountry Kennels
Terrill Schukraft
4246 Roundtop Road
Elizabethtown PA 17022-9035
(717) 533-3301

Bearhill Kennel
Bonita Hewes
RD 1 Box 321
Elverson PA 19520
(215) 469-6014

Horton's Boarding Kennel
Lisa H. Martin
P.O. Box 54
Ephrata PA 17522
(717) 733-4544

Proud Land Kennels
Joan M. Wienczkowski
6001 W. Sterrettania Road
Fairview PA 16415
(814) 838-9187

Fern Valley Farm
Jane B. Anderson
PO Box 12
Fenelton PA 16034
(412) 445-3679

T.L.C. Pet Resort
Betty J. Aoun
1372 Pittsburgh Road
Franklin PA 16323
(814) 437-3192

Animals' Choice
Molly Kirwan
2273 Lovi Road
Freedom PA 15042
(412) 728-1484

Vir-Del Kennel
Virginia & Del Austin
36 Randolph Rd. RR#1
Great Bend PA 18821-9720
(717) 879-2709

Danilchak's Redwood Kennels
Richard & Joan Danilchak
RD #10 Box 227
Greensburg PA 15601
(412) 834-0213

Laurel Hill Kennels
Melanie R. Mitchell, Owner
RD 3 Box 448-S
Hanover PA 17331
(717) 632-1440

Roberts Boarding Kennel
Gary L. Roberts
2663 Wilson Rd.
Hermitage PA 16148
(412) 346-3612

Cammeo Kennels
Don & Cathy Schwartz
RD 3 Box 281
Hollidaysburg PA 16648
(814) 695-5233

Country Pet
Jeffrey Sorber
RR #3 Box 152-B
Hunlock Creek PA 18621
(717) 675-7777

Connie Winters Knl/ Stable
Connie Winters
Rd. 3, Box 79 Airport Rd.
Indiana PA 15701
(412) 465-6120

Country Kennels
Sharon W. Long
1005 Almshouse Road
Jamison PA 18929
(215) 343-5587

Stone Ridge Kennels, Inc
Peter F. Treat
RD 6 Box 6119
Lake Ariel PA 18436
(717) 689-4244

Spotlight Kennel
Barbara L. Kauffman
2120 Columbia Ave.
Lancaster PA 17603
(717) 393-7192

Town & Country Kennels
William & Linda Lowney
393 Langhorne Ave
Langhorne PA 19053
(215) 752-3661

Animal Crackers
Dr. Robert & Carol Huber
1240 Snyder Rd.
Lansdale PA 19446
(215) 855-8378

Molly's Run Country Knls Inc.
Robert & Valerie Payne
2205 Wentz Church Rd
Lansdale PA 19446
(215) 584-6515

Roselynde Kennels Inc.
Barbara J. Weiss
695 Keeler Road
Lansdale PA 19446
(215) 855-8026

Wofford's Pet Hotel
Christy Wofford
RD 1 Box 3625
Leechburg PA 15656
(412) 845-2477

Gochenauer Kennels
Bud & Pat Gochenauer,CKO
995 Fruitville Pike
Lititz PA 17543
(717) 569-6151

McGarvey's Boarding Kennel
Donald & Shirley McGarvey
520 W. 28th Div. Highway
Lititz PA 17543
(717) 626-6961

Cloud Nine Country Knl Inc.
Donna & George C. Galanti
R.D. #1 Box 422 A
Macungie PA 18062
(215) 845-7330

Sun Hill Kennels
Glenn & Crystal Adams
346 S. Erisman Rd.
Manheim PA 17545
(717) 653-6060

Brickyard Road Kennels
Mr. & Mrs. Donald J. Casey
38 Brickyard Road
Mars PA 16046
(412) 625-1475

Kel-View Kennels
John F. & Pauline T. Kelso Jr.
926 Eppley Road
Mechanicsburg PA 17055
(717) 790-9465

Kinship Kennel Inc.
Molly McCarty
331 E. Lisburn Rd.
Mechanicsburg PA 17055
(717) 697-6508

Ernest Hill Kennels
Jay & Dale Ernest
RD #3 Box 847
Mifflintown PA 17059
(717) 436-9267

Grocott's Hayastan Farm Knl
Larry & Dorothy Grocott
RD #2 Box 93
Millville PA 17846
(717) 458-5915

Buck Hollow Kennels
Julia M. Carroll
RD 3 Box 3636
Mohnton PA 19540
(215) 856-7840

Springbrook Kennels Inc
Dr & Mrs Keith C. Dorton
Rt 7 Box 7415 Swartz Vly Rd
Moscow PA 18444
(717) 842-4502

Laurel Lane Farm
Courtney Carter
PO Box 549
Newtown PA 18940
(215) 968-2500

Ridge Crest Farm
Bob & Beth Sheldon
189 A Upper Ridge Rd.
Pennsburg PA 18073
(215) 679-8606

The Golden Bone Pet Resort Inc
David E. Anderson
6890 Fifth Ave.
Pittsburgh PA 15208
(412) 661-7001

Noah's Pet Farm & Motel
Allan & Carol Peppelman
RD.#2 Rte. 100
Pottstown PA 19464
(215) 323-2206

Mill Pond Kennel
Steve & Vicki Babylon
2245 Mill Pond Rd
Quakertown PA 18951
(215) 536-4443

Holly Farms Kennels
Joel L & Jeanette M Ward
601 Route 113
Sellersville PA 18960
(215) 723-4992

Misty Pines
Jeffrey C. Woods
2523 Wexford-bayne Road
Sewickley PA 15143
(412) 364-4122

Oak Hill Kennels
Robert L. Steup
Blackburn Road
Sewickley PA 15143
(412) 741-6421

Mountain's View Kennel & Brdg
Susan Bobersky
RD #3 Box 76
Shickshinny PA 18655
(717) 864-3761

Barmyre Kennels
Barbe Jo Myers
434 Pinola Road
Shippensburg PA 17257
(717) 532-7588

Pocono Creek Kennels
John A. Foca
RD 3
Stroudsburg PA 18360
(717) 629-2688

Pin Oak Pet Motel
Joan Rauhauser
Box 766 R2
Thomasville PA 17364-9622
(717) 792-0278

Kochems' Kennel
Kathleen Kochems, CKO
RD 1, Box 143 Birchwood Dr.
Transfer PA 16154
(412) 962-9291

Kamp K9
Robert Sterling
PO Box 2174
Wilkes-Barre PA 18703-2174
(717) 829-4644

Dona-Shirl Pet Motel
Shirley Hoffman
RD #2 Box 245
Windber PA 15963
(814) 487-5288

Yardley Animal Kennel Inc.
Maryanne Widenmeyer
1085 Reading Ave
Yardley PA 19067
(215) 493-2717

Millstone Kennels
Kathryn & Charles Fishel
RD #28 Box 396 - Trinity Rd.
York PA 17404
(717) 792-3049

RHODE ISLAND

East Bay Kennels, Ltd.
Karl & Jennifer Correia
Broad Common Road
Bristol RI 02809
(401) 253-0082

Colvintown Kennels
Philippe Van Couyghem
99 Colvintown Road
Coventry RI 02816
(401) 828-6395

Kandy Kane Kennels
Leo J. Saucier
Boswell Rd.
Foster RI 02825
(401) 647-2130

Mini Manor Kennel Inc.
A. Anderson & F. Irwin
1011 Shermantown Road
North Kingstown RI 02852
(401) 295-1222

Smithfield Kennels
Eugene and Jane Tetreault
15 Richard St.
Smithfield RI 02917
(401) 231-9250

SOUTH CAROLINA
Powderhouse Kennels
Kandy Boatwright
1155 Powderhouse Road
Aiken SC 29801-6238
(803) 648-0779

Chapin Pet Lodge
Allen & Vernell Murray
Rt. 5, Box 417
Chapin SC 29036
(803) 345-5082

Bradford Veterinary Clinic
Patricia Bradford
2517 Ashley River Road
Charleston SC 29414
(803) 763-3230

Haywood Road Pet Motel Inc.
Wayne Creel, D.V.M.
594 Haywood Rd.
Greenville SC 29607
(803) 288-7472

Hollycrest Kennels
Joyce H. Walpool
381 Liberty Hill Rd.
Greer SC 29651
(803) 877-6948

ADandie Kennels, Inc.
Danielle McCallum
1629 Creekbank Lane
Johns Island SC 29455
(803) 559-0769

Red Barn Kennel
Dale & Monroe Lindler
180 West Hwy 378
Lexington SC 29072
(803) 359-9045

Cedarwood Kennel
Virginia Carrier
PO Box 623
Little River SC 29566
(803) 249-5307

Sun-Glo Kennels
Lynn A. Powell
1019 1st Ave. S.
N. Myrtle Beach SC 29582
(803) 249-1263

Willow Pines Pet Resort
Martin & Bunty Volls
Rt. 1, Box 610
North SC 29112
(803) 247-5855

Allcare Kennel
G.A. Dobslaw
2948 E. Main Street
Spartanburg SC 29302
(803) 579-0391

Noah's Ark Kennels
Jane C. Hughston
121 S. Blackstock Road
Spartanburg SC 29301
(803) 576-0760

Companion Kennel
Pat Heinemann
103 Edgebrook Drive
Summerville SC 29483
(803) 873-6848

My Buddy Brdg. Inn For Pets
Dayle Fersner
1140 South Guignard Dr.
Sumpter SC 29150
(803) 773-2501

Deer Springs Kennels
Hildegard or Graydon Watkins
3099 Pine Tree Lane
Westville SC 29175
(803) 432-2980

TENNESEE
DeVoe Kennels
11800 Finch Rd
Farragut TN 37922
(615) 435-4487

Countryview Kennels
Joseph & Sierra Grumme
1703 Airways Blvd.
Jackson TN 38301
(901) 427-8585

Stonebridge Kennels
Virginia R. Hobby
209 Col. Heights Rd
Kingsport TN 37663
(615) 239-7331

Dog Woods
Jo Ann Geeslin
3088 Winchester
Memphis TN 38118
(901) 795-8242

Pleasant View Kennels
Jeff W. Reichen
5758 Pleasant View Rd.
Memphis TN 38134
(901) 386-3232

The Claridge Kennels, Inc.
Terrell C. Jones
3262 Hickory Hill
Memphis TN 38115
(901) 365-3500

Custom Kare Kennels
Faye McKnight
130 Thompson Lane
Murfreesboro TN 37130
(615) 893-8959

Boone Wood Kennel
Jennifer Flake, Mgr.
381 J.A. Hodge Rd Rt 2
Piney Flats TN 37686
(615) 538-8648

Crikett Lane
Diane Poore
5456 Crikett Lane
Walland TN 37886
(615) 983-1322

TEXAS
Abilene Pet Regency
Dr. R. Dale or Marsha Hembree
1126 Tracy Lynn
Abilene TX 79601
(915) 677-7387

Pampered Pet Inn
Mark & Cathy Kelley
5933 South First
Abilene TX 79605
(915) 692-2802

Ambassador Pet Resort
Dr. Dudley
12419 Metric Blvd.
Austin TX 78758
(512) 832-1012

Arrow Valley Kennel/Aquarius
Joe & Geri Gambino
2227 E. Ben White Blvd.
Austin TX 78741
(512) 441-0259

Best Of Breed Kennels, Inc.
Lee Ana Dorsett
10800 N. Lamar Blvd.
Austin TX 78753-3053
(512) 836-1174

Canine Hilton
John N. Ramsey
7509 E. MLK Blvd.
Austin TX 78724
(512) 926-8905

Exmoor Kennels
Babette Ellis
7107 Brodie Lane
Austin TX 78745
(512) 443-9393

Highmark Kennel
Linda Willard
8301 Hwy 71 West
Austin TX 78735
(512) 288-0515

Hill Country Kennel
Ross & Roseann Curtis
13412 Fitzhugh Road
Austin TX 78736
(512) 288-4696

Onion Creek Kennels
Elizabeth A. Garza
804 Canyon Wren Dr.
Buda TX 78610
(512) 295-4593

Country Clip
Dolores Baccus, CKO
Rt. 1 Box 1594
Burleson TX 76028
(817) 295-1039

Toothacres Pet Care Center
Bettye C. Clem
Rt 2 Box 220
Carrollton TX 75008
(214) 492-3711

Pets of Perfection
Karla Minyard
1104-1108 S. Hwy 67
Cedar Hill TX 75104
(214) 291-9939

Colleyville Knl/Pet Ctr
Dale R. Hodgson
4404 Colleyville Blvd
Colleyville TX 76034
(817) 498-6410

Boykin Kennel
Mary Organ
2705 Coombs Creek Dr.
Dallas TX 75211
(214) 330-1500

Cat Connection
Lana Mos
14233 Inwood Rd.
Dallas TX 75244-3920
(214) 386-6369

Deer Park Pet Hotel
Kathleen Stegall
801 Center Street
Deer Park TX 77536
(713) 479-1384

Canine Fitness Camp
Diana & Donald Shelton
6C Mitchell Bend,
Granbury TX 76048
(817) 573-1207

Mans Best Friend
Gary Bolander
2129 S Grt SW Pkwy #306
Grand Prairie TX 75051
(214) 988-0991

American Pet Care
Elmer C. Belssner
320 W. Main Street
Gun Barrel City TX 75147
(214) 887-7387

Animal House
Linda Belssner
320 West Main
Gun Barrel City TX 75147
(214) 451-2161

The Valley Pet Motel
Tracy & Lynnea Mathes
Rt #5 Box 262-X
Harlingen TX 78552
(512) 428-5400

Animal Care Center
Dr. Brent N. Melloy
6321 Bissonnet
Houston TX 77074
(713) 774-7688

Animal Inn, Inc.
Paul B. & Louise Abt
706 St. Ives Court
Houston TX 77079
(713) 277-2727

Memorial Red Oak Kennels
David & Hazel Arnold
1214 Sherwood Forest
Houston TX 77043
(713) 467-0535

Pet Hotel
Irvin A. Harrison
5602 Royalton
Houston TX 77081
(713) 664-6111

Pet Spoilers Hometel
Steve & Cindy Brock
11206 Cedarhurst
Houston TX 77096
(713) 721-6945

Sharon's Pampered Pet Inn
Bill Gordon
2411 Bissonnet
Houston TX 77005
(713) 522-7387

The Pampered Pet Inn Inc.
Selma R. Leiber
2922 Hillcroft Ave.
Houston TX 77057
(713) 783-7387

Atascocita Brdg & Grmg
Roseann Ear, CKO
5722 FM 1960 East
Humble TX 77346
(713) 852-7387

Animal Medical & Surg Hosp Inc
Richard Thomes D.V.M.
600 W. Airport Frwy
Irving TX 75062
(214) 438-7113

Roomin 'N' Groomin
G. Coleman & T. Conner, CKOs
424 W. Rancier
Killeen TX 76541
(817) 634-8076

Animal Crackers Royal Pet Htl.
Mr & Mrs. T. J. MacGillivray
796 Russell Palmer Rd.
Kingwood TX 77339
(713) 358-9723

Sea Dog Inn
Carolyn & Jack Hosmer
310 Ellen
League City TX 77573
(713) 554-2068

Family Pet Center
Anna & Marty Diggs, CKO's
1357 Morningside Dr.
Lewisville TX 75057
(214) 221-4292

Animals Etc, Inc.
Barbara Woodall, CKO
Rt. 2, Box 1595A
McAllen TX 78504
(512) 682-3806

Lake McQueeney Boarding
Jennifer McClaugherty
PO Box 486 - FM 725
McQueeney TX 78123
(512) 557-6335

P'etcetera
Paul R. Freese
4320 N. Galloway
Mesquite TX 75150
(214) 279-8887

Deb's Dog House/Pet Care Cntr
Deborah Hedges
1209 N. Washington
Mt. Pleasant TX 75455
(214) 572-0008

Canterbury Inn For Pets
Connie Stegen
22155 W. Magnolia Forest
Navasota, TX 77868
(409) 894-2913

Hollidog Inn
Denny Mounce/Peggy Lloyd
4612 Richmond Foster Rd.
Richmond TX 77469
(713) 342-7946

Kennel Kare
Sherry Gray
Rt 1 Box 480
Roanoke TX 76262
(817) 379-0737

Char-Rich Kennel, Inc.
Mr. & Mrs. Leroy Taylor
109 E. North Loop Road
San Antonio TX 78216
(512) 494-5334

Dal Acres
M. Dusek/D. LaGassie, CKO's
4280 Jung Road
San Antonio TX 78247
(512) 496-1767

Holiday Boarding Kennel Inc.
Carl W. Gibbs
323 E. Nakoma
San Antonio TX 78216
(512) 494-7649

Robcary Kennels
Caryl Fennell/Lynn Trevino
14824 Bulverde Road
San Antonio TX 78247
(512) 494-7787

Classical Canine Camp
Jo Ann Yuttal
142 Chaparral
Shady Shores TX 76205
(817) 497-4732

Hideout Acres Pet Care Center
Gerald & Rhonda Dalton
1100 N. Shady Oaks Drive
Southlake TX 76092
(817) 488-5184

Boulevard Kennels
D.W. Wisdom
2405 Texas Blvd.
Texarkana TX 75501
(214) 793-1193

R & R Farm
Alice Engel
Rt 10 Box 833
Tyler TX 75707
(214) 566-8352

Clearlake Kennels
Elyse Griffin
18520 S. Hwy 3
Webster TX 77598
(713) 332-4870

Jan's Grooming & Pet Supplies
Janet Allison
RR 1 Box 146X
Wimberley TX 78676-9801
(512) 847-3990

Magics Boarding Kennel
Scott Sherman
3216 Parker Road
Wylie TX 75098
(214) 442-7396

UTAH

Don's Pet Care
Don Sellers
1481 Gibson Ave
Ogden UT 84404
(801) 393-5143

Idlewire Pet Care Centers
Verl & Saundra Hansen
2374 Harrison Blvd
Ogden UT 84401
(801) 394-2260

Willow Creek Pet Center
Rick Campbell D.V.M.
7997 So. Highland Drive
Salt Lake UT 84121
(801) 942-0777

Rocky Willows Stables & Knls
Peggy Wilkes
10700 S 1700 E
Sandy UT 84092
(801) 571-1100

Animal Inn Of Utah
Steve Hailstone
909 N. Frontage Rd.
Springville UT 84663
(801) 489-8888

VIRGINIA

Highlands Animal Hospital
Clay Brinson, DVM
Intersection Rt 11 & 58
Abingdon VA 24210
(703) 628-4115

Stonehead Dog Ranch
Riccardo Wright
RT 1 Box 163-A
Aldie VA 22001
(703) 471-1073

For Pet's Sake Hotel
Jeffrey L. Hollabaugh
3208 Colvin Street
Alexandria VA 22314
(703) 823-3647

Yopaka Kennels
Paul M. Harris
Rt.2, Box 2050
Ashland VA 23005
(804) 798-8248

Clarke's Country Kennel
John & Frances Clarke
Rt 3 Box 3565
Bumpass VA 23024
(703) 872-3928

Dulles Gateway Kennels Ltd.
Kathy Doyle
4500 Upper Cub Run Drive
Chantilly VA 22021
(703) 631-9590

Pleasant Valley Kennel
Dr. Thomas Roehr
Box 103 Rt 1
Chantilly VA 22021
(703) 471-9617

Dominion Kennels
Al Bianchi
505 Dominion Blvd.
Chesapeake VA 23323
(804) 547-5922

Mountain Run Kennel
Jane Kelso
Rt 8 Box 70
Culpeper VA 22701
(703) 547-2961

Danville Pet Lodge
Marion Wardle
215 Ash Street
Danville VA 24540
(804) 836-1245

Calypso Boarding Kennels Inc.
Jeff Chaffin
7 Hillside Lane
Fredericksburg VA 22401
(703) 720-0050

Commonwealth Kennel Ltd
Mr.Beverly R. Bowles
4660 Pouncey Tract Rd
Glen Allen VA 23060
(804) 360-2065

Holiday Barn Pet Hotels
P. Emerson Hughes
P.O. Box 1065
Glen Allen VA 23060
(804) 262-8667

Colvin Run Pet-Otel Inc.
Jim Morrison
10127 Colvin Run Road
Great Falls VA 22066
(703) 759-3311

ABKA Kennels

Armistead Animal Inn
Michael & Beverly Silkey
531 N. Armistead Avenue
Hampton VA 23669
(804) 723-8571

Puppy Luv
Gay E. Roderick
RR 10 Box 147
Harrisonburg VA 22801
(703) 833-6901

Lake Jackson Kennels
Julie Hogan
9929 Lake Jackson Drive
Manassas VA 22110
(703) 361-7550

Manassas Animal Hospital
Carol Todd
8307 Yorkshire Lane
Manassas VA 22111
(703) 368-9241

Shadetree Kennel
Paul & Catherine Cooper
Hwy 57 East
Martinsville VA 24115
(703) 632-4969

Great Falls Boarding Kennels
Janet G. Wyant
8920 Old Dominion Drive
McLean VA 22102
(703) 759-2620

Fursman Kennels
Pamela Mary Dickson
Box 625, Rt. 709
Middleburg VA 22117
(703) 687-6990

Broughton's Kennel
Judith M. Middlebrooks
929 Otterdale Rd.
Midlothian VA 23113
(804) 794-6923

Animal Care Center
1228 W. Little Creek Rd
Norfolk VA 23505
(804) 423-3900

Countryside Kennel
Margaret Shults
3244 Judes Ferry Road
Powhatan VA 23139
(804) 794-8702

Holiday Barn Pet Hotel
Donald W. Ford, CKO
900 Southlake Blvd.
Richmond VA 23236
(804) 794-5400

Aberdeen Acres Knl & Pet Care
Cheryl L. Anderson
PO Box 220 (State Rt 836)
Stephenson VA 22656
(703) 667-7809

Crest Hill Animal Inn
Doloris Wells, Proprietor
PO Box 116 / St Rt 653
Troutville VA 24175
(703) 992-3950

Bostic Owl Creek Pet Hotel
Donald W. Bostic, Mgr
587 South Birdneck Road
Virginia Beach VA 23451
(804) 425-5349

Animal Clinic/Williamsburg
Meryl Lessinger-Bely V.M.D.
7316 Merrimac Trail
Williamsburg VA 23185
(804) 253-0812

VERMONT
Sandy Pines Kennel
James W. Roche
PO Box 134
Essex VT 05451
(802) 878-2636

Mountain View Animal Inn
Carol Skon/Claudia Cook
RD 1 (1980 Bessette Rd.)
Fairfax VT 05454
(802) 524-4574

Crossover Kennels Inc
Nancy A. Cross
Lee River Rd
Jericho VT 05465
(802) 899-3877

WASHINGTON
Schulhaus Kennels
Janet Thomas
525 Valley Road
Aberdeen WA 98520
(206) 532-8003

Creature Comforts Kennel
Debra Ferguson
36215 55th Ave. So.
Auburn WA 98001
(206) 833-5177

Fairhaven Pets' Western
Chris Hamer
2401 Fairhaven Parkway
Bellingham WA 98225
(206) 738-1302

The Plush Pooch
C. Prince/J. Hazel, CKO
913 Bass Street
Bellingham WA 98226
(206) 676-0430

Penny Creek Kennels
Julie Kirk
102 Carol Ave.
Benton City WA 99320
(509) 588-6955

Tails-A-Waggin
Leroy & Donna Hasenyager
19816 19th Ave. S.E.
Bothell WA 98012
(206) 481-3214

Fairinall Kennels
P. Chardon - L. Martinez
14637 NW Holly Rd.
Bremerton WA 98312
(206) 830-4427

Pantara Kennels
Terry Lee Panteleef
515 Bryden Ave.
Centralia WA 98531
(206) 736-4290

Longview Kitty Inn
Frances L. Middleton
PO Box 627 (815 S Engle Rd)
Coupeville WA 98239
(206) 678-4285

The Animal Inn
F. Milene Henley
497 Boyce Road
Friday Harbor WA 98250
(206) 378-4735

Happy Camp Kennel
Spence Killian
Rt 14 Box 3038
Kennewick WA 99337
(509) 582-8244

The Pet Ritz of Toklat Kennels
Debra White
4328 Columbia Heights Rd
Longview WA 98632
(206) 577-0234

Frolic'n Kennel
Stephen & Charlotte Johnson
116-214 Avenue Southeast
Redmond WA 98053
(206) 883-8186

Atwood's Pet Trans/Kelly's
Lee Atwood/Sue Atwood, CKO
2040 South 142nd
Seattle WA 98168
(206) 241-0880

Marcinda Kennels
Marc McIntosh
North 11024 Forker Road
Spokane WA 99207
(509) 928-6662

Sumner Veterinary Hospital
M.K. Sheeran DVM
15215 Main Street
Sumner WA 98390
(206) 863-2258

Atwoods/Waggin Wheel Inn
Barb Gresso
3602 112th St. East
Tacoma WA 98446
(206) 531-0779

Corporate Kennels, Inc.
Preston W. Bennett
7718 Portland Ave.
Tacoma WA 98404
(206) 531-7732

Deer Meadows Kennel
Susan M Lowder
4898 Luther Rd (Deer Meadows
Rc
Valley WA 99181
(509) 258-7210

Cascade Kennels
Andrea & Joel Woods
20004 178th Northeast
Woodinville WA 98072
(206) 483-9333

WISCONSIN
Pine Hill Boarding Kennel
Anna M. Meinholz
1212 Highway 12
Altoona WI 54720
(715) 834-8205

Bed & Biscuit Brdg Kennel
Jan L. Rudenborg
RR 1 Box 622
Balsam Lake WI 54810
(715) 485-3084

Ker-Mor Kennels
Mr. & Mrs. Ernest E. Keirsey
3070 Hickory Grove Rd
Belgium WI 53004
(414) 994-4523

Animal Motel
Diane & Don Gutknecht, CKO
P.O. Box 228
Butler WI 53007-0228
(414) 781-5200

Malagold Kennels
Connie Gerstner
3953 Hwy. 19
De Forest WI 53532
(608) 249-0033

Arnstad's Pine Tree Kennel
Ed & Terri Arnstad
598 Florist Drive
De Pere WI 54115
(414) 869-1267

Calico Kennels
Ellie Kosmoski
4860 Court Rd.
Egg Harbor WI 54209
(414) 868-3804

Cedar Dale Kennels, Inc.
Janice Skender
Rt 1 Box 553 B
Genoa City WI 53128
(414) 279-3900

Shady Glen Kennels
Shirley Seal
W188 N9808 Appleton Ave.
Germantown WI 53022
(414) 251-1920

Golrusk Pet Care Center
Jan & Ken Grosskopf, CKO
1991 Allouez Ave.
Green Bay WI 54301
(414) 468-7956

Thistlerose Kennels Reg'd
Eleanor Jolly
6801 W. Loomis Road
Greendale WI 53129
(414) 425-2434

Timberlawn Pet Care Center
John & Madonna Stedman
Rt 8 Box 8264
Hayward WI 54843
(715) 634-8712

Shel-Ray Shepherds, Inc.
William & Diane Mayer
18018 Horton Rd.
Kenosha WI 53142
(414) 857-2163

Camp K-9 Pet Care Center
Lori Campbell
4934 Felland Road
Madison WI 53704
(608) 249-3939

Kandamor Kennels
David & Ellen Luckow
8730 English Lake Road
Manitowoc WI 54220
(414) 758-2777

Allens Pet Lodge Inc
Sandra Allen
2332 Pinehurst Dr.
Middleton WI 53562
(608) 831-8000

The Puppy Lodge Brd Kennels
Dick & Sara Bernier
7311 N. Granville Rd.
Milwaukee WI 53224
(414) 353-9387

Chalet Hill Kennel Ltd
Richard D. Wheeler
PO Box 109
Nashotah WI 53058
(414) 367-4111

Barkshire Pet Care Center
Jane Collen
6438 County Hwy A
Neenah WI 54956
(414) 729-6382

Sandhill Kennels
Theodore S. Plautz
2065 Sandhill Road
Oregon WI 53575
(608) 835-7600

The Dog House & Pet Center
B.J. & Scott Nerenhausen
2275 Omro Road
Oshkosh WI 54904
(414) 231-5232

Rodak Kennel
Roger D. Keepers
2421 Silvernail Rd.
Pewaukee WI 53072
(414) 542-3209

Silverwood Kennel
Elizabeth Fredrick
4703 E. St. Croix
Superior WI 54880
(715) 398-7188

Best Care Pet Motel
Mara D. Kloes/Mgr.
918 W. Sunset Drive (Rear)
Waukesha WI 53186
(414) 547-7905

WEST VIRGINIA
Cat & Canine Camp
Emma L. Reynolds
204 Rutledge Rd.
Charleston WV 25311
(304) 345-6369

Shamrock Stables Brdg Knl,Inc.
Tom & Ruth Kirk
Rt 2 Box 340
Charleston WV 25314
(304) 744-1101

Crosby's K-9 Country Club
Lilabeth Crosby
Rt 4 Box 193
Fairmont WV 26554
(304) 366-0894

Brackenbriar Kennel Inc.
Betty J. Grandel, CKO
Rt 1 Box 370
Kearneysville WV 25430
(304) 725-0554

Brookview Pet Lodge
George & Jean Oliver
Rt 1 Bx 382(Brown's Creek Rd)
St. Albans WV 25177
(304) 727-9849

WYOMING
Broadmoor E. Brdg & Grmg
Michael P. Driscoll
4214 E. Pershing Blvd
Cheyenne WY 82001
(307) 632-66-7

The National Association of Pet Sitters consists of over 300 member pet sitters who will come into your home to care for your pet. The association promotes professional, at-home pet care and will help you find a pet sitter in your area.

As with hotel/motel reservations and kenneling, if you're interested in finding a pet sitter, be sure to <u>plan ahead</u> and call well in advance.

The National Association of Pet Sitters can be contacted by phone at:

(919) 723-PETS
       (7387)

or write:

Patti Moran
Executive Director
National Association of Pet Sitters
632 Holly Ave.
Winston-Salem, NC 27101

PETS-R-PERMITTED IS YOUR PASSPORT TO TRAVEL <u>WITH</u> OR <u>WITHOUT</u> YOUR PET!

- Over 1,000 quality ABKA boarding kennels for extended vacation boarding or day-sitting during trips

- Nationwide location service for experienced pet-sitters

- Success tips for kennel stays

- Plane, train, & auto travel information

- A crucial 23 item checklist to fill your pet's travelkit

- Practical pointers on proper hotel & motel pet etiquette

- Over 3,000 hotels & motels across the US which allow pets

- Toll free nationwide veterinary location service

- Tips for safe and happy pet travel

- Pet boarding facilities at & near major U.S. theme parks & attractions

- Handy mileage chart to calculate destination distances

- Nationwide pet recovery services

- 15 item list for your pet's first-aid kit

- Personal travel guide which includes toll free numbers for:
  - state tourism bureaus
  - hotel & motel chains
  - state road conditions
  - national rental cars
  - auto & travel clubs
  - major US airlines

Please send me ___ copies of Pets-R-Permitted!

Name _____

Address _____

City _____ State _____ Zip _____

Phone (optional) _____

I have enclosed $11.00 ($9.95 + $1.05 postage) for each copy ordered. Make checks payable to ACI.

CA residents must add sales tax

HOW TO ORDER

1. Fill in the desired number of copies of Pets-R-Permitted
2. Enclose $11.00 per copy ordered
3. Mail this completed form to ACI, P.O. Box 3099, Lakewood, CA 90711-3099

CA residents must add sales tax

Order a Copy of Pets-R-Permitted for a friend! Only $9.95.

(+ $1.05 US postage)

Please fill out the gift label with your friend's name & mailing address, and send $11.00 to:

(CA residents must add sales tax)

ACI
P.O. Box 3099
Lakewood, CA 90711-3099

Happy Trails & Happy Tails!

prices good through 6/1/92

A Very Special Gift for You!

from: _____

to: _____

_____

_____

_____

_____

To order the Pets-R-Permitted Hotel & Motel Directory, send $11.00
(CA residents must add sales tax) to:
ACI Reorders
P.O. Box 3099
Lakewood, CA 90711-3099

.